Digital Government: Principles and Best Practices

Alexei Pavlichev
North Carolina State University, USA

G. David Garson
North Carolina State University, USA

IDEA GROUP PUBLISHING
Hershey • London • Melbourne • Singapore

Acquisition Editor:	Mehdi Khosrow-Pour
Senior Managing Editor:	Jan Travers
Managing Editor:	Amanda Appicello
Development Editor:	Michele Rossi
Copy Editor:	Terry Heffelfinger
Typesetter:	Jennifer Wetzel
Cover Design:	Michelle Waters
Printed at:	Integrated Book Technology

Published in the United States of America by
    Idea Group Publishing (an imprint of Idea Group Inc.)
    701 E. Chocolate Avenue, Suite 200
    Hershey PA 17033
    Tel: 717-533-8845
    Fax: 717-533-8661
    E-mail: cust@idea-group.com
    Web site: http://www.idea-group.com

and in the United Kingdom by
    Idea Group Publishing (an imprint of Idea Group Inc.)
    3 Henrietta Street
    Covent Garden
    London WC2E 8LU
    Tel: 44 20 7240 0856
    Fax: 44 20 7379 3313
    Web site: http://www.eurospan.co.uk

Library of Congress Cataloging-in-Publication Data

Digital government : principles and best practices / [edited by] Alexei
Pavlichev and G. David Garson.
        p. cm.
Includes bibliographical references and index.
    ISBN 1-59140-122-4 (hardcover) -- ISBN 1-59140-123-2 (ebook)
    1. Internet in public administration--United States. I. Pavlichev,
Alexei. II. Garson, G. David.
    JK468.A8D53 2004
    352.3'8'0973--dc21

                                                            2003008879

Paperback ISBN 1-59140-218-2

British Cataloguing in Publication Data
A Cataloguing in Publication record for this book is available from the British Library.

NEW from Idea Group Publishing

Excellent additions to your institution's library! Recommend these titles to your Librarian!

Digital Government: Principles and Best Practices

Table of Contents

Preface

E-government has emerged not merely as a specialization in public administration, but as a transformative force affecting all levels and functions of government. This volume, written by a mix of practitioners and researchers, provides an overview of the management challenges and issues involved in seeking a new form of governance — digital government. An initial introductory section presents the hopes for e-government and outlines its history in the United States and globally. Section II, "The New Face of Government," examines *FirstGov*, the premiere example of e-government and surveys its political implications. Section III, "Issues in Digital Governance," discusses such management challenges as privacy rights, e-procurement, e-commerce, and ethics in e-government. Section IV, "Preparing for Digital Government," discusses data warehousing and related prerequisites for e-government, including the education and training of the public service. Finally, Section V, "The Future of E-Government," discusses the digital divide, citizen participation, and factors that will determine the eventual success or failure of the e-government model.

INTRODUCTION

In "The Promise of Digital Government" Garson notes that e-government advocates promise that not only will e-government bring the convenience of online transactions, it will reverse citizens' disaffection from government, create dramatic savings, and reinforce rather than erode traditional American freedoms and liberties. E-government, however, is better thought of not as a revolution but as what it is: an attempt to bring the e-business model into the public sector. A component-by-component examination of the e-business model shows that it is fraught with problems, challenges, and limitations as well as opportunities. The promise of digital government will be fulfilled only by a new generation of public managers who are generalists, not technocrats, capable of integrating the disparate fields of consideration that are necessary aspects of the vision of e-government as whole.

In "A Brief History of the Emergence of Digital Government in the United States," Relyea and Hogue outline the evolutionary progression of information technologies from the printing and distribution of Senate and House journals in 1813 down to the e-government services of today. The authors show the impact of the Privacy Act of 1974, the Computer Security Act of 1987, the Electronic Freedom of Information Amendments of 1996, and other pieces of legislation pertinent to fashioning the proper management of information technologies and the systems they serve, their protection from physical harm, and the security and privacy of their information.

Forlano, in "The Emergence of Digital Government: International Perspectives," presents an overview of the extent to which e-government has been adopted internationally by reviewing major comparative studies and case studies by international organizations. The characteristics of the five stages of e-government (emerging, enhanced, interactive, transactional, seamless) are outlined with international examples of innovative practices and potential obstacles. She concludes that currently, adoption of e-government strategies worldwide is varied, but many countries are making rapid progress in implementing their strategies.

THE NEW FACE OF GOVERNMENT

In "Portals and Policy: Implications of Electronic Access to U.S. Federal Government Information and Services," Diamond Fletcher evaluates the emerging electronic "portal" model of information and service delivery to U.S. citizens, businesses, and government agencies. The portal model is being used as a technology framework in the U.S. federal government to carry out the electronic government strategies set out in the President's Management Agenda for 2002 and the subsequent 24 electronic government initiatives included in the Budget of the United States Government for 2003 and the E-Government Strategy. FirstGov.gov is the official federal government portal for all information and services delivered by the federal executive agencies. The legal and organizational framework for FirstGov, based on an in-depth case study, is presented and evaluated as a model for future electronic government initiatives.

Franzel and Coursey, in "Government Web Portals: Management Issues and the Approaches of Five States," discuss further web portals as the dominant organizational motif for e-gov service delivery. To date, most reviews of government portal experiences focus on the types and technical sophistication of delivered services as well as design issues, such as usability. Management issues, like commercialization and centralization, have received relatively little attention. The authors define and argue for a more management-oriented perspective. Several major issues are explained and then the experiences of five states are used to demonstrate how they present a different view of portal strategies for researchers.

In "The Organizational Culture of Digital Government: Technology, Accountability & Shared Governance," Allen and her associates examine the characteristics of government organizations that influence their capacity to employ information technology (IT) in a strategic manner such that it assists them in their quest to meet the governance challenges they face. They explore the organizational factors, architectural and cultural, that impede large government departments from moving beyond the adoption of IT as a mere instrument that assists the execution of routine tasks in the traditional way and move into new forms of governance that alter the relationships between individuals and units within the organization and between the organization and its external environment. Our objective is to provide a useful framework for the analysis of the barriers to, and potential catalysts of, an IT-mediated transformation of the governance of large government departments.

In "Political Implications of Digital Government," Baker and Panagopoulos show that while citizen participation-driven e-government is, in theory, a desirable objective of government, it is complex on a variety of dimensions. From a design standpoint, considering the implementation aspects of access, and awareness; from a baseline assessment of what *has* been implemented to date empirically; and in terms of a meaningful design of responsive policy. Much of the observed variations in e-government applications is still descriptive in nature, and given the rapidly emerging technological and political ramifications is not unexpected. Panagopoulos continues these themes in an essay on "Consequences of the Cyberstate: The Political Implications of Digital Government in International Context. "

ISSUES IN DIGITAL GOVERNANCE

Mullen, in "Digital Government and Individual Privacy," shows how the growth of the Internet and digital government have dramatically increased the Federal government's ability to collect, analyze, and disclose personal information about many private aspects of citizens' lives. Personal information, once available only on paper to a limited number of people, is now instantly retrievable anywhere in the world by anyone with a computer and an Internet connection. Over time, there has also been a declining level of trust by Americans in government, and currently, many perceive the government as a potential threat to their privacy. Given these forces at work in our society, one should not be surprised to read the results of surveys that show privacy as a top concern of citizens in the 21st century. Privacy issues discussed in this chapter include challenges regarding (1) protecting personal privacy; (2) ensuring confidentiality of data collected; and (3) implementing appropriate security controls.

In "E-Procurement: State Government Learns from the Private Sector," Krysiak and his associates examine the effect of leveraging and integrating the power of the Internet as a tool in the total procurement process and its relationship to the supply and demand for goods and services. This work will be of interest to both informed and uninformed readers who wish to broaden their understanding and the effect of e-procurement within the process of government purchasing. The chapter begins with a discussion of legacy systems and past practice purchasing methods. It is followed by sections on public sector versus private sector business practices, business models for e-procurement, culture changes, legislative changes allowing for adoption of e-procurement and advisory committees. A case study of eMaryland Marketplace, the State of Maryland's e-procurement portal, is discussed with particular attention given to theoretical use versus "real life" experience associated with implementing an e-procurement system. Finally, recommendations are made for other state or local jurisdictions that are considering implementation of e-procurement.

Stowers, in "Issues in E-Commerce and E-Government Service Delivery," examines three issues emerging in the fields of e-government service delivery and e-commerce — the need for and a potential structure for performance measures, the heightened need for security awareness around e-government and e-commerce, and the need for e-government web design centered on usability. Beginning these discussions are some basic definitions, a review of the current literature on e-government and a discussion of the stages of e-government development is undertaken. The chapter concludes with a discussion of a future research agenda in e-service delivery and e-commerce.

In "Digital Government and Criminal Justice," Holland outlines the history of digital government in criminal justice starting with the Johnson Administration's findings concerning automation in its report "The Challenge of Crime in a Free Society," the development of the national criminal justice network, and the creation of SEARCH Group, a consortium of states that led the effort to create computerized criminal histories of individual offenders.

Richardson, in "Digital Government: Balancing Risk and Reward Through Public Private Partnerships," notes that the modern focus on the application of business principles to the running of government is unique due to an escalated emphasis on divesting the public sector of as many service provision responsibilities as possible. This divestiture is being accomplished through an array of arrangements alternatively described as privatization, contracting out, outsourcing and public/private partnerships. There are three fundamental challenges to this process: (1) defining those responsibilities which cannot and should not be turned over to the private sector; (2) ensuring that such arrangements balance both the risks and rewards between the parties involved; and (3) getting the best deal for the public. This chapter focuses on the second point: achieving a reasonable balance that should, if implemented successfully, result in that elusive "best deal."

Finally in this section, Anderson in "Ethics and Digital Government" considers the high costs to digital government of inadequate ethical choices and reviews the role of ethics in government generally. While codes of ethics may not go far toward resolving ethical challenges, they provide bases for ethical discourses and embody key ethical principles. Selected principles from the Code of Ethics of the Association for Computing Machinery (ACM) are applied to contemporary ethical issues in the context of digital government. In the rapidly evolving environments of digital technology, it is impossible to anticipate the leading-edge ethical issues; however, there are solid ethical or moral imperatives to use it working toward resolution of the issues.

PREPARING FOR DIGITAL GOVERNMENT

In "Data Warehousing and the Organization of Governmental Databases," Harper outlines how data warehousing is a technology architecture designed to organize disparate data sources into a single repository of information. As such, it represents a strategy for creating the architecture necessary to support the vision of e-government. Data warehousing enables a new type of "decision intelligence" by providing access to historical trend data, typically difficult to retrieve through operational database systems. Government data warehousing is complex, expensive, and often fraught with data privacy and security issues. E-government goals may be met through a successful data-warehousing project, be it in the form of a more efficient, informed government or as a result of increased public access to information. But given the substantial barriers to success, a thorough planning and investigation process is necessary.

Gant and Ijams, in "Digital Government and Geographic Information Systems," focus on how government agencies are deploying geographic information systems (GIS) to enhance the delivery of digital government. Outlining critical technological advances enabling government agencies to use GIS in web-based applications, they illustrate the approaches that state and local governments of the United States are taking to deploy GIS for e-government applications using examples from Indianapolis, Indiana, Tucson, Arizona, Washington, D.C., and the State of Oregon's Department of Environmental Protection.

In "Training for Digital Government," Howle Schelin argues that while the use of digital government applications has increased exponentially in the past decade, the training that should accompany it has not. This chapter seeks to offer insight into the current need for and state of training for digital government, as well as to highlight key models at each level of government. Additionally, it attempts to outline a training methodology for federal, state, and local employees and officials in order to reduce the information asymmetry that occurs within the context of digital government.

Similarly, Pavlichev, in "The E-Government Challenge for Public Administration Education," emphasizes that as public sector agencies use the e-government model to improve delivery of their services, it is important that this model become integrated into education of future leaders of the public service. A fully-scaled implementation of e-government requires more than simple automation of the existing processes. It can affect significantly the overall organizational structure of public agencies, their missions and goals, and the way they interact with customers and with each other. Because of its profound impact on the functions and even structure of government, implementing e-government involves significant challenges, including resistance to change and the problem of lack of information technology skills among public managers. To address these challenges, public affairs programs must include in their curricula courses that would prepare qualified graduates for the era of e-government. Survey results are presented, outlining efforts of graduate public affairs programs to meeting demands related to the e-government model. Major components of the model are outlined and the extent to which these components are covered in graduate courses in leading public affairs programs is assessed.

THE FUTURE OF DIGITAL GOVERNMENT

In "Digital Government and the Digital Divide," Groper discusses how the digital divide has negatively impacted the ability of minority groups to accumulate social capital. This chapter compares Internet access rates in California and the United States in order to test the premise that race is the primary influence upon Internet access. In California, the data explicitly depicts a stronger relationship between Internet access and education and income than it does with Internet access and race. Across the United States, the results are not as stark. However, education and income are increasingly becoming important variables. The policy implications of this study are dramatic. Since most governmental and non-profit efforts in the United States have put resources and money into decreasing the racial divide, this study suggests that at least some of those resources should be shifted to alleviating the educational and economic discrepancies that exist among the American people.

Holzer and his colleagues, in "Digital Government and Citizen Participation in the United States," address the topic of citizen participation via digital government in several sections: the academic literature, best practices, principles and implications from these best practices; and potential problems of digital citizen participation in terms of further research. The best practices described in this chapter include Minnesota's Department Results and Online Citizen Participation Opportunities, Santa Monica's Budget Suggestions, California's California Scorecard, Virginia Beach's EMS Customer Satisfaction Survey, and others.

An international perspective on the crucial issue of citizen participation in e-government is provided by Geiselhart in "Digital Government and Citizen Participation in International Context." Geiselhart observes that the shift towards digital government is part of a sweeping set of changes. These are best viewed holistically, as they relate to pervasive shifts in the locus and purpose of many forms of control. These changes are visible in the gradual shift of terminology from 'government' to 'governance'. This chapter outlines the implications of this shift at the international level, and the role of digital technologies in global citizenship. Participation in these new regimes of global governance includes individuals as well as corporations, international institutions and non-government agencies.

Finally, in "The Future of Digital Government," Corbett explores the challenges that we will collectively face as we make choices about the use and implementation of enabling technology for e-government. The construction of informed government policy that protects citizens' freedoms while accomplishing the critical work of a professional civil service within a democratic government will be the central theme of public administration in the next decade.

Alexei Pavlichev and G. David Garson
North Carolina State University
15 November 2002

Section I

Introduction

Chapter I

The Promise of Digital Government

G. David Garson
North Carolina State University, USA

ABSTRACT

E-government promises to mark a new era of greater convenience in citizen access to governmental forms, data, and information. Its advocates promise that not only will e-government bring the convenience of online transactions, but it will also reverse citizens' disaffection from government, create dramatic savings, and reinforce rather than erode traditional American freedoms and liberties. E-government, however, is better thought of not as a revolution, but as an attempt to bring the e-business model into the public sector. A component-by-component examination of the e-business model shows that it is fraught with problems, challenges, and limitations as well as opportunities. The promise of digital government will be fulfilled only by a new generation of public managers who are generalists, not technocrats, capable of integrating the disparate fields of consideration, which are necessary aspects of the vision of e-government as a whole.

THE PROMISE OF DIGITAL GOVERNMENT

The promise of e-government is not, as some suppose, putting existing paper-based processes of bureaucracy into digital form. Rather, the promise is really nothing less than a profound transformation of the way the government does business. E-government advocates envision a future in which citizens have 24 hour, 7 days a week interactive access to all important government bureaus; where online transactions with government can be conducted from the comfort of home; where government officials make all purchases online; where there are one-stop web portals for businesses seeking to deal with regulatory requirements, students seeking assistance, and ordinary citizens seeking tourist information. As essays in the present volume demonstrate, we are already well on our way to such a future.

The second promise of e-government is that new, improved, and transformed governmental processes will cut transaction costs, thereby reducing the expense of government. E-government advocates cite as a model the 90% transaction cost savings of the financial industry's implementation of online banking (Atkinson and Ulevich, 2001). It is also hoped that e-government will allow flatter organizational structures as government is re-engineered to eliminate process pass-offs, which are better handled through online process control, and this, too, promises to yield impressive cost savings. Likewise, abandoning the department-focused "stovepipe" approach to implementation in favor of a cross-agency client-focused "smart" or integrated approach is thought to be a strategy that will improve long-run cost/effectiveness ratios. Cost savings may be passed back to citizens in the form of online rebates and discounts for governmental transactions, or passed back in the form of lower taxes. This future, however, is not yet here and evaluation research on the cost savings of e-government has yielded more ambiguous results than has research on service enhancement.

A third promise of e-government is of a future where the long-term loss of social capital in the United States is reversed, along with reversal of corresponding public opinion trends that have been associated in the past decades with ever lower faith in the efficacy of government as a tool for solving social problems. The same technology that implements interactive transactions for e-licensing, e-procurement, and e-commerce can be used to promote government-citizen interactions on proposed regulations, policy changes, and laws. Proponents envision everything from online suggestion boxes to online national voting for president and everything in between. Numerous federal agencies are experimenting with participative e-rulemaking and the Office of Management and Budget is poised to mandate such initiatives, institutionalizing a new form of citizen participation. Political leaders like Senator Joseph Lieberman (D, CT) have launched online policy discussion forums to explore new methods of political engagement. Empowerment is a common theme of the widespread community computing center movement as well as of cyber-activists of all stripes. Again, however, research suggests that e-democracy will raise as many questions as it answers — the verdict is not in on this aspect of the promise of e-government.

The final promise of e-government is that all of this will come about in a way that enhances the freedoms that Americans enjoy. With regard to digital privacy, the Supreme Court has already ruled that governmental sale to commercial interests of individual-level data records, such as driver license records, is unconstitutional. Individual privacy is said be further enhanced by several processes associated with e-government: the formalization of data stewardship practices and norms; the standardization that is required for data integration across agencies; and by heightened security practices in the post-9/11 era. Moreover, fear of liability in a litigious world combined with the rise of risk management functions in federal agencies is a further protection. A formal mandate of the current Bush administration's FirstGov initiative is that it be a "trusted" portal, toward which end the Office of Management and Budget has issued detailed data quality control and privacy standards.

A recent report of the Pew Internet and American Life Project was titled *The Rise of the E-Citizen* (Larsen and Rainie, 2002a). It is interesting that revolutions reconceptualize citizenship, from the rights of "national citizens" proclaimed in the French Revolution to idealistic, ultimately failed visions of the "new socialist citizen" of the Russian Revolution to the democratic and empowered "e-citizen" of today. The Pew report found 42 million Americans have used government web sites to research public policy issues, 23 million have used the Internet to send comments to public officials about policy choices, and 14 million have used the web to gather information in order to cast a more informed vote. Some 13 million have even engaged in online lobbying activities. E-citizens are satisfied (80% find what they are looking for on the web) and more favorable to government as a result (60% say e-government has improved their interactions with at least one level of government). Herein, a vision emerges of e-government creating a new citizenry that is more knowledgeable, more political engaged, better served, and more content with their government.

A related report by the same authors (Larsen and Rainie, 2002b) reflected the first Internet-related survey of mayors and city council members. This survey found that 88% of local elected officials used email and the Internet in their official duties. Of those online, 90% used e-mail weekly and 61% used it daily. Seventy-nine percent of all municipal officials reported receiving e-mail from citizens or local groups about civic issues. Twenty-five percent stated they received e-mail from constituents every day. Three-quarters use the web for research and other official duties, including 34% who use the Internet daily. The report concluded, however, "while the use of email adds to the convenience and depth of civic exchanges, its use is not ushering a revolution in municipal affairs or local politics" (p. 2). At this time, traditional communications media, notably the telephone, constitute more important links between local officials and citizens. Only 14% of officials said that they assign a significant amount of weight to email. Silicon Valley lobbies still urge supporters to contact Congress by fax, not e-mail, because e-mail seems to make no impact on Congressmen (Levy, 2002: 42).[1] If e-government is a revolution, it is one that most studies have found, if anything, to both reflect and reinforce powers that be. If it upsets the political apple cart, it will be because of unintended consequences of technological change.

To the extent that the political implications of the promise of e-government have been recognized, there has been caution. West (2000) surveyed e-government and found "there are problems in terms of access and democratic outreach" (p. 2) and that "some states have been slow to put accountability-enhancing material such as legislative deliberations, campaign finance information, and ethics reports online" (p. 5). While 68% of websites did post e-mail addresses so citizens could interact in this way, only 15% provided for posting of citizen comments. West also found relatively few governmental websites had posted a privacy policy: in the best-rated, Michigan, only 20% of state government websites had some sort of privacy policy. Even the nation's premiere institutionalization of e-government, the FirstGov portal at firstgov.gov, headlined "Citizens Interacting with Government," but in fact all links were to one-way provision of information or at best transactional forms, such as IRS tax forms. An obscure "Contact Us" button, viewable only by scrolling to the very bottom, led only to a librarian-like offer to help citizens find information not listed. Politically speaking, e-government is cautious government quite removed from the dreams of cyber-activists.

E-GOVERNMENT AS THE NEXT AMERICAN REVOLUTION

"What has the greatest potential to revolutionize the performance of government and revitalize our democracy?" asks the opening sentence in Hart-Teeter's (2000: 1) report, *E-Government: The Next American Revolution*. This document explicitly sees e-government reality today as what "would have seemed a utopian dream just a decade ago" (p. 1), citing examples such as remote reading of x-rays for rural patients or members of the armed services communicating with their families even while on duty in the Mideast. Much of the report expounds on the four promises of e-government discussed in the introduction to this essay. "E-government...puts ownership of government truly in the hands of all Americans" (p. 2) is the belief of its authors. But this belief is rooted in a premise, "if government embraced information technology with imagination and bold leadership" (p. 2). The likelihood of this premise being fulfilled is little examined by the authors, for whom it is simply a hope.

Revolutionaries create revolutions. Marx believed these revolutionaries would come the oppressed working class. We are accustomed to think of revolutions in terms of hordes of students and ordinary people in the streets, confronting tanks, soldiers abandoning their regime to join with the people in a mass uprising. What is striking about the rapid rise of e-government is precisely the opposite: the impetus has come from above with very little *a priori* demand from below. Truly, once services are offered, millions use them. But these same millions rarely join in any politically effective manner to demand that e-government be used to "revitalize democracy" or achieve any of the other lofty ideals of e-government's more enthusiastic proponents.

The revolutionary possibilities of e-government have titillated into action a large coalition of strange bedfellows, including activists, philanthropic foundations, progressives, Silicon Valley futurists, management reformers, and idealists. Behind their energy has marched a second, much more moderate phalanx of public managers and some elected officials who see e-government as an inevitable and desirable set of tools to improve government services and save money at the same time. Far behind the masses that would give meaning to the e-government "revolution" are indeed coming along, not with revolutionary zeal but merely as occasional and casual, largely passive users of a free service. One cannot picture trying to convince Karl Marx that this is a revolution.

Hart-Teeter surveys seek to further the e-government bandwagon through surveys that show public support for e-government. Thus, the above-cited report documents that Americans think e-government should be a high priority for the Bush administration by a 3:1 majority. Never mind that e-government does not even appear on the list when citizens are asked more open-ended questions about what issues concern them in the 2000 or 2002 elections. Hart-Teeter also shows 2:1 support for appointment of a White House "technology czar" to lead e-government innovation. Never mind that when Casey Coleman was actually appointed in the General Services Administration to be Chief Technology Officer in July 2002, or when Mark Forman became the OMB's Associate Director for Information Technology and E-Government a year earlier, the public took no note at all. Hart-Teeter also shows that 2:1 favor accomplishing e-government through public-private sector partnerships, a favorite theme of "reinventing government" reformers. Never mind that with regard to these would-be partners, in the Enron era of corporate scandals the public also has a negative attitude toward corporate irresponsibility not seen since the New Deal.

The "new American revolution" is fraught with other problems:

- *The promise of access.* The public has little support for (or understanding of) the Universal Service fee on their phone bills, and the Bush administration de-funded "digital divide" access programs from its FY 2003 budget without fear of public backlash or even public notice.

- *The promise of cost savings.* e-procurement, a cornerstone of this promise, is in deep trouble as an April 2002 survey by the National Institute of Governmental Purchasing showed virtually no increase in the percent of government purchasing agencies using e-procurement between 2001 and 2002, and South Carolina even abandoned its e-procurement system in June, 2002.

- *The promise of privacy:.* This is not really an issue as a post-9/11 public supports unprecedented electronic eavesdropping, computer matching, and governmental removal of information to "cleanse" websites in ways that would have been, at the least, very controversial a few years ago.

- *The promise of e-democracy?:* Santa Monica's seminal and much-vaunted example of e-democracy, PEN, which could be said to have started it all, after an initial tsunami of publicity and flurry of actual use soon fell into relative disuse as elected officials came to see it as a vehicle for hecklers and political junkies not representative of the community and not helpful as a forum for their exposure for purposes of re-election.

The purpose of mentioning these negatives of e-government is not to rebut the "new American revolution" view of e-government as utopia realized with an equally extreme argument about e-government as a failure. However, in considering e-government there is a need for a "reality check," not accepting every claim for it at face value. Perhaps the greatest enemies of e-government at the moment are its own proponents, by claiming more for it than realistically can be delivered.

E-GOVERNMENT AS REENGINEERING THE FEDERAL GOVERNMENT

If e-government is something a little less than a revolution, perhaps it is at least a re-inventing or re-engineering of government. This, in fact, is the dominant view of academics and consultants. "Reinventing government" was already a popular academic management theme when the Clinton administration seized upon it, making it central to Vice President Gore's National Performance Review (NPR). The central themes of this perspective are (1) making government more business-like, including more reliance on markets and public-private partnerships; (2) using technology to replace existing hierarchical agency-centered government processes with flexible results-centered alternatives; and (3) achieving cost savings through shrinking the overall size of government (a dramatic but largely unacknowledged outcome of the NPR). These perspectives have been reformulated for current consumption in the reports of the Harvard Policy Group (2000-2002) and in an immensely popular book by one of Harvard's faculty, Jane

Fountain's *Building the Virtual State: Information Technology and Institutional Change* (2001).

The concept of re-engineering the federal government has evolved over the last decade. A precursor was the Paperwork Reduction Act of 1980 (PRA), which mandated an Information Resources Management (IRM) approach to federal data, a concept in which lay the seeds of the contemporary e-government strategy of replacing departmentalized "stovepipe" data processes with cross-agency integrated ones. The National Performance Review (NPR) was created March 3, 1993, and represented the Clinton Administration's emphasis on information technology as a tool to reform government. Its report, *Creating a Government that Works Better and Costs Less: Reengineering Through Information Technology,* illustrated that the reinventing government movement, originated with a focus on decentralization/devolution, had come to see e-government as major reform thrust. NPR was later renamed the National Partnership for Reinventing Government (NPRG). In 1993, the Government Information Technology Services Board was created to help implement NPR in information technology areas. Also in 1993, the Government Performance and Results Act (GPRA) required agencies to prepare multi-year strategic plans and these, of course, included strategic IT plans. The 1995 amendment to the Paperwork Reduction Act of 1980 (sometimes called the Paperwork Reduction Act of 1995) formally established strategic planning principles for information resources management, including setting IT standards, applied life cycle management principles, mandating cross-agency information technology initiatives, and set technology investment guidelines. The Act designated senior information resources manager positions in the major departments and agencies and created the Office of Information and Regulatory Affairs (OIRA) within OMB to provide central oversight of information management activities across the federal government. OIRA was mandated to "develop and maintain a government-wide strategic plan for information resources management." The OIRA director became, in principle, the main IT advisor to the director of the OMB.

In 1996, the Clinger-Cohen Act (originally named the Information Technology Management Reform Act of 1996) established a chief information officer (CIO) in every agency, making agencies responsible for developing an IT plan. It mandated top management's involvement in IT strategic planning, using IT portfolio management approaches. Later, when e-government became a priority, the existence of the CIO strategic planning structure was an important element facilitating e-government implementation at the federal level. The Clinger-Cohen Act also (1) encouraged federal agencies to evaluate and adopt best management and acquisition practices used by both private and public sector organizations, and (2) required agencies to base decisions about IT investments on quantitative and qualitative factors associated with the costs, benefits, and risks of those investments and to use performance data to demonstrate how well the IT expenditures support improvements to agency programs, through measurements such as reduced costs, improved employee productivity, and higher customer satisfaction.

Also in 1996, President Clinton issued Executive Order 13011, a companion to the Clinger-Cohen Act. EO 13011 sought to improve management through coordinated approaches to technology in the Executive Office, calling for an alignment of technology goals with strategic organizational goals and calling for interagency coordination of technology applications. EO 13011 created the CIO Council, an advisory body from 28 federal agencies plus senior OMB/OIRA personnel. It represented the presidential "seal of approval" for e-government.

In 1998 the Government Paperwork Elimination Act was passed, authorizing the OMB to acquire alternative information technologies for use by executive agencies (Sec. 1702); support for electronic signatures (Secs. 1703-1707); electronic filing of employment forms (Sec. 1705). Electronic filing of most forms must be in place by 21 October 2003. The GPEA is the basis for accepting electronic records and electronic signatures as legally valid and enforceable. It also represents Congressional endorsement of the e-government strategy. In 2000, the President's Management Council adopted digital government as one of its top three priorities.

In a Presidential Memo of 17 December 1999, titled "Electronic Government," Clinton endorsed the concept of a federal government-wide portal and in June 24, 2000 delivered the first presidential Internet address, in which he reiterated the call for what later became FirstGov.gov.

FirstGov.gov was launched on 22 September 2000 as a Clinton management initiative. It is the official U.S. government portal, designed to be a one-stop gateway to federal services for citizens, businesses, and agencies. At launch, it was a gateway to 47 million federal government web pages. FirstGov.gov also linked to state, local, DC, and tribal government pages in an attempt to provide integrated service information in particular areas, such as travel. It is managed by the Office of Citizen Services and Communications, within the General Services Administration.

In Election 2000, both candidates (Gore and Bush) advocate digital government concepts. In August 2001, the Bush administration issued *The President's Management Agenda*, committing the Administration to five major management objectives, one of which was electronic government. In June 2001, OMB created the position of Associate Director for Information Technology and E-Government. This gave the OMB a "point man" to give higher priority to IT initiatives. In essence, this position had a mandate to provide leadership to all federal IT implementation, including a special emphasis on e-government. Mark Forman became the first incumbent. On the General Services Administration side, the first Chief Technology Officer (CTO) for the Federal government was appointed, located in the Office of Citizen Services, charged with overseeing the implementation of e-government initiatives. The first incumbent was Casey Coleman.

Acting on a February 2002 recommendation from the Federal CIO Council, the OMB established the Federal Enterprise Architecture Program Management Office (FEAPMO) on February 6, 2002.[2] In 2002, FEAPMO issued "The Business Reference Model Version 1.0," which created a functional (not department-based) classification of all government services with a view to its use by OMB for cross-agency reviews to eliminate redundant IT investments and promote re-usable IT components. A Performance Reference Model (forthcoming) is to set general performance measurement metrics. A Data and Information Reference Model is to detail data needed to support Enterprise Architecture. Overall, these models are quite reminiscent of program planning and budgeting (PPB) in the 1960s, with their similar focus on functional rather than line item budgeting, emphasis on empirical measurement of performance, and strengthening of top management oversight capabilities.

On 27 February 2002, the OMB issued *E-Government Strategy*. This document set forth Bush administration e-government principles: citizen-centric, results-oriented, and market-based. It also called for increased cross-agency data sharing. Thirty-four projects were identified for funding. The E-Government Act of 2002 passed by the Senate in July 2002 but awaiting House action at this writing mandated the establishment of a federal CIO in the Office of Management and Budget, along with funds for inter-agency e-government initiatives. A new Office of Electronic Government is to oversee setting of cross-agency standards, including privacy standards, and to assure new e-government initiatives are cross-agency in nature. As such, the EGA represented a direct attack on the agency-centric "stovepipe" approach to IT of prior years. Two other 2002 actions included the OMB calling for a uniform protocol for e-rulemaking by end of 2003, and OMB issuing a revision of Circular A-76, encouraging outsourcing, in line with the Bush administration's goal to outsource 15% of "non-inherently governmental jobs" as part of his "market-based" strategy for public information technology.

Likewise, at the state level, the last five years has had a dramatic expansion of digital government. Most, if not all, state governments now have formal e-government plans and extensive gateway portals. In terms of e-democracy, Washington and Missouri were first to show legislative hearings via the Internet, in 1996. Gene Rose, public affairs director of the National Conference of State Legislatures, indicates that almost every state broadcasts at least some of its hearings over the web and a majority broadcast floor sessions. For instance, all hearings and committee sessions of the Michigan Legislature are now broadcast in streaming video, live over nine channels. Some 700 legislative staff members now find it crucial, using it to filter committee work while still able to work in their offices (Bhambani, 2002). The Center for Digital Government and *Government Technology Magazine* ranked state legislatures on citizen ease of following legislative bills and hearings and making online input. The winner was the Arizona legislature, whose Arizona Legislative Information System (ALIS) lets the public create a free, individualized bill-tracking system to select bills on which to receive alerts.[3] All bills are online and searchable by keyword, bill number, title, or sponsor. Citizens can find complete e-mail addresses for legislators and can search for representatives by zip code or map. Anyone can access streaming video of all committee hearings and legislative floor activities (Peterson, 2002).

THE E-GOVERNMENT BUSINESS MODEL

The OMB and others promoting e-government are guided by an e-government business model. Fulfillment of the promise of e-government is contingent on the realism of this model. A business model in the private sector is the core strategy of the firm that defines its place in the market. In the public sector, a business plan is the core strategy of a governmental entity, defining the basis for its long-range support by citizens and superordinate governmental entities. The business plan is not about implementation tactics or even about strategy. Rather it is about the architecture of components that will exploit opportunities for the organization. That architecture is system-dependent, not people-dependent, and as such can be translated into standard operating procedures thought to bring success.

In the private sector, the business plan describes how the enterprise makes money - its market targets, the benefit of its products or services to those targets, its basic architecture and process flow in delivering products or services, and its revenue stream. For instance, the McDonald's business model offers an instantly recognizable brand based on consistent-tasting popular foods served quickly in a colorful and circus-like atmosphere consistent across a large number of restaurants, such that there is always one nearby. It seeks to be more convenient, better value, and higher in performance than other fast food vendors. This plan is embedded in a book of standard operating procedures that specify in some detail how the individual restaurant is to carry out the business plan. In another example, Dell Computer's business model is to have suppliers linked electronically to deliver components on a just-in-time basis. Dell manufactures customized PCs for sale at a low price, delivering through independent shippers like UPS. Web pages and 800 numbers provide information and ordering; customers make payments on the phone or online.

Many private-sector e-business models have only partial applicability to the public sector environment:

1.   *Direct sales models* center on savings via disintermediation, eliminating middlemen between the producer and the public. In education, defense, highways, welfare, and other public arenas, there is no layer of intermediating wholesalers and retailers to eliminate.

2.   *Virtual storefront e-tailing*: While e-government seeks to emulate the "click-and-order" convenience of e-business models like Amazon.com, the private sector focus is on increased sales at reduced cost. In the public sector, the focus is only on reduced paper transaction costs. Moreover, the bulk of governmental services cannot be delivered online.

3.   *Online malls.* E-government seeks to emulate the "one-stop shopping" of Yahoo! Stores, but in the private sector, the mall owner profits from listing fees, transaction fees, setup fees, advertising, and commissions. In the public sector, the portal ("mall") owner must foot the expense in most cases, undermining the incentive logic of the business plan.

4.   *Online brokers.* An e-business model is to bring buyers and sellers together to negotiate and finalize transactions, with the broker taking a small percentage for arranging the buys, as E-Trade or AutoTrader do. The public sector cannot charge brokerage fees and most governmental services are not germane to servicing purchasing transactions.

5.   *Auctions.* Another e-business model is auctioning, popularized by E-Bay. Auctioning is a special case of brokering, with the same differences for the public sector.

6.   *Infomediaries.* In this e-business model, a fee is charged for aggregating and distributing information of value, and/or advertising is rented in exchange for traffic exposure. While many aspects of government lend themselves to the infomediary model in theory, in practice there are strong traditions and even legislation preventing agencies from generating net revenues from the sale of information, much less advertising.

7.   *Content sponsorship.* This e-business model provides entertainment or freebies (Freesamples.com) to generate traffic for the purpose of soliciting information on consumer interests and permission to send advertising. Selling advertising space and promotions for advertisers, which is foreign to the public sector, supports the model.

If so many e-business models have little or no applicability to the public sector, it may be asked, "What *is* an e-government business model?"

In the public sector, a General Services Administration Roundtable sought to bring out some of the ideas behind a public sector e-government business model (Steyaert, 2002). As articulated by Joan Steyaert, Deputy Associate Administrator of the Office of Information Technology, Office of Governmentwide Policy, GSA, the e-government business plan shared by Roundtable participants is based on several key premises:

1. There a "new economy" attributable to technology and reflected in the extraordinary economic growth of the 1990s.
2. Technology allows decisions to be made "just in time," improving delivery, reducing work hours, and increasing efficiency.
3. As in the Dell business plan, risk is minimized by pursuing only those technologies clearly demanded by customers. Customer satisfaction should be a test of CIO performance.
4. As at IBM, large savings can be gained by replacing paper records with digital ones.
5. By standardizing hardware and software, "huge productivity gains" are possible.
6. Public-private partnerships, like EDS's aid in establishing data sharing networks for law enforcement in Ontario, illustrates the financial benefits of partnering
7. While there is a lower tolerance for failure in the public sector and while incentives for risk-taking are much less clear and agency cultures are risk-averse, and this is being overcome by the GSA requiring portfolio management starting in 2001, shifting from a project-centric form of risk management to a portfolio approach encouraging a mix of low-risk and higher-risk, higher-payoff project.

In the e-government business plan, it is thought that government will become customer-oriented, working in partnership with the private sector to deliver paperless just-in-time services using standardized hardware and software developed as part of a portfolio approach to IT investment, allowing greater risk-taking and greater payoffs. In this way, the public sector will reap the dramatic gains seen by the technology-driven economy of the 1990s.

Examination of each of these seven points in the e-government business plan suggests there are limitations.

1. **Lack of an equation for prosperity.** While it is true that the 1990s economy coincided with large investments in technology, economists are far from agreeing that these economic good times are the result of IT. Massive borrowing, Reagan's or Clinton's economic policies, the reorganization of the economy primarily to serve shareholders, the tripling of the balance of payments deficit, international trade considerations, and many other factors also played a role in this period of prosperity. If anything, massive private borrowing and spending is seen as the engine of the 1990s economy. Though technology is also among the growth factors, there is no simple IT investment = prosperity equation. Government cannot blithely assume that IT investment "will do for government in the 2000s what it did for the private sector in the 1990s."
2. **Just in time (JIT) inputs and outputs** have less applicability in governmental organizations. For one thing, public organizations budget inputs are often concentrated in personnel (public universities, for instance, may have over 90% of their budget in personnel lines), which is not very amenable to just-in-time procedures. The single largest agency, Defense, is illustrative of a range of agencies which must have pre-positioned resources not delivered on demand. Another huge govern-

mental component, the federal-state-local roads agencies, do not fit well with the notion of a "customer" appearing to "buy" a service that the agency then goes out and orders "just in time" and "delivers" to the customer. JIT methods can be a cost-saving aspect of e-government in certain circumstances but hardly with the impact JIT has had in the private sector.

3. **Customer-orientation** is certainly a battle cry for e-government reformers. But in government, "customers" can be hard to identify: Soldiers in the Army? Criminals in the corrections system? Taxpayers for the IRS? Children in schools? Will it really help matters if CIOs in government are rated in terms of consumer satisfaction, even where "customers" can be identified, such as vacationers in state and national parks? We all agree that public service should have the orientation of being of service to the public, not to the bureaucracy, and that this requires feedback about public satisfaction with services. E-government can facilitate this feedback (though thus far agencies have been slow about soliciting public evaluation). But whereas customer-orientation in the private sector seeks to increase consumer demand, there is no corresponding purpose in the public sector.

4. **Digital record-keeping and electronic access** is one aspect of the business plan which GAO studies do show can reap substantial savings in the public sector (Schwartz, 2000). While the greater needs of public agencies for accountability mean greater need for a "paper trail," and while government consumes more paper than ever, nonetheless this aspect of electronic government is an area where reforms have been successful.

5. **Standardization of hardware and software** is a complex area in which the pendulum has swung back and forth several times. Economies of scale can be gained by standardization of hardware and software. On the other hand, interoperability requires less standardization of data formats and platforms than was the case ten years ago. Also, past efforts at government-sanctioned standardization have not infrequently left agencies straight-jacketed with outdated requirements and have prevented them from participating in the march of technology. Current plans for a Department of Homeland Security (DHS), uniting dozens of agencies, has led OMB to freeze agency IT investments in anticipation of DHS-wide IT systems and standards. For instance, INS (Immigration and Naturalization Service) has frozen its new financial system, which is still running in tandem with its legacy system. Now INS faces the prospect of having to run both of these systems while trying to build toward some new unified DHS system. DHS systems for finance and other objectives not directly related to fighting terrorism may be lower in priority, meaning agencies like INS may be in IT limbo for years (Ryan, 2002). In the long run, standardization may save money, but this aspect of the e-government business plan is unsure and could even backfire.

6. **Public-private partnerships.** The law enforcement public-private partnership with EDS may well have been very beneficial to Ontario, just as there have been public-private law enforcement data efforts in the U.S., partnering with IBM, Microsoft, and ESRI. Firms find it useful to model their products and services in real-world governmental settings so that subsequently they can better market to the public sector. Such seeding is part of a corporate business plan. However, while it should be taken advantage of when possible, such partnerships are problematic when proposed as part of a government business plan because of the conceptual

mismatch involved. Partnering for firms is seeding, but it is proposed for government as a general strategy for jurisdictions across the board, glossing over the fact that the 114th law enforcement jurisdiction to come along and propose an innovative partnership to provide a model of data sharing is not apt to receive as warm a welcome as the early models so much discussed by e-government proponents. When the 114th jurisdiction comes along (and the U.S. has over 40,000 jurisdictions in law enforcement alone), "public-private partnership" means not corporate-subsidized projects but rather simply a cozy relationship with a vendor. The 114th jurisdiction would do much better to read the literature not on partnership but rather on effective procurement and contracting, particularly since the evaluations of outsourcing show a very mixed picture.

7. **Portfolio management.** The intent of a portfolio approach to IT investment is to develop a critical mass of investment funds, to invest them in a way that maximizes cross-agency benefits, and to do so using a mix of safer lower-payoff investments and riskier higher-payoff investments that involve more entrepreneurial risk-taking than agency project managers could contemplate. Investment in e-government infrastructure is one aspect of portfolio management, enabling things that no single agency could afford. Without disparaging portfolio management, it too brings with it some cautionary considerations. It involves centralization of IT funding, making it more challenging to get agencies to feel they "own" the information processes that are addressed. It involves closer oversight of and performance standards for those lower in the IT food chain, making it more difficult to maintain morale in an environment where the public sector is already at a personnel disadvantage. While the portfolio manager can afford to take some risks (have losing projects), it is not clear the same can be said of the individual project managers and agencies saddled with high-risk projects. By definition, portfolio management has the potential to reap large rewards through large projects. Of course, the history of large IT projects in government is not a good one, but investment in e-government infrastructure promises to be one of the success stories. This, however, is not the same as saying that the portfolio management aspect of a e-government business plan will allow reduced budgets for agencies using that infrastructure. Initially at least, it will involve substantial increased costs, not actual dollar savings. Rather, the "savings" come from improved quality and quantity of transactions. This is quite in contrast to private-sector business plans, which are designed to raise actual dollar revenue.

In summary, while there are aspects of business planning that can be imported into the public sector in its quest for e-government, Bozeman and Bretschneider (1986) remain correct that MIS and PMIS (public management information systems) operate on different dynamics. Ignoring these differences will undermine rather than enhance the long-range success of e-government.

CONCLUSION

As Patricia Diamond Fletcher notes elsewhere in this volume, the federal government is the world's largest creator, maintainer, and disseminator of information. Its portal model of e-government, reflected in the FirstGov.gov website, is not only central to the management agenda of the current presidential administration but promises to mark a new era of greater convenience in citizen access to governmental forms, data, and information. Its advocates promise that not only will e-government bring the convenience of online transactions but it will also reverse citizens' disaffection from government, create dramatic savings, and reinforce rather than erode traditional American freedoms and liberties.

E-government, however, is better thought of not as a revolution but as what it is: an attempt to bring the e-business model into the public sector. A component-by-component examination of the e-business model shows that it is fraught with problems, challenges, and limitations, as well as opportunities, for those who would attempt to implement it in government. This, of course, makes those of us who are academics smile, for it means there is a great deal to research and discuss! E-government is not "apple pie" or "motherhood," immune from criticism and controversy. Indeed, it is not "a" thing at all but rather a large set of options that can go in many directions, not all of them productive or even desirable.

The purpose of this volume of essays on e-government is both to call attention to the transformational potential of e-governance and also to focus on the ethical, policy, and managerial issues that it raises. Some essays in the volume also document the need for a realignment of educational and training programs in public service to meet the needs of the coming era of e-governance. Other essays dwell on policy issues such as the digital divide, implications for international affairs, the potential of e-democracy, and the threat to privacy, to name a few. More managerial topics are covered as well, such as the organization of government databases and the administration of public-private partnerships. The promise of digital government will be fulfilled only by a new generation of public managers who are generalists, not technocrats, capable of integrating these disparate fields of consideration, which are necessary aspects of the vision of e-government as whole.

ENDNOTES

[1]   This citation specifically refers to DigitalConsumer.com's grassroots lobbying efforts against the proposed Peer to Peer Privacy Act and the Consumer Broadband and Digital Television Promotion Act.

[2]   The Web site is www.feapmo.gov/resources/fea_brm_release_document_rev_1.pdf.

[3]   The Web site is www.azleg.state.az.us.

REFERENCES

Atkinson, R. D. & Ulevich, J. (2000). Digital government: The next step to reengineering the federal government. Washington, DC: Progressive Policy Institute. Retrieved on 10/1/02 from http://www.ppionline.org/documents/Digital_Gov.pdf.

Bhambhani, D. (2002). Michigan lawmakers give birds-eye view of session. *Government Computer News*, (October 21), 32.

Bozeman, B. & Bretschneider, S. (1986). Public management information systems: Theory and prescription. *Public Administration Review, 46*, 475-487.

Fountain, J. E. (2001). *Building the virtual state: Information technology and institutional change*. Washington, DC: Brookings Institution.

Hart-Teeter, Inc. (2000). *E-government: The next American revolution*. Washington, DC: Council for Excellence in Government. Retrieved on 10/1/02 from http://www.excelgov.org/egovpoll/report/poll_report.PDF.

Harvard Policy Group on Network-Enabled Services and Government. (2000 - 2002). *Eight imperatives for leaders in a networked world*. Cambridge, MA: Harvard University. An overview and eight additional reports, issued between 2000 and 2002. Retrieved on 10/1/02 from http://www.ksg.harvard.edu/stratcom/hpg/.

Larsen, E. & Rainie, L. (2002a). *The rise of the e-citizen: How people use government agencies' web sites*. Washington, DC: Pew Internet & American Life Project.

Larsen, E. & Rainie, L. (2002b). *Digital town hall: How local officials use the Internet and the civic benefits they cite from dealing with constituents online*. Washington, DC: Pew Internet & American Life Project.

Levy, S. (2002). Glitterati vs. geeks: Two heavyweights. Hollywood and Silicon Valley, take the fight over content to the Supremes. *Newsweek,* (October 14), 40-42.

Peterson, S. (2002). Digital legislature. *Electronic Government, 3*(3), 8-12.

Ryan, S. M. (2002). Homeland agencies will be wards of OMB. *Government Computer News* (September 09), 42.

Schwartz, A. (2000). Cost. Washington, DC: Center for Technology and Democracy. Retrieved on 10/15/02 from http://www.netcaucus.org/books/egov2001/pdf/cost.pdf.

Steyaert, J. (2002). Public and private sector innovation risk and return in information technology. *Government Computer News,* (October 14). Retrieved on 10/15/02 from http://www.gcn.com/partners.html.

Tonn, B. E., Zambrano, P. & Moore, S. (2001). Community networks or networked communities? *Social Science Computer Review, 19*(2), 201-212.

West, D. M. (2000). *Assessing e-government: The Internet, democracy, and service delivery by state and federal governments*. Providence, RI: Brown University. Retrieved on 10/1/2002 from http://www.insidepolitics.org/egov/egovtreport00.html.

Chapter II

A Brief History of the Emergence of Digital Government in the United States

Harold C. Relyea
Library of Congress, USA

Henry B. Hogue
Library of Congress, USA

ABSTRACT

Digital government may be regarded as the most recent development in the evolving application of electronic information technology to the performance of governmental functions. In the United States, that evolutionary progression is rooted in the Federal, state, and local government use of such information technologies as the telegraph and the telephone. This history, however, considers more than the mere introduction and adaptation of such technologies by governmental entities. Other important aspects include the development and migration of the technologies, as well as imaginative applications of information technology in support of government operations. Also, new policies have been fashioned to ensure the proper management of these technologies and the systems they serve, their protection from physical harm, and the security and privacy of their information. These matters are concisely explored in this overview.

INTRODUCTION

Effective communication was essential for the new Federal government, for various reasons, when it began functioning in the spring of 1789. Because it was a democracy, communication between the citizen and the state was required. Because it was based upon federalism, communication between the national government and subnational governmental entities was necessary; because it was constitutionally comprised of three separate and coequal branche, communication among them was also requisite. The early establishment of Federal records management and publication policies was an initial attempt, of no small importance, at facilitating communication. These included statutes providing for the printing and distribution of laws and treaties,[1] the preservation of state papers,[2] and the maintenance of official files in the new departments.[3] The printing and distribution of both the Senate and House journals was authorized in 1813.[4] Congress arranged for a contemporary summary of chamber floor proceedings to be published in the *Register of Debates* beginning in 1824. It then switched in 1833 to the weekly *Congressional Globe*, which sought to chronicle every step in the legislative process of the two houses, and then established a daily publication schedule for the *Globe* in 1865.[5] Subsequently, the *Congressional Record* succeeded the *Globe* in 1873 as the official congressional gazette.[6] It was produced by a new Federal printing agency, the Government Printing Office, created by Congress in 1860 to produce all of its literature and to serve, as well, the printing needs of the executive branch.[7]

The permanent location of the Federal government in the District of Columbia in 1800 contributed significantly to the development of the Washington community and to communication both among the three branches of government and by them, directly and indirectly (through the press), with the America people. Communication was also facilitated by a gradually increasing number of government workers. At the White House, a single personal secretary, usually a relative, assisted the President, who personally compensated this assistant. It was not until 1857 that Congress appropriated funds for the hiring of official presidential staff.[8] A modest number of clerks began to assist with the work of the new departments and the courts. By 1816, 535 paid civilian employees worked for the executive branch in Washington, DC; 243 were in the legislative branch; and 115 in the judicial branch (U.S. Department of Commerce, 1975, 1103). Their numbers would grow as a consequence of not only added institutional responsibilities, but also increased interaction with a growing populace seeking government information, benefits, and services.

Before long, a revolutionary communications technology presented itself to this bureaucracy of handwritten communiqués, ledgers, and logs — the telegraph. Samuel F. B. Morse opened the first long-distance line, connecting Washington and Baltimore, in 1844. Twelve years thereafter, Hiram Sibley consolidated several fledgling telegraph businesses to create the Western Union Telegraph Company. A transcontinental line was completed on the eve of the Civil War. Recognizing the significance and value of the new technology, the Federal government seized commercial telegraph facilities in April 1861, and created the United States Military Telegraph, a quasi-military organization, to operate them during the war. The Army Signal Corps ran war zone telegraphs and tapped Confederate telegraph lines. Telegraph censorship was managed at different times by the Departments of the Treasury, State, and War, and the President had a telegraph office in close proximity to the White House (Plum, 1882, 64-66; Randall, 1951, 481-482). With the end of the war, telegraph facilities outside of the South were returned to commercial operators, Western Union counting some 4,000 offices. The war experience, however, had taught Federal officials the value of this new electronic communication technology for a variety of governmental functions other than military and law enforcement activities.

Soon, another electronic communication technology — the telephone — would prove useful for government. Shortly after Alexander Graham Bell obtained his 1876 telephone patent, telephone networks began a steady growth in size and complexity. The first telephone exchange was begun in Boston in May 1877; it was linked with New York in March 1884; connections to Philadelphia, Washington, and Albany, NY, were realized a few years later. Technical improvements amplifying long-distance signals enabled the inauguration of a truly transcontinental telephone system in 1915.

The extent to which the Federal government had become permeated by the telephone was reflected in the official *U.S. Congressional Directory* of January 1906, which, for the first time, listed telephone numbers for almost all of the agencies and institutions of the three branches. Presidents Grover Cleveland and Benjamin Harrison, "for temperamental reasons," were reportedly infrequent users of the telephone, but William McKinley "revelled in the comforts of telephony," while Theodore Roosevelt regarded the instrument as being "mainly for emergencies." These presidential tidbits were proffered in 1910 by the respected Canadian editor and writer Herbert N. Casson, who characterized the "sweeping revolution" resulting from public officials' growing acceptance of the new technology as "Government by telephone!" (Casson, 1910, 201-203). A couple of decades would lapse, however, before the elements of another such revolution would begin formulation.

TECHNICAL DEVELOPMENTS

The electronic computer was the result of efforts to develop a better computational device — one that initially performed calculations, but soon was perfected to sort, file, edit, or otherwise process information or data.[9] One of the more elaborate and sophisticated analog computers — called a mechanical differential analyzer because of its ability to solve differential equations — was built in 1930 at the Massachusetts Institute of Technology (MIT) by Vannevar Bush, who would later come to prominence in the administration of President Franklin D. Roosevelt (Flamm, 1988, 32).

A prototype of an experimental all-electronic computer was created at Iowa State University in 1939 by John V. Atanasoff, followed by an upgraded model in 1942, but further work ceased later that year when Atanasoff and his associates left the university for other war-related endeavors. Atanasoff's efforts, and those of George R. Stibitz at the Bell Telephone Laboratories developing electromechanical calculators, were significant for making use of "circuitry that processed numbers in digital form, as sequences of binary, on-off electrical pulses that were stored in switches and counted in adders" (Flamm, 1988, 32).

Sometime in 1941, Atanasoff demonstrated his computer for physicist John W. Mauchly, who wrote a memorandum proposing the construction of an all-electronic, general-purpose computer. This memorandum subsequently came to the attention of Army Ballistic Research Laboratory staff at the Moore School of the University of Pennsylvania in 1942, which decided to accept the proposal. Among those involved in the ENIAC (Electronic Numerical Integrator and Computer) project were director Herman H. Goldstein, university liaison officer J. G. Brainerd, and chief engineer J. Presper Eckert, Jr., with Mauchly in a consultant role. Completed in the winter of 1944-1945, the ENIAC had a computing speed of about 300 multiplications per second while other digital machines at the time had multiplication speeds of approximately one per second. In contrast, today's 1.7GHz P4 computer has multiplication speeds of 1.7 billion per second.

In August 1944, Goldstine, Eckert, Mauchly, and mathematician John von Neumann, among others, began work on an ENIAC successor, the EDVAC (Electronic Discrete Variable Computer), which would result in a number of basic ideas that would govern computer development for the next two decades. First generation machines (1952-1958), characterized by vacuum-tube circuits, huge size, and exorbitant cost, gave way to second-generation machines (1959-1963), distinguished by individualized transistor circuits and the exclusive use of magnetic-core storage systems. Third generation machines (1964-1975), not always clearly distinguishable from those of the previous generation, saw the introduction of integrated circuits and large-scale integration. With fourth generation machines (mid-1970s) making use of very large scale integrated circuits, multiprocessors, and networks (and less costly memory chips) came the development of minicomputers, which led to high-performance personal computers and workstations.

In the decade following the end of World War II, the Federal government dominated computer development. Thereafter, a commercial, business-oriented market began to emerge, with private sector developers producing first and second generation computers. Third generation technology was the product of a maturing and highly competitive commercial computer market. At this time, the Federal government increasingly became a purchaser of commercially produced computers, but its research and development support was confined to high-end, very large scale computers, and later "shifted to advanced, pre-commercial, leading-edge concepts, more exotic technologies, and support for basic research" (Flamm, 1987, 43).

The roots of the Internet lie in the development of computer networking through Federally funded projects, beginning in the 1960s.[10] The Advanced Research Projects Agency (ARPA, later renamed the Defense Advanced Research Agency or DARPA), a Department of Defense entity that supported military-related research and development of technology, funded the development of ARPANET by Bolt, Beranak, and Newman (BBN) of Cambridge, MA. ARPANET responded to the need to make efficient use of expensive computing resources among ARPA research contractors; networked computers could be shared. The existing telephone network provided a conduit for electronic communications, although networking required additional innovations. The development of ARPANET drew on a number of technological developments, including "packet switching," which, rather than sending a complete communication along a predefined route, breaks the communication into a number of smaller units and allows each packet of information to be individually delivered to its destination along the best path available at the time. This innovation was developed in parallel by several different researchers in the early 1960s.

ARPANET became operational in 1969, and continued to evolve during the following decade. The Telnet Protocol (a standardized method of information transmission) enabled a user to log onto another computer through the network. A group at MIT led by Abhay Bhushan created the File Transfer Protocol (FTP) in 1971, which allowed the transfer of files from one machine to another. E-mail, developed in early 1972 by Ray Tomlinson of BBN, became the most popular use of ARPANET. In the mid-1970s, Robert Kahn and Vinton Cerf developed the Transmission Control Protocol (TCP), with Internet Protocol or IP added later. Whereas previous protocols allowed for communication among computers on a single network, TCP/IP created a standard of communication between computers on different networks, and thus allowed the interconnection of multiple networks and the creation of an Internet.

During the 1970s, ARPANET was accessible only to ARPA contractors; other networks were developed to serve other constituencies. Two Duke University graduate students, Tom Truscott and Jim Ellis, together with students from other universities, are credited with beginning, in 1979, the development of Usenet, which grew to be a grass roots network of tens of thousands of discussion groups (newsgroups). [For a history of Usenet and its relationship to the Internet, see Hauben & Hauben (1996).] Other institutional networks were developed as well. In 1980, the National Science Foundation (NSF) provided a grant that launched the development of CSNET, planned to provide network access to university computer science departments lacking access to ARPANET. Later, in the 1980s, NSF developed NSFNET, a larger project that formed the infrastructure foundation of the Internet. NSFNET evolved into a network of regional networks, which were, in turn, connected to institutional systems. The Internet continued to grow, and, for the most part, has been transferred from NSF management to the private sector.

By the early 1990s, the Internet was used by hundreds of thousands of people from around the world. The simultaneous creation of the World Wide Web (WWW) greatly broadened the use of the Internet by facilitating its use by people with little technical knowledge or aptitude. It also allowed the Internet to move beyond simple text transfers to multimedia exchanges. The Web is based in the document format Hypertext Markup Language (HTML), created by Timothy Berners-Lee and Robert Cailliau at CERN, a particle physics laboratory in Geneva, Switzerland. Hypertext Transfer Protocol (HTTP) was designed to aid in the retrieval of such documents. The development of Web browsers and search engines, which help the user navigate through the Web and search for information, further facilitated the spread of Internet use.

VISIONS

Often individuals struggling with immediate problems and needs will imaginatively discern a scheme of resolution employing plausible techniques or technologies. Indeed, "plausible" may mean the technique is not available or perfected at the moment, but is foreseeable in terms of technology developments. It is the character of technologies to "alter and control the material conditions of life" and to "create a reality according to our design" (Grove, 1980, 294, 311).

As the world erupted in war in 1939, Vannevar Bush was thinking about the creation of a personal aid to memory. At that time, he was president of the Carnegie Institution of Washington, DC, would soon be called to chair the National Defense Research Committee, and then be named the head of the Office of Scientific Research and Development where he would serve as President Franklin D. Roosevelt's highly influential science adviser. By training, Bush was an engineer, with doctorates from Harvard University and MIT. He taught at the latter school for many years. While there, Bush, in 1930, invented a differential analyzer, a predecessor of the analog computer. Five years later, he began work on an advanced model of his earlier machine, and would continue to experiment actively with such technology until arriving at the Carnegie Institution in 1938 (see Burke, 1994; Nyce & Kahn, 1991).

The problem that Bush was considering was the inability of human memory to contend with the growing difficulty of too much information. Late in 1939, he sent an initial draft of his thoughts about this matter to *Fortune* magazine. Undecided about the appropriateness of the essay for that publication, an editor encouraged Bush to rewrite the piece for a popular magazine. Overtaken by his responsibilities for the war effort, Bush did not return to the essay until 1944, when, late in the year, he sent it to the editors of *The Atlantic Monthly*, who accepted it for publication in July 1945 (Bush, 1945).

In all likelihood, Bush's war experience reinforced his sense of the mounting difficulties of information overload. In posing a solution, he proffered that, "every time one combines and records facts in accordance with established logical processes, the creative aspect of thinking is concerned only with the selection of the data and the process to be employed, and the manipulation thereafter is repetitive in nature and hence a fit matter to be relegated to the machines." The particular machine he envisioned was "a sort of mechanical private file and library," which he called a "memex." It would have consisted of a work desk (presumably operable from a distance), viewing screens, a keyboard, and other mechanization controls which would facilitate the easy and rapid retrieval of images — book pages, records, and communications — stored on microfilm. "Associative indexing" would be a central feature of its operations: "any item may be caused at will to select immediately and automatically another." Thus, the memex, in Bush's view, would be "an enlarged intimate supplement to . . . memory."

Calling Bush's vision "breathtaking," his biographer has observed that Bush offered "a careful description of the benefits to ordinary people of automating thought;" understood the crucial importance of programming and human-machine interaction as limiting factors to the spread of information processing machines; described, in plain language, a set of problems to be overcome in the effort to mechanize cognition; and posed information technology challenges for a generation of inventors (Zachary, 263).

A few years after the publication of Bush's article, Joseph Carl Robnett Licklider, another MIT professor and an experimental psychologist, was exploring psychoacoustics, the study of the conversion of air vibrations into the perception of sound by the human ear and brain. His research required an enormous amount of data analysis, and he was rapidly coming to the realization that his mathematical models of pitch perception were becoming too complex to solve with available analog computers. In his search for a better computational tool, he became acquainted with one of the first minicomputers, a Digital Equipment Company PDP-1. As a consequence of his experience with this technology, he realized that minicomputers were becoming sufficiently powerful to support the kind of mechanical private library envisioned by Vannevar Bush (see Licklider, 1965). Moreover, he also recognized that interactive computers had potential well beyond this library function. In a 1960 essay, he described a "man-computer symbiosis" in which computers, as automated assistants, would facilitate formulative thinking by answering questions, producing simulated models, graphically displaying results, and drawing upon past experience to extrapolate solutions for new situations. He also envisioned, some "10 or 15 years hence," something he called a "thinking center," incorporating both the functions of libraries and the symbiotic man-computer functions described earlier in his essay. Furthermore, he anticipated a network of these centers connected by wide-band communications lines and leased-wire services, the cost for the system being shared by the users (Licklider, 1960).

Two years later, Licklider and his MIT faculty colleague, Welden E. Clark, produced a paper entitled "On-Line Man-Computer Communication," which is widely regarded as providing one of the first conceptions of the future Internet (Licklider & Clark, 1962). This was followed in 1968 with another essay, coauthored by Licklider and psychologist Robert W. Taylor, which discussed "interactive multi-access computer communities." The next step, in the authors' view, was to interconnect these separate communities so as to transform them into a "super community" in which all members of all the communities would commonly share the data resources and programs of the super community. The result would be an organic effect: each community member would contribute more to the super community than they receive, so that the resources of the super community are greater than what any community member alone could create (Licklider & Taylor, 1968; see, generally, Waldrop, 2001).

During the next 20 years, the utilization of information technology (IT) slowly became pervasive within the Federal government, extending beyond the Department of Defense, National Aeronautics and Space Administration, and General Services Administration, which were among the initial major users. Reviewing this development in 1986, a congressional oversight committee observed that an "ongoing revolution in computer and telecommunication technology is producing major changes in the way that the Federal Government collects, maintains, and disseminates information." The situation was one of clear significance: "Information and the ability to access it quickly and reliably have become a source of political and economic power" (U.S. Congress, 1986, 2). The panel offered a number of prescient findings:

- "Increasing amounts of information — both private and public — are being maintained in electronic data bases," and this "trend will both continue and accelerate."
- "Electronic collection, maintenance, and dissemination of information by Federal agencies can undermine the practical limitations and legal structures" governing public access to, as well as government collection, creation, and dissemination of, such information.
- "Electronic information systems offer the opportunity to make more government information readily available" to the public, and this same information "technology also permits government information to be used in ways that are not possible when the information is stored on paper records."
- "The development and installation of an electronic information system requires advanced planning and may require sizable capital expenditures."
- "The Federal Government must understand the consequences of electronic information systems and must recognize the need for new policies that will prevent these systems from being used in unintended ways."
- "There is little communication among Federal agencies about electronic information activities, and there is little central administrative guidance." (U.S. Congress, 1986, 10-11)

These findings revealed a relatively new technology of growing use and application, one conveying considerable discretionary capability to Federal agencies concerning government information management, while simultaneously outstripping the existing practical limitations and legal structures governing many aspects of the government information life cycle.

Two years later, an Office of Technology Assessment (OTA) report gave further testimony to the impact of evolving IT upon existing government information policy and practice. Identified in the OTA study were the following "problems and challenges":

- A blurring or elimination of "many distinctions between reports, publications, databases, records, and the like, in ways not anticipated by existing statutes and policies";
- Electronic technology permitting "information dissemination on a decentralized basis that is cost-effective at low levels of demand, but in ways that may challenge traditional roles, responsibilities, and policies";
- Electronic technology "eroding the institutional roles of government-wide information dissemination agencies"; and
- Electronic technology that "has outpaced the major government-wide statutes that apply to Federal information dissemination." (U.S. Office of Technology Assessment, 1988, 8)

The emerging vision highlighted the need for new policies and administrative arrangements to plan and manage an emerging electronic information phenomenon and make effective use of IT.

Observing that the "automation of Federal agencies and programs has been under way for three decades," and noting that some "agencies, in recent years, have moved beyond internal automation to the application of computers and telecommunications for delivering services and interacting with clients," a September 1993 OTA report identified powerful forces that were thought to be "so strong that the transition toward ever greater use of electronic delivery is inevitable." These included:

- Intensified demands for a more responsive, more productive, and less costly government;
- Relentless fiscal pressures at all levels of government;
- Increasing recognition that service delivery is a core business of government;
- Declining cost-performance ratios and growing user-friendliness of information technology; and
- Increasing use and acceptance of information technology. (U.S. Office of Technology Assessment, 1993, 4-5)

This vision, however, also had a negative dimension: "The Federal Government," said the report, "lacks an overall strategy or vision of electronic service delivery," so that "many opportunities for technology and program integration, common technical standards and delivery platforms, partnering with state and local governments, and use of off-the-shelf commercial technology may be lost," and "Federal leadership in electronic service delivery will be in jeopardy" (U.S. Office of Technology Assessment, 1993, 6, 9). Congress was seen as a primary agent for correcting this deficiency. The report indicated that Congress and the administration could require that certain strategic elements, specified in the report, "be included in all Federal agency plans and budgets for electronic service delivery, and provide agencies with guidance for directives on implementation."

Also, "Congress could, at a minimum, reinforce the importance of these strategies through general statutory language, and perhaps more specific report language, to accompany the reauthorization of the Paperwork Reduction Act (PRA) and through annual appropriations"; "could work with and monitor OMB [Office of Management and Budget] to develop detailed guidance for agency information technology planning and budgeting on electronic delivery"; and its "committees with government-wide oversight (Senate Committee on Governmental Affairs and House Committee on Government Operations) may find it helpful to hold annual oversight hearings on electronic delivery activities of Federal agencies" (U.S. Office of Technology Assessment, 1993, 17-18).

That same month, a task force — the National Performance Review (NPR) — under the leadership of Vice President Al Gore delivered its first report to the President. Filled with recommendations to fulfill its title and theme of "creating a government that works better and costs less," the report and the NPR would give impetus to the more widespread and effective use of IT to manage the operations and information of Federal agencies and to deliver services to the American people (U.S. Office of the Vice President, 1993). The NPR vision of "electronic government" appeared in its most developed form in a February 1997 report, where, in an introduction, Vice President Gore wrote:

> *Taken together, the recommendations here paint a picture of the kind of government we should have as we begin the next century. It will be a government where all Americans have the opportunity to get services electronically and where, aided by technology, the productivity of government operations will be soaring.* (U.S. Office of the Vice President, 1997, 2)

So-called electronic or digital government — "where all Americans have the opportunity to get services electronically" — was a reality when the new century arrived, and will, in all likelihood, develop, in many dimensions, in the years ahead. However, for the lack of a measure, if not for other reasons, some uncertainty exists about characterizing the productivity of government operations as "soaring," a reminder that IT is a tool for realizing efficient, economical, and effective government, but not a guarantee of that desired end.

THE EVOLVING POLICY FRAMEWORK

The nurturing of the technology that would contribute to the realization of digital government in the United States began with Federal government funding of computer research and development during the decade following the end of World War II. This support shifted as a maturing and highly competitive commercial computer industry evolved. Similarly, federal funding fostered the development of computer networking, such as ARPANET, CSNET, and NSFNET, underlying the Internet, which would not be managed by the Federal government.

The High-Performance Computing Act of 1991 set goals and authorized funding for a high performance computing and communications program, which Federal, industrial, and academic interests had been seeking since 1989. The statute also mandated the National Research and Education Network (NREN) to support broadly communication and resource sharing among institutions and individuals engaged in unclassified research in the United States. In many regards, NREN was an addition to NSFNET, which served as the primary cross-continental backbone for it, but at the time, the Internet was operational and evolving into its mature, international form.

Plans for aiding that transformation were unveiled on September 15, 1993, when the Clinton Administration released its agenda for realizing a national information infrastructure — "a seamless web of communications networks, computers, databases, and consumer electronics that will put vast amounts of information at users' fingertips." Government would enhance the realization of the "information superhighway," make its information holdings available, and perhaps "itself improve through better information management" (U.S. Department of Commerce, 1993, 3, 11). Thus, the plan for realizing electronic or digital government was set.

The creation and operation of digital government owes much to a variety of legal authorities that seek to promote the use of IT by governmental entities with a view to improving the efficiency and economy of government operations, and to ensuring the proper management of these technologies and the systems they serve, their protection from physical harm, and the security and privacy of their information. Among the major policy instruments are the laws and directives described below.

Privacy Act

With the Privacy Act of 1974, Congress sustained some traditional, major privacy values; created arrangements whereby American citizens and permanent resident aliens could gain access to and, for corrective purposes, emend records maintained on them by most, but not all, Federal agencies; and established a number of principles of fair information practice. These principles constrain the government's use of personally identifiable information and, thereby, to some extent, protect individuals from invasions of their privacy. This act coincided with the growing use of electronic databases in government, and continues to play an important role in information policy with the growth of the Internet and the transfer of information it facilitates. The act provides both civil and criminal enforcement arrangements.

Paperwork Reduction Act

The original Paperwork Reduction Act of 1980 (PRA) was enacted largely to relieve the public from the mounting information collection and reporting requirements of the Federal government. It also promoted coordinated information management activities on a government wide basis by the director of OMB, and prescribed information management responsibilities for the executive agencies. The management focus of the PRA was sharpened with amendments in 1986 which refined the concept of "information resources management" (IRM), defined as "the planning, budgeting, organizing, directing, training, promoting, controlling, and management activities associated with the burden, collection, creation, use, and dissemination of information by agencies, including the management of information and related resources such as automatic data processing equipment." This key term received further definition and explanation in the PRA of 1995, making IRM a tool for managing the contribution of information activities to program performance, and for managing related resources, such as personnel, equipment, funds, and technology.

The evolution of the PRA reflects the beginning of an effort to manage better electronic information and supporting IT. The PRA of 1995 specifies a full range of responsibilities for the director of OMB for all government information, regardless of form or format, throughout its entire life cycle. Agency responsibilities regarding government information policy and IT are also established by the act.

Computer Security Act

Recognizing the increasing use of computers by Federal agencies and the vulnerability of computer-stored information, including personal information, to unauthorized access, Congress enacted the Computer Security Act of 1987. The statute requires each Federal agency to develop security plans for its computer systems containing sensitive information. Such plans are subject to review by the National Institute of Standards and Technology (NIST) of the Department of Commerce, and a summary, together with overall budget plans for IT, is filed with OMB. NIST is authorized to set security standards for all Federal computer systems, except those containing intelligence, cryptologic, or certain military information, or information specifically authorized under criteria established by an executive order or statute to be kept secret in the interest of national defense or foreign policy. Each Federal agency is directed to provide all employees involved with the management, use, or operation of its computer systems with mandatory periodic training in computer security awareness and accepted computer security practice.

Computer Matching and Privacy Protection Act

Congress amended the Privacy Act in 1988 to regulate the use of computer matching — the computerized comparison of records for the purpose of establishing or verifying eligibility for a Federal benefit program or for recouping payments or delinquent debts under such programs — conducted by Federal agencies or making use of Federal records subject to the statute. The amendments, denominated the Computer Matching and Privacy Protection Act of 1988, regulate the use of computer matching by Federal agencies involving personally identifiable records maintained in a system of records subject to the Privacy Act. Matches performed for statistical, research, law enforcement, tax, and certain other purposes are not subject to such regulation. In order for matches to occur, a written matching agreement, effectively creating a matching program, must be prepared specifying such details, explicitly required by the amendments, as the purpose and legal authority for the program; the justification for the program and the anticipated results, including a specific estimate of any savings; a description of the records being matched; procedures for providing individualized notice, at the time of application, to applicants for, and recipients of, financial assistance or payments under Federal benefits programs and to applicants for and holders of positions as Federal personnel that any information they provide may be subject to verification through the matching program; procedures for verifying information produced in the matching program; and procedures for the retention, security, and timely destruction of the records matched and for the security of the results of the matching program. Every agency conducting or participating in a matching program must establish a Data Integrity Board, composed of senior agency officials, to oversee and coordinate program operations, including the execution of certain specified review, approval, and reporting responsibilities.

Electronic Freedom of Information Amendments

Congress enacted the original Freedom of Information Act (FOIA) in 1966. It replaced the public information section of the Administrative Procedure Act (APA), which was found to be ineffective in providing the public with a means of access to unpublished executive agency records. Subsection (a) of the FOIA reiterates the requirements of the APA public information section that certain operational information — e.g., organization descriptions, delegations of final authority, and substantive rules of general policy — be published in the *Federal Register.*

Subsection (b) statutorily establishes a presumptive right of access by any person — individual or corporate, regardless of nationality—to identifiable, existing, unpublished records of Federal agencies without having to demonstrate a need or even a reason for such a request. The subsection lists nine categories of information that may be exempted from the rule of disclosure. The burden of proof for withholding material sought by the public is placed upon the government. Denials of requests may be appealed to the head of the agency holding the sought records, and ultimately pursued in Federal court.

The FOIA was subsequently amended in 1974, 1976, 1986, and 1996, the last alterations being the Electronic Freedom of Information Amendments (E-FOIA), which, among other modifications, confirm the statute's applicability to records in electronic form or format, require that responsive materials be provided in the form or format sought by the requester, and mandate so-called electronic reading rooms which the public may access online to examine important and high visibility agency records.

Clinger-Cohen Act

In 1996, the PRA was modified by new procurement reform and information technology management legislation resulting from the merger of two similar bills into a single measure, which was included in the National Defense Authorization Act for FY1996. Set out in two divisions of the statute as the Federal Acquisition Reform Act of 1996 and the Information Technology Management Reform Act of 1996, the duo was subsequently denominated the Clinger-Cohen Act in honor of the legislators who had sponsored the original legislation.

The Clinger-Cohen Act makes each agency responsible for its own IT acquisition, and requires the purchase of the best and most cost effective technology available.[11] It mandates a chief information officer (CIO) for each executive agency and specifies certain duties and qualifications for these officials. Other provisions gloss some of the responsibilities prescribed in the PRA. For example, the capital planning and investment control duties assigned to director of OMB by the Clinger-Cohen Act are to be performed, according to that statute, in fulfilling the director's IT responsibilities under the PRA. Similarly, the director is to "encourage the use of performance-based and results-based management" in fulfilling these same responsibilities.

Executive Order No. 13011:
Federal Information Technology Management

Following the enactment of the PRA of 1995 and the Clinger-Cohen Act, President William Clinton issued Executive Order No. 13011 of July 16, 1996, to improve Federal IT management and promote a coordinated approach to its application and use across the executive branch. In addition to improving the management of their information systems, including the acquisition of IT, by implementing the relevant provisions of the PRA and the Clinger-Cohen Act, agencies were directed to refocus IT management to support their strategic missions, and rethink and restructure the way they perform their functions before investing in IT to support that work. Other immediate objectives for the agencies included cooperation in the use of IT to improve the productivity of Federal programs and to provide a coordinated, interoperable, secure, and shared government wide infrastructure that is provided and supported by a diversity of private sector suppliers and a well-trained corps of IT professionals. Skill and career development opportunities for IT professionals also were to be expanded.

New responsibilities for agency heads included effectively using IT to improve mission performance and service to the public, and strengthening the quality of decisions about the employment of information resources to meet mission needs through integrated analysis, planning, budgeting, and evaluation processes.

The order tasked the director of OMB, among other duties, with evaluating agency IRM practices and, as part of the budget process, analyzing, tracking, and evaluating the risks and results of all major capital investments for information systems. The Administrator of General Services was given responsibility for developing, maintaining, and disseminating for agency use, as requested by OMB or the agencies, recommended methods and strategies for the development and acquisition of IT.

Presidential Decision Directive 63: Critical Infrastructure Protection

On May 22, 1998, the White House issued Presidential Decision Directive 63 (PDD 63), a security classified policy instrument on critical infrastructure protection.[12] It was the product of an interagency evaluation of the recommendations of the President's Commission on Critical Infrastructure Protection.[13] The directive set a goal of a reliable, interconnected, and secure information system infrastructure by 2003, and significantly increased security for government systems by 2000. To assist with the realization of this goal, PDD 63 established a National Coordinator for Security, Infrastructure Protection, and Counter-Terrorism, whose responsibilities include not only critical infrastructure protection, but also safeguarding against foreign terrorism and threats of domestic mass destruction, including biological weapons; a National Infrastructure Protection Center at the Federal Bureau of Investigation to provide the principal means of facilitating and coordinating the Federal response to an incident, mitigating attacks, investigating threats, and monitoring reconstitution efforts; a National Infrastructure Assurance Council, composed of private sector experts and state and local government officials, to provide guidance for a national plan for critical infrastructure protection; and a Critical Infrastructure Assurance Office to provide support for the National Coordinator's work with government agencies and the private sector in developing a national plan for critical infrastructure protection, and to help coordinate a national education and awareness program, and legislative and public affairs activities.

The centerpiece of the efforts launched with PDD 63 is a national plan to serve as a blueprint for establishing a critical infrastructure protection capability. Version one, the National Plan for Information Systems Protection, was unveiled on January 7, 2000.[14]

Since the arrival of the Bush Administration in 2001, PDD 63 has been under reevaluation with a view to upgrading. Terrorist attacks of September 11, 2001, gave added impetus to improving critical infrastructure protection, with the result that a variety of policy and administrative reforms are under consideration.

Rehabilitation Act Amendments

A provision of the 1998 amendments to the Rehabilitation Act of 1973 requires Federal agencies to procure, maintain, and use electronic and information technology that provides individuals with disabilities, including both Federal employees and members of the public, with accessibility comparable to what is available to individuals without disabilities.[15] The Architectural and Transportation Barriers Compliance Board, known as the Access Board, was tasked with developing access standards to implement the new requirement. After some delay, these were issued on December 21, 2000, for agency compliance by June 2001 (Guidelines, 2000).

Government Paperwork Elimination Act

Additional amendments to the PRA were enacted in 1998 as the Government Paperwork Elimination Act (GPEA), which was included in the Omnibus Consolidated and Emergency Supplemental Appropriations Act, 1999. The statute makes the director of OMB responsible for providing government wide direction and oversight regarding "the acquisition and use of information technology, including alternative information technologies that provide for electronic submission, maintenance, or disclosure of information as a substitute for paper and for the use and acceptance of electronic signatures."[16] In fulfilling this responsibility, the director, in consultation with the National Telecommunications and Information Administration (NTIA) of the Department of Commerce, is tasked with developing, in accordance with prescribed requirements, procedures for the use and acceptance of electronic signatures by the executive departments and agencies. A five-year deadline is prescribed for the agencies to implement these procedures.[17]

The director of OMB is also tasked by the GPEA to "develop procedures to permit private employers to store and file electronically with Executive agencies forms containing information pertaining to the employees of such employers" (GPEA of 1998 at 2681-750). In addition, the director, in cooperation with NTIA, is to conduct an ongoing study of the use of electronic signatures under the GPEA, with attention to paperwork reduction and electronic commerce, individual privacy, and the security and authenticity of transactions. The results of this study are to be reported periodically to Congress.

Finally, electronic records submitted or maintained in accordance with GPEA procedures, "or electronic signatures or other forms of electronic authentication used in accordance with such procedures, shall not be denied legal effect, validity, or enforceability because such records are in electronic form." The act further specifies: "Except as provided by law, information collected in the provision of electronic signature services for communications with an executive agency . . . shall only be used or disclosed by persons who obtain, collect, or maintain such information as a business or government practice, for the purpose of facilitating such communications, or with the prior affirmative consent of the person about whom the information pertains" (GPEA of 1998 at 2681-751).

Children's Online Privacy Protection Act

Enacted as part of the Omnibus Consolidated and Emergency Supplemental Appropriations Act, 1999, the Children's Online Privacy Protection Act of 1998 (COPPA) requires the operator of a commercial website or online service targeted at children under the age of 13 to provide clear notice of information collection and use practices; to obtain verifiable parental consent prior to collecting, using, and disseminating personal information about children under 13; and to provide parents access to their children's personal information and the option to prevent its further use. A June 22, 2000, OMB memorandum on website privacy, discussed below, prescribed, as a matter of policy, compliance with the COPPA standards by Federal agencies and contractors operating on behalf of agencies.

OMB Memoranda: Federal Website Privacy

A June 2, 1999 memorandum from the director of OMB to the heads of executive departments and agencies requires the posting of clear privacy policies on Federal websites and provides guidance for this action.[18] Such policies "must clearly and concisely inform visitors to the site what information the agency collects about individuals, why the agency collects it, and how the agency will use it." Also, they "must be clearly labeled and easily accessed when someone visits a website," according to the memorandum. Agencies are reminded that, pursuant to the Privacy Act, they must protect an individual's right to privacy when they collect personal information.

A June 22, 2000, follow-up memorandum was issued by OMB after press disclosures that the National Drug Control Policy Office, an agency within the Executive Office of the President, was secretly tracking visitors to its website through the use of computer software known as "cookies" (Harris & Schwartz, 2000; Gay, 2000). Reminding the agencies that, under the earlier guidance, they "could only use 'cookies' or other automatic means of collecting information if they gave clear notice of those activities," the new memorandum said "'cookies' should not be used at Federal websites, or by contractors when operating websites on behalf of agencies, unless, in addition to clear and conspicuous notice, the following conditions are met: a compelling need to gather the data on the site; appropriate and publicly disclosed privacy safeguards for handling of information derived from 'cookies'; and personal approval by the head of the agency." "In addition," it declared, "it is Federal policy that all Federal websites and contractors when operating on behalf of agencies shall comply with the standards set forth in the Children's Online Privacy Protection Act of 1998 with respect to the collection of personal information online at websites directed to children."[19]

CONCLUSION

As in the past, IT has been applied of late in fulfillment of realizing the efficient, economical, and effective performance of government functions. The result of these applications has been denominated electronic or digital government. Ultimately, however, the important consideration is that IT applications are consistent with, if not supportive of, the form of government guaranteed by the Constitution of the United States. A government failing to honor these guarantees, we have been warned, "is not worth the cost of preservation."[20]

ENDNOTES

1   1 Stat. 68 and 443; 1 Stat. 519; 1 Stat. 724; 2 Stat. 302; 3 Stat. 145; 3 Stat. 439; 3 Stat. 576.

2   1 Stat. 168.

3   1 Stat. 28, 49, and 65; these and similar provisions were consolidated in the Revised Statutes of the United States (1878) at section 161, which is presently located in the United States Code at 5 U.S.C. 301.

4   3 Stat. 140.

5   13 Stat. 460.

6   17 Stat. 510.

7   12 Stat. 117.

8   11 Stat. 228.

9   The digital computer processes discrete quantities of information, such as digits or characters, while analog computer operations are based on continuously variable quantities, such as lengths, weights, or voltages. On the development of computers, see Flamm (1987), Flamm, (1988), and National Research Council (1999).

10 This overview of the development of the Internet provides only a brief summary of a complex and rich process that involved the efforts of many individuals and institutions. More detailed treatments can be found at, among other sources, National Research Council (1999), Leiner, Cerf, Clark, Kahn, Kleinrock, and Lynch (2000), and Moschovitis, Poole, Schuyler, and Senft, (1991).

11 110 Stat. 186.

12 At the time of the issuance of PDD 63, the White House made available to the public a fact sheet, a white paper, and a press-briefing transcript. The full text of PDD 63 was retrieved on 7/17/02 from http://www.fas.org/irp/offdocs/pdd/pdd-63.htm.

13 U.S. President's Commission on Critical Infrastructure Protection, 1997. This report and other documents relevant to the commission's activities were available, as of 8/8/02, at http://www.ciao.gov/PCCIP/pccip_documents.htm.

14 The full text and executive summary of the national plan were available, as of 10/1/02 at http://www.ciao.gov/resource/strategy.html.

15 The Rehabilitation Act Amendments of 1998 constituted Title IV of the Workforce Investment Act of 1998, 112 Stat. 936; the electronic and information technology access requirement was appended to the Rehabilitation Act as section 508, 112 Stat 1203, at 29 U.S.C. 794(d); the Rehabilitation Act was originally enacted in 1973, 87 Stat. 355, at 29 U.S.C. 701 et seq.

16 44 U.S.C. 3504(a)(1)(B)(vi), as amended.

17 The final version of OMB procedures and guidance for implementing the GPEA was published in *Federal Register*, vol. 65, May 2, 2000, 25508-25521.

18 Office of Management and Budget memorandum M-99-18, "Privacy Policies on Federal Web Sites," (6/2/99). Retrieved 10/1/02 from http://www.whitehouse.gov/omb/memoranda/m99-18.html.

19 Office of Management and Budget memorandum M-00-13, "Privacy Policies and Data Collection on Federal Web Sites," (6/22/00). Retrieved 10/1/02 from http://www.whitehouse.gov/omb/memoranda/m00-13.html.

20 *Ex parte Milligan*, 71 U.S. 121 (1866).

REFERENCES

Administrative Procedure Act of 1946, 60 Stat. 237.

Burke, C. (1994). *Information and secrecy: Vannevar Bush, ultra, and the other memex.* Metuchen, NJ: Scarecrow Press.

Bush, V. (1945). As we may think. *Atlantic Monthly, 176*, 101-108. Retrieved on 3/21/02 from http://www.theatlantic.com/unbound/flashbks/computer/bushf.htm.

Casson, H. N. (1910). *The history of the telephone.* Chicago, IL: A. C. McClurg.

Children's Online Privacy Protection Act of 1998, 112 Stat. 2681-728; 15 U.S.C. 6501-6506.

Clinger-Cohen Act of 1996, 110 Stat. 3009-393.

Computer Matching and Privacy Protection Act of 1988, 102 Stat. 2507.

Computer Security Act of 1987, 101 Stat. 1724.

Electronic Freedom of Information Act Amendments of 1996, 110 Stat. 3048; 5 U.S.C. 552.

Executive Order (E.O.) 13011: Federal Information Technology Management, 3 C.F.R., 1996 Comp., 202-209.

Federal Acquisition Reform Act of 1996, 110 Stat. 642.

Flamm, K. (1987). *Targeting the computer: Government support and international competition.* Washington, DC: Brookings Institution.

Flamm, K. (1988). *Creating the computer: Government, industry, and high technology.* Washington, DC: Brookings Institution.

Freedom of Information Act of 1966, 80 Stat. 250; 5 U.S.C. 552.

Gay, L. (2000, June 21). White House uses drug-message site to track inquiries. *Washington Times*, p. A3.

Government Paperwork Elimination Act of 1998, 112 Stat. 2681-749.

Grove, J. W. (1980). Science as technology: Aspects of a potent myth. *Minerva, 18*, (1980, Summer, pp. 294-312).

Guidelines to force federal agencies to redesign Web sites. (2000, December 22). *Washington Times*, p. A5.

Harris, J. F. & Schwartz, J. (2000, June 22). Anti-drug Web site tracks visitors. *Washington Post*, p. A23.

Hauben, M., & Hauben, R. (1996). *Netizens: On the history and impact of Usenet and the Internet.* Retrieved on 8/8/02: http://www.columbia.edu/~ hauben/netbook/.

High-Performance Computing Act of 1991, 105 Stat. 1594.

Information Technology Management Reform Act of 1996, 110 Stat. 679.

Leiner, B.M., Cerf, V. G., Clark D.D., Kahn, R. E., Kleinrock, L., & Lynch, D. C. (2000). *A brief history of the Internet.* Retrieved 8/8/02 from http://www.isoc.org/internet/history/brief.shtml.

Licklider, J. C. R. (1960). Man-computer symbiosis. *IRE transactions on human factors in electronics, 1*, 4-11. Retrieved 3/21/02, from http://memex.org/licklider.pdf.

Licklider, J. C. R. (1965). *Libraries of the future.* Cambridge, MA: MIT Press.

Licklider, J. C. R. & Clark, W. E. (1962). On-line man-computer communication. *Proceedings of the American Federation of Information Processing Societies, 21*, 113-128.

Licklider, J. C. R. & Taylor, R. W. (1968). The computer as a communication device. *Science and Technology, 76*, 21-31. Retrieved 3/21/02, from http://memex.org/licklider.pdf.

Moschovitis, C. J. P., Poole, H., Schuyler, T., & Senft, T.M. (1991). *History of the Internet: A chronology, 1843 to the present*. Santa Barbara, CA: ABC-CLIO.

National Research Council, Committee on Innovations in Computing and Communications. (1999). *Funding a revolution: Government support for computing research*. Washington, DC: National Academy Press.

Nyce, J. M. & Kahn, P. (Eds.). (1991). *From memex to hypertext: Vannevar Bush and the mind's machine*. Boston, MA: Academic Press.

Paperwork Reduction Act of 1980, 94 Stat. 2812; 44 U.S.C. 3501 et seq.

Paperwork Reduction Act Amendments of 1986, 100 Stat. 3341-336.

Paperwork Reduction Act of 1995, 109 Stat. 165-166.

Plum, W. R. (1882). *The military telegraph during the civil war in the United States (1)*. Chicago, IL: Jansen, McClurg.

Presidential Decision Directive 63 (PDD 63), Retrieved on 4/17/02, from http://www.fas.org/irp/offdocs/pdd/pdd-63.htm.

Privacy Act of 1974, 88 Stat. 1896; 5 U.S.C, 552a.

Randall, J. G. (1951). *Constitutional problems under Lincoln* (revised ed.). Urbana, IL: University of Illinois Press.

Rehabilitation Act of 1973, 87 Stat. 355.

Rehabilitation Act of Amendments of 1998, 112 Stat. 936.

U.S. Congress, House Committee on Government Operations. (1986). *Electronic collection and dissemination of information by federal agencies: A policy overview*, 99th Congress, 2nd session, (H. Rept. 99-560). Washington, DC: Government Printing Office.

U.S. Department of Commerce, Bureau of the Census. (1975). *Historical statistics of the United States*. Washington, DC: Government Printing Office.

U.S. Department of Commerce, Information Infrastructure Task Force. (1993). *The national information infrastructure: Agenda for action*. Washington, DC: Government Printing Office.

U.S. Office of Technology Assessment. (1988). *Informing the nation: Federal information dissemination in an electronic age*. Washington, DC: Government Printing Office.

U.S. Office of Technology Assessment. (1993). *Making government work: Electronic delivery of federal services*. Washington, DC: Government Printing Office.

U.S. Office of the Vice President. (1993). *From red tape to results: Creating a government that works better & costs less, report of the National Performance Review*. Washington, DC: Government Printing Office.

U.S. Office of the Vice President. (1997). *Access America: Reengineering through information technology, report of the National Performance Review and the Government Information Technology Services Board*. Washington, DC: Government Printing Office.

U.S. President's Commission on Critical Infrastructure Protection. (1997). *Critical foundations: Protecting America's infrastructures*. Washington, DC: Government Printing Office.

Waldrop, W. M. (2001). *The Dream Machine: J.C.R. Licklider and the revolution that made computing personal*. New York: Viking.

Zachary, G. P. (1997). *Endless Frontier: Vannevar Bush, engineer of the American century*. New York: Free Press.

Chapter III

The Emergence of Digital Government: International Perspectives

Laura Forlano
Columbia University, USA

ABSTRACT

This chapter gives an overview of the extent to which e-government has been adopted internationally by reviewing major comparative studies and case studies by international organizations. The characteristics of the five stages of e-government — emerging, enhanced, interactive, transactional, and seamless are outlined and international examples of the innovative practices and potential obstacles faced. Of particular interest are studies on countries that have implemented transactional e-government strategies with service-delivery to citizens as the main priority. Currently adoption of e-government strategies worldwide is varied; however, many countries are making rapid progress in implementing their strategies.

INTRODUCTION

This chapter will introduce digital government in the international context and evaluate the extent to which e-government strategies have been adopted worldwide. Enthusiasm for digital government has been widespread among both developed and developing countries, but the opportunities and challenges differ from country to country. Developing countries face particularly acute challenges in designing and implementing e-government strategies.

Internationally, the push towards digital government is a combination of several factors: the use of information and communication technology by citizens and non-governmental organizations to influence policymakers; the migration of information including draft government legislation and services on-line; and the availability of the necessary telecommunications infrastructure. In addition, e-government strategies have grown, in part, out of a need for public sector reform and the promise of information and communication technology to increase government efficiency. Both domestic and international pressures for increased accountability, transparency, human rights and financial management have influenced national government adoption of e-government strategies (UNESCO, 2002).

However, currently there is no international standard approach to the development and implementation of e-government strategies. By analyzing recent benchmarking reports and detailed case studies of several countries at each stage of digital government development, this chapter will serve to highlight a wide range of international best practices in digital government. These case studies, most of which have been conducted by international organizations, bring to life common classifications of e-government stages with specific examples of the potential opportunities for improved efficiency, better information, new technology and increased interaction and services for citizens, businesses and among government agencies.

METHODOLOGY

This chapter uses the United Nations' (UN) "Benchmarking E-government" classification of the five stages of e-government presence, which builds on previous classifications as proposed by other international organizations, private sector consulting firms and *The Economist*. For each stage of e-government, one national Web site is showcased and the URL is provided in order to give readers a sense for international government Web sites and their services and encourage further exploration of country Web sites. While the use of the terminology of five stages is not ideal due to their heavy focus on service delivery in lieu of other national goals for e-government, it is a useful tool for students, researchers and practitioners alike.

The countries surveyed in this chapter appeared in more than one international study and were selected because of the existence of well-documented case studies by international organizations and private sector consulting firms. In addition, the countries chosen represent a diversity of world regions including North America, Latin and South America, Africa, Europe and Asia and a range of economic development levels.

OVERVIEW OF MAJOR INTERNATIONAL E-GOVERNMENT STUDIES

In recent years, there have been a number of major international benchmarking studies on e-government by university research centers, international organizations and private sector consulting firms. Benchmarking surveys have become important so that government agencies can compare their e-government progress with their peers in other countries. The following section will summarize the main findings of these studies before moving on to specific examples of e-government initiatives at varying levels of development later in this chapter.

According to a study by World Markets Research Centre and Brown University, which analyzed on-line services of 2,288 government Web sites in 196 countries in Summer 2001, "e-government is falling short of its true potential." Among other things, the study claims that the income disparities and information infrastructure requirements of e-government are hampering its development globally. Thus, while some regions including North America, Europe, Asia and the Middle East are ranked highly, other regions have much less well-developed sites and services.

In another study conducted by Accenture, only 23 countries were analyzed and benchmarked according to the availability of 169 government services in nine sectors. In general, the countries that they selected are those with the most developed e-government services. For these countries, governments "are becoming increasingly sophisticated, both in their articulation of what e-government is, and in how best to implement e-government initiatives to maximize benefits to citizens, businesses and government alike."

Finally, perhaps the most comprehensive study on global e-government, the UN "Benchmarking E-government" report, surveyed the Web sites of all 190 UN member states for content and services. An index was developed. The study concluded that national e-government programs for most countries are still at the information provision stage. Among the findings of this report are: a country's e-government capabilities and its social, political and economic level are highly correlated; national e-government strategies are still uncoordinated across government agencies; Internet access and technological resources are not the only factors necessary to transform government services; citizens are still not aware of many on-line government services; and e-government success is tied to political will. In addition, one important aspect of e-government is that it transforms governance. According to UN surveys of government officials, "E-government potentially empowers individual citizens by providing them with an alternative channel for accessing information and services and interacting with government," (Ronaghan, 2002). International e-government strategies are driven by a number of goals including open communication with and participation of citizens, increased efficiency and transparency, and improved democracy and governance.

Policies for E-Government

On-line privacy, security and special services for disabled populations are lacking in the majority of government Web sites. For example, only 6% of sites surveyed had privacy policies and only half that number had security policies according to the World Markets study. Governments need to "...create the right regulatory and public-policy environment for the digital economy — a competitive communications market, universal access, digital signatures, light taxation, on-line privacy, consumer protection for web shoppers and so on," (The Economist, 2000). This is an important concern if governments are going to introduce services that require sensitive information to conduct transactions. Governments must balance their need to unique identification of users necessary to deliver secure services with citizen expectations of privacy (Accenture, 2002).

For many countries, computer penetration, Internet access, telecommunications cost, lack of real services, lack of security and cultural resistance to technology are the key factors in hampering the implementation of e-government according to UNESCO's "Global Survey on On-line Governance." These concerns are valid both for developed

Table 1: Top 20 global e-government leaders

World Markets (2001)	Accenture (2002)	United Nations (2002)
United States	Canada	United States
Taiwan	Singapore	Australia
Australia	United States	Canada
Canada	Australia	New Zealand
United Kingdom	Denmark	Singapore
Ireland	United Kingdom	Norway
Israel	Finland	United Kingdom
Singapore	Hong Kong	Netherlands
Germany	Germany	Denmark
Finland	Ireland	Germany
France	Netherlands	Sweden
Lesotho	France	Belgium
St. Kitts	Norway	Finland
Vatican	New Zealand	France
Bahamas	Spain	Korea
Malaysia	Belgium	Spain
Iceland	Japan	Israel
Belgium	Portugal	Brazil
Bolivia	Brazil	Italy
Argentina	Malaysia	Luxembourg

Source: World Markets, 2001; Accenture, 2002; Ronaghan, 2002

and developing countries. Thus, policies that will help to overcome the lack of infrastructure and resources, including investment policies, competition policies, customs duties, telecommunications tariffs and revenue generation for e-government are vital for effective implementation. In addition, UNESCO recommends the development of integrated policies on ICT and governance, additional research and benchmarking on e-government, international harmonization of laws related to telecommunications and the Internet and public-private partnerships (UNESCO, 2000).

Generating a Return on Investment in E-Government

According to the OECD, in the short-run, e-government may not generate significant savings due to the necessary investments required to implement a successful strategy. These investments include the technology, training and human resources. In addition, since e-government requires the streamlining of the public sector, government officials are may resist the adoption of e-government strategies that threaten their job security. However, in the long-term, e-government is highly likely to result in a significant cost savings due to streamlining of the government bureaucracy and greatly increased efficiency.

Challenges for Developing Countries

Developing countries face particularly keen challenges in implementing e-government strategies due to the lack of an advanced information infrastructure and necessary resources to fund e-government initiatives. Specifically, while "developed countries are evidently on an accelerating spiral of knowledge acquisition and application, as well as the transformation of governance, developing countries are facing formidable hurdles — other than acquiring and deploying ICTs" (UNESCO, 2000).

The UN has identified a number of obstacles to the implementation of an effective e-government strategy in developing countries. These include unclear objectives, lack of trained staff, underestimated project costs, lack of local technology vendors, and shortages of technology (Ronaghan, 2002). In addition, developing countries may be forced to choose between providing services for their business community or for their citizens. As a result of their constraints, developing countries must be even more innovative in designing their e-government strategies using technologies such as telecenters and mobile e-government centers, which may be less common in developed countries. According to the UNESCO study:

> Data from developed countries may be construed as a road map for the less-developed, it is vital to concurrently examine the contextual issues in developing countries if we are to achieve a truly participative society — not simply one of leaders and followers. Transforming global governance, therefore, is the ultimate challenge.

As we will see later in this chapter, there are a number of very innovative e-government projects in developing countries such as China, India and Brazil. These projects do not necessarily involve the delivery of government surveys through a Web interface and thus have been left out of many international studies.

THE FIVE STAGES OF E-GOVERNMENT

The UN "Benchmarking E-government" report builds on earlier studies by international organizations and private sector consulting firms to identify five stages of e-government presence. The following chart provides a brief summary of these stages and their major characteristics:

Stage 1: Emerging Presence

In the first stage of e-government, the country establishes a Web presence through select government Web sites with static information. In this case, the Internet functions as a brochure for posting government information on-line. While contact information

Table 2

Stage of E-government	Description of Government Web Sites	Number of Countries
Emerging	Limited and static information	32
Enhanced	Regularly updated information	65
Interactive	Downloading and communication is possible	55
Transactional	Payment for services is possible	17
Seamless	Total integration of all services across administrative and departmental boundaries	0

Source: Ronaghan, 2002

may be available, it is not possible to interact on-line or conduct transactions for government services. Countries at an emerging level of e-government presence include Botswana (see case study), Ethiopia, Madagascar, Myanmar and Syria (Ronaghan, 2002). To access government Web sites other than those referenced in this chapter, refer to this database of government Web sites: http://www.gksoft.com/govt/en/world.html.

Stage 2: Enhanced Presence

In the second stage, the number of official government Web sites increases and sites contain regularly updated information including publications, legislation, newsletters, links, a search engine and e-mail capabilities. Countries at an enhanced level of e-government presence include Bangladesh, Ecuador, Iran, Tanzania (see case study) and Vietnam (see case study) (Ronaghan, 2002).

Stage 3: Interactive Presence

In the third stage, many interactions and services with a large number of government agencies are possible. In addition, e-mail, message posting, data downloading and document submission are possible. Countries at an interactive stage of e-government presence include China, Estonia, India, and Malaysia, all of which are profiled later in this chapter (Ronaghan, 2002).

Stage 4: Transactional Presence

In the fourth stage, a wide variety of government transactions can be conducted on-line. These include visa and passport applications, birth and death certificate requests and payments for licenses, fines, fees, bills and taxes. In addition, more sophisticated functions including digital signatures, passwords and encryption are also provided. Countries at a transactional stage of e-government presence include Brazil, Singapore, Mexico and the United Kingdom all of which are profiled later in this chapter (Ronaghan, 2002). While the United States is also in the fourth stage of its e-government development, the US case is not presented since it will be discussed in detail in the following chapters of this anthology.

Stage 5: Seamless or Fully Integrated Presence

In the most advanced stage, all services can be accessed instantly from one portal without differentiation between government agencies. There are no countries that have a fully integrated presence as of the time of writing. According to the World Markets study, as of Summer 2001, only 6% of e-government sites used a one-stop services portal and only 8% offered services that could be completed on-line. Portals are viewed as an emerging platform for interaction with citizens and businesses because of their "uniform, integrated and standardized navigational features" (World Markets, 2001). Accenture's report also supports the importance of portals, however states:

> Their true potential continues to be unrealized due to the barriers to cross agency cooperation. There is some evidence that these barriers are starting to be dismantled, while governments, businesses and citizens acknowledge that the benefits of common platforms and information sharing outweigh the perceived costs.

Currently, only 36 UN member states have single-entry portals. Only 17 are equipped to handle on-line transactions. Thus, continued efforts are needed by countries with the most advanced e-government programs to provide seamless services to their citizens.

Examples of E-Government Web Sites and Portals

The following chart provides some examples of Web sites for countries whose case studies will be discussed later in this chapter.

EMERGING

Botswana: Internal Development of E-Government Services

Botswana is still in the very early stages of an emerging e-government presence. According to 1999 statistics, the country had 77 telephone lines and 31 personal

Table 3

Stage of E-Government	Country	Country Web Sites
Emerging	Botswana	www.gov.bw/home.html
Enhanced	Vietnam	www.invest.mpi.gov.vn/ www.hcminvest.gov.vn/
	Tanzania	www.tzonline.org
Interactive	China	http://www.gov.cn/ (Chinese only) www.zhongguancun.com.cn
	Estonia	www.riik.ee/en/
	India	http://goidirectory.nic.in/
	Malaysia	http://www.mampu.gov.my/mampueng/Ict/flagship.htm http://www.moe.gov.my http://www.jpn.gov.my httP//www.rilek.com.my
Transactional	Brazil	http://www.redegoverno.gov.br Portal (Portuguese only) http://www.brasil.gov.br/ http://www.brasiltransparente.gov.br
	Singapore	http://www.gov.sg Portal http://www.iras.gov.sg/ http://www.ecitizen.gov.sg/ http://www.onemotoring.com
	Mexico	http://www.precisa.gob.mx/splash.php Portal (Spanish only) http://www.e-mexico.gob.mx http://www.sat.gob.mx
	United Kingdom	http://www.ukonline.gov.uk Portal http://www.hmce.gov.uk http://www.consignia-online.com

computers for every 1,000 people, nine Internet hosts for every 10,000 people and 30,000 Internet users total in its population of 1.5 million. In Botswana, basic infrastructure remains the main barrier to increased e-government services (UNESCO, 2002).

Despite this, there are a number of opportunities for the implementation of IT that the government of Botswana is actively pursuing in accordance with its ICT Vision 2003 plan. These include: plans to become a regional IT leader; targeting IT systems on the private sector and key government agency where clear efficiency gains are possible; training of officials; decentralized development of IT systems across government agencies with collaboration between them; the reduction of excess paperwork and long lines for public services in government agencies; and the use of geographic information systems (UNESCO, 2002).

Currently, the government has no plans to interact with its citizens on-line due to the high cost of Internet access, low telephone density and lack of personal computers. However, some e-government services have been developed for specific groups such as government officials who are more likely to have Internet, telephone and computer access. In addition, the government is planning to develop its IT infrastructure with a specific focus on increasing access for citizens by wiring public schools and developing interactive applications for distance learning, telemedicine and video conferencing in the near future (UNESCO, 2002).

Graphic 1

Source: http://www.gov.bw/home.html

ENHANCED

Vietnam: Government-to-Business Services

In 2000, two of Vietnam's business services agencies, the Hanoi Ministry of Planning and Investment and the Ho Chi Minh Department of Planning and Investment launched interactive Web sites targeted at foreign investors. These agencies issue investment licenses to insure that new investment projects meet Vietnam's development goals. Prior to the availability of on-line investment license applications, foreign investors faced costly delays in obtaining investment licenses. Currently, license applications are processed in one day (Desai, 2001).

Some advantages to the Web site development project include Web site management by non-technical experts, technical assistance from the Multilateral Investment Guarantee Agency (MIGA) part of the World Bank Group. One sign of the project's success was that the Web site template was also implemented in Laos and Cambodia. However, challenges include a low level of support from senior officials, a reluctance to share information and an over-reliance on outside consultations (Desai, 2001).

This project illustrates Vietnam's ability to conduct interactions over a government Web site, a capability typical of the third stage of e-government development. It is a positive sign that Vietnam is offering targeted interactive services at the foreign investment community because alleviating obstacles to investment could help increase economic development in Vietnam and thus the country's ability to offer expanded services to its citizens in the future.

Tanzania: Internal Development of E-Government Services

As of 1999, the country had five telephone lines and two personal computers for every 1,000 people and very few Internet hosts (UNESCO, 2002). Again, as in the case of Botswana, the availability of an information infrastructure stands as the main obstacle in developing e-government services.

However, Tanzania does have a number of Web sites and services that are worth mentioning. First, both the parliament and the central bank have Web sites and human resources and financial management software has been implemented to streamline government expenditures. Second, an innovative project that has been successful over the long-term is the Kibidula Farm Institute, a non-government organization, which provides e-mail and Internet access via a solar-powered satellite. Finally, Tanzania Online, a Web site about development issues, is a cooperative project between the UNDP/UN, the Government of Tanzania and the Economic and Social Research Foundation (ESRF). The site is targeted at providing policy makers, academics, civil society, government officials and the donor community with documents and data about Tanzania's progress in development (UNESCO, 2002).

INTERACTIVE

China: Government-to-Business Services

In 2000, as part of the "Digital Beijing" initiative, China launched one of its first e-

Graphic 2

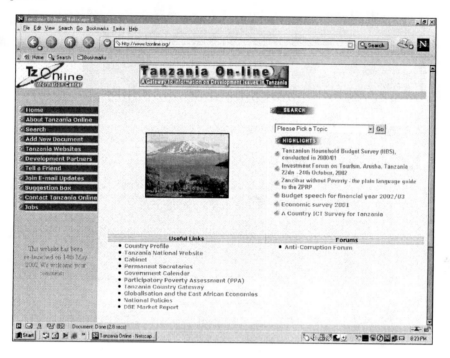

Source: www.tzonline.org

government pilot projects, Zhongguancun E-Park. The project has enabled more than 6,000 businesses to apply for licenses, file financial statements and submit taxes in addition to 32 other government services. The E-Park was strategically placed to complement the nation's largest science park which was established in 1988 and is now home to the Chinese research and development centers of IBM, Motorola, Microsoft, Lucent, Hewlett-Packard and Epson (Lin, 2001).

The main benefits of the E-Park system is that it has increased government transparency and efficiency while limiting opportunities for corruption. E-Park has greatly increased information sharing between twelve local government departments that interact with the business community in Zhongguancun. Similar to the Vietnam case, prior to the E-Park system, companies were burdened by extremely complicated procedures that often required fifteen appointments and took up to three months. Since these companies generated $12 billion in revenue and attracted $200 million in investment for China's economy, the hurdles faced by the companies in obtaining licenses inhibited China's economic development (Lin, 2001).

The E-Park system includes five main functions for businesses: e-application, e-registration, e-reporting, e-administration and e-consulting. These functions assist businesses in complying with government requirements. In addition, the E-Park includes an application status reminder system, a monitoring system, a statistics and query system, optical, voice and hand writing recognition software, and standard forms and templates (Lin, 2001).

Graphic 3

Source: *http://www.zhongguancun.com.cn/en/default.asp.htm*

However, the E-Park system also faced a number of obstacles including resistance among government officials, difficulty in cooperating across government agencies and the need for staff retraining. Finally, since China has no digital governance laws, the legal status of electronic documents is unclear. Thus, hard copies of licenses must be retained for legal purposes. Despite these barriers, E-Park has been extremely successful in increasing efficiency and transparency and encouraging interaction between businesses and the Chinese government. Currently, 90% of government services are performed on-line and in the first year, approximately 1,200 new companies applied for their licenses on-line and 4,400 have submitted financial information to the government on-line (Lin, 2001).

Estonia: Government-to-Citizen Services

Estonia has a well-developed information infrastructure with 35.4 phone lines and 31.5 mobile phones per every 100 people. The wireless network covers 99% of the countries populated areas and 28% of the population report having used the Internet in the last six months. In addition, the backbone network connects 550 government institutions and departments; the current focus is on connecting schools and libraries to the Internet (UNESCO, 2002).

For the past eight years, the government of Estonia has been dedicating 1% of its budget to information technology development. This has enabled the country to streamline the public sector, produce and share information and focus on services for their citizens. Currently, all government information and services are provided through a single integrated portal and, in the future, the on-line barriers between departments will disappear as the portal becomes focused on services. Estonia has also developed its digital governance policies on issues such as digital signatures, freedom of information, IT standardization, data security and language technology. In addition, a clear IT management organization is in place (UNESCO, 2002).

India: Government-to-Citizen Services

As part of India's e-government efforts, rural Internet kiosks have been used to connect farmers with market information and increase efficiency in getting payment for their goods. The Gyandoot project which implemented community-owned kiosks in rural areas won the Stockholm Challenge IT Award in 2000 in the Public Service and Democracy category and the CSI-TCS National Award for Best IT Usage in the same year. According to the jury of the Stockholm award, Gyandoot is:

a unique government-to-citizen Intranet project...with numerous benefits to the region, including a people-based self-reliant sustainable strategy. 'Gyandoot' is recognized as a breakthrough in e-government, demonstrating a paradigm shirf which gives marginalized tribal citizens their first ever chance to access knowledge, with minimum investment (Bhatnagar, 2000).

The network of 31 Internet kiosks serves over 600 villages, 500,000 people and was accessed 55,000 times during the first 11 months of operation. The main services offered at the kiosks include agriculture prices, land records, applications for government certificates, public complaint filing, village auctions and advertisements, information about government grants, distributions and services. Similarly, rural Internet kiosks are being used in dairy and sugar cane cooperatives in order to calculate the amounts due to farmers for their products, speed up the amount of time it takes for them to receive payments and reduce opportunities for fraud and corruption (Bhatnagar, 2000).

The E-government Centre at the Indian Institute of Management, the Prime Minister's Office of Information Technology, the private sector, trained volunteers and local civil servants have been important in the successful implementation of these projects. In addition, offering content in the local language, assessing the information needs of the community and targeting initiatives at women and the poor is vital for knowledge transfer. Some obstacles facing the implementation of rural Internet kiosks include the lack of support from local civil servants whose fear job loss and unreliability of Internet connections (Bhatnagar, 2000).

Malaysia

Malaysia has a well-developed information infrastructure as a result of the government's investment in the Multimedia Super Corridor which connects Malaysia with Japan, ASEAN, the US and Europe over a high-speed network. As of 1999, 23.2% of Malaysians had a telephone, but the country is actively pursuing a 50% penetration rate (UNESCO, 2002).

Currently, the government has six e-government pilot projects that range from e-procurement to electronic human resources management. The Malaysian government's goals included public-private partnership, information sharing, customer satisfaction and information and data security. While there are currently multiple applications, Web sites and platforms being used, the government plans to streamline these and move towards a portal format. Like China, Malaysia faced the problem of getting support for e-government projects from the government bureaucracy and their commitment to implementing the necessary changes.

TRANSACTIONAL

Brazil: Government-to-Citizen Services

In the Brazilian state of Bahia, federal, state and municipal services are offered through Citizen Assistance Service Centers (SACs) located in shopping malls and at transportation hubs. These centers greatly limit the need for citizens to make multiple trips to different government agencies in order to get a driver's license or national identification card, file a legal claim or business complaint, or apply for unemployment or retirement benefits. The SACs allow citizens to conduct up to 500 services with 29 different agencies including those responsible for social security, agriculture, labor and sanitation. Currently, there are 23 SACs of varying sizes and service offerings from large ones housing services for over 20 government agencies to small ones with services for only eight agencies. In addition, there are mobile SACs with basic services that travel to remote areas and connect to the Internet through the nearest telephone line (Rinne, 2001).

The implementation of SACs required strong pressure from the government of Bahia in order to persuade many government agencies to comply. In addition, SAC employees are not civil servants; instead they work on a contractual basis. One would expect conflicts with government employees. But this has not been an obstacle for the SAC project (Rinne, 2001).

Despite these potential threats, the SACs have been extremely successful and 32 million services had been delivered by April 2001 with 175,000 services delivered in a single month. In addition, 89% of citizens evaluated the SACs as "excellent" (Rinne, 2001). Similarly, in São Paolo "Poupatempo" or Time Saver Centers are providing similar services for Brazilians.

Singapore: Government-to-Citizen Services

Singapore's government has made a strong commitment to information technology and has aspirations to become one of the world's "high-tech capitals" by 2010. The country's eCitizen Center, centralizes government services on-line making them more convenient and easy-to-use. According to *The Economist*, "Singapore's eCitizen center is the most developed example of integrated service delivery in the world."

Since 1992, Singapore has been carefully phasing in its electronic taxation services moving from telephone to Internet tax filing. In the long run, the country plans to link data from many different government agencies so that taxpayers will not need to file a tax return at all. As of 2000, 30% of taxpayers filed electronically and slightly less than half of that number filed over the telephone. In addition, 60% of taxpayers pay their taxes with electronic fund transfers, by phone, via Internet banking, at kiosks or at service centers (Bhatnagar, 2000).

Mexico: Government-to-Citizen Services

The main focus of Mexico's e-government strategy is to decrease the digital divide and increase citizen participation. As of 2002, Mexico had 112 telephone lines and 44 computers per every 1,000 people and 41 Internet hosts for every 10,000 people. One project developed by the President's Office, Mexico On Line, aims to transform the relationship between the Mexican government and its citizens and foster a democratic participatory culture by increasing transparency and credibility of political leadership. To this end, the President's Web site includes links to live Internet streaming of "phone-in" discussion, radio program and 24-hour news channel. In addition, the government is increasing access to laws, regulations and other official documents (UNESCO, 2002).

Some transactional services such as payment of motor taxes and polling are also possible via the Internet. For example, as part of the 2001- 2006 National Development Plan, the government solicited citizen's participation in drafting the priorities on 110 national issues in the following areas: human and social development, economic growth and quality, and law and order. The government received questionnaires from 117,040 people both on-line and by mail and incorporated many of the citizen's suggestions into the plan. Finally, the eMexico project aims to reduce the digital divide by upgrading the country's information infrastructure so that small communities can get on-line. The government plans to target content and applications on priority areas of education, health, commerce and other community services (UNESCO, 2002).

United Kingdom: Government-to-Business Services

The United Kingdom is often cited as having one of the most advanced e-government strategies. One reason for the UK's success in implementing its e-government strategy is its strong support from the highest levels of government and its clear management structure. Prime Minister Tony Blair has committed to putting 100% of government services on-line by 2005. The Office of the E-Envoy and the Central Information Technology Unit (CITU) have the main responsibility for the country's e-government strategy in coordination with individual government agencies. The CITU manages the portal site through which businesses and citizens can access all government services.

The UK's portal approach integrates all government services for businesses and citizens to a single Web site. The country has placed a particular priority on serving the needs of small and medium sized enterprises. The benefits of e-government to businesses include faster interactions, decreased transaction costs and a lightening of the regulatory burden. Here are examples of the types of transactions that businesses can conduct on-line: research and renew patents, trademarks and designs; receive information about small businesses, employee training and worker's rights, social benefits and environmental issues; file taxes and licenses. In addition, services for citizens will be offered over customizable interfaces via kiosks, cell phones and digital television.

Graphic 4

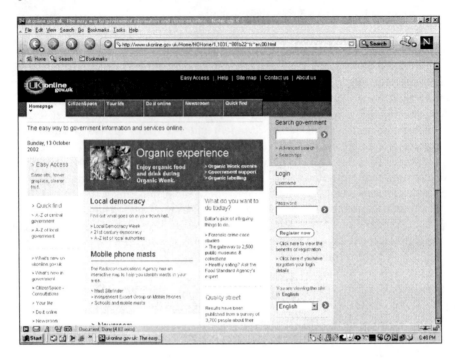

Source: www.ukonline.gov.uk

CONCLUSION AND POLICY RECOMMENDATIONS

This chapter introduced digital government in the international context and evaluated the extent to which e-government strategies have been adopted worldwide. The five stages of e-government presence — emerging, enhanced, interactive, transactional and seamless — were discusses and detailed case studies of countries in each stage were presented.

Through analysis of a number of case study 'snapshots' of e-government developments around the world, several policy recommendations have emerged. These include:

- Strong support from highest levels of government
- Obtaining support from local government employees in areas targeted by e-government strategies
- Targeting e-government initiatives on specific communities that stand to gain the most due to increased efficiency (i.e., businesses, farmers, women and the rural poor)
- Creating local language content and assessing community information needs

- Implementing e-government strategies gradually based on individual country needs with the long-term goal of providing fully-integrated access to government services

Knowledge of international e-government strategies as well as their unique opportunities and challenges is vital for a full understanding of the political implications of e-government, specific policies of digital governance including privacy, security, e-commerce and the digital divide and citizen participation in digital government in the future, all of which will be discussed in later chapters of this anthology.

REFERENCES

Accenture. (2002). *E-government leadership: Realizing the vision.* New York: Accenture.

Bertelsmann Foundation and Booz Allen Hamilton. (2002). *E-government: Connecting efficient administration and responsive democracy.* Bertelsmann Foundation Publishing House.

Bhatnagar, S. (2000). *Empowering dairy farmers through a dairy information & services kiosk.* Washington, DC: World Bank.

Bhatnagar, S. (2000). *Modernizing tax administration in Singapore.* Washington, DC: World Bank.

Bhatnagar, S. & Vyas, N. (2001). *Gyandoot: Community-owned rural Internet kiosks.* Washington, DC: World Bank.

Cecchini, S. & Raina, M. *Village information kiosks for the Warana cooperatives in India.* Washington, DC: World Bank.

Daugherty, S., Forlano, L., Mele, V., & Van der dys, V. (2002). *Italy.gov: Strategic recommendations for e-government in Italy.* Unpublished manuscript.

Deloitte Research. (2000). *At the dawn of e-government: The citizen as customer.* New York: Deloitte Consulting and Deloitte & Touche.

Desai, M. & de Magalhaes, N. (2001). *Vietnam's tale of two cities.* Washington, DC: World Bank.

Forlano, L. (2000). *To vote or not to vote: Shifting the balance of power in the information age.* Unpublished manuscript.

Fountain, J. (2001). *Building the virtual state.* Washington, DC: Brookings Institution Press.

Garson, G. D. (1999). *Information technology and computer applications in public administration: Issues and trends.* Hershey, PA: Idea Group Publishing.

Holmes, D. (2001). *e.gov: E-business strategies for government.* Naperville, IL: Nicholas Brealey Publishing.

Institute of Public Finance Limited. (2000). *E-gov: Electronic government services for the 21st century: A performance and innovation unit report.* Croydon, UK: Institute of Public Finance Limited.

Institute of Public Finance Limited. (2000). *E-government: A strategic framework for public services in the information age.* Croydon, UK: Institute of Public Finance Limited.

Lin, M., Zhu, R. & Hachigian, N. (2001). *Beijing's business e-park.* Washington, DC: World Bank.

Lips, M. (2001). Designing electronic government around the world: Policy develop-
      ments in the USA, Singapore, and Australia. In J.E.J. Prins (Ed.), *Designing e-
      government: On the crossroads of technological innovation and institutional
      change*. Boston, MA: Kluwer Law International.

OECD. (2001). *Information technology projects in the public sector*. Paris: OECD.

O'Looney, J. A. (2002). *Wiring governments: Challenges and possibilities for public
      managers*. Westport, CT: Quorum Books.

Orrego, C., Osorio, C. & Mardones, R. (2000). *Chile's government procurement e-system*.
      Washington, DC: World Bank.

Rinne, J., Benvinda Teixeirra Lage, A., & Andrade, E. (2001). *Citizen service centers in
      Bahia, Brazil*. Washington, DC: World Bank.

Ronaghan, S. A. (2001). *Benchmarking e-government: A global perspective, assessing
      the progress of the UN member states*. New York: United Nations Division for
      Public Economics and Public Administration and American Society for Public
      Administration.

The next revolution: A survey of government and the Internet. (2000, June 24). *The
      Economist*, 1-34.

UNESCO and COMNET-IT. (2000). *Global survey on on-line governance*. Paris: UNESCO.

UNESCO and COMNET-IT. (2002). *Study of e-governance: Development of country
      profiles*. Paris: UNESCO.

World Markets Research Center and Brown University. (2001). Global e-government
      survey. Providence, RI: World Markets Research Center.

Section II

The New Face of Government

Chapter IV

Portals and Policy: Implications of Electronic Access to U.S. Federal Government Information and Services

Patricia Diamond Fletcher
UMBC, USA

ABSTRACT

This chapter evaluates the emerging electronic "portal" model of information and service delivery to U.S. citizens, businesses, and government agencies. The portal model is being used as a technology framework in the U.S. Federal government to carry out the electronic government strategies set out in the President's Management Agenda for 2002 and the subsequent 24 electronic government initiatives included in the Budget of the United States Government for 2003 and the E-Government Strategy. FirstGov.gov is the official Federal government portal for all information and services delivered by the Federal executive agencies. The legal and organizational framework for FirstGov, based on an in-depth case study, is presented and evaluated as a model for future electronic government initiatives.

INTRODUCTION

The United States Federal government is the world's largest creator, maintainer and disseminator of information. The Federal government's information technology (IT) portfolio of investments for fiscal year 2003 is approximately $52 billion; a portion of this includes the development of 900 major IT projects, which account for $18 billion of the total IT budget for fiscal year 2003. This makes the United States the largest investor in IT in the world (*Budget of the United States Government, Fiscal Year 2003*).

Under the current Bush administration, the development and further enhancement of electronic government applications is one of the five government-wide Presidential management initiatives highlighted as critical for improving government performance. This continues the strategic focus on information technology that began in the Clinton Administration with the creation of the National Performance Review. The implementation of FirstGov.gov, the first Federal government-wide portal, was a major project endorsed, developed, and launched under the aegis of the Clinton administration.

The portal concept of electronic commerce has become a dominant theme in today's Internet environment. At its most basic, a portal is the main doorway for users to access the Web. It is somewhat analogous to a homepage as Internet users see it as a personal entry point to the Web. Further, it becomes a place Internet users routinely access, meeting a range of their information and commerce needs (Kalakota and Robinson, 2001). Government is moving towards a portal model of business in an effort to offer a more integrated or horizontal view of government — one that minimizes the "agency" or stovepipe aspect of services and information and capitalizes on the "content" or subject of the information or service need. The development and use of a single point of access application to government is seen as a necessary condition in the move to a more citizen-centric Federal government. It is envisioned that an electronic government portal will transform the citizens' relationships with their government. Governance will also be facilitated; with portals creating communities of interest that will meet around issues of democracy, politics, and electronic interaction with elected officials, enabling an unprecedented flow of conversation between citizen and government. FirstGov.gov was designed to enable government-to-citizen (G2C), government-to-business (G2B), and government-to-government (G2G) interactions and transactions to occur.

FirstGov.gov was launched on September 22, 2000, with 47 million U.S. Federal government web pages. FirstGov.gov is the only official U.S. Federal government Web portal. The intent is to be a single, trusted, point-of-service for citizens and businesses to the services and information resources of government. The Presidential Memo of December 17, 1999, *Electronic Government*, was the impetus behind the development of FirstGov.gov, calling for a government-wide portal that would be accessible by type of service or information needed. The vision for this portal was described as a high-speed, 24 hour-a-day, seven days-a-week, user-friendly entry point to every online resource, be it information, data, or service, offered by the Federal government, and ultimately, to all levels of government in the United States. FirstGov.gov was also seen as the vehicle to substantively reduce government bureaucracy, create a more responsive and customer-focused government, and enable a new and active citizen participation in democratic processes. Today (September, 2002) FirstGov.gov contains information and services from more than 51 million Federal, state, local, District of Columbia, and tribal government web pages of information, services and transactions.

This chapter will examine the policy framework that enabled the creation and continued support of this Federal government portal. The relevance of a portal to government users will be delineated as well, tying in the conceptual notion of a portal to the actual practice of information access and dissemination in Federal government. The data for the analysis of FirstGov.gov came from a case study funded by the National Science Foundation Digital Government grants program.

THE DEVELOPMENT OF THE FIRSTGOV.GOV PROJECT

FirstGov.gov was created to be the single point of access for citizens and business to the U.S. Federal government. The Internet was perceived as becoming a major enabler of access to government, and the use of a portal model to the Federal government was deemed the most appropriate way to provide electronic information and services to the public. The development of FirstGov.gov is a singular example of changing the manner in which government routinely operates in order to meet an executive mandate. Contributing to its success are three key variables: top level support, an enabling policy environment, and the necessary diffusion of the technology. It was the combination of these three variables that facilitated the success of the Federal portal, and led the way for electronic government in the United States.

Top Level Support

First, the project had visible and formal support from the Clinton Administration. On June 24, 2000, President Bill Clinton, in the first presidential Internet address to the public, called for the development of a Federal government portal, or single point of entry, that would provide easy and open access to the online services and information available to the public. Many saw this FirstGov.gov initiative, as transformational to the conduct of government. This attention from the Executive Office of the President was one of the critical success factors which enabled to portal to be "open for business" in such a short period of time. The portal was given 90 days to "open" — no mean feat for government agencies to accomplish — and it did.

A favorable project running prior to and coincident with the development of FirstGov.gov was the "e-Government Project" (http://www.senate.gov/~gov_affairs/ egov/), launched by Senators Joseph Lieberman (D-CT) and Fred Thompson (R-TN). The e-Government Project was developed as an experiment to see how the Internet could be used to enhance the governance process. At the website, users can express their opinions on ten broad topic areas related to the creation of an electronic government. This site represents an early, high-level effort to involve citizens more actively in legislation. It is still in existence. This effort, with the backing of the Chairman and Ranking Member of the Senate Committee on Governmental Affairs, was an additional sign that people placed in high-level government positions saw the potential in an electronic Federal government.

The current Bush administration is also showing signs of top-level support for electronic government. *The President's Management Agenda* (PMA) (August, 2001) has five stated goals for the administration, one of which is electronic government. In the

PMA, President Bush states that "his administration will advance e-government strategy by supporting projects that offer performance gains across agency boundaries, such as e–procurement, e-grants, e-regulations, and e-signatures" (*The President's Management Agenda*, 2001, p. 23). The expected results include increased citizen access to government, along with enhanced government efficiency and accountability. In specific to the FirstGov.gov portal, the PMA states, "It will expand and improve the FirstGov (www.FirstGov.gov) website to offer citizens a convenient entry to government services. OMB will engage the agencies and state and local governments in this venture, to help citizens find information and obtain services organized according to their needs, and not according to the divisions created by the government 's organizational chart" (p. 23).

There were other, visible high-level political activities which also lent support to the development and implementation of FirstGov.gov. At a hearing before the House Subcommittee on Government Management, Information, and Technology (October 2, 2000), Senator Horn (R-CA) noted the criticality for government to be up-to-date in its information management, be well organized for information retrieval, and be accessible to the public. In his comments, the Congressman stated that "FirstGov is an important step in making Government information and services available to the public seven days a week, 24 hours a day. FirstGov.gov, and electronic government in general, offer the potential to revolutionize the way citizens and businesses interact with their Government." In her testimony to the same House Subcommittee, Sally Katzen, then Deputy Director for Management, Office of Management and Budget, praised the early efforts of the FirstGov.gov website. Katzen made reference to the quarter of a million users that visited the site in its first four days of business. She also reinforced the concept that searching at FirstGov.gov be intuitive to citizens, with access organized by information or service need and not by the agency that provides the information or services. The idea here was to get the citizens fast answers to their questions or problems. Someone looking for information to reserve a campsite at Glacier National Park should not need to know what Federal agency is in charge of this service. They should be able to enter their request and seamlessly have their reservation made.

Two recent appointments made by the Bush Administration gave another signal of on-going support and credibility for the FirstGov.gov portal — the first being the June 2001 appointment of an Associate Director for Information Technology and E-Government. This appointment was to ensure that the administration's goal of a citizen-centric electronic government would be met. In January 2002, the appointment of a Chief Technology Officer (CTO) for the U.S. Federal government was made. This position was developed to oversee the implementation of the President's e-government strategy and facilitate Federal agencies' move to electronic government. The creation of both of these positions was a clear signal from the President that the Internet was to be used as a primary point of access to government for the public. It also signaled that access to information and services was to be done on a cross-agency basis, with the Associate Director for Information Technology and E-Government, as well as the CTO, working with agencies to create this new approach to information management and use.

It is clear that using the Internet as an access mechanism for the American public has had top level support now for a number of years. The Clinton administration's Access America program and the National Partnership for Reinventing Government were visible programs that promoted information access via the Internet. Clinton's creation of the FirstGov.gov portal was a strong, visible manifestation of the commitment to public access to government. The Bush administration has continued to give FirstGov.gov, and the move to an electronic government top level attention as well, with the development of the e-government strategy in *The President's Management Agenda*, and the appointment of two top-level officials in OMB to nurture this structure along. Congress has also taken an active interest in electronic access for the public, most noticeably in the Senate Committee on Governmental Affairs. The role of a technology champion or the importance of top organizational support has long been noted as an IT enabler (Caudle, Marchand, Bretschneider, Fletcher, and Thurmaier, 1989; Fletcher, Bretschneider, and Marchand, 1991; Bensaou and Earl, 1998; Applegate, McFarlan, and McKenney, 1999). Recognition of the value of IT from organizational leaders is critical to any successful development and use of technology. This has become a standard critical success factor for IT implementation, so much so that it has been taken for granted in many private sector organizations. The government — with the backing of two presidential administrations — has created an atmosphere whereby the use of the Internet for public access to government is a top-level mandate now for Federal agencies.

The Policy Environment

Looming large in the policy arena was the enactment of the Government Paperwork Elimination Act (GPEA) (P.L. 105-277), signed into law October 21, 1998. GPEA represents a major legislative endorsement of electronic government. It requires the Federal executive agencies, no later than October 21, 2003, to allow individuals and businesses that interact with Federal agencies the opportunity to do so electronically. GPEA goes on to state that electronic records and their electronic signatures are to have the full force of legal effect and validity. It encourages Federal agencies to promote an electronic information management environment that includes recordkeeping, filing, maintenance, submission, and archiving. This opens up a wide array of possible types of electronic information interactions between government and the public. The submission of bids and proposals for government contracts, application for licenses, loans, and benefits, requests for government records, receipt of benefits such as social security, online procurement, and citizen interaction in legislation are a few examples of possibilities enabled by GPEA.

The policy environment for electronic government has also been set forth in S. 803, the E-government Act of 2001, introduced by Senator Joseph Lieberman (D-CT). While it was not successful in 2001, an amended version of the Act was reintroduced and reported out of Committee March 21, 2002. The amended version of the E-Government Act sets up a broad policy framework for an electronic government strategy that will enable citizens to access their government information and services electronically, over the Internet. The Act recognizes the effect the Internet has already had on U.S. society and seeks to avail both government and citizens of the benefits already being realized by businesses and individual Internet users. The Act further includes the creation of a Federal Chief Information Officer housed in the Executive Office of Management and Budget (OMB) and the establishment of an Office of Electronic Government housed in OMB. The Federal Chief Information Officer is to be appointed by the President with the advice and consent of the Senate. The creation of an Office of Electronic Government is to ensure that electronic initiatives are sound investments, and, more important, that these new e-government initiatives are cross-agency in nature. This is a serious effort to dismantle the unwieldy "stovepipe" structure that is predominant today across government. Cross-agency initiatives are seen as reducing the information burden on the public, while making access simplified, universal, and not time-limited.

There are many other laws that frame the electronic government environment. The following brief note is not meant to be exhaustive of the policy framework that informs an electronic government. Rather, it depicts the key legislation that has enabled an electronic government to evolve. The Paperwork Reduction Act of 1995 (44 U.S.C. chapter 35) creates the strategic framework for information resources management in Federal agencies. This act gives OMB the responsibility for setting policy and guidance for the Federal agencies in their information resources management activities. It also requires the agencies to strategically plan for their IT investments. The Clinger-Cohen Act of 1996 (40 U.S.C. 1401(3)) requires top-level agency support for all IT investments and investment management. It further requires that Federal agencies tie their IT investments to their actual performance, and establish integrated systems architectures. The Government Information Security Reform Act (GISRA) of 2000 (P.L. 106-398) mandates Federal agencies to routinely assess the security of classified and non-classified information systems and to include risk assessment and security needs with each agency budget request. GISRA establishes a risk-based framework for agencies to manage their information security. The Computer Security Act of 1987, as amended (P.L. 100-235, 15 U.S.C.), creates a secure environment for sensitive information in Federal computer systems. The act defines "sensitive information" to include any unclassified information that, if lost, misused, or accessed or modified without authorization, could adversely affect the national interest, conduct of Federal programs, or the privacy to which individuals are entitled under the Privacy Act. The Privacy Act of 1974 (5 U.S.C. 552a) is the primary law regulating the Federal government's collection and maintenance of personal information. The act is a comprehensive privacy statute that provides certain safeguards to protect individuals' personal privacy. The act limits the collection, maintenance, use, and dissemination of personal information by Federal executive agencies. The Computer Matching and Privacy Protection Act of 1988 (P.L. 100-503) amended the Privacy Act to establish procedural safeguards regarding a Federal agency's use of Privacy Act records in performing certain types of computerized matching programs. The Telecommunications Act of 1996 (P.L. 104-104) reinforced the importance of universal service to information. This act mandates that high quality telecommunications services, at reasonable and affordable rates, be made available to the American public. Altogether, these laws and other guidance support GPEA, which in turn supports the creation and implementation of an electronic government.

The February 27, 2002, release of the *E-Government Strategy* (Executive Office of the President), was yet another bright signal that electronic government was on the policy agenda of the Bush administration. This report sets out a vision that is citizen-centered, results-oriented, and market-based in nature. It called for cross-agency sharing of data to simplify access to government. There are four citizen-centered groups that serve as a focus for cross agency e-government projects: government-to-citizens, government-to-business, government-to-government, and intragovernmental to improve internal efficiency and accountability. An initial group of 34 projects were singled out for the first round of funding, with completion dates scheduled no later than 18 to 24 months. All the projects represented cross-agency applications. The haste to get them online is a further measure of the import of electronic government to the administration's overall policy.

Policy is a critical tool in framing the operational environment for government (Dawes, Bloniarz, Kelly, and Fletcher, 1999; Fletcher and Westerback, 1999). Policy related to information and the management of information resources has had a defining influence in the evolution from a paper-based to a computer-based, to an electronic government in the U.S. When viewed from the perspective that the U.S. Federal government is the world's largest creator, disseminator, and user of information, the critically of having a strong policy framework is obvious. Harlan Cleveland (1986) asserted, "Government is information." The importance and value of information to government mandates a high-level attention to ensure that it will be used for the public good. This policy framework serves to highlight and unify information issues such as management, planning, privacy, security, access, property rights, and electronic commerce.

The Technology Environment

A convergence of computers, the Internet, and government information has occurred creating an environment conducive to an electronic government. A recent report from the Department of Commerce on the digital economy (February, 2002) notes that in spite of an economic slowdown, the United States continues to build upon its strong IT industries, services, and workforce, resulting overall in a stronger more vibrant economy. The report states that the migration of businesses and services to the Internet is an ongoing activity, the recession non-withstanding. This diffusion of technology is evident in the growth in users of the Internet. Not only are more people using the Internet, but also they are using it in a more diverse manner. Online banking, travel reservations, and drivers' license renewals are but a few of the activities that are becoming commonplace on the Internet. The National Telecommunications and Information Administration (Department of Commerce, February, 2002) recently reported that we are a "nation online." Previous reports in this series focused on the digital divide in the United States; the current report indicates that the divide is decreasing as more than half of America is now online. The reported noted that approximately 54% of the U.S. public, or 143 million Americans, are now connected to the Internet at home, at work, or though schools, libraries, and other public Internet facilities. The rate of growth for the Internet in the U.S. is about 2 million new users per month. One major trend noted in this report is that the use of broadband is significantly increasing in residential areas. The Internet has not only gained entrance in U.S. households — but high-speed access is expanding. Another statistic from this report is the number of Americans who use email — 45%. These two Department of Commerce reports point to the ubiquity of Internet use in the U.S. This acceptance and use of the technology is critical to the development of an electronic government. With more and more Americans going online, using e-mail, making transactions, seeking information, the time is right for government to take advantage of the benefits of the Internet.

As noted earlier in the chapter, a portal concept of electronic commerce has become a dominant theme in today's Internet environment. Businesses have turned to portals for engaging in their value chain activities (Kalakota and Robinson, 2001). Individuals are taking advantage of Internet portals as a place they come back time and again, meeting a wide range of their information needs. The tendency to make repeat visits to a site is often referred to as *stickiness*, the ability of a portal site to keep users faithful to repeated use of their services. In a business sense, portals are viable in their ability to aggregate thousands of Internet users to one "home" location. Given the Department of Commerce statistics above, it makes sense to engage in this model of Internet use in order to capture a wide or deep population of Internet users. Recent IBM data (May, 2001) indicates that there are more than two billion web pages currently populating the Internet universe and that number is expected to double by the year 2002. This magnitude of Internet resources makes good sense of the notion of aggregating and providing a common entry guide to the Web. Such extensive market penetration and the enhanced 24/7 access to information and services in the business sector makes government's move to an electronic presence a sensible next move. The idea of using a portal to simplify access to government information builds on the experience of the private sector. It enables the government to take advantage of the business sector's experiences and best practices as the development of FirstGov.gov evolves.

WHEREFORE FIRSTGOV.GOV

FirstGov.Gov is the official Internet portal to U.S. Federal government. The U.S. General Services Administration, Office of Citizen Services and Communications manages it, although it represents an interagency effort across the Federal government. It is touted as the "easy-to-search, free-access website designed to give you a centralized place to find information from U.S. local, state and Federal government agency websites. It is YOUR first click to the U.S. government!" (www.firstgov.gov). Today, FirstGov.gov provides informational and transactional government-to-citizen, government-to-business, and government-to-government electronic services. It covers all three branches of government; executive, judicial and legislative. It has as its vision statement: "Our work transcends the traditional boundaries of government and our vision is global — connecting the world to all U.S. Government information and services."

FirstGov.gov offers a powerful search engine that searches every word of every U.S. government document in a quarter of a second or less. It also features a topical index, online transactions, links to state and local government, options to contact government directly, and other tools so the user does not have to know the name of the government agency to get the information they need. This is a major accomplishment. FirstGov.gov further creates and maintains a number of content-specific mini-portals geared to special audience needs, such as students.gov, seniors.gov, workers.gov, science.gov, and consumers.gov. These specialty, cross-agency portals are organized in a manner consistent with the topic or needs-oriented approach to government that FirstGov.gov uses. Access is enhanced when, as noted earlier, problems can be addressed by the user's information need — not by the agency organization structure.

The portal has also won wide recognition and diverse awards for excellence. These include the:

- Industry Advisory Council, E-Gov, and the Federal Chief Information Officer Council's **Excellence.Gov Award Finalist**, January 2002;
- *Government Executive* magazine's **2001 Grace Hopper Government Technology Leadership Award**, December 2001;

- 2001 Innovations in American Government Award Finalist, August 2001 and Semi-Finalist, April 2001; and
- **Yahoo! Internet Life Magazine's** 50 Most Incredibly Useful Sites, July 2002.

The future for this government wide portal is bright. The top-level support for electronic government has carried over from the Clinton to the Bush administration. The policy environment supports its continued development and maintenance. The American public is online and taking advantage of government websites. A report issued by the Council for Excellence in Government (Hart-Teeter, 2002) indicates that 76% of all Internet users and 51% of Americans have accessed a government website. It also noted that overall, Americans are more positive in their outlook towards electronic government than they were the previous year, and that they had high expectations for government as it went online.

The FirstGov.gov website has won numerous awards and has strong visibility and usage. It is poised to play a critical role in the implementation of the *President's Management Agenda* and the electronic government initiatives funded in the 2003 Budget of the United States. The 2003 Budget recognizes that the U.S. government will mix its use of Internet and physical assets to become a "click and mortar" enterprise. The agencies that serve citizens, businesses, internal Federal government functions, and inter-governmental needs will, thus, become more accessible, effective and efficient. In adopting a "click-and-mortar" model, the Federal government will use the best practices of industry. The Bush administration's goal is that services and information will rarely be more than three clicks away from citizens and business.

A final thought here has to do with the initial idea of access to government information. This principle has been the driver behind information policy and management in Federal government. But it is hindered by the perpetual inefficiencies of data redundancy, data duplication, and data error, which abound in government information systems. The creation of FirstGov.gov does not mean that all government information will reside in one format, in one location. Rather, the portal makes use of existing Federal agency databases for its content. It is no secret that these agency web developments are often less than optimal (McClure, Sprehe, and Eschenfelder, 2001). What we have seen is government agencies putting their paper products online, without first thinking about reengineering their activities for an online environment. Initially, there was no attention to thinking about what data should to be provided and in what format. Thus, in many instances, we are receiving the electronic version of our paper government rather than seeing government reengineered for an electronic environment. There are further complications and complexities when we add into this mix the state and local government websites. All U.S. state governments have websites, many of these being all-inclusive gateways to state government. One need only go to North Star, the official home of Minnesota government (http://www.state.mn.us/) or AccessWashington (http://access.wa.gov/) to see innovative and diverse approaches to online information access and service delivery. Cities such as New York and Chicago are also making use of the portal concept, offering a "mygov.gov" approach for their users. States and local governments also operate under different information management policies and environments when it comes to public records, privacy and security, and infrastructure concerns. This further compounds the difficulties of merging all U.S. government websites into one mega-portal such as FirstGov.gov. There are many important questions to be thought through and problems to be solved as we move forward in our electronic world. Our portal to electronic government has been constructed — what remains to be seen is how the rest of the structure will develop.

REFERENCES

Applegate, L. M., McFarlan, F. W., & McKenney, J. (1999). *Corporate information systems management.* New York: McGraw-Hill.

Bensaou, M., & Earl, M. (1998). The right mind-set for managing information technology. *Harvard Business Review,* (September/October).

Caudle, S.L., Marchand, S.I., Bretschneider, S.I., Fletcher, P.T., & Thurmaier, K. (1989). *Managing information resources: New directions in state government.* Syracuse, NY: Syracuse University.

Cleveland, H. (1986). Government is information (but not vice versa). *Public Administration Review,* 46, 605-607.

Dawes, S.S., Bloniarz, P.A., Kelly, K. L., & Fletcher, P.D. (1999, March). *Some assembly required: Building a digital government for the 21st century.* Albany, NY: Center for Technology in Government.

Executive Office of the President, Office of Management and Budget. (2001). *The President's management agenda.* Retrieved on March 15, 2002 from http://www.whitehouse.gov/omb/budintegration/pma_index.html.

Executive Office of the President, Office of Management and Budget. (February 27, 2002). *E-government strategy: Simplified delivery of services to citizens.* Retrieved on March 1, 2002 from http://www.whitehouse.gov/omb/inforeg/egovstrategy.pdf.

Executive Office of the President, Office of Management and Budget. (n.d.). *Budget of the United States government, fiscal year 2003.* Retrieved on June 6, 2002 from http://www.whitehouse.gov/omb/budget/index.html.

Fletcher, P.T., Bretschneider, S.I., & Marchand, D.A. (1992). *Managing information technology: Transforming county governments in the 1990s.* Syracuse, NY: Syracuse University.

Fletcher, P.D., & Westerback, L. (1999). Federal information policy: Management to measurement. *The Journal of the American Society for Information Science,* Special Issue on the National Information Infrastructure, 50(4), 299-304.

Hart-Teeter for The Council for Excellence in Government. (2002, February 26). *E-government to protect, connect and serve us.* Retrieved on March 20, 2002 from http://excelgov.xigroup.com/displayContent.asp?Keyword=ppp022602.

Horn, Congressman S. (October 2, 2000). *FirstGov: Is it a good idea?* Retrieved on September 12, 2001 from http://www.house.gov/reform/gmit/hearings/2000hearings/001002.FirstGov/001002sh.htm.

IBM. (n.d.). *Fast growing cyveillence analyzes millions of web pages daily.* Retrieved May 20, 2001 from http://www2.software.ibm.com.

Kalakota, R., & Robinson, M. (2001). *E-Business 2.0.* NY: Addison-Wesley.

McClure, C.R., Sprehe, T., & Eschenfelder, K. (2001, October). *Performance measures for Federal agencies: Final report.* Retrieved December 13, 2001 from http://www.access.gpo.gov/su_docs/index.html.

Presidential Memo of December 17, 1999. *Electronic Government*. Retrieved January 3,
    2000 from http://whitehouse.gov.
Remarks by the President in the First Internet Webcast (June 24, 2000). Retrieved
    October 10, 2000 from http://www.whitehouse.gov/WH/new/html/internet2000-
    02-24text.html.
U.S. Department of Commerce. (2002, February). *Digital Economy 2002*. Retrieved on
    September 15, 2002 from http://www.esa.doc.gov/508/esa/pdf/DE2002r1.pdf.
U.S. Department of Commerce. (2002, February 5). *A nation online: How Americans are
    expanding their use of the Internet*. Retrieved on July 22, 2002 from http://
    www.ntia.doc.gov/opadhome/digitalnation/index.html.
U.S. General Accounting Office. (2000, September 12). *Year 2000 computing challenge:
    Lessons learned can be applied to other management challenges*. (AIMD-00-290).
    Washington, DC: U.S. Government Printing Office.

Chapter V

Government Web Portals: Management Issues and the Approaches of Five States

Joshua M. Franzel
American University, USA

David H. Coursey
Florida State University, USA

ABSTRACT

Web portals are the dominant organizational motif for e-government service delivery. To date, most reviews of government portal experiences focus on the types and technical sophistication of delivered services as well as design issues, such as usability. Management issues, like commercialization and centralization, receive relatively little attention. The authors define and argue for a more management-oriented perspective. Several major issues are explored and then the experiences of five states are used to demonstrate how their consideration presents a very different view of portal strategies for researchers.

INTRODUCTION

As of February 2002, more than 143 million Americans, or 54 percent of the total population of the United States, have used the Internet. This number continues to increase at a rate of approximately two million users per month (NTIA, 2002). The Internet is, and will continue to be, a major tool disseminating information worldwide. From hospitals to police stations, from private firms to schools, millions of Americans in every state in the nation have daily access to the Internet and use it regularly.

Given this level of public access, Web-based government services are critical to service delivery. Most government efforts began as single agency sites, usually informational more so than direct services, but in the late 1990s, the idea of a centralized site to navigate the offerings of a government unit developed: the web portal.

Today, web portals are arguably the leading organizational strategy for the provision of online government services. Every state government has a web portal. However, understanding exactly what a portal is and how such a strategy is developed, is hampered by the very definition. Consider this definition:

"A web portal serves as the integrated gateway into state government web sites and provides visitors with a single point of contact for online service delivery within the state. Because portals integrate state e-service, they can improve access to government, reduce service-processing costs, and enable state agencies to provide a higher quality of service. (Gant et al., p. 10)"

This typical definition stresses that a portal provides (1) a single site for accessing all government services and (2) e-service applications. Early "portals" were mostly just homepages with links to various agencies and perhaps a search engine. A true portal presumes some organization around service and not agencies. Such an approach appears to be heavily influenced by private sector websites.

Web portals, regardless of their form, are virtual requirements for Web-based government access. However, despite their rapid adoption, such an approach carries significant management and policy issues, aside from the obvious concern about their effectiveness in meeting their goals of improved citizen access, reduced service costs, and better quality service

In this chapter, we seek to create a boilerplate for future, more evaluative research focused on major management and policy issues with the web portal approach. Specifically, we begin by reviewing some existing literature, then outline major management and policy issues, and follow with more in-depth reviews of the efforts of five states (Florida, Kansas, Illinois, Pennsylvania, and New Mexico) as demonstrations of how such issues create important research questions for future evaluations.

PREVIOUS STUDIES

There are two primary studies to date on state Web portals. The Center for Digital Government (http://www.centerdigitalgov.com/) and the Progress and Freedom Foundation's (http://www.pff.org) release of the *Digital State* study documenting state government progress in online service delivery. Also relevant to the topic of state portals is the report, *State Web Portals: Delivering and Financing E-Service*, by Gant et al. (2002).

The *Digital State 2001* study evaluates each state's web portal using eight categories of criteria (Lassman, 2002) for use of the Internet:

1.   To locate and file paperwork;
2.   To retrieve tax information, forms and filing and for digital recordkeeping;

3.   To find program information, eligibility requirements and processing applications for administrative Intranet, and applications used for electronic benefit transfers and child support payments;

4.   In conjunction with two-way multimedia applications: for law enforcement, judicial and corrections officials as well as to provide public information;

5.   Measures for online or digital access to, and promotion of, information about state government and the electoral process;

6.   Measures of institutional arrangements for digital policy decision-making and long-term infrastructure management;

7.   The use of digital technologies for education, including functions in the areas of administration, instruction and reporting; and

8.   The use of geographic information systems and data — intra-governmental and in transportation policy — as well as institutional arrangements for collecting and making it available to the public.

Digital State 2001 was based on a comprehensive survey distributed to the Chief Information Officer (CIO) or equivalent official of each participating state. The answers given by respondents were measured against benchmarks based on past studies and a standardized ranking was produced for each state (Lassman, 2002). The two states ranking first and second in the study respectively were Illinois and Kansas.

While valuable, the *Digital State* suffers from two major drawbacks. First, it is overly focused on what services are being provided with surprisingly little effectiveness assessment. Second, the over-reliance on CIOs for their data is highly suspect. CIOs are increasingly politically appointed, with strong loyalties to make their Governor (who was also their appointer) look good. Even if the *Digital State* begins including more management and policy issues, it is unlikely that answers from CIOs alone could be very reliable.

The second study, *State Web Portals: Delivering and Financing E-Service* (Gant et al., 2002, p. 8), was meant to "assess the level of functionality for each of the 50 U.S. state web portals and to provide a benchmark by which future developments in e-service can be judged." The study assessed all 50 state web portals on four dimensions:

1.   *Openness*: the level at which the site offers comprehensive information and services;

2.   *Customization*: the level at which user can uniquely tailor views of the portal content;

3.   *Usability*: the level of accessibility to portal content to a range of users; and

4.   *Transparency*: the level at which users can assess the legitimacy of the information offered (Gant et al., 2002).

The Gant and Associates (2002) study relies on their personal evaluations. While immune to some of the problems of relying on CIOs, it does not provide much inside information from managers and developers in the states. Furthermore, their study is more focused on usability issues and still not very attuned to management and policy concerns.

MANAGEMENT AND POLICY ISSUES

Web portals present a variety of seemingly overlooked management and policy issues. To date, studies have tended towards reporting how well government is implementing e-services and building usable interfaces to such services. We believe at least some attention should be placed on what we see are key issues outside of service delivery:

- Client definition
- Political uses
- Centralization
- Commercialism
- Outsourcing
- Performance measurement

Client Definition

Web portals almost universally presume that it is helpful to the citizen to have a one-stop shop for government services. The argument goes that having agencies with separate sites, web addresses, and interfaces is confusing and presumes that citizens know which agency handles what service. Therefore, a central portal is viewed as optimal.

The primary problem with this approach is it makes a very questionable assumption: citizens think government first and then service. The presumption is that citizens know that a certain level of government performs the service, just not what unit. This becomes a serious problem when portals require agencies to use only the portal address for service access and marketing, an approach that was attempted in Florida for example. Portals may actually make it harder to find such services.

The reason, in part, relates to search engines like Yahoo! stressing homepage addresses and titles more than page content. For example, it is far more likely a user will easily find a site for state hunting permits if such a service is given a separate web address than located as a subdirectory under a state web portal address. If nothing else, having a domain name specific to the service provides more visibility.

A second problem is assuming all citizens need to access all services. The very idea of a common branding, navigation, and interface is based on such a fallacy. While this is a significant issue, attempts have and are being made to create tailored user interfaces (for citizen, state employee, business, etc.) to address this concern.

A third difficulty arises from the assumption that government is a coherent, single entity. This questionable position comes from the adoption of web portals from business sites. The problem is that government is best viewed, if it has to be compared to the private sector, as a conglomerate, not a single business. Like a conglomerate, it is not reasonable to expect clients of one company or agency to have anything to do with another company or agency. Agencies have very different types of clients, not just in their expected level of service demands, but also their web skills. Such dramatic differences may be far greater than tailored user interfaces can service and call for a more decentralized approach to online service design than most web portals currently support.

Last, and perhaps most important, a government-centric model for service delivery is arguably fundamentally flawed. The simple reason is citizens do not spend much time at all on government sites (Eggers, 2002). Making a user come to a government site for any service is the electronic equivalent to forcing them to drive to a government office instead, say, of using an innovative one-stop physical government service center in a mall. If users spend the vast majority of their time on MSN, AOL, then why not have the services primarily accessible (or at least assume that is the access) there? Why spend millions of dollars to market a government web portal address?

The Gartner Group argue in their, "Why Today's Government Portals are Irrelevant," (2002) report that portals will soon be obsolete, estimating that less than 20 percent of government web transactions by 2006 will be conducted via portals. Instead, outside service providers will dominate. For example, AOL has recently signed a deal with NIC, a large private provider of government web services, to deliver many of the current e-government applications via AOL's Government Guide (Eggers, 2002).

Political Issues

Political implications in the provision of information technology services have been a key issue in public administration IT literature. As the classic URBIS studies (e.g., Kraemer and King, 1986, 1989) found, political leadership may be technologically challenged, but they always seem to understand the political implications of how technology is deployed and managed. Early government web page adoption was strongly pushed by political necessity as agency heads and political leadership felt they had to have a web page to appear technologically current. Politics continue with today's web portals.

Web portals have become a very attractive publicity outlet for governors, even in so-called "weak" governor states, where the portal function is assigned under the office's control. In Florida, the Bush administration's portal development was part of a significant centralization of information technology management away from the agencies to the Governor's office. California experienced the same situation under the Davis administration. Usually, the argument is made that such centralized control is necessary for a coherent and consistent government presence. However, a brief look around portals such as Florida's (http://www.myflorida.com) makes it clear how arguably biased such sites have become as a political tool if not more than service delivery. In some cases, the state homepage/portal was, or still is, designated as the Governor's homepage.

The political use of state web portals is a serious management and policy issue. Besides the ethical considerations, such use can threaten the very presumed legitimacy of information, a critical issue in the Gant and Colleagues (2002) study. It also misinforms citizens by implying the governor is responsible for all state services. Of course, separating self-promotion from "objective" information is difficult. Is an e-mail list derived from a web portal and maintained by the governor too political? In Florida, legislators are banned from placing almost any content other than basic personal and legal information on their state-hosted pages for this very reason.

Centralization

How centralized should the management and policy making of government services be and exactly what should be centralized versus decentralized? These centralization, or loci of control, issues are nothing new in government information technology. Web portals, by their very nature, all but assume some centralized control over interface and basic management policies to the portal site. But, how much control should still remain with the agencies providing the services? Should agencies be required to use the portal address for all access? If there is a trend, it appears web portals strive toward centralization of basic design elements, use policies, and e-commerce infrastructure (e.g., what vendor, if any, and how transactions are processed).

There are certainly areas where centralization can help, especially in standardization of payment technologies (viz., it makes little sense for agencies to have differing online purchasing vendors and systems). However, content development and management policy for an agency's site might be better left decentralized. First, content is likely more accurate if provided as close to the source as possible. Second, giving an agency a sense of ownership of the materials can encourage better site design and service delivery. Both assumptions are debatable, but the point is that there is considerable question as to how and what parts of web portals should be centralized and the resulting implications.

Commercialism

Commercialism issues in web portals take many forms: (1) naming conventions, (2) advertising/placement, and (3) user fees. How to name the web portal is an ongoing issue: should a state adopt a standard "state.**.us" address or go for a commercial name, such as Florida uses with www.myflorida.com? The arguments of the .com advocates tend to include that .com implies the site provides commerce/e-services and that the "state.**.us" approach is cryptic to citizens and more difficult to market. The first argument is invalid because .com means it is a commercial entity and has nothing to do, directly, with commerce. Second, the idea that somehow "state.**.us" is more difficult to find is highly questionable as the experiential evidence of states like Pennsylvania which have aggressively marketed such names suggests otherwise.

The major problem with using a .com name for a portal site is legitimacy. It is not easy for a citizen to know if the site is official. This is especially problematic for local governments where citizens may get lots of "hits" off search engines from related private sites to their queries. It is perhaps more logical to use a "state.**.us" name as the primary page address, then use various .com names as alternatives for marketing. There is no reason why such .com names cannot just forward (or "resolve") to the official state address. The .com names are also subject to expiration. A government may forget to renew their domain and find it taken by a private vendor (which recently happened to a Florida government .com site).

There is also the issue of advertising and placement. Some states (like Florida) have considered selling advertisements as a way to offset the cost of service provision. But such advertisements have significant policy questions. Will an ad on a state portal site suggest to a citizen that the state endorses a vendor? Will ads, especially on .com portals, make the site look less legitimate? Will conflicts of interest arise between the regulatory relationship with vendors and their advertising contracts?

Lastly, there is the user fee issue. Should portals charge for services? How should such services be charged? Issues of cost recovery, service promotion, and market signals, among others, arise. The issue is hardly new to portals as the debate about the appropriateness of user fees for government information services is a long-standing one in the literature.

For example, the Florida Legislature originally sought to encourage citizens to use online services by waiving any fees associated with various permits and license applications shifted from paper-based to the Web. The idea was that such incentives would encourage citizens to adopt the more cost-effective online approach. The Legislature did not worry about lost revenues on the presumption that the efficiency gains would outstrip the losses and/or the long-term savings would offset lost revenue. However, this policy became a strong disincentive for agencies to convert permit and license applications to the Web as they feared the loss of such revenues that were used to support more than just administrative processing costs.

Such a totally free approach has been abandoned. Now, Florida is charging online fees in such areas as hunting permits and in some cases, requiring clients to use online versions in replacement of traditional processes. Larger businesses, for example, will soon be required to file many of their state tax returns electronically.

Outsourcing

Should web portal development, maintenance/hosting, and content generation be outsourced? What are the implications? As our example states will show, outsourcing portal development is a popular option. A recent study from the International City/County Management Association (2002) found about 17 percent of e-government services are outsourced, with an additional 46 percent between consultants and local government staff. Partly, this is due to the difficulty governments have in acquiring and maintaining the in-house expertise. Some states, like Florida, that had developed a solid in-house staff and supportive infrastructure have virtually dismantled it in favor of outsourcing on the ever-questionable presumption that it can be done more cheaply and effectively by the private sector.

Besides the usual questions surrounding cost and effectiveness, outsourcing yields other major issues. First, web portal outsourcing usually involves large contracts. Such contracts are very tempting political plums for elected officials to award campaign contributors. Such issues have clearly occurred in California, Florida, and other states. For example, in Florida, upon entering office, the Bush administration took web portal development away from arguably the country's finest state development team and gave it to a small web development firm that had worked on his campaign page.

Second, there are the issues of public information access and privacy. How can a citizen be sure that their protected, private information is safe if content is developed or hosted by a private company? Information access is especially an issue when a government chooses to provide a service via a vendor for a user fee. In such cases, the result can actually be less access to information. For example, in Tallahassee, Florida one cannot get notices on upcoming bid opportunities except through a paid online service under contract with the city.

Performance Measurement

Portals are presumed to increase service effectiveness, citizen access, and reduce service costs. Despite the fact that those goals often conflict in any service provision, the problem remains there are few attempts at even the most elementary evaluation of portal effectiveness. The assumption that portals are good is quite dominant and questionable. A recent National Audit Office analysis condemned the lack of any real, meaningful attempts to measure portal cost-benefits (Perry, 2002).

Of course, simply assuming that an information technology will yield positive results is an old problem as are the difficulties in developing effectiveness measures. Probably the most commonly cited measure is the number of "page hits," or better yet, the number of "user visits." These are hardly measures of service effectiveness. Even as a measure of citizen demand or use, such indicators are imperfect. For example, the number of page hits can go up just by having a disorganized site and/or confusion from the user on how to access a service.

It is sometimes argued that performance measurement simply is not cost effective, too time consuming, and yields questionable results due to research design weaknesses. However, web services can be quickly evaluated in rather low cost quasi-experimental, even experimental, approaches.

For example, an animal shelter creates an online kennel with pictures of animals for adoption. The shelter can track before and after adoption rates or, as Santa Rosa County, Florida did, randomly assign animals for web publicity and compare their adoption rates to the control group to see if the approach is effective before investing in such an approach for all animals in its care. These measurements would be neither time consuming nor very costly, yet have the usual strengths associated with experimental and quasi-experimental evaluations.

CURRENT STATE EFFORTS

Exactly how do these management and policy issues change the way we evaluate government web portals? To demonstrate the types of research questions focused by such a lens, we chose five states, with varying administrative situations, to discuss: Florida, Kansas, Illinois, Pennsylvania, and New Mexico. We based our selection on the two primary studies to date on state web portals — *The Digital State 2001* study by The Center for Digital Government and the Progress and Freedom Foundation and *State Web Portals: Delivering and Financing E-Service* (Gant et al., 2002).

The two states ranking first and second respectively in the *Digital State 2001* study were Illinois and Kansas. These states have interesting, contrasting administrative schemes. Illinois's portal is fully developed and maintained by the Illinois Technology Office's state employees, while Kansas's portal is outsourced to the Kansas Information Consortium (KIC), Inc., a subsidiary of National Information Consortium (NIC), Inc.

Pennsylvania's portal was selected based on its high rating in the Gant et al. (2002) study and, due to its medium-large size, its situation with regards to resources and needs is applicable to many other states. Also selected were the portals of New Mexico and Florida. Both are currently in the process of changing portal phases by using private companies for development and implementation. Such parallel situations offer more insight into portal phases, decision-making, and varying alternative situations.

The State of Florida's Web Portal

Roughly $3,000,000 of Florida's FY2001 ($1,000,000,000) IT budget was used to maintain the previous http:///www.myflorida.com portal phase that was used since 1999 (for developments before 1999, see Coursey and Killngsworth, 2000). The portal was the responsibility of the State Technology Office (STO) that is located within the Department of Management Services, a part of the state's executive branch (D. Glouser, personal communication, February 12, 2002). The main portal was used as an unofficial standard for the 13 agencies directly under the control of the Governor's office. Each of the agencies were responsible for maintaining their own sites and had their own webmaster(s) loosely follow the look and feel of the main portal (placement of logos, header design, etc.) and provide information related to their agencies to be integrated into the main portal (D. Glouser, personal communication, February 12, 2002). This phase consisted mainly of a search area, general categories and topics sections, a current news section, small list of links to government services pages, links to specific government offices/agencies, and space available for state related advertising. All of these sections were updated regularly by the STO's web developers based on availability of information and governor's office requests (D. Glouser, personal communication, February 12, 2002).

In 2001, the State of Florida contracted the next phase of MyFlorida to Yahoo! Inc. The three-year contract is for $5.21 million with an indefinite $750,000/per year maintenance fee option after the initial three years. During the first three years, Yahoo! Inc. provides, on their official portal (http://www.yahoo.com), a half-million dollar's worth of Florida tourism advertising and easier navigation to Florida's portal through its main portal. Upon the completion of Yahoo! Inc.'s portal construction, the majority of the content and maintenance will be the responsibility of the STO Web developers (under the Governor's Office), as was the case with the previous phase. Most of the content is the same as Florida's previous portal phase but is structured using Yahoo! Inc.'s portal style of one main portal with one web address that distributes users to other portal pages and outside pages. All state agency, department, and office pages are given standardized URLs that can only be found by first going through the main portal page and follow a uniform design style and structure.

Political Issues

Given that the Governor's office continues to have much input, by way of requests, on what is put on the portal, one might assess the portal's usage and effectiveness around political issues. Such an analysis, for instance, would highlight whether particular accomplishments of the state administration are highlighted (particularly around an election cycle) and/or potential partisan agendas undermine the legitimacy of the portal. Areas of inquiry like these may offer more insight into the optimal way to offer information on the portal and subsequent sites while operating the portal in an obvious political environment.

Centralization

Assessment of the modified centralization approach of Florida's portal might shed light on the relative effectiveness of the Yahoo, Inc., and similar groups' approach of one portal, with one style for all pages, with one web address. With this, one might find whether such standardization (non-uniqueness) of look and feel of agency sites promotes or inhibits attracting of new clientele and/or information distribution. Another aspect that could be explored would be if this type of centralization contributes to the validity and reliability of the information offered.

Commercialism

Florida's and similar situations might call for portals to be evaluated around commercialism issues. In this respect, studies might examine whether state advertisements on a site, such as private Yahoo Inc. sites, portray the state's endorsement of all advertisements/services on a specific site. Also, another area worth studying would be how advertising in a commercial setting detracts from or contributes to the credibility of the state's portal as an official state entity. In regards to difference between public and private entities, other commercialism issues that could be looked at are how private firms (like Yahoo) categorize and create useful links to all state e-services, given that they might not have a full grasp of government administration and services.

The State of Kansas's Web Portal

The current Kansas portal phase is structured with situational links, quick links to specific information sources (state phone directory, calendar, sitemap, etc.), links to current news/feature sites/popular services sections, and links to up-to-date information from Kansas's Governor's office, state interest articles, and feedback pages.

The Information Network of Kansas (INK) was created by an act of the Kansas State Legislature in 1990 for the purpose of providing equal electronic access to state, county, local and other public information (State of Kansas web portal, 2002). This venture, the first of its kind in the United States, led to INK's board of directors' selecting the private firm, Kansas Information Consortium (KIC) to develop, implement, maintain, and host the state information network including Kansas's main portal (L. Counts, personal communication, February 12, 2002). From the beginning of the contract with KIC, the state of Kansas has allotted no annual funding to the company for Kansas's state network; this continues today. Instead, selling subscriptions to the Information Network of Kansas generates funds. Currently the rates are $75 for an initial annual fee and an annual renewal fee of $60. The subscriptions provide the ability to use AccessKansas fee services (which account for 10 percent of total Kansas portal services — 90 percent of the total services offered on the portal are free to all users). (State of Kansas web portal, 2002). Examples of online services currently available exclusively to subscribers are: (1) search for and print drivers' license records, (2) search for, track, and print legislative bills, and (3) search the Board of Nursing database. Examples of online services currently available and free to all users include: (1) purchasing trucking permits, (2) searching statistics, contributions, contributors, or candidates that pertain to the House, the Senate, state-wide races, or the Board of Education, and (3) filing Kansas state income tax.

One of the areas Kansas improved in its current portal over the previous phase was its links (L. Counts, personal communication, February 12, 2002). Kansas's old portal was found (through user interviews and testing) to have a very poor linkage from the main portal page to specific government services. In the previous version, often a user looking for information on a specific state government service would logically click on a government link on main portal page and then be given six link options to choose from: (Legislative, Elected Officials, State Agencies, Judicial, Local Government, State Committees). The user would likely select the state agencies option. He would then be presented with a long list of agencies under a "Public Services" heading. If the user were unfamiliar with roles of each of the agencies, he might not know in which agency site to look for information. To correct this problem, the current version offers sections based on the type of user (visitor, student, etc.), which contains links to services categorized by type of service, not by agency.

Political Issues

As is the case in other states, with the Governor's office being a significant source of input of the information offered on the portal, it might be useful to assess such cases around political use issues. The Governor's office of Kansas provides for postings such as weekly columns, news releases, executive order information, proclamations, and appointment information. Currently, the information is posted to the portal without a formal review, political or any other type. An analysis of this area might offer a further understanding of the levels of use and intended effectiveness at which the portal is being provided.

Outsourcing

The Kansas Information Consortium is responsible for developing and administering Kansas's main portal. As discussed in the management and policy issues section, it may be beneficial to assess such cases around outsourcing issues. One might use levels of investigation that would offer further insight into how content and aesthetic decisions are made. Which are by state personnel and which are made by KIC? As INK and KIC have been partnered together since 1991, it might be beneficial to assess the cost efficiency of the current portal and also price and evaluate other portal alternatives.

Client Definition

E-services, like the ones offered by Kansas, point to the need for evaluation of a portal around the client definition issue. More specifically, one might evaluate such a portal on how easily a person is able to find a specific e-service given its location, reference from other sites, and its ability to be found through external search engines. Also, a portal could be assessed on how well it accommodates for varying Internet (and overall technology) skill sets of users when attempting to link specific clientele with the e-services they need. To date, such a review has not been carried out.

The previous portal version made it difficult for someone who did not know the structure and responsibilities of government to find information on services. Recognizing these difficulties of client definition, this problem was corrected by using the new layout of situational categories and then organizing links to services by type, not by which entity responsible for them. The initial problem and solution were discovered and addressed based on user interviews and testing. Such an approach surfaces as a type of assessment tool of the relative effectiveness of a portal, both from the perspective of the agency providing the services and the citizen using them. This is a valuable tool for improvement of the web portals of other states.

Commercialization

Unlike Florida, Kansas is far less commercial. For example, Kansas is very reluctant of posting advertisements on its site. The INK is currently discussing the issue, carefully examining the issues involved including legal and policy issues, such as whether to allow outside (the state) companies to advertise when they might be in competition with resident firms (Peterson, 2002).

The State of Illinois's Web Portal

Created on February 19, 1999, the Illinois Technology Office (ITO), which is located within the Office of the Governor, is responsible for developing all of the state's portal phases and contracts its services out to individual agencies to develop, maintain, and host their sites. In regard to the cost of the portal, the actual expenditures on staff or hardware for the portal were not available at the time of this chapter. But previous state studies comparing outsourcing options to "in-house" state employee development and maintenance with state provided training and organization have concluded that the "in-house" model was more cost efficient (M. Davis, personal communication, February 8, 2002).

Outsourcing Issues

With the ITO contracting its service to other state offices and agencies, an interesting area of inquiry may be whether the entities solely utilizing the ITO are sacrificing the diversity, breadth of information, and originality of multiple, non-government providers, for the ease of access to the centralized services. To date, a published report has not covered such points in regards to Illinois's portal and state web sites. While this area of analysis may be based to a large extent on stylistic and content opinion, assessing the portal and subsequent sites around these outsourcing issues may shed light on the optimal balance between a centralization approach (using an ITO-like office) and the individual creation of portals and web sites by state offices and agencies.

The Commonwealth of Pennsylvania's Web Portal

In February of 2000, Pennsylvania entered into a contract with Microsoft Corporation and the Pennsylvania IT firm, Peripherals Plus Technologies (PPT). The three entities released the latest portal phase on October 12, 2000 (PPT's web site, 2002). Microsoft designed the portal and it was created/coded by PPT. Peripherals Plus Technologies was and continues to be responsible for providing training every two months to the state employees who maintain the portal. The state's Office of Information Technology directly oversees the portal and the webmasters from each of the state's agencies and offices who are responsible for maintaining the content on the portal and associated sites. The entire portal is hosted by the Governor's office and is administered by both state employees (Governor's Office, Office of Information Technology, etc.) and the private sector partners (T. Horley, personal communication, February 7, 2002).

The new portal improved on several aspects of its previous version. One of the biggest areas of improvement was in the main page organization (T. Horley, personal communication, February 7, 2002). There had been a large number (100+) of links on the main portal page which would often be very confusing and overwhelming to the user. Also, given the large number of links in the small screen space of the main page, it would often be difficult for the user to notice new, potentially useful links, when the main page was updated. To make the portal easier to navigate, situational links are used and newer updated portions of the portal are highlighted.

Navigation for specific users was also improved by using an imagemap of the state. With this map, users can click on the portion of the state in which they live or work and access information about weather, news, regional services, etc. Also, the new portal phase allows users to set up an account with login/password to the portal. This allows users to format the page with information pertinent to them and easily view such topical information updates.

Client Definition

Situational links, highlighted updates, and personally tailored options are aimed at allowing users to more easily find information. With these models of self directed client definition, it would be useful to assess how successful this design is in connecting the desired areas to end users while eliminating problems that arise in other portals. Often other portals offer information that is both pertinent and not pertinent to users. It may be the additional unneeded information that confuses the user, inhibiting portal use. If portals like Pennsylvania's are analyzed along client definition lines and are found to increase the effectiveness due to their attributes that reduce extraneous information, such attributes might be applied to other portals.

The State of New Mexico's Web Portal

New Mexico's current portal version has been in use since January 16, 2002. It was created and maintained in house by Web developers in the Information Services Division located within New Mexico's General Services Department (GSD). The state's Web Portal Committee of the Chief Information Officer's (CIO) office oversees portal development. The current version cost $10,000 to develop and implement (D. McCuthcheon, personal communication, February 7, 2002).

In February 2002, the state government and IBM (at a cost of $750,000 — mostly provided through a Federal grant) began working on the next phase of New Mexico's portal. IBM is developing the new portal and providing servers for hosting it. Upon the portal's completion, it will become the responsibility of the GSD for updating, further development, and hosting. Although the new phase has not yet been completed, it is slated to offer user login options (similar to Pennsylvania's) that will identify specific users and allow them to tailor the main portal page with personally pertinent information. Also, users will have an option to have their personal information follow them throughout the site and automatically fill out forms when the user is applying or registering for services (D. McCuthcheon, personal communication, February 7, 2002).

Another option that was considered, but not chosen, was using state employees to develop the new portal. It was estimated by employees within the GSD that it would cost roughly $500,000 ($250,000 less than the IBM contract) and require a small team of five to ten developers to create a new portal phase that would be very similar to the current version in look and feel but include features comparable to the IBM version. This option would have taken between six to nine months to develop, test, and implement. The time length was unacceptable to the CIO, but IBM was able to reduce the time frame (D. McCuthcheon, personal communication, February 7, 2002).

Outsourcing

Moving from the wholly in-house development of New Mexico's current portal to the outsourcing of its development to IBM would permit an assessment of relative cost factors associated with portal development and implementation as well as whether the use of outside developers has a significant impact on the other areas of inquiry. Specifically, the impact that the nongovernmental developers have on the portal's organization is based on services rather than agencies or departments. Also, another area would be the effect the non-governmental developers have on the level of political uses of the site.

CONCLUSION

Management and policy issues are often overlooked in regards to web portals. Currently, the major portal studies tend to report on levels of how well government is implementing e-services, using the associated technologies, and building usable interfaces to such services. While useful, such an approach provides little real management guidance and clearly assumes the portal strategy is an effective one for all governments. Web portals suffer from their own litany of presumed success.

In this chapter, we have outlined several major management and policy issues that should be part of the ongoing portal evaluation process: (1) client definition — needs and resources of types of citizens, (2) political uses — level at which portals are able to be used for/altered on purposes and political grounds, (3) centralization — defining point(s) of control over portal, (4) commercialism — extent to which public portals follow private conventions, (5) outsourcing — decisions on extent to which portal is the responsibility of a public or private organization, and (6) performance measurement — assessment of portal effectiveness in relation to mission.

Our review of five state web portals demonstrates very different management and policy approaches and significant questions for government IT researchers to ponder. These topics are not simply about assessing web portals, but also about the very core of much of traditional government IT research concerns such as the political implications of IT management (e.g., Garson, 2000). Furthermore, the clear lack of significant evaluative research of the true effectiveness of such portals reflects a typical problem with government IT ventures. The challenge is for researchers to develop reasonable measures than can be applied in a cost-effective manner. Whether or not one is an advocate of the portal approach, there is little doubt that such issues are critical to improving e-government services.

REFERENCES

Americans with Disabilities Act of 1990, 42 U.S.C. Sec. 12131, et seq.

Center for Digital Government. (n.d.). Center for Digital Government index page. Retrieved on March 5, 2002, from the World Wide Web: http://www.centerdigitalgov.com.

Commonwealth of Pennsylvania. (n.d.). PA PowerPort. Retrieved on January 19, 2002, from the World Wide Web: http://www.state.pa.us/PAPower.

Counts, L. (2002). Web developer and project coordinator — Kansas Information Consortium. Personal communication, February 12, 2002.

Davis, M. (2002). Public Information Officer — State of Illinois. Personal communication, February 8, 2002.

Department of Justice — The American with Disabilities. (n.d.). Information and technical assistance on the Americans with Disabilities Act. Retrieved on February 25, 2002, from the World Wide Web: http://www.usdoj.gov/crt/ada/adahom1.htm.

Eggers, W. (2002). The invisible state. *Government Technology*. Retrieved on March 1, 2002, from the World Wide Web: http://www.govtech.net/magazine/story.phtml?id=3030000000005508&issue=02:2002.

Gant, D. B., Gant, J.P., & Johnson, C.L. (2002). State web portals: Delivering and financing e-service. *IBM Endowment for the Business of Government*. Retrieved March 1, 2002, from the World Wide Web: http://endowment.pwcglobal.com/pdfs/JohnsonReport.pdf.

The Gartner Group. (2002). *Why today's government portals are irrelevant*.

Glouser, D. (2002). Portal Program Manager — State of Florida. Personal communication, February 12, 2002.

Horley, T. (2002). Program Manager, Governor's Office of Administration — Commonwealth of Pennsylvania. Personal communication, February 7, 2002.

International City/County Management Association. (2002). 2002 Electronic government survey results. Retrieved on November 14, 2002, from the World Wide Web: http://icma.org/go.cfm?cid=1&gid=4&sid=8&did=1680.

Lassman, K. (2002). The digital state 2001.*The Progress & Freedom Foundation*. Retrieved on February 1, 2002, from the World Wide Web: http://www.pff.org/publications/digitalstate2001.pdf.

McCuthcheon, D. Web developer — State of New Mexico. Personal communication, February 7, 2002.

National Telecommunications and Information Administration. (2002). A nation online — How Americans are expanding their use of the Internet. National Telecommunications and Information Administration. Retrieved on March 15, 2002, from the World Wide Web: http://www.ntia.doc.gov/ntiahome/dn/html/anationonline2.htm.

Peripherals Plus Technology. (n.d.). People, power, technology. Retrieved on January 15, 2002, from the World Wide Web: http://www.pptnet.com.

Perry, M. (2002). NAO report finds flaws in e-gov plans. Accountancyage.com. Retrieved on April 26, 2002, from the World Wide Web: http://www.accountancyage.com.

Peterson, S. (2000). This space for rent. *Government Technology*. Retrieved on November 1, 2002, from the World Wide Web: http://www.govtech.net/magazine/gt/2000/dec/140.html.

Rehabilitation Act of 1973, 29 U.S.C. Sec. 794d.

State of Florida. (n.d.). MyFlorida.com Homepage. Retrieved on February 1, 2002, from the World Wide Web: http://www.myflorida.com.

State of Illinois's State Technology Office. (n.d.). Technology in Illinois. Retrieved on February 1, 2002, from the World Wide Web: http://www100.state.il.us/tech/technology.

State of Kansas. (n.d.). accessKansas Home page. Retrieved on January 12, 2002, from the World Wide Web: http://www.accesskansas.org.

Waddell, C. & Thomason, K.L. (n.d.). Is your site ADA-Compliant or a lawsuit-in-waiting? *The International Center for Disability Resources on the Internet*. Retrieved on January 25, 2002, from the World Wide Web: http://www.icdri.org/CynthiaW/is_%20yoursite_ada_compliant.htm.

Chapter VI

The Organizational Culture of Digital Government: Technology, Accountability & Shared Governance

Barbara Allen
University of Ottawa, Canada

Luc Juillet
University of Ottawa, Canada

Mike Miles
University of Ottawa, Canada

Gilles Paquet
University of Ottawa, Canada

Jeffrey Roy
University of Ottawa, Canada

Kevin Wilkins
University of Ottawa, Canada

ABSTRACT

This chapter examines the characteristics of government organizations that influence their capacity to employ information technology (IT) in a strategic manner such that it assists them in their quest to meet governance challenges. We explore the organizational factors, architectural and cultural, that impede large government departments from moving beyond the adoption of IT as a mere instrument that assists the execution of routine tasks in the traditional way and move into new forms of governance that alter the relationships between individuals and units within the organization and between the organization and its external environment. Our objective is to provide a useful framework for the analysis of the barriers to, and potential catalysts of, an IT mediated transformation of the governance of large government departments. Our insights are based on explorations of the issues surrounding the development of new governance models for data and informatics management within Fisheries and Oceans Canada, the federal department with a leading role in a wide range of activities relating to Canada's marine environment. As one of the world's leading marine science institutions, this case underscores the fact that technical competence alone is insufficient to facilitate a shift towards digital government. Using IT strategically is a governance challenge that is contingent upon organizational structure and culture.

Science and engineering produce 'know-how'; but 'know-how' is nothing by itself; it is a means without an end, a mere potentiality, an unfinished sentence. 'Know-how' is no more a culture than a piano is music.

E.F. Schumacher

INTRODUCTION

This chapter examines the characteristics of government organizations that influence their capacity to employ information technology (IT) in a strategic manner such that it assists them in their quest to meet the governance challenges they face. We explore the organizational factors, architectural and cultural, that impede large government departments from moving beyond the adoption of IT as a mere instrument that assists the execution of routine tasks in the traditional way and move into new forms of governance that alter the relationships between individuals and units within the organization and between the organization and its external environment.

Our objective is to provide a useful framework for the analysis of the barriers to, and potential catalysts of, an IT mediated transformation of the governance of large government departments. Our insights are based on explorations of the issues surrounding the development of new governance models for data and informatics management within Fisheries and Oceans Canada, the federal department with a leading role in a wide range of activities relating to Canada's marine environment. As one of the world's leading marine science institutions, this case underscores the fact that technical competence alone is insufficient to facilitate a shift towards digital government. Using IT strategically is a governance challenge that is contingent upon organizational structure and culture.

In the next section, we outline the challenges of a socio-economic environment driven by heightened change, complexity and turbulence — outlining the important role that IT can have in coping with a turbulent conditions. In the section following that, we explore organizational factors that act as barriers to the strategic employment of IT in a manner that is consistent with and contributes to the principal governance challenges of government agencies in a digital world. The obstacles explored include those that inhibit government departments from developing information systems that integrate across their organizational units and those that inhibit a more strategic design of accountability and technology within the context of digital government. The third section continues this emphasis on the alignment between the evolution of information systems and an organizational structure and culture that is appropriate to the context. We conclude with some potential and preliminary strategies through which IT may be employed to enable governance transformations.

INFORMATION, GOVERNANCE AND DIGITAL GOVERNMENT

Intervening in the area of marine resources presents an intractable problem to many governments for reasons that include the size of the area to be governed, the natural complexity of marine ecosystems, and the numerous and conflicting demands of resource users. Government agencies charged with the task of stewarding marine resources must generate and integrate a vast amount of scientific and social data to support decision-making and the policy processes: they must also develop and adapt knowledge networks that build on the tacit forms of information tied to the cognitive resources that exist within and external to their organization.

The result is a need to employ technology strategically, and to do so within an environment that facilitates interpersonal exchanges. The challenge is well illustrated by Canada's situation.

Managing Complexity and IT

With the second largest offshore territory in the world and the world's longest coastline, Canada also has a vast oceanic area to survey and govern. Canada's coast touches the Atlantic, Pacific, and Arctic oceans and is thus the home of numerous vastly different ecosystems demanding different management approaches. Scientists and managers are therefore presented with the difficult task of building a knowledge base sufficiently complete to assist the decision-making process in each of these environments.

However, oceans are first and foremost a complex entity characterized by considerable natural environmental variability and significant scientific uncertainty regarding resource conditions. The controversy surrounding the role of changes in water temperature, water salinity, and habitat damage as contributors to the collapse of the Northern Cod fishery in the early 1990s attests to this fact. Moreover, the uncertainty regarding the role that seal predation had on the cod population underscores the lack of understanding of interspecies relationships in marine ecosystems. There is also much uncertainty regarding the impact of land-based anthropogenic activities on aquatic life forms. There are therefore an enormous amount of variables to consider when predicting and interpreting the impacts of environmental changes or altered patterns of human activity.

Managing for sustainability requires an approach based upon the integration of scientific, socio-economic, and management knowledge. It is therefore not surprising that information drives the programs and services of Fisheries and Oceans Canada and, as such, it is one of their most valuable assets. The ministry recognizes that nearly all data collected is analyzed and transformed into information that ultimately drives their decision-making process. The department is therefore a heavy user of current and historic data for operational, tactical, and strategic decision-making.

Meanwhile, new information and communication technologies (ICT) are enhancing demands on DFO to provide information to clients and partners in a timely fashion and to release more information. As Osborne and Gaebler (1992) note: "today information is virtually limitless, communication between remote locations is instantaneous, many public employees are well educated, and conditions change with blinding speed. There is no time for information to go up the chain of command and decision to come down." For example, in some fisheries the nature of the species, the environment, and the technical capacities of fishermen are such that decisions are made regarding opening and closing the fishery in the space of days and at times hours. Environmental turbulence (natural and socio-economic) is therefore pushing the department to make operational decisions in shorter time frames, a task that is proving difficult to perform with information that is of questionable quality or is difficult to assemble.

Within the organization there has therefore been a growing realization that effective information management frameworks will be an essential component of efforts to meet current and future policy objectives. In response to this realization, Fisheries and Oceans Canada has embarked on the development of a comprehensive strategy to guide the activities that impact the generation of information and the application of information towards the achievement of policy objectives.

The initiative was also precipitated by the convergence of afferent factors that include the directives of central government agencies to develop information management frameworks that promote greater transparency and efficiency. The department has also been the subject of direct criticism stemming from a much-debated inability to reconcile the scientific, management and political functions of the department, a failure that may have contributed toward the collapse of the Cod fishery on Canada's eastern coast.

Multi-Stakeholder Governance and New Accountabilities

However, information management is only one of the pillars of improved governance of marine resources; the other is multi-stakeholder collaboration. Coastal regions are often the seat of numerous marine based industries including commercial fishing, aquaculture, transport, shipbuilding, tourism, mining, and oil and gas exploitation and exploration. Access to the oceans is also required for scientific investigation, defense, and recreational purposes. Resource management agencies with jurisdiction over oceans are thus faced with multiple and conflicting demands.

Since the adoption of the adoption of the *Oceans Act* in 1997, Fisheries and Oceans Canada has seen their responsibility extended from fisheries and marine mammals to encompass all ocean related activities. The ministry is charged with the development of a national strategy for Canada's oceans that considers both the economic importance of marine resources to communities and the need to conserve ecosystem integrity. For Fisheries and Oceans Canada this translates into a need to manage stakeholder relationships and the ensemble of incentives created by markets, social forces, and other government programs.

This represents a major challenge for Fisheries and Oceans Canada as they, like many of their counterparts in other nations, have adopted an approach over their evolution that presumed that they had all the relevant information, power and resources to do the job themselves. The traditions that developed favoured a paternalistic approach and hierarchal management. As described by Wondolleck and Yaffee (2000, p. 11), "The industrial era […] produced a way to manage organizations that emphasized top-down control, production, and measuring objectives by narrow criteria, and the public resource agencies adopted those approaches as they sought to deal with the rising demands facing them."

Such a model, with centralized knowledge and resources had definite advantages in a world with more primitive information and communication technologies and a less educated public (Osborne and Gaebler, 1992). In the current context, this model is proving to be of limited value. The increased interdependence and interconnectedness of organizations that has resulted as more organizations communicate with one another has changed the landscape.

The rapid diffusion of information through communication networks "has accentuated the difficulty for individual actors, even powerful states, to understand the nature of the socio-environmental problems that they face and severely curtail their ability to control all the necessary factors to ensure an appropriate governance response" (Paquet and Juillet, 2001). This has been particularly true in the area of natural resource management.

The proliferation of information and communication technologies and widespread public concern over environmental issues has diminished the ability of these agencies to maintain their legitimacy through their 'technical wisdom' (Wondolleck and Yaffee, 2000, p. 13). Moreover, the increasing distrust of public agencies that has developed over the last few decades, compounded by the failures of many agencies to protect resources has increased the demand for increased public involvement in the decision-making process.

With non-government actors rapidly developing the capacity to perform many of the ministry's analytical functions and to critique decisions, government departments are subject to increasing pressure to be accountable for the decisions they make and the outcomes of their programs. Collaboration and transparency are therefore quickly becoming central objectives of natural resource agencies.

It is within this context that Fisheries and Oceans Canada has engaged in processes that clarify their strategic objectives and establish performance objectives. The ministry is increasingly aware that annual reports to parliament that outline their intentions and their spending against the budget are insufficient; the impact of those investments must be outlined. Moreover, in order to secure the support of stakeholders and increase the range of information brought into the decision-making process, they have committed to augmented levels of public consultation and to engage in more partnerships with industry and civic organizations.

The shift towards measuring performance relative to strategic objectives and the complex set of relationships between public servants and the public that is flourishing is impacting the accountability structures within government. In the Canadian case this is reflected in the new management models being embraced, including modern comptrollership, which attempts to connect fiscal and performance accountabilities, with the implication that the focus on results shifts accountability away from a strictly upwards focus to include the client and co-workers. The changing relationship between government and the public is therefore changing the internal structure of government, or at least pressuring governments to adapt.

Parallel and Interdependent Governance Challenges

Fisheries and Oceans Canada is faced with the challenge of employing IT strategically such that the information employed within the organization and shared with the public is accurate and timely. Moreover, they must do so within a context that, in addition to being complex, is increasingly oriented towards collaboration with outside stakeholders and the adoption of new forms of public interaction that are more transparent and participative. Finally, these challenges must be met within the context of diminishing financial resources, more elaborate and extensive demands on internal accountabilities, and in an environment that is increasingly complex.

The struggles of Fisheries and Oceans Canada in this respect are therefore representative of those of many government departments. Too often however, governments, as with Fisheries and Oceans Canada, fail to connect these issues. The stakeholder and accountability questions are considered governance issues, while the IT issue is perceived as separate and technical. Investments in IT are primarily cost and efficiency oriented, geared to fit within linear policymaking and service delivery models. That IT can deployed within an organization in a manner that alters its governance, moving it beyond the integration of data for decision-making and fundamentally changes the dynamics and extent of relationships that exist within and external to organizations is rarely recognized.

Governance is concerned with guiding: it examines the processes in organizations that determine how they steer and co-ordinate themselves and shape their evolution when resources, power and information are distributed (Paquet, 1999). It is about the full set of relationships between an organizations management, employees, and stakeholders and the formal and informal structures that shape those relationships. It follows that the principal governance challenge of an organization is the leveraging and shaping of the structures and processes that determine how they coordinate their interaction with the environment such that knowledge and resources are applied in a fashion that best aligns the internal and external worlds.

Figure 1: Governance is fundamentally about relationships

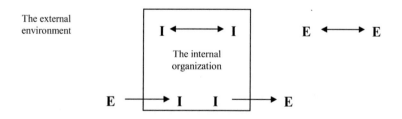

Governance is concerned with the mixture of mechanisms employed to shape stakeholder relationships. Those relationships exist internal to the organization (I) and in the external world (E). The extent and nature of those relationships impacts the learning capacity of the organization; that is, the information the organization can extract from the outside world and the ability of the organization to develop strategies and implement plans, therefore shaping its evolution.

DIGITAL AMNESIA

Structural amnesia describes the tendency for an organization to disregard problems that threaten their values or hasten their deconstruction (Clark and Munn, 1986, p. 433). This self-preservation mechanism has its origins in the cultural nature of risk. Because institutions select the problems and risks worthy of consideration (Braybooke and Paquet, 1987), there is not necessarily a link between new facts and institutional attention: There is therefore no guarantee that facts that confirm new risks translate into a socially defined problem that is acknowledged (Douglas and Wildavsky, 1982; Douglas, 1986). The culture of government organizations is therefore an important determinant of the degree to which self-preservation mechanisms will retard their reaction to a changing environment.

'Digital amnesia' may therefore be an accurate term to describe the cultural factors that prevent governments from employing IT in a manner that facilitates a transformation of their governance structures. While the heightened concern for security and scrutiny of the public service can be accredited in a large part to the reluctance to change, the tardiness of governments is also rooted in an adherence to traditional controls and decision-making processes (Paquet and Roy 2000). The acknowledgment that one must move beyond doing the same things in a different way, to doing new things, and questioning what is done and not done can be an arduous process when the structures and cultures of an organization are resistant to creative destructionism.

The struggles of Fisheries and Oceans illustrates the importance for governments to realize not only that they must alter their relationships with the external world, but also they may need to modify the levers within their organization that shape internal relationships in order to respond to this change. The challenge is both technical and social. Structures and processes developed over the past century that have shaped the distribution of power and accountability, as well as the organizational culture, are having a significant impact on the ability of the organization to employ IT in a manner that transforms its governance.

With approximately 9,000 employees, Fisheries and Oceans Canada is one of the largest of the federal departments in Canada. The central features of the organization's structure are its matrix design (see Figure 2) and its highly decentralized nature. The central features of the organization's culture are hierarchal forms of accountability and a paternalistic approach to stakeholders. Each has significantly influenced the ability of the organization to develop information systems that employ IT strategically.

With approximately 90 percent of its employees located in the five regional offices, and significant autonomy enjoyed by regional bureaus the department has had the ability to approach common problems with management approaches tailored to the local contexts. In many cases, this has meant information systems and informatics architectures unique to each region. The consequence of this decentralized approach has been much local innovation. However, there is little sharing of this innovation between regions or from the region to the centre. As a result, there is less organizational learning than this demanding context merits.

The limits to the sharing of learning across regions or between the line functions are largely vertical accountability structures and a culture of control that discounts horizontal collaboration. In fact, these same hierarchal forces have impacted the amount of innovation that each region has displayed; to the extent to which each has overcome

Figure 2: The matrix structure of Fisheries and Oceans Canada

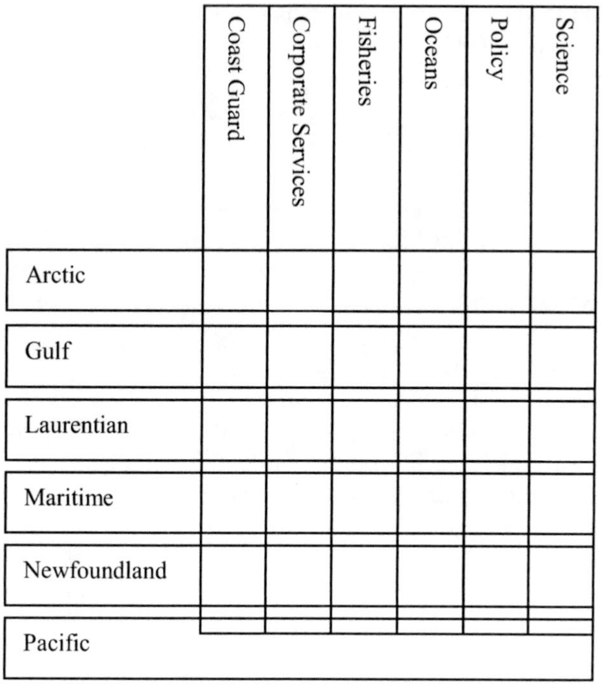

	Coast Guard	Corporate Services	Fisheries	Oceans	Policy	Science
Arctic						
Gulf						
Laurentian						
Maritime						
Newfoundland						
Pacific						

those forces they developed more integrated information systems. That organizational factors could inhibit naturally existing interdependencies is unfortunate. For example, the fishery is regulated by the fisheries branch, which monitors to determine if catches are as per the quotas defined by policy, which are based on the estimates of stock populations determined by science. Nonetheless, management structures have impeded a free flow of information and created divisions.

The chasms that have resulted due to these physical and structural separations are the driving force behind the national information strategy previously mentioned. It is particularly important to the informatics component of the strategy. The autonomy that each branch and region has exercised in the development of its informatics systems and policies has made it difficult to determine the extent of department's information holdings. Concern is therefore high that knowledge is not adequately shared and possibly not generated cost-effectively.

The centrality of the cost concerns is important, in addition to less informed decision-making through incapacity to share data. The lack of central direction regarding informatics systems has produced a situation where it is conceivable and probable that information would be lost, ignored, or maintained when not required; in the process of generating data there could be duplication or a lack of data generation as the pressures to avoid the humiliation of having repeated the work of others. Moreover, information systems could be built too big or too small for the data within. The frequent recourse to the services of external consultants has left much of the organization without the tools to reconfigure their systems.

The consequences of this lack of alignment between the informatics and policy and operational functions of the department are important. It is in fact the possibility that this incongruence could lead to new crises, such as that which resulted when the Northern Cod Fishery was closed in 1992, that has motivated the push to develop an information strategy. Some primary concerns include: the legal consequences of disseminating inaccurate information (a concern that augments as the government on-line agenda advances); the loss of legitimacy and public embarrassment of not meeting obligations to partners and stakeholders efficiently; the continued criticism of central government agencies and parliament due to the inability to produce the outcomes intended due to lost corporate memory and inability to integrate diverse data sources; the environmental degradation that may result if policies lead to irreversible consequences on species and ecosystems; and the disastrous socio-economic impacts of mismanagement on the lives of Canadians.

Improved integration of IT into departmental operations therefore represents a major element of the information strategy currently in development by Fisheries and Oceans Canada. The ministry recognizes that from the storage of electronic data to the integration of the information within the various information systems into decision-making frameworks, technology plays an important role in information management. The aim of the informatics strategy is to reduce the time spent gathering and integrating data from different sources, improve access to data for clients and stakeholders, and achieve a more cost effective employment of resources over the long-term.

The objectives of the informatics component of the information strategy are largely at the level of retooling. The informatics strategy is largely centred upon data and the IT employed to treat data. Data management issues include the lack of a common language in the form of standard codes and data definitions, invalid assumptions regarding variables used and shared in different systems, the overall lack of awareness of available data, and the difficulties experienced in obtaining access to some data.

The informatics strategy envisioned is therefore mainly concerned with leveraging IT in a manner that allows them to deliver their current programs more effectively and efficiently. Within the department there is much concern over the fact that difficulties in accessing data, and a lack of current and reliable data hamper the department's ability to integrate various forms of data to execute their activities within the current operational framework and develop strategies. The possibility of enabling more innovation through IT is a secondary concern at best.

The limited vision of the ministry in this regard is unfortunate, as it prevents the acknowledgment that IT can also alter relationships, facilitating the creation of links between people that would not otherwise be made. The scope and scale of those links are important elements of the amount of organizational learning that can occur. As those interactions intensify and a diversity of stakeholders (internal or external) are included in the dialogue, perspectives are shared and values are contrasted, there can be enhanced understanding and reconsideration of what the organization is in relation to its environment.

Within the ministry several units have demonstrated their ability to employ IT creatively to restructure relationships. For example, in some regional offices integration across sectors is occurring to a greater and greater degree, especially as the sectors get into forensic types of enforcement and cross-verification of information sets. As contextual factors that create interdependencies enhance the capacity of the branches to collaborate, they discover new opportunities for collaboration.

In other cases, the relationships between the ministry and its stakeholders can be restructured. In a parcel of water on Canada's east coast, managers of a small part of the herring fishery and industry exchange information daily in order to make determinations of daily quotas and restricted and permitted fishing zones that are based on detailed measures about the physical environment and the stock characteristics.

The result is not only more reliable data but an improved relationship between government and industry; as noted by Stephenson et al. (1999) "the gap between regulator and regulated has been reduced." Again, environmental factors that include uncertainty regarding resource conditions and a lack of resources have prompted innovation. For more widespread innovation to occur, the ministry must adopt bottom-up approaches.

Micro-Level Resistance

That the organization has made progress in the innovative use of IT is promising. However, in the cases where it has occurred the support of management and the IT professionals has facilitated the progress of projects. In essence, the traditional gaps between staff described by Heeks and Davies (1999) as the 'ITernal triangle' have been surmounted.

Figure 3 outlines how the differing perceptions of how different staff see IT fitting into the organization impact its level of adoption. Most commonly those unfamiliar with the technology feel threatened by its adoption and offer resistance while the literates (often at the operational end) develop an agenda that may not fit with the broader goals of the organization and may undermine integration efforts because it represents a form of interference (Davies and Heeks, 1999).

Figure 3: The ITernal triangle (adopted from Heeks and Davies, 1999)

Senior Management
Hesitant to integrate IT into reform
because they misunderstand the technology
and the role of information in government
and thus fear a loss of control

IT professionals
Technical outlook that lacks a strategic
emphasis. Often find themselves
defending the IT unit.

'Mainstream' Staff
Increasingly aware of IT and the
importance of information
management and are impatient to
adopt it and are doing so in a limited,
piecemeal fashion.

The stereotypes defined by Heeks and Davies (1999) would appear to reasonably approximate the situation of Fisheries and Oceans Canada. The IT department is a unit of corporate services that is consumed in the same struggle for resources as the other sectors of the department. A sense of the broader strategy of the department then gets lost in the quotidian challenges of the sectoral tug-of-war.

Moreover, despite their positioning as a shared service unit, a lack of resources and their preclusion from the majority of the regional or sectoral IT initiatives has largely diminished them to the status of the stewards of major servers and occasional technical support. The top management of the department is largely wary of the technology; it has not grasped the imperative of information management. There is, therefore, no vision for IT, for the IT department or the mainstream staff around which it can orient their activities.

Large-scale innovation at the level of the department is unlikely as long as this gap in perception of the potential role of IT and information management in transforming government persists. To move towards a comprehensive governance change, governments must acknowledge that IT can enable the reforms they desire.

Governance systems are information systems (Paquet, 1999), they are composed of formal and informal connections that stimulate the formation of codified and tacit knowledge. IT can certainly modify the formal and codified elements of the system, but can also have a subversive effect on the informal and tacit elements. As the ITernal triangle emphasizes, organizational structure and culture have a powerful effect on the ability of the organization to build new information systems. As the remainder of this section outlines, culture and structure also contribute to resistance to change for political reasons.

In most instances where IT-based innovations have occurred at Fisheries and Oceans Canada, it has been in the local offices and it has evolved in spite of the efforts of the national office rather than because of it. The strong departmental emphasis on the political motives of the minister and deputy minister the accountabilities created at this level permeate the organization, creating silo-like structures where the vertical emphasis predominates and the horizontal exchanges required to stimulate creativity are attenuated.

The financial constraints of the last decade have compounded norms within the organization that discourage horizontal collaboration. The department is structured and managed around the budget. The struggle for resources that results impedes horizontal networks from emerging. When it comes to data management and informatics, for all projects and activities, sectoral and regional needs are met and implemented before cross-sectoral or inter-regional requirements are identified.

Although each unit agrees that greater integration is desirable, it seems that once provided with funds there is a greater tendency to take the money and build parallel systems. In this fragmented and financially constrained environment, sectoral and regional priorities take precedence over departmental ones; each sector is focused on their objectives and funding is the ultimate lever.

The fixation on controlling spending generates an environment where data and informatics activities represent an expense rather than an asset. This mindset has a great impact on this inability to get organized around outcomes rather than resources. Data management and informatics issues lose out to other priorities because executives are rewarded according to budget management. It is thus that accountabilities relate to spending rather than outcomes in many instances. The problem is particularly acute for sectoral representatives in the national office as most of the information required to perform their functions is generated in the regions in order to meet regional objectives.

The problem of reluctance to share information is accelerated by a mentality that holds that information is power and encourages individuals to protect information to preserve power. Government departments are thus faced with the challenge of establishing accountability structures that support horizontal collaboration and accelerate an emerging process of cultural change away from an aversion to share information that sometimes prevails in populations not accustomed to the instantaneous availability of information.

With accountabilities based upon the narrow concerns of particular units of an organization, it is difficult to adopt IT at a level that extends beyond retooling. The system must ultimately connect people. Without a culture and accountability structures that emphasize collaboration requests from other units then become horizontal demands on vertical priorities. For governments, the move away from hierarchal structures is a nearly intractable task without significant cultural and structural changes. This is certainly the case for Fisheries and Oceans Canada.

Macro-Level Resistance

With its heavy emphasis on science and a rational approach to management, the structure and culture of Fisheries and Oceans Canada is in many ways a reflection of the industrial period in which it was established and flourished in. In the ministry, the science focus has at times been to the detriment of the non-scientific elements of their operations. For example, when faced with budget cuts in a fiscally motivated program review in the mid-1990s, most cuts occurred in other areas, which left the department barely able to manage socio-economics. This is an unfortunate situation when it is behaviours that the ministry ultimately attempts to influence.

The bias towards science has naturally dominated the informatics strategy development. The notion that informatics is a part of the assumed 'technical fix' that is required to tackle the dilemmas the ministry faces dominates the discussion. The notion that all is data ultimately transformed into forms of information that translate into knowledge; ultimately leading to the wisdom required to manage marine resources. There is in this tidy pyramidal model little acknowledgment of the fact that the 'wisdom' that can be extracted from data may be compromised by the fact that science is a social construction, subject to systematic errors in the conception and execution of experiments, and perhaps most importantly in the models employed to interpret observations. Moreover, there is little acknowledgment of the fact that tacit knowledge is an important component of the 'wisdom' of organizations.

In an organization that mediates between an incomplete scientific understanding of the environment and human behaviour, the limits of science must be recognized. There needs to be space to appreciate the local, the contextual, and the tacit. Management in such contexts demands an iterative approach where managers acknowledge that objectives are moving targets and employ probabilistic models. IT can impact the formal and informal knowledge systems that have an important role to play in developing an adaptive approach but it is only one piece of the puzzle; the relationship between those with the technology and those with the knowledge and/or problem must also be nourished.

In addition to the internal dynamics that impede units of the organization from collaborating to the necessary degree to strategically adopt IT, a reluctance to change the relationship with stakeholders outside the organization also is proving to be an impediment to digital government. There are mounting concerns, for instance, over the legal impacts of disseminating inaccurate information as government on-line stresses enhanced transparency in this regard. Also, the possibility for public embarrassment from not meeting obligations to partners and stakeholders efficiently, and the continued criticism of central government agencies and parliament due to the inability to produce the outcomes intended due to faulty corporate memory and fragmented data systems are all indicative of the existence of self-preservation mechanisms and an insular culture that must be overcome.

For governments to reinvent themselves into digital governments they need to embrace the increasingly blurred lines that separate them from the private and civic sectors. The fact is, digital government depends on a highly informed citizenry. The creation of an 'informational commons' is an important element of the transition. The informational commons is built upon the idea that the public domain is more than just a physical space; it also consists of the information that is publicly available to citizens (Roberts, 2000). If governments adopt defensive behaviours that inhibit the expansion of the information in the public sphere they will be doomed to continue to operate in a less collaborative manner. Without such collaboration, the extra-organizational information systems available to governments will remain untapped.

Alasdair Roberts argues that cultural, economic, and political forces are combining to limit the types and amount of information that is publicly available, a dynamic that creates tensions with the countervailing view of deeper transparency in public institutions.

> *The informational commons is contested terrain. Governments and corporations — and citizens themselves — have all taken steps to preserve secrecy, often spurred to do so by the power of new modes of surveillance, or by the desire to gain economic advantage by asserting their property rights over the central commodity of the new information economy (Ibid., 2000).*

The new restraints are, in addition to being the product of the advancing capabilities of the technology, in some cases a consequence of the diffusion of power over a wide variety of actors and the diminished influence of governmental agencies. In other cases, the reduced financial means of governments has prompted direct reductions in the resources devoted to or peripherally related to access to information. Moreover, the indirect consequence of the shift towards increasing privatization of government agencies, outsourcing of standard government tasks, and private-public partnerships have brought new restrictions on accessibility (Roberts, 2000).

These factors are playing out in the Canadian government and are becoming increasingly apparent. The executive branch of the governing party has resisted efforts to broaden the Access to Information Act (Bronskill, 2000) while federal agencies have augmented the prices of the information they provide the public and partnered with the private sector to sell government information (Morton and Zinc, 1991; Nilsen, 1994; Hubbertz, 1999). Moreover, there is a trend towards increasing privatization of some government-owned agencies that has in some cases seen access to information eliminated (Roberts, 2000). The increased pressures to release information have provoked even more defensive postures from the government in a cyclical pattern, reminiscent of a form of paranoia (Juillet and Paquet, 2002).

Should Fisheries and Oceans adhere to this trend towards secrecy to protect the 'interests of the government' their required governance reforms may stall. As with most government departments, participative governance structures and governance processes will be required to move from a technical conception of the benefits of IT to restructured relationships and a potential reframing of the organization as a whole. In many cases, this will demand more stakeholder collaboration in the form of private-public partnerships, outsourcing, exchanges, etc.

TRANSFORMING GOVERNANCE

In Fisheries and Oceans Canada, micro- and macro-level changes in the fundamental structure and culture of the organization are required if the organization is going to adopt IT in a strategically significant way. At both levels, innovation must be embraced. Innovation means more than automating; it entails the generation of new dynamics and the development of new models of decision-making.

The organization must learn to overcome barriers that prevent collaboration between branches and regions *and* they must acknowledge that a more open approach to stakeholders is required. The remedy rests in connectivity and bravely accepting the new accountability structures that connectivity demands. The opportunity for an IT-mediated transformation lies in the development of new forms of coordination and collaboration between internal and external stakeholders.

That such a transformation is possible is inherent in the fact that all organizations are essentially creatures that transform certain inputs into outputs. While it is obvious that manufacturers turn raw materials into finished products, one rarely recognizes that programs and policies of public institutions also take shape based on inputs and technologies, both social and technical, that the organization employs. Because IT can influence both the social and technical aspects of the organization, it can be levered to shape the organization.

In the case of Fisheries and Oceans Canada, the individuals that are the organization have an immense amount of knowledge and dedication to the mandate of the organization. Moreover, they represent a highly skilled workforce capable of meeting the challenges of the tasks they must perform, despite the inherent complexity of the task at hand and the intangible rewards involved in dealing with a complex adaptive system. The governance challenge involves the transformation processes that depend on the formal (structure, accountabilities and reward systems, methods) and the informal or cultural (norms, interpersonal relationships, management practices) elements of the organization.

Using IT strategically is an essential component of each of those transformation processes. IT can rewire the physical and social network of the organization, changing not only methods, rather the way the organization learns and interacts with its environment needs to be altered. A change in either the structure or culture is insufficient, the four basic transformation processes must be altered, all four must align with each other and with the mission of the organization.

For a public sector organization to be able to alter its use of IT in a strategic and holistic manner, it must:

- acknowledge that information is an asset and that information systems are social systems where learning occurs both formally and organically,
- adopt more horizontal and shared forms of accountability to complement and co-exist with more traditional patterns of vertical decision-making and authority.

Information as an Asset

Information is the main resource of governments. In pursuing the democratic/ political process, in managing resources, executing functions, measuring performance and in service delivery, information is the basic ingredient. The tendency to treat information systems and information management as an expense must be overcome. Acquiring such an understanding is a cultural challenge. Heeks outlines four models of IT mediated reform taken by public sector managers:

- *Ignore*: IT not a factor of planning or reform.
- *Isolate*: IT is included in planning and reform but is seen as primarily a technical issue.
- *Idolize*: IT alone is thought to be the answer to the need for reform.
- *Integrate*: IT is seen as a valuable means to an end, as part of a larger system that includes personal communication networks (1999, pp. 26-27).

Public sector managers need to be educated to become conscious of the barriers within their organization that prevent them from taking an integrative approach to IT. The realization of the central role that information has in an organization leads to two major cultural shifts; the creation of accountabilities for performance relative to information generation and management; and, a valorization of the contribution that external actors can make to the information generation and flow. Both of these consequences help the organization change from one that primarily has financially oriented governance to one that is more participative and stakeholder oriented.

Fisheries and Oceans Canada requires not only such a cultural shift that acknowledges that information is their *raison d'être*, but a widespread awareness of the fact that they must tap the resources external to their organization — that the complexity of the environment can only be managed by supporting the conflicting logics of numerous actors in different spheres. Governments must become the facilitators of processes that build information networks within their departments and with their departments and the external world.

Facilitating such a change is a daunting task, but possible. Using specialized training sessions, public service agencies have been able to develop a widespread appreciation of the organization as an information system and an appreciation of the power of organizational structure and culture in building information systems. Effective sessions ask the managers and staff, over the course of a few hours, to create a complex task within the confines of their present structure and processes that control resources and restrict collaboration. Upon failure, the organization is redesigned to manage the fragmented information flow and complexity of their task, and equally as importantly, to clarify their objectives and values.

Without such holistic design measures, IT systems are likely to continue to be a fragmented array of automation systems. It is important to note that a centralized system is not necessarily the solution to fragmentation; the issue is the uncoordinated nature of the systems and the objectives they pursue. In fact, greater control is likely to hinder the innovation required to function in a complex environment. It is for this reason that the IT system that one needs to view as a part of, and as an enabler of a social system based upon information.

Moreover, information systems are social systems; that is to say, information systems are rooted in a context of people and of social structures and are themselves made up partly of people and social structures (Heeks, 1999, p. 55). Information systems are the ensemble of processes employed to provide inputs for managerial decision-making. IT is but one component of an information system. It can however, be an integral component of that social system if it can lead to new productive relationships.

The appreciation of information systems as social systems demands an appreciation of the tacit and the informal. It demands that managers "move beyond the formal, quantitative and technical aspects of organizations" (Anderson in Heeks, 1999, p. 321). This necessitates a complementary culture of ongoing learning and adaptation. It therefore presents a significant challenge for Fisheries and Oceans Canada, but greater stakeholder collaboration and horizontal forms of accountability could support it.

Shared Accountability

Information systems must be connected to the strategy functions of the department. The informatics systems constructed, the data sought and analyzed, and the resulting relationships and interdependencies that result need to be continually aligned to the mission of the organization. This link between the technical infrastructure and the extent to which it contributes to objectives needs to be constantly evaluated in order to ensure that feedback loops required to facilitate its evolution are maintained and continually utilized and strengthened.

To maintain such a planning and feedback cycle, appropriate accountability structures are required. Accountability, in the context of digital government, refers to the degree to which individuals and groups are made responsible for IT management and the extent to which such management is integrated into the broader organizational objectives of the entity.

It can imply autocratic processes, however, as noted earlier, they are generally more effective when supported by mechanisms such as incentives, rewards, monitoring, and audits that ensure adherence to those commitments. Rather than devising rules, the leadership should provide only supporting policy frameworks, standards, resources (financial and human) and moral support for IT-related activities. Policies are useful but not compelling.

It is more important to connect rewards to outcomes. Under such a system, where accountabilities are softer and the relationship between the activities of individuals and groups is clearly connected to the mission of the organization, bottom-up systems can develop. If centralized structures are designed, they should be imposed from the bottom. Fisheries and Oceans has demonstrated, through the development of department-wide science databases, that the units of the organization can come to consensus on national standards.

IT can support the development of a organization built on horizontal accountability by enhancing connectivity. Where information does flow in Fisheries and Oceans Canada, it does so because people have developed interpersonal rapports. These connections are largely within regions and occasionally across regions. For innovation to flourish, connections will need to be established that allow interdependencies to be explored and for tacit knowledge to be communicated. In addition, as with most governments the need to develop partnerships with agents outside the department underpins a growing imperative of generating and sustaining the level of trust that exists between the department and its stakeholders.

It is important in the establishing of a performance-based approach that a horizontal network of accountability supported by a team approach dominates. The experience of Fisheries and Oceans Canada shows us that if the vertical mode of accountability predominates, then it is possible to hinder organizational learning. Organizational units or even professionals in the same unit will continue to work at cross-purposes. Rather, temporary teams of a multidisciplinary nature need to be supported. Increasingly, this horizontal form of accountability based on reciprocity and moral contracts sustains collaboration on IT projects.

CONCLUSION

The establishment of a corporate mechanism to ensure the alignment and leverage of information management decisions with business and operational strategies, plans and priorities presents an important challenge for all large organizations today — and governments are no exception. Experiences at Fisheries and Oceans Canada underscore the fact that information systems are complex social systems: as such, the coordination of IT strategy within the context of large government departments requires holistic thinking in order to undertake both the cultural and structural transformations necessary to overcome the political and bureaucratic inertia of traditional, and primarily vertical mechanisms of control and accountability.

It is extremely important to underscore that alone, new and more digital technology infrastructures cannot enhance organizational learning. The requisite amount of coordination, sharing and collective action also depend on organizational structure and culture and how they are adapted simultaneously. Coordination processes will therefore be critical elements of the establishment of new governance frameworks that aim to truly reform internal governance arrangements and improve performance.

To achieve this end, all stakeholders must be both willing and able to collaborate, to work in groups, to engage in constructive dialogues and negotiate in the internal and external worlds. As in the case of Fisheries and Oceans Canada, this requires a cultural shift and a move away from traditional hierarchal modes of operation and vertical accountability structures that inhibit horizontal collaboration. Such a shift begins with more information sharing — as well as its integration into better decision-making processes that underpin collective learning.

As is the case internally, an open IT architecture alone cannot enhance social learning externally. Such a capacity is dependent as well on the deployment of new and more collaborative governance mechanisms that join together actors in the public, private and civic spheres. This external alignment also requires a cultural shift towards more participative governance structures and processes and a willingness to accept the fact that the organization does not have all the necessary power, knowledge, and resources to tackle complex problems. Rather, they must be facilitators of processes that temporarily assemble a broad range of actors for an integrated and iterative approach to problem solving.

The aim of an IT strategy for government should be heavily rooted in the idea of enhancing human interactions and forming alliances within and external to departments, bringing in new perspectives and incorporating opposing values. Digital government depends on such governance changes in order to avoid the structural amnesia that prevents an IT-mediated renewal of the public service.

REFERENCES

Anderson, K.V. (1999). Reengineering public sector organizations using information technology. In R. Heeks (Ed.), *Reinventing Government in the Information Age: International practice in IT-enabled public sector reform*. New York: Routledge (pp. 22-48).

Braybooke, D. & Paquet, G. (1987). Human dimensions of global change: The challenge to humanities and the social sciences. *Transactions of the Royal Society of Canada*, 5(2), 271-291.

Bronskill, J. (2000). Senior liberals shoot down broader access act. *Ottawa Citizen*. Ottawa, Canada. (June 7).

Clark, W.C. & Munn, R.E. (Eds.) (1986). *Sustainable Development of the Biosphere*. Cambridge University Press.

Douglas, M. (1986). *How Institutions Think*. Syracuse, NY: Syracuse University Press.

Douglas, M. & Wildavsky, A. (1982). *Risk and Culture*. Berkeley, CA: University of California Press.

Heeks, R. & Davies, A. (1999). Different approaches to information age reform. In R. Heeks (Ed.), *Reinventing Government in the Information Age: International Practice in IT-Enabled Public Sector Reform*. New York: Routledge (pp. 22-48).

Hubbertz, A. (1999). Responses to "closing the window." *Government Information in Canada*, *17*, (Web Ed.).

Juillet, L. & Paquet, G. (2002). The neurotic state. In G.B. Doern (Ed.), *How Ottawa Spends 2002-2003: The Security Aftermath and National Priorities*. Don Mills: Oxford University Press (pp. 69-87).

Morton, B. & Zink, S. (1991). Contemporary Canadian federal information policy. *Canadian Public Administration*, 34(2), 312-328.

Nilsen, K. (1994). Government information policy in Canada. *Government Information Quarterly*, 11(2), 191-209.

Osborne, D. & Gaebler, T. (1992). *Reinventing Government: How the Entrepreneurial Spirit is Transforming the Public Sector*. New York: Plume/Penguin.

Paquet & Roy (2000). Information technology, public policy and Canadian governance: partnerships and predicaments. In D. Garson (Ed.), *Handbook of Public Information Systems*. NY: Marcel Dekker, Inc. (pp. 53-70).

Paquet, G. (1999). *Governance Through Social Learning*. Ottawa, Canada: University of Ottawa Press.

Roberts, A. (2000). The informational commons at risk. In D. Drache & R. Higgott (Eds.), *Recovering the Public Domain: Moving the Boundary Between the Market and the State*. London: Routledge.

Stephenson, R., Rodman, K., Aldous, D. & Lane, D. (1999). An in-season approach to management under uncertainty: The case of the SW Nova Scotia herring fishery. *ICES Journal of Marine Science, 56*, 1005-1013.

Wondolleck, J.M. & Yaffee, S.L. (2001). *Making Collaboration Work*. Washington: Island Press.

Chapter VII

Political Implications of Digital (e-) Government

Paul M. A. Baker
Georgia Institute of Technology, USA

Costas Panagopoulos
New York University, USA

ABSTRACT

Citizen participation-driven e-government is, in theory, a desirable objective of government. However, it is complex along a variety of dimensions: from a design standpoint, considering the implementation aspects of access, and awareness; from a baseline assessment of what has been implemented to date empirically; and in terms of a meaningful design of responsive policy. Much of the observed variations in e-government applications is still descriptive in nature and given the rapidly emerging technological and political ramifications, is expected. Following an overview of several examples of different types of participation-related e-government applications, we present preliminary results of an examination of the relationship between state e-government initiatives and underlying demographic, cultural or economic variables. While the population of a state appears to be related to the presence of e-government applications, beyond this, curiously, few of the expected relationships appear, or appear to operate in conflicting manners depending on the dataset used. As such, additional research drawing on larger dataset and more robust instrumentation is needed.

OVERVIEW

The diffusion and adoption of innovative digital information and communication technologies (ICTs) by government and other public sector entities has been relatively well documented. This recognition has been especially true in terms of uses oriented at the internal implementation of administrative systems to achieve managerial efficiency, and to enable more robust and broader delivery of service to the citizens (Bellamy & Taylor, 1998; Dutton, 1999; Fountain, 2001).

In many respects, this distribution is a logical extension of the literature dealing with organizational studies., It has resulted in the development of best practices and recommendations appropriate to fine-tuning of administrative systems (Fountain, 2001; Hague & Loader, 1999; Garcon, 2000). For instance, the World Bank website on E*Government[1] delineates the following goals for e-government: Better Service Delivery to Citizens, Improved Services for Business, Transparency & Anticorruption, Empowerment through Information, Efficient Government Purchasing. While two of the three goals do somewhat relate to the "politics" of these technologies, the thrust has more of an administrative, rather than participatory flavor.

Given the relatively recent deployment of the technologies for communication, policymaking and collaborative purposes, the literature on the application and implication of adoption of these systems is much thinner. In part, this can attributed to the fact that many of the most established and connected actors in the political system already had adapted to the efficiency of communication technologies, the use of newer digital ICTs provided merely evolutionary advantages. However, in the broader political sphere, these systems can be expected to provide a greater variety of tools to less "connected" groups, especially at state and local levels, and to groups characterized as less resource rich and those not generally well versed in the use of modern technologies for accessing the political system. While digitally based, ICT-related tools designed to boost general citizen participation exist, they appear to be more common at local and municipal levels, or show a greater variation in implementation (Larsen & Rainie, 2002; Larsen & Rainie, 2002b; West, 2002a, 2002b). It is a bit more problematic to ascertain the connections between the variations that occur between the states and underlying demographic, cultural or economic variables. An examination of some of the extant data about the implementation of e-government, presented below, suggests that population of a state appears to be correlated with degree of e-government applications, but beyond this, curiously, very little of the expected relationships appear. We discuss this below.

At a state and Federal level, the tools that appear to have been implemented are frequently specialized for specific input or comment on regulation (i.e., the FCC's solicitation of comment on pending regulation[2]), or are oriented toward a specialized class of user, such as lobbyists (i.e., Lobbyist in a Box[3]). While the latter might not necessarily come to mind immediately as a type of citizen participation, it does represent a positive movement toward increased involvement in government. The significance is less the groups represented, but rather that these ICT-based tools offer potential for increased kinds of interaction between citizens and governments.

GOVERNMENT, TECHNOLOGY AND KEY STAKEHOLDERS

The complex interaction between technology, society and government embodied in digitally-based interactions suggests that a variety of disciplines can contribute to understanding the implementation and operation of e-government (Hague & Loader, 1999; Garcon, 2000; Hacker & van Dijk, 2000). The cost of technology is still somewhat of a barrier for some groups (if not in terms of technology, then in terms of awareness of the possibilities of information). Overall, efficiencies provided by the technology should allow a greater variety of participants to attempt to influence the policy systems, *ceteris paribus*.

E-government, in its various implementations, still represents a relatively new component in the tool chest of governance, although recognition of the importance of information architectures to enhance communication between governments and citizens is not new (Anderson et al., 1995; Katz & Aspden, 1997). Mounting a website on the Internet is simple enough technically so that a wide array of individuals have managed the task; anything more than simple posting of information poses somewhat of an unknown quantity for policymakers, especially when the focus is citizen participation (Larsen & Rainie, 2002a; Larsen & Rainie, 2002b; O'looney, 2001; West, 2000a).

The production and distribution of information by governments, while routine, is an enterprise that can be both labor- and resource-intensive. However, the benefits of networked information systems include the potential for reduced production costs for new and more useful products, new highly cost-efficient distribution channels, and the opportunity for increased citizen input into the governance and policy making process (Anderson et al., 1995). Yet, the adoption and implementation of new networking technologies, straightforward technically, has begun to generate complex policy issues with respect to usage of the technologies (Anderson et al., 1995; Brudney & Selden, 1995; Ghere & Young, 1998; Simon, 2000; Baker & Ward, 2002). Public sector policies toward information networks and databases vary greatly across the spectrum, with the wide array of alternative substrates for delivery (cable, standard telephone lines, fiber, and a spectrum of wireless alternatives) creating uncertain environments for policymakers and administrators at all levels of government.

While networked technologies have existed for quite some time (e.g., the telephone) the explosive growth of the Internet has drawn attention to information networks as a new type of infrastructure offering significant cost advantages over other types of information delivery mechanisms. As the Internet continues to grow and develop, it has moved through a variety of shapes, capacities and forms. Generally thought of in terms of a global information infrastructure, paradoxically, its networked structure allows development of a local component that can serve as a delivery channel for the provision of local information content and multi-modal communication. It is also at the local level that citizens have the most frequent contact, and thus a primary interface between government and the residents of a locality.

Given the opportunity presented by a new communication media and channel for citizen and engagement, and delivery of services, surprisingly few governments have actually implemented significant e-government efforts to any degree, beyond static broadcast websites and straightforward transactions processing applications (West, 2002a). Once past the initial implementation, many public (primarily municipal in this case) websites remain unchanged or permanently "under construction" giving rise to the image of "ghost towns" in cyberspace (Kanfer, 1997). While additional local government websites have continued to appear, early research (Krasilovsky, 1998) found little new use of the communication possibilities of the medium beyond what could be considered the Internet equivalent of "test patterns," a condition that continues today.

Progress in implementing e-government has been made, generally at higher levels of government. Recent assessments of e-government efforts have found governments are taking security and privacy much more seriously than they did in 2000 and 2001 (West, 2000a; Larsen and Rainie, 2002a). An increase in the presence of "restricted areas" on government websites that require registration and passwords for entrance (plus occasionally premium payments), can partially be attributed to a concern with security, although these restricted areas exist for a variety of reasons, including provision of premium services, personalized service delivery, and e-commerce applications. These developments raise problems for the future of e-government, including differential classes of users, in this case, citizens, based on ability to pay for public services, as well as simple access to these services[4].

From a policy standpoint, studies (Guthrie & Dutton, 1992; Guy, 1996; Cohill & Kavanaugh, 1997; Tsagarousianou et al., 1998; Baker, 2000; Cantinat & Vedel, 2000; Baker & Ward, 2002; among others) have provided some indication of the interaction of environmental and political factors influencing e-government innovation. From an administrative viewpoint, making use of the Internet either as an infrastructure provider, or simply as a content/service provider offers the opportunity for information and services to be rapidly and cost-effectively distributed in modes distinctly different from the traditional broadcast (or one-to-many) model. This of course can be either a significant opportunity or pitfall depending on the political and cultural components of the local government environment.

The ability to link or network into complex information systems appears to have significant geographic spillover effects interrelated with those generated by increased density of telecommunication infrastructures (Graham, 1992; Glaeser, 1994; OTA, 1995; Stough, 1996). From a citizen participation standpoint, networked information technologies represent a new policy opportunity for government, in that they present the opportunity for new channels for citizen participation and a solution for local governments to address the complaints that it "doesn't listen." Specifically, various components of electronic communication, such as the well established mode of e-mail, provide citizens with a capacity to query and to influence local governmental officials (Anderson et al., 1995; Larsen & Rainie, 2002a, 2002b; West, 2002a). However, the relatively immediate nature of e-mail demands a more rapid response than do other forms of communications, and carries the additional concern of being in a written, and potentially actionable format.

In contemplating the use of networked technologies for the delivery of local services, local government policymakers have recognized that websites only become viable alternatives for service delivery, or communication, when the number of users reaches a significant threshold to be "politically viable," offsetting the cost of implementing another channel of communication. On the cost side of the equation are more readily identifiable issues such as liability, equity and technical implementation difficulties. Looking at just liability, for instance, raises the question of responsibility not only for the content of a website, (provision of services), but also in terms of communication — answering questions that arrive directly to the local government through the communication mode. Another concern relates to technical questions of integration. Once a locality begins to deliver information through networked channels, the demand for new or increased services may well be overwhelming. How does the MIS department deal with interfacing legacy systems, or extracting this sort of data to make it available? How do policy makers address issues of access, and cost of services?

What variables might influence the range of implementations of e-government? Given the cost of implementing e-government applications both in terms of technical and human resources, a reasonable assumption would be that the governments with the largest populations might have the most elaborate websites, and be most likely to have implemented citizen participation and other policy process related tools. Further, size of a given governmental entity is somewhat related to the underlying population, all things being equal, population can be used for a surrogate for organizational size (Smith & Taebel, 1985). While the literature presents somewhat mixed findings with respect to the importance of organizational size (see Damanpour, 1987) as an explanatory factor, studies with a public sector orientation seem less ambiguous (Brudney & Seldon, 1995). Never the less, while population offers some explanation for the e-government implementation it appears to be one a range of organizational, technological and socio-cultural factors (see below).

Difficulty also arises in the attempt to assess the influence of more qualitative variables such as target constituencies, or role of stakeholders in the e-government implementation process. These factors may be geographically influenced, and difficult to measure, and therefore less generalizable (Gray et al., 1999; Baker & Ward, 2002). They can include for instance economics/income factors such as per capita income, education level, activities of interest groups, dominance of political parties and political participation in the electoral process.

SOCIAL CONSIDERATIONS:
THE DIGITAL DIVIDE

Early evidence of economic and social change related to the diffusion of a number of information and communication technologies (ICTs) suggests that governments and other public sector actors face significant opportunities, as well as some unexpected barriers in the implementation of e-government. While the benefits of e-government applications and services are generally recognized, the *use* of these technologies occurs in a distressingly uneven manner. This variation, which for the sake of simplicity has been described by extending the information superhighway metaphor as "gaps" or "divides" in the development of the "information highway," the technological and communication infrastructure that provides a substrate for e-government. Some disservice is done in reducing the apparent inequities in the diffusion of the technologies to a simple socioeconomic concern. Rather than a one-dimensional "digital divide," more accurately, there is a policy problem related to the use and deployments of ICTS with multiple geographic, social, economic and organizational dimensions.

Given the recognition of the problem, a legitimate question might be raised as to the necessity of assessing its parameters. Federal, state and philanthropic efforts are increasingly funding efforts to address the digital divide — the term commonly used to describe an personal and communal lack of access to computers and online resources. Data from the U.S. Department of Commerce (1999a, 1999b) show that the digital divide currently breaks along many "fault lines," including education, geography, race and income (GCATT, 2001). Access to computers and the Internet and the ability to effectively use information and communication technologies (ICTs) have become increasingly important for full participation in America's economic, political and social life. The U.S. Department of Commerce estimated in 2000, that approximately 60 percent of jobs require skills with technology. As a result, the digital divide has effects that go to the heart of issues concerning economic participation and equality.

To further obscure the picture, use of digital technologies for e-government presents policymakers with an array of complex issues that extend beyond purely technological concerns (such as the purpose and design of information systems) to the nature and extent of communication that the institutional entity undertakes. Rather than answering the question of how should public sector functions respond to the changes made possible by diffusion of ICTs; a more critical effort seems to be to accurately assess the specific objectives of digital government, and how various digital and non-digital approaches can be optimally employed to facilitate citizen engagement with government.

In terms of attempting to establish parameters for discussing the digital divide, one framework for analysis, used recently in assessing the digital divide in Georgia (GCATT, 2001), considers the demand side (user/citizen) and the supply-side (provider/government). In this case, the digital divide can be conceptualized from a user standpoint as a suboptimal condition of

- **access to technologies** (the initial conceptualization of the digital divide), oriented to hardware, networking and access to advanced IT/Telecom services;
- **available content**, that is, what services and information can be accessed; and,
- **awareness/utility** that relates to the actual value as well as the perceived value or awareness of the user/citizen/business of the use of ICTs and associated services.

From the supplier (or public sector side) the consideration alters slightly depending on what the specific function, or service under discussion is. Depending on the organizational/political culture of a governmental unit, use of ICTs might lean toward provision of services and transaction orientation, currently the most common examples of e-government implementation. Alternatively, digital technologies might be employed as a communication channel focused toward increasing citizen participation, input into the policymaking process, and transparency in government. Of course, various types of combinations exist in between.

In terms of public participation, this leads to a key question for assessment, and system design. What is the objective of the system? Is it to provide communication (which can be one way, bi-directional, broadcast, or many to many-networked), information (say, access to library information, ordinance, tax filing information, city council minutes) services (online payment of taxes, telephone directories of officials, e-mail to officials, answers to question from citizens, feedback to officials, or economic development efforts)? In one sense, even the provision of information about the operation of government, reflecting a commitment to transparency can be thought of as a movement in the direction of participation-oriented digital government.

One quite possible outcome of deployment of these technologies is that like-minded citizens will use the communication abilities of the networks to aggregate and focus political influence, a key rationale driving the effort to reduce the digital divide. Another could parallel the occurrence in the United States of significant outsourcing of public sector functions. Imagine a situation where a networked citizenry simply chooses to bypass the local public sector to tap into regional or even global resources for many of the functions performed by the public sector. To date, a number of states have begun to implicate state-wide policies to begin to address some of the policy issues generated by ICT deployment.[5]

IMPLEMENTATION CONSIDERATIONS

While there are any number of approaches to developing e-government applications, the two primary methods are top down (this is what we want to do/can do) and bottom up (this is what the users seem to want). From a citizen participation standpoint, the latter method would appear to be ultimately more effective approach both politically, as well as in terms of utility to the end user. From a design perspective, e-government application design can be driven by the same factors identifiable in the digital divide question - access, content and awareness.

Access can be said to be the manner in which the end user connects to the system, which could be through a home computer, through a public terminal at a public library or through a secondary node such as a business (an access primarily for other purposes). This component takes into account a variety of methods to provide primary connectivity to the ICTs, reducing this barrier to access to information, services and communication with institutions and officials. Content can be considered the substance of the information or the organization of it, such as providing access to city council minutes, economic development information or an online database of tax records. Alternatively, it can take the form of venues for communication of input into the policy-making process for increased citizen participation. Awareness/utility, perhaps the most complex to address, concerns the desire of citizens to participate, engage in the process, or simply, to even become cognizant of the potential and benefit of access to information.

The optimal design of any type of e-government related application would ideally be a response to an assessment of the underlying access, content and awareness variables. All too frequently, this aspect is neglected in the rush to "get online." Assessment tools to gather broad operational parameters include focus groups; solicitation of e-mail-based comments to policymakers; in-person public listening sessions;

Figure 1: E-government communication matrix

	Internal Function	**External Functions**
Local	Administrative (i.e. HR, Budget)	Information (Procedures for Licensing)
	Information (Procedure Manual)	Transactions (i.e., Permits, Taxes)
	Transactions (i.e., Requests for leave)	Communications (Bulletins, Council Agendas)
	Communications (Bulletins)	Example: Citizens, local business
	Example: Local agencies	
Global	Administrative (i.e. HR, Budget)	Information (Procedures for Licensing)
	Information (Interagency Procedures)	Transactions (i.e., Permits, Taxes)
	Transactions (i.e., Requests for Actions)	Communications (Bulletins, Council Agendas, Incentives)
	Communications (Bulletins/News)	Example: Out of State Businesses
	Example: State agencies	

and, survey of other governmental websites for "best practices." Unfortunately, these are generally more widely discussed than used. Yet they provide rich input into the development of ICT based systems, and in turn, allow participation related e-governmental efforts to be more tightly focused on citizen utility rather than convenience to the provider.

Looking at the "audience" or system user, and using a website as the delivery mode (though it might well be a telephone response system) we ask, who is the constituency that we are trying to reach? A simple yet useful model breaks this down into a four-way matrix, which can be envisioned on one axis as an internal/external orientation, and on another as a local/global orientation.

While these examples are not necessarily pure examples of citizen participation, they do reflect various aspects of underlying governmental communication, central to any model of participation. Respectively, examples might be: administrative personnel communicating with the human resources department (internal, local), or with other governmental non-local personnel, such as the state office of labor (internal global). In terms of external constituencies (non governmental in this sense), examples might include local government interacting with local citizens or civic groups (external, local) and engaging in economic development efforts such as attracting outside business to the community (external, global).

In terms of targeting or developing e-government objectives, the governmental unit might choose to emphasize a certain subset of the matrix. Citizen participation might take a back seat to economic development in a rural area, where e-government might orient toward an external (potential new businesses) and global (outside of the community) focus as a way of generating new jobs. Here, the need might be to try to bring new business into the area, and where with smaller populations, citizen engagement is viewed as a luxury that can be developed when resources permit. In this case, the objective might be to communicate to outsiders the benefits the community offers rather than in facilitating digitally based communication. The difficult here lies in generating messages powerful enough that they can compete effectively with other efforts. Networked technologies represent one effective means of accomplishing this. However, this falls more within developing content, than in developing overall system objectives, and is the subject of another paper.

Alternatively, when government is focused on interventions in highly urbanized areas, an effort might be at extending architecture into the community via technology centers, public libraries or the school system. Here the focus is local, and external to the classic model of government, yet one where e-government might be used to bridge community/digital divide issues along the access/awareness dimensions.

REPRESENTATIVE CASES

The political landscape is developing in several interesting directions because of the use of information technologies. According to a report released in April 2002 by the Pew Internet and American Life Project, 42 million Americans last year used the internet to conduct public policy research, 23 million sent comments to public officials about policy choices, 13 million participated in an online lobbying campaign, and 68 million visited a government website (Larsen & Rainie 2002a). Conversely, local officials, unlike

Congressional representatives, have generally report found e-mail to be useful and are not generally overwhelmed by incoming e-mail. E-mail has a clear civic payoff as more groups are being heard, and recognized, thanks to e-mail communications. The exchange is generally viewed as supplemental and adding to the extant communication rather ushering "a major revolution" (Larsen & Rainie, 2002a). This, of course, offers a promising counterpoint to the experience of Federal and Congressional users.

While these applications are not mature examples of well-developed interactive citizen participation process, they do represent attempt to provide information that can help the citizen be more informed about governmental processes that frequently lack transparency. They represent the first step, provision of policy and legislative related information, and point in the direction of fully interactive citizen participation systems.

Political Process — Congressional Online Project

Improvements in information technology and greater access to communications technologies, as noted above, increasingly provide Americans opportunities to interact directly with their representatives. Emerging communication technologies continue to redefine the relationship between the governors and the governed. Congressional representatives today are "swimming in a sea of online communication." According to research conducted by George Washington University and the Congressional Management Foundation, members of Congress received an unprecedented 117 million inbound e-mail messages in 2001. On an average day, House offices receive 234,245 e-mail messages and Senate offices 88,009. These numbers appear to be on the increase. Inbound e-mail to members of the U.S. House of Representatives increased 186 percent between 1999-2002. Inbound e-mail to Senators increased 69 percent during the same period (Congress Online Project Report, 2002)[6].

The report reveals significant variation, however, in the level of website quality within Congress. Examining over 605 sites (all member offices, committees, leadership offices), investigators rated only 10% of sites with either an A or a B score, while 90% received scores of C or lower. (A=2.5%; B=7.4%; C=58.8%; D=26.3%; F=5.3%.) Researchers based their analysis on five criteria used to evaluate congressional websites. These included: Audience (the office clearly identified potential and targeted web audiences and built sites around these audiences); Content (updated and geared around audience demands); Interactivity, Usability and Innovation.

The report, however, finds a gap between what audiences want from representative's websites and what most Capitol Hill sites provide online. While constituencies seek basic legislative information including position statements, rationales for key votes, status of pending legislation and educational information of congress and legislative processes, congressional offices are using websites primarily as promotional tools, posting press releases, descriptions of members' achievements and photos of members at events (Congress Online Project Report, 2002).

The public seems to be increasingly interested in obtaining information about Congress online. House sites received over 500 million hits to their sites in 2001. Even as competition from non-congressional sites that provide information about Congress is on the rise, members can realize significant benefits from strong online presence: enhanced constituency service, visibility, the ability to target and recruit target audiences, unfiltered communication with constituencies, new opportunities to build coalitions and grassroots support and increased office productivity (Congress Online Project

Report, 2002). To date, the research reveals that the Senate seems to be doing a better job overall with online communications than the House. (Consider that the average score for Senate member offices is a 2.12 (out of four) compared to 1.67 for the House.) In the Senate, Democrats seems to outperform Republicans (2.61 average versus 2.10, respectively), while in the House, Republicans fare better (1.76 to 1.58, respectively.)

Legislative — "Lobbyist-In-A-Box"

An interesting case of legislative service provision is an application "Lobbyist-In-A-Box"[7] (LIAB) developed by the Virginia Division of Legislative Automated Systems, in partnership with the Virginia Information Providers Network, to enable people to monitor the status of bills as they move through the General Assembly [http://leg1.state.va.us/liabtutorial.htm]. The system has been adopted in several other states including Arkansas, Georgia and Kansas.

The Lobbyist-in-a-Box application accesses legislative information from the division's Legislative Information System database each hour, and if a user indicates interest in a bill and action was taken, the system uses "push technology" to notify the user. The system also pushes information about new bills that meet user-specified criteria. The fast pace of legislative sessions means private lobbyists and public representatives rarely have immediate access to their computers, so Lobbyist-in-a-Box is also available for handheld computers. A free version for citizens also has been implemented [http://www.vipnet.org/liab/citizen.htm]. Since the implementation of Lobbyist-in-a-Box, division staff members have fielded fewer telephone inquiries regarding the bill status and special requests for enhanced or customized legislative reports.[8]

Administrative Portals — "My Virginia"

My Virginia (http://www.vipnet.org/vipnet/myvahomepage) was the nation's first customizable homepage offered by a state portal. My Virginia enables citizens to select links to the specific state and local government entities they want to see on their customized state homepage. Citizens have the option to update or remove various channels or links within categories such as a commonwealth calendar, local governments, local media, lottery numbers and traffic information. Additional customization includes the ability to obtain weather, selection of the color scheme of the page, and the ability to update user information. While a cookie is placed on an individual's PC to store the personalization choices, no information is saved, tracked or sold by VIPNet.

My Virginia is an alternative form of navigation that allows users to select only the government information they wish to have on their personalized homepage, but does not replace the official state site. My Virginia also uses "push technology" with several of its special features. For example, citizens can choose the public meetings of which they wish to receive notification, and the meeting date, time, location and host will appear on their homepage. Another special push technology feature enables users to track the status on 20 bills.

Virginia has also added a wireless, PDA-based state portal, "My Mobile Virginia," according to the website "the nation's first wireless state portal."[9] The My Mobile Virginia portal offers services and information regarding state government, online Services, and emergency information, and some additional applications including access to Lobbyist-In-A-Box, election returns, and a "polling place lookup." By using additional software (a special channel of AvantGo), it is possible to obtain the Commonwealth Calendar, and "the Event and Official Meeting Announcements for the Commonwealth."

NGO/Non-Profit Case — OMB Watch

OMB Watch Plugged In, is an interesting example of what could be called "ancillary e-government," a nonprofit origination that monitors and analyzes the activities of government, it enables citizen participation by providing information and hence, increases transparency and accountability. Thus, it essentially amount to "indirect" e-government. OMB Watch recently undertook an analysis of state level websites "Tuning Up: An Assessment of State Legislative Websites." It notes, "The Internet is increasingly considered a central element of revitalized civic participation in the United States. One aspect of this powerful force is "e-government," the idea that effective information exchanges and efficient service transactions between citizens and government can occur online. The potential for e-government raises a set of expectations of citizens, and a host of considerations for government itself — including accessibility, security, privacy, and relevancy of content" (OMB Watch, 2001).

The report observes for e-government to become a efficacious, that governments must ensure access, as well content and services to the public. As citizens increase their use of the internet, for policy related matters, there will be greater demands for legislative content and services online, as well as increased access into the workings of the legislatures themselves.

The report catalogues state rather than Federal level websites in order to provide a starting point for citizens, public interest groups and legislatures to evaluate and develop online resources. Our assessment covers whether a site provides information on:

- Legislators and How to Reach Them
- Explanations of Legislative Process
- Legislative Tracking and Monitoring
- Administrative Entities within the Legislature
- State Resources
- Statements Addressing User Expectations
- Site Design
- Site Navigation

Findings include:
- Ninety-two percent of state legislative websites provide contact information for legislators, but only 12 percent provide the means to address concerns directly to legislators while online
- Seventy-six percent explain the legislative process, and 65 percent provide access to the rules for legislative bodies, but only 49 percent present definitions of legislative terminology
- More than half of the states provide no information on legislative calendars, committee schedules, floor schedules, or a legislative session report

- Most states only provide information on the majority and minority leadership, but not the oversight, ethics, or legislative research bodies
- While 84% of the legislatures provide access to their constitutions online, only about a quarter provide links to the other branches of state government
- Fifty-one percent of state legislatures use cookies on their sites, but 96% do not have a statement about their use. Though 75% of legislatures have some method of collecting information or allowing users to interact with the legislative body, nearly all states lack a clearly defined privacy policy on their site.
- No state provided clearly identifiable compliance with commonly accepted web design principles for accessibility to those with disabilities
- More than half of the legislative websites lacked a clear set of tools to help users navigate the volume of content available (OMB Watch, 2001)

The finding raises some interesting questions. For instance, designers of the services needs to take into account the capabilities and facilities of the users, in terms of access. This includes both electronic access as well as "accessibility" considerations due to disabilities — the unacknowledged aspect of the digital divide. Another barrier to citizen participation is cost, especially when critical content is classified as "premium, fee-based services." The following section explores the data generated by OMB Watch, examining potential variables that might help explain the variation observed among state level websites.

E-DEMOCRACY IN THE U.S. STATES: EMPIRICAL ANALYSIS

A more robust examination of the OMB Watch analysis reveals much variation between states. Evaluating the five categories the report examined, we find that scores range from zero to four (no state provides all five offerings) and that, on average, states provide only two of the five services. This variation is hard to explain, both theoretically and empirically. A multivariate statistical analysis conducted to explain these differences yields few conclusive results. The findings (below) do show, however, that the level of what we term "e-democracy" (scores created from the OMB Watch data) depends on at least a couple of variables that are statistically significant even if somewhat puzzling. Specifically, the results show that the greater the percentage of Democrats in a state, the less likely the state is to have higher levels of e-democracy. In addition, higher levels of per capita spending in the state are likely to yield lower levels of e-democracy. Additionally, the higher the percentage of households with Internet access in a state, the lower the level of e-democracy. Key variables that we may expect to be strongly explanatory — including, population, percentage of senior citizens, blacks and education levels, for example, are not statistically different from zero.

In his study of states' e-government offerings, Darrell West ranked each state according to the level of services provided online. It is interesting to note that while there appears to be a positive relationship between West's rankings and the e-democracy

Table2: Determinants of e-democracy level

Dependent Variable: E-Democracy Level

Independent Variables	Coefficient	Standard Error	t-score
Population	1.49e-08	3.00e-08	0.50
Black Population (%)	2.36	1.88	1.25
Internet Access (%)	-.08**	.035	-2.38
Senior Citizen Population (%)	-.26	9.75	-0.03
Education (% with Bachelor's)	-1.45	3.60	-0.40
Democrats (%)	-.12***	.029	-4.18
Party Competition	2.51	2.05	1.22
Interest Group Involvement	.11	.23	0.49
State Spending (per capita)	-.43*	.24	-1.78
Constant	9.21***	2.99	3.09

* p<.10, ** p<.05, *** p<.01
N=44. R-squared=.40. Adjusted R-squared=.24.
Data sources: E-Democracy Level: OMB Watch Report: http://www.ombwatch.org/article/articleview/395/1/3/. Population, Education, State Spending: US Census (2000). Internet Access: "Falling Through the Net: Toward Digital Inclusion" Report, 2000, Democrats: Erikson et al., *Statehouse Democracy*, 1993. Party Competition: Ranney Competition Index source: Gray et. al ,1999. Interest Group Involvement source: Gray et. al, 1999.

scores, it is not as high as we may expect. (The Pearson correlation is .20, N=50.) That is to say, higher levels of e-government provision in a state do not necessarily imply higher levels of e-democracy (as defined above.) There are some states, like Indiana, that excel on both counts. Others, like Washington State, score high on West's rankings (47.6) but low on e-democracy (0). Moreover, Hawaii goes in the opposite direction, scoring four on e-democracy but only 38.1 on West's scores.

We believe that both of these elements are key ingredients in the overall level of digital government in a state. When we combine both West's scores with e-democracy scores into a composite index (Overall Level of Digital Government), we find some compelling results that may help us to better understand what the political underpinnings of the levels of digital government provisions may be. The multivariate analysis findings presented below show that variation in the overall level of digital government in a state would depend on a few variables. First, the greater the population, the more likely states will be to exhibit higher overall levels of digital government as we have defined such levels. Similarly, the more Democrats in a state, the lower the overall level of digital government. (This is especially perplexing given that West finds this to be a statistically significant variable in the opposite direction in explaining variation in his rankings.) Furthermore, the more states spend per capita, the lower the level of digital government. One additional variable becomes statistically significant; however, that warrants particular attention. The findings show that the higher the level of party competition in a state (Ranney Index of Party Competition by State), the greater the overall level of digital government. This finding has important political implications. It appears that state governments provide additional services, greater transparency and enhanced opportunities for citizen participation in the political process where there is greater competition between parties for control of state government.

Table 3: Determinants of overall level of digital government by state

Dependent Variable: Overall Level of Digital Government

Independent Variables	Coefficient	Standard Error	t-score
Population	3.84e-07***	1.37e-07	2.81
Black Population (%)	5.39	8.57	0.63
Internet Access (%)	-.19	.16	-1.18
Senior Citizen Population (%)	4.55	44.48	0.10
Education (% with Bachelor's)	3.28	16.43	0.20
Democrats (%)	-.27**	.13	-2.01
Party Competition	17.72*	9.34	1.90
Interest Group Involvement	-.83	1.03	-0.81
State Spending (per capita)	-1.80	1.09	-1.65
Constant	52.53***	13.62	3.86

* p<.10, ** p<.05, *** p<.01
N=44. R-squared=.41. Adjusted R-squared=.26
Data sources: Overall Level of Digital Government: OMB Watch report and West, 2002a.

Political Implications

The data enables us to test theories posited by experts about the political implications of digital government. Two of the more prominent arguments follow. One hypothesis advanced is that increased levels of digital government — by generating greater transparency of government proceedings, access to government services and the perception of greater efficiency — will engender increased citizen support of their governments. The other, perhaps related, hypothesis is that higher levels of digital government will result in greater participation amongst citizens. Using voter turnout by state during the 2000 presidential election and survey results on public confidence in government from the 2000 National Election Study, we test these propositions.

The Impact of Digital Government on Confidence in Government Levels

The results below indicate no clear relationship between the overall level of digital government and citizens' confidence in government. Confidence appears to be explained by median income in a state and the degree of competition between the political parties in a state (in both cases, a positive, statistically significant relationship). It is important to point out that this finding does not indicate that the relationship does not exist. It may be that the relationship will emerge over time as citizenries' access to and awareness of digital government provisions increases and as we collect more data.

The Impact of Digital Government on Political Participation Levels

We measure political participation as voter turnout in elections. (Other indicators of participation may also be relevant, but they are not included in our analysis.) When

Table 4: Impact of digital government on confidence in government

Dependent Variable: Confidence in Government (NES 2000)

Independent Variables	Coefficient	Standard Error	t-score
Population	-3.43e-09	3.91e-09	-.88
Median Income	.00001*	6.05e-06	1.76
Black Population (%)	-.04	.30	-.13
Internet Access (%)	-.00	-.01	-.06
Senior Citizen Population (%)	1.15	1.31	.88
Education (% with Bachelor's)	-.70	.45	-1.57
Democrats (%)	-.00	.00	-.01
Liberals (%)	-.01	.01	-.65
Party Competition	.49*	.26	1.89
Interest Group Involvement	.00	.04	.12
State Spending (per capita)	-.04	.04	1.08
Overall Digital Government Level	-.08	.31	-.26
Constant	-.38	.60	-.64

* p<.10, ** p<.05, *** p<.01
N=39 R-squared=.39. Adjusted R-squared=.10.
Data sources: Median Income: US Census (2000) Liberals: Erikson et al. (1993)

we consider the impact of the overall level of digital government on political participation, the relationship appears to be positive, as we may expect, but it does not achieve statistical significance. Thus, while we cannot draw any conclusive inferences from this finding with certainty, we have reason to believe that a positive relationship will eventually result. This expectation is strengthened when we consider that turnout is expected to be higher in states where citizens have greater access to the Internet. Turnout also appears to vary depending on population (where turnout is lower in states with higher populations) and age (higher in states with greater proportions of senior citizens). While not directly relevant to our study of the impact of digital government, the results

Table 5: Impact of digital government on political participation

Dependent Variable: Political Participation (Turnout)

Independent Variables	Coefficient	Standard Error	t-score
Population	-3.30e-07**	1.68e-07	-1.97
Median Income	-.00	.00	-.28
Black Population (%)	-.64	10.22	-.06
Internet Access (%)	.44*	.24	1.83
Senior Citizen Population (%)	120.96**	50.43	2.40
Education (% with Bachelor's)	-38.15**	17.52	-2.18
Democrats (%)	-.05	.15	-.30
Liberals (%)	-.15	.27	-.54
Party Competition	2.67	10.42	.26
Interest Group Involvement	-2.60**	1.29	-2.01
State Spending (per capita)	1.57	1.31	1.19
Overall Digital Government Level	10.93	10.36	1.05
Constant	30.38	18.91	1.61

* p<.10, ** p<.05, *** p<.01
N=44 R-squared=.61. Adjusted R-squared=.46.

also reveal two other interesting findings. First, turnout is lower in states with greater education levels (percent of the population with a bachelor's degree), a finding that runs counter to the results of many studies voter turnout. Second, participation seems to be lower where the impact of interest groups is high. No other variables included in the analysis are statistically significant.

CONCLUSIONS

It is apparent that the adoption of citizen participation-driven e-government is a desirable objective of government. However, it is complex along a variety of dimensions. From a design standpoint, it is complex considering the implementation aspects of access, and awareness; from a baseline assessment of what *has* been implemented to date empirically. Participation-driven e-government is also complex in terms of a meaningful design of responsive policy, in analysis of some of the variables involved in the focus and orientation of e-government initiatives. Much of the observed variations in e-government applications is still descriptive in nature, and given the rapidly emerging technological and political ramifications is expected. This chapter presented the preliminary results of an examination of the relationship between the state level e-government initiatives and underlying demographic, cultural or economic variables. Of note, population of a state appears to be correlated to some extent with the presence of e-government applications, but beyond this, curiously, very little of the expected relationships appear, or appear to operate in conflicting manners depending on the dataset used. This suggests that the observed phenomena may be (1) more complex than is captured in the observed data, (2) that there are interaction effects that may be confounding the analysis; and/or (3) the unit of analysis (state level data) may represent indirect policy and technological factors not captured in the underlying selected independent variables. In any case, this suggests that more robust instrumentation is called for.

While this chapter has focused primarily on the practical and policy aspects of the use of networked information technologies to support e-government, it is important to at least note the risks that these technologies pose for the information driven transformation of public discourse. An example of the potential changes that may occur as an unintended consequence of government adopting or aggressively promoting the wide-scale use of networked information technologies relates directly to the disadvantaged. If the "Market" becomes the dominant force driving either the functioning or provision of e-government applications, it may become cost-prohibitive for governments to serve the needs of all its citizens. If this happens, it is likely that those with means will rely on the private sector to meet their needs while those with limited resources may be able only to turn to government, one that has shifted commitment to digital and information-related technologies, thereby by increasing efficiency at the cost of equity. Digital democracy, poorly conceptualized runs the risk of decreasing rather than increasing the involvement of an array of stakeholders.

E-government focused on the delivery of services *is* useful, however the most valuable effect of networked technologies is the potential it offers for policymaking, hence, governance, in a distributed and participatory manner. While this has the potential of generating administrator anxiety over loss of "power," a shift in conceptual thinking from governance as top-down to one of networked participatory engagement may alleviate some of the policy concerns connected with liability of information flows. Conversely, not anticipating the tremendous potential of these communication technologies may well result in the diminishing influence or even role of policymakers, as the flow of "political will" shifts from official public sector governmental channels to less predictable "quasi-public" venues of political expression. Policymakers can choose to support and learn to take advantage of these new channels of public participation, or risk reduction to ancillary actors in the new world of networked public sector governance (Baker & Ward, 2000; Baker, 2000).

"Correct approaches," while possible in an ideal world can be approximated by thoughtful assessment and planning of any technologically related initiatives central to e-government. The desire of policymakers to take action in the face of obvious social disconnects runs the risk of acting first and fixing later. This suggests an alternative is to "ask first" consider the benefits and then act. Assessment of fundamental dimensions of the citizen participation can be effectively achieved by using standard "survey techniques" of baseline assessment, objective determination and desires of the users in order to develop policy initiatives that more clearly target the limited resources and energies of government.

REFERENCES

Anderson, R., Bikson, T., Law, S., & Mitchell, B. (1995). *Universal E-Mail: Feasibility and Societal Implications*. Santa Monica, CA: Rand Corp.

Baker, P. M.A. (2000). The role of community information in the virtual metropolis: The co-existence of the virtual and proximate terrains. In M. Gurstein (Ed.), *Community Informatics: Enabling Communities with Information and Communications Technologies*. Hershey, PA: Idea Group Publishing.

Baker, P. M.A., & Ward, A. C. (2000). Searching for civitas in the digital city: Community formation and dynamics in the virtual metropolis. *National Civic Review, 89*(3), November.

Baker, P. M.A., & Ward, A. C. (2002). Bridging temporal and spatial gaps: The role of information and communication technologies in defining communities. *Information Communication and Society, 5*(2), June.

Bellamy, C. & Taylor, J. A. (1998). *Governing in the Information Age*. Bristol, PA: Open University Press.

Brudney, J. L. & Selden, S. C. (1995). The adoption of innovation by smaller local governments: The case of computer technology. *American Review of Public Administration, 25*(1), 71-86.

Cantinat, M. & Vedel, T. (2000). Public Policies for Digital Democracy. In K. L. Hacker & J. van Dijk (Eds.), *Digital Democracy: Issues of Theory and Practice*. Thousand Oaks, CA: Sage Publications.

Castells, M. (1996). *The Rise of the Network Society*. Cambridge, MA: Blackwell.

Congressional Online Project. (2002). Congress Online: Assessing and Improving Capitol Hill Web Sites. Washington, D.C.: George Washington University and the Congressional Management Foundation (CMF). Online at http://www.congressonline project.org/aboutus.html

Damanpour, F. (1987). The adoption of technological, administrative and ancillary innovations: Impact of organizational factors. *Journal of Management, 13*(4), 675-688.

Damanpour, F. (1992). Organizational size and innovation. *Organization Studies, 13*(3), 375-402.

Dutton, W. (1999). *Society on the Line: Information Politics in the Digital Age.* New York: Oxford University Press.

Erikson, R S., Wright, G. C. & McIver, J. P. (1993). *Statehouse Democracy: Public Opinion and Policy in he American States.* New York: Oxford University Press.

Fountain, J. E. (2001). *Building the Virtual State: Information Technology and Institutional Change.* Washington D.C: Brookings Institution Press.

Garson, G. D. (2000). Information systems, politics, and government: Leading theoretical perspectives. In G. D. Garson (Ed.), *Handbook of Public Information Systems.* New York: Marcel Dekker, Inc.

Gaw, J. (1999). Government Slow to Get Online - Internet: Although Services like Traffic Ticket Payment Get Rave Reviews, they Remain a Rarity. *Los Angeles Times* (26 August). Online at http://www.latimes.com

Gray, V., Hanson, R., & Jacob, H. (1999). *Politics in the American States.* Washington D.C.: CQ Press.

Guthrie, K. K., & Dutton, W. H. (1992). The Politics of Citizen Access Technology: The Development of Public Information Utilities in Four Cities. *Policy Studies Journal, 20*(4), 574- 597.

Hacker, K. L. & van Dijk, J. (2000). What is Digital Democracy? In K. L. Hacker & J. van Dijk (Eds.), *Digital Democracy: Issues of Theory and Practice.* Thousand Oaks, CA: Sage Publications.

Hague, B. N., & Loader, B. D. (1999). Digital Democracy and Introduction. In B. N. Hague & B. D. Loader (Eds.), *Digital Democracy: Discourse and Decision Making in the Information Age.* New York: Routledge.

Hale, M. L., Musso, J. A., & Weare, C. (1999). Developing Digital Democracy: Evidence From California Municipal Web Pages. In B. N. Hague & B. D. Loader (Eds.), *Digital Democracy: Discourse and Decision Making in the Information Age.* New York: Routledge.

Katz, J. E., & Aspden, P. (1997). A Nation of Strangers? *Communications of the ACM 40*(12), 81-86.

Larsen, E. & Rainie, L. (2002a). *The rise of the e-citizen: How people use government agencies' Web sites.* Washington, D.C.: Pew Internet & American Life Project Online at: http://www.pewinternet.org/reports/toc.asp?Report=57

Larsen, E. & Rainie, L. (2002b). *Digital town hall: How local officials use the internet and the Civic benefits they cite from dealing with Constituents online.* Washington, D.C.: Pew Internet & American Life Project. Online at: http://www.pewinternet.org/reports/toc.asp?Report=74

O'Looney, J. (2000). *Local Government On-Line: Putting the Internet to Work..* Washington D.C.: International City Management Association.

O'Looney, J. (2001). *The Future of Public-Sector Internet Services for Citizen Participation & Service Delivery.* Athens, GA: Carl Vinson Institute of Government/ University of Georgia. Online at: http://www.cviog.uga.edu/govtech/cybsur.htm

OMB Watch. (2001). Plugged In, Tuning Up: An Assessment of State Legislative

Websites. Washington D.C.: OMB Watch. Online at: http://www.ombwatch.org/article/articleview/395/1/3/

Rand Institute. (1995). *The Feasibility and Societal Implications of Providing Universal Access to Electronic Mail (E-mail) Within the U.S.* Santa Monica, CA.: Rand Institute.

Simon, L. D. (2000). *NetPolicy.com: Public Agenda for a Digital World.* Washington D.C.: Woodrow Wilson Center Press.

Smith, A. C. & Taebel, D. A. (1985). Administrative Innovation in Municipal Government. *International Journal of Public Administration, 7*(2), 149-77.

Tsagarousianou, R., Tambini, D., & Bryan, C. (1998). *Cyberdemocracy: Technology, Cities, and Civic Networks.* London: Routledge.

U.S. Department of Commerce (1999a). *The Emerging Digital Economy II.* Washington D.C.

U.S. Department of Commerce (1999b). *Falling Through the Net: Defining the Digital Divide.* Washington D.C.

West, D. M. (2002a). *State and Federal E-government in the United States, 2002.* Providence, RI: Center for Public Policy, Brown University. Online at: http://www.insidepolitics.org/egovt02us.pdf

West, D. M. (2002b). *Urban E-government, 2002.* Providence, RI: Center for Public Policy, Brown University. Online at: http://www.insidepolitics.org/egovt02us.pdf

World Bank. E-government website. Online at: http://www1.worldbank.org/publicsector/egov/

ENDNOTES

[1]   http://www1.worldbank.org/publicsector/egov/

[2]   For instance: https://svartifoss2.fcc.gov/cores/CoresHome.html

[3]   The Virginia Division of Legislative Automated Systems, in partnership with the Virginia Information Providers Network, developed Lobbyist-in-a-Box to enable people to monitor the status of bills as they move through the General Assembly. Online at: http://leg1.state.va.us/liabtutorial.htm. A more in-depth description follows in a subsequent section.

[4]   West (2002a) reported that of the websites examined this year, the most frequent services were filing taxes online, applying for jobs, renewing driver's licenses and ordering hunting and fishing licenses online. Of note also was an access issue; twenty-eight percent of government websites have some form of disability access, up slightly from 27 percent last year.

[5]   See for instance, the Digital Georgia Project online at: http://digitalgeorgia.org; Virginia's policy at: http://www.sotech.state.va.us/gcoit/gcoit.htm#about; Arizona at: http://gita.state.az.us/sitplan99/index.htm; Texas at: http://www.state.tx.us/DIR/ssp95.html; or, a summary of state level policy at: http://www.westgov.org/smart/policy.html

[6]   http://www.congressonlineproject.org/webstudy2002.html

[7]   http://www.vipnet.org/vipnet/liab/infopage.html

[8]   Virginia Offers Do-It-Yourself site, civic.com (7.21.00). Online at: http://www.fcw.com/civic/articles/2000/0717/web-1myva-07-21-00.asp

[9]   http://www.vipnet.org/cmsportal/services_869/wireless_1101/

Chapter VIII

Consequences of the Cyberstate: The Political Implications of Digital Government in International Context

Costas Panagopoulos
New York University, USA

ABSTRACT

Emerging technology has provided public sector leaders with unprecedented opportunities to redefine the relationship between citizens and the state. Yet, even as leaders embrace the promise and possibilities afforded by digital government, there is little consensus about the political implications of digital government. While some experts expect little impact, others claim that advances in digital government will have significant political implications. This study assesses the political implications of digital government from an international perspective. Using data recently compiled by the United Nations (U.N.), the findings indicate that digital government is likely to produce significant political implications. Specifically, advances in digital government are likely to engender greater citizen support for government as well as higher levels of political participation.

INTRODUCTION

Emerging technology has recently provided public sector leaders with unprecedented opportunities to redefine the relationship between citizens and the state. Even as leaders grapple with alternatives over how best to incorporate technologies in their provision of services, there is little doubt that progress has been made and that, in many cases, the "rhetoric" of e-Government is becoming a reality. Yet, even as leaders embrace the promise and possibilities afforded by digital government, there are fewer consensuses about the political implications of e-Government.

Two camps have emerged in the debate about the political implications of digital government. On one side, experts argue that digital government will have few, profound political implications. Implementation barriers, concerns about privacy and security, and reliability and access issues, they argue, will perpetually limit the possibilities of e-Government and compromise its efficiency. Digital government may supplement the government's current system, but it is unlikely to replace it entirely. It may add a spoke in the governmental wheel, so to speak, but it will not reinvent it. As a result, the implications for politics and for democracy will be minimal, at best.

Proponents of the opposite viewpoint argue that digital government will fundamentally reshape citizens' interactions with government. The benefits of greater efficiency and reduced costs are likely to engender favor towards the government amongst the citizenry, perhaps even encouraging increased participation in the political process. Consequently, they believe the political implications of digital government will be profound.

This selection will analyze the global status of digital government. It presents a balanced summary of each perspective and of the major arguments that each camp uses to advance its claims. Then evidence is presented that speaks to the political implications of digital government in international context. This analysis will focus on two aspects of political life: the public's level of confidence in government and political participation. In the end, the findings reveal that digital government has important political implications on these two critical components of politics.

THE GLOBAL GROWTH OF DIGITAL GOVERNMENT

Governments throughout the world have been consistently leveraging emerging technologies to enhance the lives of citizens and to improve the governing process since the mid-1990s. Most recently, the global growth of digital government has been impressive. A comprehensive, worldwide study commissioned by the United Nations (Benchmarking E-government, 2002) and released in May 2002 claims that "[f]rom Armenia to Zaire, the concept of e-government is being openly embraced (5)." The report finds that 2001 saw a greater expansion of government online presence than during the previous five years combined. It estimates that over 50,000 official government websites exist worldwide, compared to only 50 in 1996. Of the U.N.'s 190 member states, 169 are providing some level of information and services online. Each of these states has an official government website, 84 have a national government website, 36 have a single entry portal, 84 have sub-national government websites, and 17 have online transaction capacity. A separate study of 22 nations, conducted by *Accenture* in 2001, claims that "online service delivery has never been higher on the political agenda than it is today. From the United Kingdom to the United States, Belgium to Brazil and Malaysia to Mexico, governments are talking about the significant benefits that can be realized by migrating traditionally paper-based and face-to-face services to the Internet" (Rhetoric vs. Reality-Closing the Gap, 2001). Experts estimate citizens will be able to conduct electronic transactions with more than 60 percent of government agencies in OECD countries by 2003 (Abramson and Means, 2001).

RECENT DEVELOPMENTS, INITIATIVES AND PIONEERING PRACTICES

Across the globe, nations are clearly augmenting their levels of providing government services online. Beyond that, however, governments are striving to enhance citizens' overall experience with digital government. "There is a growing recognition," reports *Accenture*, "that e-Government is not just about technology, but about harnessing technology as just one of the tools to transform the way governments operate. Governments are learning that transformation comes not from moving services online, but from redesigning the organization and processes to put the citizen at the center, integrating across agencies to simplify interaction, reduce cost and improve service (Rhetoric vs. Reality, 2001). Canada for example, which earns top marks from *Accenture* as the global e-Government leader, achieves this largely as a result of its commitment to a citizen-centric model of online services. The Canadian government's commitment to Customer Relationship Management (CRM) views citizens as consumers and uses techniques developed initially by the private sector to recast service delivery around customer-citizen intentions. Lucienne Robillard, Canada's Treasury Board President and the government's e-Government champion, claims: "Too often in the past government services designed from the inside out; they reflected the structures of government organizations rather than the needs and priorities of citizens. We cannot stop until all Canadians can have seamless access to all government services quickly, simply and with a minimum of fuss" (e-Government Leadership-Realizing the Vision, 2002). This approach is echoed in the recommendations to governments to incorporate customized and value-added services into their sites, offering cross-agency services, information and even entertainment features that help solidify the relationship with the user (Abramson and Means, 2001).

Canada is not alone in recognizing the importance of citizens' experience with digital government. Setting the standards for the citizen-centric approach are also Singapore, Hong Kong, the United States, and Ireland. France, another leader in this area, is poised for new achievements with a new initiative — mon.service-public.fr — that will provide each French citizen with a personalized portal. Australia provides free online services and information for businesses (www.business.gav.au) and permits users to manage online transactions with the Commonwealth, state/territory and local government agencies via the Business Entry Point Transaction Manager. The United States has made a strong commitment to inter-agency projects that improve citizen access to Federal services (e-Government Leadership-Realizing the Vision, 2002).

E-DEMOCRACY: A SPECIAL CATEGORY OF DIGITAL GOVERNMENT INITIATIVES

Broadly conceptualized, e-Government typically includes features that we could more specifically characterize as e-Democracy. E-Democracy encompasses all forms of electronic communication between government and its citizens, or, between the electorate and the elected. E-Democracy initiatives can facilitate good governance and contribute directly to making the processes of government transparent and responsive to public preferences. E-Democracy initiatives are typically predicated along the following principles for information management: *access, convenience, awareness, communication and involvement* in political processes. Such programs aim to transition citizens from passive information access to active participation. In his report, Electronic Governance: Re-inventing Good Governance, Rogers W'O Okot-Uma suggests that e-Democracy is predicated along the following five dimensions: *Informing, Representing, Encouraging, Consulting and Involving the Citizen.* Successful e-Democracy initiatives are a key ingredient in the digital government program and can play a critical role in determining the degree to which digital government will impact politics. For this reason, it is useful to consider examples of e-Democracy initiatives that have been implemented across the world (for details, see http://www1.worldbank.org/publicsector/egov/Okot-Uma.pdf).

E-Democracy programs intended to inform citizens are most abundant. Examples include efforts in: Australia (www.nla.gov.au/oz/gov), Canada (www.canada.gc.ca./main) Hong Kong (www.info.gov.hk), Singapore (www.gov.sg), Sweden (www.goteborg.se) and South Africa (www.open.gov.uk). Representation initiatives are designed to improve the accessibility of citizens to their elected officials. A common way of achieving this goal is by making digital contact details (e-mail addresses) available in the public domain. Uganda, for example, made such a directory available to citizens during the Sixth Parliament (1996-2000). The Caterbury Regional Council in New Zealand (www.govt.nz/crchrome/crchonme.asp) offers links to elected members, as does the Icelandic Parliament (www.althingi.is/eksag/nra-d/i0), the regional government of Rajasthan, India (www.rajgovt.org) and the United States Senate (www.senate.gov/senators/index.cfm). Efforts to encourage citizen participation by stimulating debate and exchanging views about voting and elections are also emerging. In Newham, London Borough, UK, for example, citizens may provide instant feedback in debate wvia www.newham.gov.uk. Along the dimension of consulting citizens, initiatives foster two-way communication and interaction between citizens and government. They seek public information, feedback and aim to increase citizen participation in decision-making. The Oxfordshire County Council in the UK provides an example of such a program. The Council solicits debate and feedback on key issues via the Internet (www.oxfordshire.gov.uk). In Brent (UK), citizens are consulted about annual budget considerations (www.brent.gov.uk). Similar interaction and consultation is also possible in New Zealand (www.govt.nz). The final dimension, involvement, is the most ambitious. Programs designed to involve citizens view the decision-making process as a partnership between citizens and elected officials. Ultimately, involvement initiatives will provide citizens and groups with direct opportunities to shape the policymaking process. In the Australian Capital Territory, citizens have such opportunities via online consultation papers (www.act.gov.au/government/reports.) Online community discussion forums, chat rooms, and bulletin boards are found in Denmark (www.naeskom.dk/danish/ addressliste/html/citynet.htm) Cape Town, South Africa, (www.cmc.gov.za/disc22frm) and in Minnestota, U.S. (www.e-democracy.org). While these efforts do not represent a transition to direct democracy by any means, they do make political processes more transparent and open to citizen scrutiny and penetration. e-Democracy initiatives are an integral part of the e-Government agenda, and they contribute meaningfully to the overall impact of e-Government on the political process. Additional data and information specifically about e-Democracy programs worldwide would allow analysts to determine the direct effects and political implications of such programs.

PERSISTENT CHALLENGES

Despite these significant advancements, powerful challenges to e-Government's global progress persist. To attempt a comprehensive analysis of these claims is beyond the scope of this study. Yet, a summary of the key arguments will produce some useful insights.

Privacy

The public's concerns about privacy and the security of information online are key impediments to the potential for digital government growth. A study of U.S. consumers conducted in 1998 by *Business Week,* Harris revealed that concerns about privacy were the biggest obstacle preventing consumers from using websites. These privacy concerns ranked above cost, ease of use and unsolicited marketing (Green et al., 1998). Perhaps that is with good reason: in a study of 1,400 U.S. websites conducted the same year by the Federal Trade Commission — all of which collect information — only between 14 and 16 percent had any disclosure statements about their policies regarding information collection or privacy (Abramson and Means, 2001). Studies consistently find that privacy concerns top the list when it comes to reasons why citizens may be skeptical of digital government (see Abramson and Means, chapter 5). Yet, governments show a commitment to addressing privacy concerns in order to instill public confidence that personal information can be protected from unauthorized use. All 23 countries surveyed by *Accenture*, for example, had some form of data protection legislation.

In Ireland, the government's plan to introduce a central Public Services Broker include security measures to prevent one public agency from gaining unauthorized access to information relating to a person's transactions with another department. The Irish government is committed to giving citizens as much control as possible over the release of personal data. Smart cards are another new development that has the potential to secure transactions between citizens and government. Smart cards are credit card-sized individual identity cards that able to contain vast amounts of information in digital format. Smart card initiatives have been implemented (with varying degrees of success) in such places as Malaysia, Finland, Italy and Hong Kong. The Malaysian government estimates that 20 million citizens will carry the MyKad by 2007; In Hong Kong, smart identity cards will be issued to all residents by 2003 (e-Government Leadership-Realizing the Vision, 2002).

Access

Access issues remain paramount in any discussion about the potential of digital government. Even as the total global online population increased 20 percent between 2001 and 2001 (to 514 million users), only about nine percent of the world's population enjoys regular Internet access. Furthermore, the "digital divide" continues to offer certain population segments (the more educated, affluent) — and certain populations (industrialized, developed nations) — greater access (Von Hoffmann, 1999). Some experts are concerned that e-Government will only exacerbate the digital divide and further marginalize the have-nots (Benchmarking E-Government, 2002). There are encouraging indicators, however, that access rates are improving across the board. Between 2000 and 2001, the online population in Africa increased 24 percent (to 4.2 million), in Asia/Pacific, 28 percent (to 143 million), in Europe, 26 percent (to 154 million), in the U.S. and Canada, 8 percent (to 181 million users), in Latin America, 32 percent (to 25 million). The Middle East experienced the fastest rate of growth during the same period, 47 percent, to 4.7 million users (www.nua.ie). Beyond that, countries are beginning to recognize the need to address accessibility issues. Brazil sets an example in this area with the establishment of its 250,000 Points of Presence program, an initiative that will enable citizens to access government services online from public kiosks throughout the country. Such programs improve access, particularly in places like Brazil, where only about 7 percent of the population has Internet access. Nevertheless, access points are not a panacea, and lack of training, familiarity with technology and distrust of digital formats continue to place limitations on access.

Cash-Based Economies

Many digital government services involve monetary transactions for such things as tax payments, fees for services etc. This may pose problems in countries whose economies remain predominantly cash-based. Such is the case in approximately 75 percent of the nations evaluated by the United Nations report (Benchmarking E-Government, 2002).

Implementation Barriers and Organizational Obstacles

Governments commonly encounter a variety of organizational obstacles at the Institutional, Managerial and Planning Areas (Benchmarking E-Government, 2002). At the Institutional/Operational level, countries are first and foremost, challenged by significant technology and infrastructure costs. Consider, for example, that in the United States, the government proposed a budget of over $200 million for e-Government initiatives, beyond what each state individually invests in developing and sustaining digital government programs. Despite the potential for a high return-on-investment in the long-term, the short-term costs of e-Government programs are often prohibitive for many nations. Beyond that, they oftentimes lack sources to support 24/7 operations. They may lack institutional support and clear policy guidelines.

At the managerial level, some countries lack the capacity to manage large-scale IT projects. Top and mid-level managers may not be fully committed to e-Government initiatives. Information mismanagement can be characteristic as are also gaps between management expectations and management realities. Furthermore, opposition by professional or union interests may be crippling. Birnbaum argues that governments are likely to face resistance from public employee's unions who may feel threatened by inevitable job reductions as e-Government initiatives are implemented (Birnbaum, 2000). At the policy level, there is often a lack of coordination or strategic planning. Furthermore, as bureaucratic leadership changes, a lack of continuity may emerge in planning and policy areas.

The Status of Global Digital Government

In a monumental study aimed to assess the level of e-Government throughout the world, the United Nations Division for Public Economics and Public Administration partnered with the American Society for Public Administration to release Benchmarking E-Government: A Global Perspective in May 2002 (http://www.unpan.org/e-government/Benchmarking%20E-gov%202001.pdf). The report evaluates the level of e-Government in 190 member states. The investigators examine over 1,900 national government websites in order to assess each country's overall level of digital government offerings. The website research was conducted from May to July and then again from October to December 2001. Investigators broken down the development of e-Government into five possible stages: Emerging, Enhanced, Interactive, Transactional and Seamless. Each stage is characterized by the following features (as summarized from the report):

Emerging (Stage 1): A country commits to becoming an e-gov player. A formal but limited web presence is established through a few independent government websites which provide users with static organizational or political information. Sites may include contact information for public officials. In rare cases, special features like FAQs may be found.

Enhanced (Stage 2): A country's online presence begins to expand as its number of official websites increase. Content will consist more of dynamic and specialized information that is frequently updated; sites will link to other official pages. Government publications, legislation, newsletters are available. Search features and e-mail addresses are available. A site for the national or ruling party may also be present that links the user to ministries or departments.

Interactive (Stage 3): A country's presence on the Internet expands dramatically with access to a wide range of government institutions and services. More sophisticated levels of formal interactions between citizens and service providers are present like e-mail and post comments areas. The capacity to search specialized databases and to download forms and applications or submit them is also available. The content and information is regularly updated.

Transactional (Stage 4): Complete and secure transactions like obtaining visas, passports, birth and death records, licenses, permits where a user can pay online for services, pay parking fines, automobile registration fees, utility bills and taxes. Digital signatures may be recognized in an effort to facilitate procurement and doing business with government. Secure sites and user passwords are present.

Seamless (Stage 5): Total integration of e-functions and services across administrative and departmental boundaries. Capacity to instantly access any service in a "unified package." Ministerial/departmental/agency lines of demarcation are removed in cyberspace. Services will be clustered along common needs.

Highlights from the United Nations' Benchmarking E-Government Report

Each government's web presence was evaluated and assigned a numerical score ranging from one to five, with one representing Emerging Presence and five, Seamless. Each stage was then further analyzed for the presence of specific features and content and measured by intervals of 0.25. (See report for details.) The results follow.

Emerging Presence

Nearly all 32 countries at this level are among the world's least developed nations. Over half are in Sub-Sahara Africa. They averaged 3.9 official websites per government. Official information for many of these countries is predominantly of a highly partisan, political nature, with a strong bias toward the ruler or the party in power. Despite limited progress, there is strong potential for advancement among some nations at this level. In Gabon, for example, the national government site (www.gabon.gov.ga) is a single-entry portal that allows users access to 14 official national government sites. Others include Guiana and Botswana.

Enhanced Presence

Of the 65 countries in this group, 58 percent are emerging or newly industrialized economies and are dispersed throughout the globe (except North America.) These include several Central American nations (El Salvador, Dominican Republic and Guatemala) as well as the majority of CIS states (Georgia, Kazakhstan, Turkmenistan). Some African countries are also at this level: Nigeria, Cote d'Ivoire, Burkina Faso and Ghana).

Interactive Presence

The delivery of service and information in this group is aimed at making the user the top priority and thus reflect strong citizen-centric e-Government programs. Portals are the preferred point of entry. Of the 55 countries at this level, 20 percent are developing nations. The remainder is evenly divided between newly emerging and industrialized economies. This group presently includes the Netherlands, Sweden and Japan.

Figure 1: 2001 stages of e-Government development (data source: Benchmarking E-Government, UN Report, 2002)

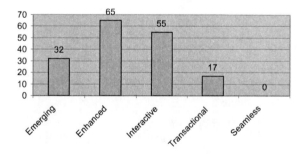

Transactional Presence

All 17 of the countries at this level are OCED countries. All use single-entry portals and have sophisticated citizen-centric features. They include Spain, Germany, Finland, Norway, the United States, Canada, the United Kingdom and France.

Seamless Presence

No nation achieved this level of web presence. According to the report, attaining this level would necessitate a considerable degree of political, administrative and managerial cooperation. For many countries, this may be an abstract or remote objective.

EXPLAINING VARIATIONS IN THE LEVELS OF DIGITAL GOVERNMENT

Before attempting to assess the political implications of the level of digital government in countries across the world, it is useful to consider the factors that may determine the level of web presence (as quantified by the U.N. report). Using the data released in the report, as well as measures of additional variables, the multiple regression analysis below reveals several key factors that influence the level of e-Government in a country.

The dependent variable (web presence) is the measure of the level of a country's e-Government as determined by the U.N. report (the range is from one to five, where five equals the highest level of e-Government). Other variables include the nation's population, annual GDP (millions of U.S. dollars), level of education (as indicated by percentage of the population that is literate) and the degree of political freedom in a country. Note that the measure of political freedom used is determined by Freedom House. The range is from one to seven, with one being the most free and seven being the least free.

Table 1: Determinants of a nation's e-Government web presence

Variable	Coefficient	Standard Deviation
Population	4.80e-07	4.61e-07
GDP	.0001167*	.0000686
Political Freedom	-.11141**	.036
Education	.02397***	.0036
Constant	.85716**	.3669
*p<.10 level, **p<.05 level, ***p<.01 level*		*N=120. R-squared=.47*

Data Sources: E-Government Web Presence: Benchmarking E-Government report, 2002. Population: World Population Bureau; GDP: World Bank; Political Freedom: Freedom House; Education: United Nations.

The findings suggest that the population in a country is not a significant predictor or the level of e-Government. That should not be especially surprising, particularly given examples like Luxembourg, Malta and Iceland, whose populations are relatively small, but whose web presence level is 3.0. Conversely, China, whose population is the largest in the world, has a web presence measure of 2.0. A nation's GDP, however, is a significant predictor of the level of e-Government. The data suggest that as the level of GDP rises, the level of e-Government in a country is likely to rise as well. The overall literacy rate is also a significant predictor. As a nation's literacy rate increases, the level of e-Government will also increase. Specifically, for every additional percentage point of literacy obtained in a country, the web presence measure will rise by .024 points. Finally, the analysis suggests that the more politically free a nation is, the higher its level of digital government is likely to be. [In this case, since the highest measure of political freedom is one (rather than seven) the coefficient is negative, suggesting that the higher the measure of the variable, the lower the web presence measure.] Therefore, nations with little political freedom are likely to have lower levels of e-Government.

Beyond simply assessing the level of e-Government for each state, the U.N. report creates E-Government Index. The index incorporates the web presence measure, but also includes other key indicators that define the core areas of an enabling e-Government environment (Benchmarking E-Government, 2002). These core areas are: the web presence measure, a measure of telecommunications infrastructure and a measure of human capital. The first measure was discussed above. The second measure — telecommunications infrastructure — incorporates six primary indicators that define a country's infrastructure capacity. These are: the number of personal computers per 100 individuals, the number of Internet hosts per 10,000 individuals, the percentage of a nation's population online, the number of telephone lines per 100 individuals, the number of mobile phones per 100 individuals, and the number of televisions per 100 individuals. 2001 International Communications Union Report and the 2001 UNDP Human Development Report.) However, possessing the education level, freedom and desire to access information — in short, human capital — is critical to e-Government's efficacy (Benchmarking E-Government, 2002). Thus, the e-Government index includes a measure of human capital that is comprised of the nation's UNDP Human Development Index (measures a society's well-being, including education, economic viability and healthcare), the Information Access Index (as determined by a combination of survey measures from Freedom House and Transparency International), and the urban/rural population ratio. Data is available for 144 countries that are included in the study. While the two measures are distinct, there is a strong positive correlation between the web presence measure and the eGov index (Correlation is 0.92)

The study reveals that the mean e-Government Global Index is 1.62. Index numbers range from a high of 3.11 (United States) to a low of .46 (Uganda). Sixty-one nations (or 42 percent) indexed above the global mean. Table 2 below shows the 2001 Global E-gov Leaders with their corresponding e-Government indexes: United States (3.11), Australia (2.60), New Zealand (2.59), Singapore (2.58), Norway (2.55), Canada (2.52), the United Kingdom (2.52), The Netherlands (2.51), Denmark (2.47), and Germany (2.46). Table 3 shows the mean indexes geographically by region. Regionally, North America leads with a mean score of 2.60. Europe places second with a mean of 2.01, South America next at

Table 2: Global e-Government leaders

State	E-Gov Index
USA	3.11
Australia	2.60
New Zealand	2.59
Singapore	2.58
Norway	2.55
Canada	2.52
UK	2.52
Netherlands	2.51
Denmark	2.47
Germany	2.46

Data Source: Benchmarking E-Government, 2002.

1.79, then the Middle East at 1.76. These regions registered an index above the global mean. Below the mean were Asia at 1.38, the Caribbean at 1.34, Central America at 1.28 and Africa at .84.

DEMOCRACY AND E-GOVERNMENT

The analysis above suggests that a nation's level of political freedom will determine the extent to which it develops an e-Government presence. While it is generally true that those societies with the greatest level political freedom tend to have greater web presence measures (as well as higher e-Government Indexes overall) than societies with the least

Table 3: Mean e-Government index by region

Region	Mean E-Gov Index
North America	2.60
Europe	2.01
South America	1.79
Middle East	1.76
GLOBAL MEAN	*1.62*
Asia	1.38
Caribbean	1.34
Central America	1.28
Africa	0.84

Data Source: Benchmarking E-Government, 2002.

amount of political freedom, those in between are much closer to (in some ways, indistinguishable from) non-democratic countries. Table 4 shows that when we categorize countries based on the classification system used by Freedom House into three groups (Free, Partly Free and Not Free), the levels of digital government in societies that are partly free resemble levels in societies that are not free at all. In fact, the mean level of web presence is actually higher in societies classified as "not free" than in "partly free" societies.

THE POLITICAL IMPLICATIONS OF DIGITAL GOVERNMENT

The impressive global growth of digital government propels one to reflect on what are the political implications of digital government. Commentators have suggested that citizens will increasingly evaluate leaders based on their ability to capitalize on the possibilities afforded by e-Government. They argue that, increasingly public officials and public sector managers will be judged on how they leverage e-commerce technologies in operating government (Abramson and Means, 2001). Citizens will expect government to use technology to achieve efficiency, savings, ease and increased revenue. In the words of the former Speaker of the U.S. House of Representatives, "e-customers will begin to carry [Internet-inspired] attitudes into their relationship with bureaucracy, and, as e-voters, they will favor politicians who work to make their lives easier and more convenient (Abramson and Means, 2001)."

THE IMPACT OF DIGITAL GOVERNMENT ON PUBLIC CONFIDENCE IN GOVERNMENT

Even if digital government achieves high levels of success, will this recast the relationship between citizens and government? Will the political implications be pro-

Table 4: E-Government levels by degree of freedom (Freedom House)

	Free	Partly Free	Not Free
Mean Web Presence	1.85	1.22	1.23
	(.56)	(.52)	(.46)
Mean E-Gov Index	2.99	2.05	2.02
	(.89)	(.89)	(.69)
N	*60*	*43*	*30*
(Standard Deviations noted in parentheses.)			

Data Source: Benchmarking E-Government, 2002; Freedom House.

found or insignificant? Speculations about the potential political implications of e-Government center around two major possibilities. First, there is the hypothesis that digital government growth will instill greater confidence amongst citizens towards government. To be sure, low levels of public confidence in government are indeed an international reality. Consider that, according to available data from 42 countries across the globe, on average, 34 percent of respondents report confidence in their respective governments. (Data on "confidence in government" reported in Plasser and Plasser, 2002.) The lowest level of confidence reported was 13 percent (Russia) and the highest — 69 percent — was reported in Norway. One of the primary explanations for low levels of confidence in government is that citizens often consider government inflated, wasteful and inefficient. In the United States, for example, where confidence in government currently stands at around 30 percent, public opinion surveys reveal a steady increase in the number of Americans who view government as wasteful since the mid 1950s (National Election Studies, 1948-2000).

The following multiple regression analysis confirms the hypothesis. The evidence indicates that improvements in the level of digital government in a country will positively affect the level of public confidence in government. Table 5 reveals that the influence of the level of e-Government in a country (as measured by the U.N.'s E-Gov Index described earlier) has a statistically significant positive effect on the level of confidence in government in a country. In fact, for every full unit (1.0) of increase in the e-Government Index, confidence in government is predicted to increase an astounding 16 percentage points. Furthermore, this analysis also shows that the level of e-Government variable (the U.N.'s E-Gov Index was used) is the only predictor whose influence is statistically significant from zero. The other independent variables included in the analysis are population size, GDP, level of political freedom (Freedom House measure, described earlier) and the type of electoral system (plurality systems, proportional list systems, mixed system, etc.) Of course, the index, as we discussed earlier, includes measures for

Table 5: Factors that influence the level of confidence in government

Variable	Coefficient	Standard Deviation
Population	-.00005	.00007
GDP	-.00025	.00237
Political Freedom	-1.3392	2.2890
Electoral System	2.3504	2.1120
E-Gov Level	16.111**	6.885
Constant	-1.6299	16.992

*$p<.10$ level, **$p<.05$ level, ***$p<.01$ level $N=41$. R-squared=.24

Data Sources: Level of Confidence in Government: Plasser and Plasser, 2002. E-Government Level: Benchmarking E-Government report, 2002. Population: World Population Bureau; GDP: World Bank; Political Freedom: Freedom House; Education: United Nations; Electoral System: Institute for Democracy and Electoral Assistance.

human development, literacy and other infrastructure measures. It is interesting to note that it serves as a more reliable predictor of the level of confidence than a country's overall economic achievement (GDP), population, degree of political freedom, or the type of electoral system used in a country. The results show a clear positive relationship between the degree of e-Government in a country and the level of public confidence in government we are likely to observe. In this respect, the political implications of improvements in digital government are significant.

Multiple explanations for these results are possible. Experts have theorized that the perceived greater efficiency of digital operations would yield such results. Possibly as more information about government becomes available online, government processes will become more transparent and citizens will feel more confident about its proceedings.

THE IMPACT OF DIGITAL GOVERNMENT ON POLITICAL PARTICIPATION

A second and perhaps more fundamental question that speaks to the potential political implications of digital government is over the question of political participation. (For the purposes of this analysis, we will limit participation to voting in elections.) Experts argue that advances in e-Government — either by reducing the barriers to participation through digital democracy initiatives or indirectly by increasing confidence in government and government officials — will result in higher rates of political participation. As it currently stands, the average *global* turnout for the past four elections (including both executive or legislative) is 59.97 percent (N=121. Standard Deviation: 18.80). While average turnout in some societies can be as high as 96 percent (as in Malta), other societies turn out at rates less than 15 percent (as in Uruguay.) Higher rates of participation are, however, associated with higher levels of digital government worldwide. (The correlation is 0.41.)

This yields the following hypothesis that we can test using data on nations' levels of e-Government (the E-Gov Index) and turnout rate measures. Increases in a country's

Table 6: Factors that influence political participation (turnout)

Variable	Coefficient	Standard Deviation
Population	.00001	.00001
GDP	-.00348**	.00164
Political Freedom	-3.3352***	.94229
E-Gov Level	7.9834***	3.1620
Constant	58.354***	6.9339
*p<.10 level, **p<.05 level, ***p<.01 level*	N=120. R-squared=.28	

Data Sources: Turnout: Institute for Democracy and Electoral Assistance; E-Government Level: Benchmarking E-Government report, 2002. Population: World Population Bureau; GDP: World Bank; Political Freedom: Freedom House.

level of e-Government will produce corresponding increases in the average level of turnout in elections. Note: that is not specifically or exclusively a discussion of digital democracy or Internet voting. While researchers have shown that such initiatives do increase turnout (Nagler and Alvarez, 2000), this is a broader discussion about the impact of the overall level of e-Government. The results of the following statistical analysis confirm this hypothesis.

As Table 6 shows, the average level of turnout in a country is impacted by three variables. As a country's level of freedom decreases (using the Freedom House scale, this means the value of the variable increases up to seven, the value of the lowest level of political freedom), average turnout also decreases by approximately three points. Population is not a statistically significant predictor. As GDP increases in a nation, there is a modest but statistically significant drop in average turnout. Turning to the level of digital government in a country, we find a strong and statistically significant relationship in a positive direction. As a nation's e-Government level (e-Gov Index) rises by a full unit, the turnout in that country is expected to rise by nearly eight percentage points. These results confirm that the level of digital government in a country is likely to have significant political implications on levels of turnout.

This analysis includes participation rates in societies that are non-democratic or just partly free. In such instances, participation may be forced or even meaningless as elections may be acclamatory or otherwise ceremonial or symbolic in nature rather than effectual. While they may not be "free and fair," however, they still take place and can serve as indicators of participation levels. The data do reveal higher turnout rates in nations that a categorized as "Free" by Freedom House. Table 7 below summarizes the mean turnout rates for each category for the four most recent elections.

The findings about the impact of digital government still hold when you consider only politically free societies. The results of the following regression analysis show that the E-Gov Index variable continues to have a statistically significant (at the $p<.01$ level) positive impact on the turnout rate. In fact, a full-unit increase in the E-Gov Index would yield a substantial increase of 15 points in the mean rate of turnout.

Table 7: Mean turnout* rates by degree of freedom

	Free	Partly Free	Not Free
Mean Turnout Rate	68.6 (15.1)	53.5 (20.6)	47.7 (11.28)
N	*59*	*43*	*19*

(Standard Deviations noted in parentheses.)

Sources: *Four most recent elections (Institute for Democracy and Electoral Assistance); Freedom House.

Table 8: Factors that influence political participation (turnout) in free societies

Variable	Coefficient	Standard Deviation
Population	-.000093	.000099
GDP	-.0017535	.0030643
E-Gov Level	15.06197***	3.551289
Constant	43.309***	6.8412

*$p<.10$ level, **$p<.05$ level, ***$p<.01$ level $N=58$. R-squared=.29*

Data Sources: Turnout: Institute for Democracy and Electoral Assistance. E-Government Level: Benchmarking E-Government report, 2002. Population: World Population Bureau; GDP: World Bank; Political Freedom: Freedom House.

CONCLUSIONS AND POLICY IMPLICATIONS

The results of the analyses above suggest that the level of digital government in a country has important political implications. Specifically, higher levels of digital government are expected to produce greater confidence in government as well as higher rates of political participation. In this study, participation was defined as the level of turnout in election. It is conceivable, however, that increases in digital government will have a similar effect on other forms of political participation that may include: involvement in party or campaign activities, making political contributions, attending meetings or gathering of a political nature, engaging in political debate and discussion more frequently, or contacting elected officials. E-Democracy, in particular, promises to provide the mechanism by which much such participation may be facilitated. While such an analysis was beyond the scope of this study, future research may well confirm this proposition.

This study also finds that higher digital government levels are likely in free and more affluent societies. However, digital government is not a phenomenon exclusive to democratic, industrialized societies. Some societies with lower levels of political freedom have achieved impressive levels of digital government and they display a commitment to expanding these services. The findings of this analysis suggest that the political implications of greater levels of digital government apply to both democratic and authoritarian governments, and authoritarian leaders may well find that they engender stronger public confidence as they expand their levels of digital government.

POLICY RECOMMENDATIONS

More Digital Government is Necessary but May Not Be Sufficient. The indicators suggest that to achieve greater levels of public confidence and political participation, governments must increase their level of digital government. Advances in digital government offerings online, however, may not be adequate. Governments must also strengthen the other elements that are incorporated in the E-Gov Index. That is, governments must increase web presence measures, but they also need to bolster telecommunications infrastructure and human capital levels. States must improve access to and proliferation of communications technologies. The digital government agenda also needs to include plans to increase literacy rates, levels of education, access to information and other human capital elements. Coordinated efforts that successfully achieve increases in all of these areas are most likely to produce the political implications this analysis suggests.

Expand e-Democracy Initiatives in Particular. E-Democracy programs are a key component in the overall e-Government agenda. While a lack of availability of data specifically about such initiatives makes it challenging to ascertain the direct political implications of e-Democracy, it is conceivable that such efforts play a special role in shaping citizens' perceptions about the transparency of political processes, its responsiveness to citizen input, and the opportunities for inclusion and involvement in political life. Such sentiment may engender greater confidence in government and higher levels of participation. Governments, therefore, would be suited to consider initiatives that inform citizens, seek input from citizens on policy matters and allow citizens to influence the political process in convenient ways.

REFERENCES

Abramson, M. A. & Grady, E. M. (2001). *E-Government 2001.* MD: Rowman & Littlefield.

Alvarez, R. M. & Nagler, J. (2000). *The Likely Consequences of Internet Voting for Political Participation.* Presented at the Internet Voting and Democracy Symposium, Loyola Law School, Los Angeles, CA. October.

Benchmarking E-Government: A Global Perspective. (2002). United Nations Division of Public Economics and Public Administration and the American Society for Public Administration (May).

Birnbaum, J. H. (2000). Death to bureaucrats, good news for the rest of us: As government moves online, jobs will disappear. but you won't have to spend hours renewing a driver's license. *Fortune, 142*(10), 241-244 (June 26).

E-Government Leadership-Realizing the Vision. Accenture. (2002). Washington, DC.

Green, H., Yang, C. & Judge, P.C. (1998). A Little Privacy Please. *Business Week* (3569), 98-99.

Plasser, Fritz & Gunda Plasser. (2002). *Global Political Campaigning.* CT: Praeger Publications, 132-135.

Rhetoric vs. Reality-Closing the Gap. (2001) *Accenture.* Washington, DC.

Von Hoffman, C. (1999). The making of e-government. *CIO Enterprise Magazine,* (November 15).

W'O Okot-Uma, R. Electronic Governance: Re-Incenting Good Governance. http://www1.worldbank.org/publicsector/egov/Okot-Uma.pdf.

Section III

Issues in Digital Governance

Chapter IX

Digital Government and Individual Privacy

Patrick R. Mullen
U.S. General Accounting Office, USA

ABSTRACT

The growth of the Internet and digital government has dramatically increased the Federal government's ability to collect, analyze, and disclose personal information about many private aspects of citizens' lives. Personal information once available only on paper to a limited number of people is now instantly retrievable anywhere in the world by anyone with a computer and an Internet connection. Over time, there has also been a declining level of trust by Americans in government, and currently, many perceive the government as a potential threat to their privacy. Given these forces at work in our society, one should not be surprised to read the results of surveys that show privacy as a top concern of citizens in the 21st century. If citizens do not believe that the government is adequately protecting the privacy of their individual information, they may be less willing to provide this information. Such reluctance could compromise the ability of government to collect important information necessary to develop, administer and evaluate the impact of various policies and programs. Privacy issues discussed in this chapter include challenges regarding (1) protecting personal privacy; (2) ensuring confidentiality of data collected; and (3) implementing appropriate security controls. Perspectives on privacy and stewardship responsibilities of agencies are also discussed.

INTRODUCTION

As discussed in earlier chapters, governments have an increasing ability to accumulate, store, retrieve, cross-reference, analyze and link vast amounts of personal information — in an ever faster and more cost-efficient manner. This is largely the result of advances in the use of information technology (IT) and the Internet, which continues to change the way Federal agencies communicate, use and disseminate information, deliver services, and conduct business. These advances have the potential to help build better relationships between government and the public by facilitating Federal agencies' timely and efficient interaction with citizens. According to a January 2001 poll, nearly half of Americans have used a government website and almost three-quarters believe that issues concerning electronic government (e-government), also known as digital government, should be a high priority.[1]

Generally speaking, e-government refers to the use of technology, particularly Web-based Internet applications, to enhance an individual agency's website, for access to and delivery of government information and service to citizens — including business partners and employees — other agencies, and entities.[2] At the Federal level, agencies have identified 1,371 electronic government initiatives, ranging from those that simply disseminate information to those that are expected to transform the way the government operates. At the state level, according to the National Association of State Chief Information Officers, government-to-business electronic interaction is well under way and government-to-citizen and government-to-government electronic interaction is rapidly increasing. At the local level, according to a survey in the fall of 2000 by the International City/County Management Association and Public Technology, Inc., about 83 percent of local governments had websites, but few local governments were providing interactive service delivery on line,[3] although many jurisdictions planned to offer such services.

While the Internet opens new opportunities for streamlining processes and enhancing delivery of services, Federal executives and managers must also be cognizant of the responsibilities and challenges that accompany these opportunities, including (1) sustaining committed executive leadership, (2) building effective e-government business cases, (3) maintaining a citizen focus, (4) protecting personal privacy and confidentiality, (5) implementing appropriate security controls, (6) maintaining electronic records, (7) maintaining a robust technical infrastructure, (8) addressing IT human capital concerns, and (9) ensuring uniform service to the public.[4]

This chapter discusses in particular the responsibilities and challenges identified in GAO reports ad studies dealing with the issues (4) and (5) above: protecting personal privacy and confidentiality, as well as implementing appropriate security controls. The sections below discuss perspectives on privacy, followed by the issues and key GAO findings associated with privacy, confidentiality, and security. This chapter concludes with a discussion on the need for agency stewardship over data collected on individual citizens.

PERSPECTIVES ON PRIVACY

In our society, there is an inherent tension between the desire for the free flow of information versus the concern for maintaining individual privacy. This tension is captured in various congressional statements in legislation, as well as in executive branch guidance to agencies on how to carry out their seemingly conflicting responsibilities under the law. For example, in passing the Paperwork Reduction Act of 1995, the Senate Governmental Affairs Committee noted its belief that "information obtained by government is a valuable and useful resource to government and society, if managed in a coordinated and systematic manner." The committee noted the importance of the free flow of information:

> *The advent of the electronic information age presents new opportunities and obligations of the Federal government as it strives to fulfill its continuing responsibility to make government information accessible to the American public. The legislation meets this need by providing for improved dissemination of government information to the public, particularly in electronic formats.[5]*

However, these same technological trends also raise concerns about information privacy. As Congress stated in passing the Privacy Act (1974):

> *...the increasing use of computers and sophisticated information technology, while essential to the efficient operations of the Government, has greatly magnified the harm to individual privacy that can occur for any collection, maintenance, use, or dissemination of personal information.[6]*

While the Privacy Act of 1974 is the primary law regulating the Federal government's collection and maintenance of personal information, the legislative intent has been clarified with subsequent Office of Management and Budget (OMB) guidance to Federal agencies. OMB's circular on "The Management of Federal Information Resources" (Circular A-130) also captures the balance between the free flow of information versus the right to privacy.[7] The circular also addresses (1) the need for agency websites to post clear and easily accessed privacy policies and (2) Federal agency use of Internet cookies, which pose privacy risks because the data contained in "persistent" cookies may be linked to individuals after the fact. A cookie is a short string of text that is sent from a webserver to a webbrowser when the browser accesses a webpage (see below for a detailed discussion of persistent cookies).[8] In addition, the Federal Trade Commission (FTC) has issued four Fair Information Principles governing on-line privacy at commercial websites that can be used as criteria to assess Federal agency websites, including proper notice, choice, access and security. Each of these topics is briefly discussed below, with a summary of problems identified in GAO reports and studies on agency implementation of OMB guidance and adherence to FTC principles. Also discussed below are personal privacy issues and solutions.

PROTECTING PERSONAL PRIVACY

The next three sections provide working definitions of three privacy concepts — personal privacy, confidentiality, and security — and a brief discussion of the relationships between these three concepts.[9] In addition, certain privacy issues associated with electronic government are addressed. Personal privacy pertains to an individual citizen's privacy status and rights. With respect to electronic government issues, the two key factors may be:

- Whether the information about an individual, including his or her personal attitudes or experiences, is known to another (privacy status), and
- Whether the individual has control over whether information is shared with anyone else (privacy rights).

Many definitions of personal privacy emphasize the second factor. Logically, however, an individual citizen's privacy may be preserved, enhanced, or reduced by the choices that he or she makes as well as by the actions of others, specifically, excessive intrusion.

The Federal government faces challenges in ensuring personal privacy while also implementing e-government. On-line privacy has become one of the key and most contentious issues surrounding the continued evolution of the Internet. In addition, record linkage[10] has sometimes been viewed as enhancing personal privacy because the collection of new data may be avoided. Conversely, record linkage is sometimes seen as reducing privacy because of the additional information provided about the individual citizen (the whole may be greater than the sum of its parts). In addition, because agency websites now make the results of research and statistical programs widely available to the public, there is an increased need to make sure that the confidentiality of personal data is strongly protected.

The Privacy Act can be viewed as striking a balance between government needs for information and individual privacy interests. In order to strike this balance, the Privacy Act contains requirements that implement the principle of "openness," which is a fair information practice that GAO has used to evaluate agency websites.[11] The openness principle dictates that an agency of the Federal government must not be secretive about its personal-data record-keeping policies, practices and systems. The requirements implementing the openness principle are intended to achieve two general goals:

(1)   Facilitate public scrutiny of Federal agency record-keeping policies, practices, and systems by interested and knowledgeable parties, and
(2)   Make the citizen aware of systems in which a record on him is likely to exist.

Specifically, the Privacy Act applies these principles only to information maintained in a system of records[12] and allows exceptions, under various circumstances, to the disclosure and use of information without the consent of the individual. The advent of electronic government has brought new challenges for Federal agencies to comply with the principles of the Privacy Act. In addition, various rules and regulations to implement the Privacy Act have been updated in attempts to make these requirements relevant in the era of the Internet and Web-based applications.

Posting Clear and Easily Accessed Privacy Policies

The government cannot realize the full potential of the Internet until citizens are confident that the government will protect their privacy when they visit its websites. To ensure that citizens have notice about how their personal information is handled when they visit Federal websites, in accordance with the openness principle, in June 1999 OMB issued a memorandum (M-99-18) that required Federal agencies to post privacy policies on their Internet websites and provided guidance for doing so. Specifically, the memorandum requires each agency to post privacy policies to (1) its principal websites, (2) any other known, major entry points to the websites, and (3) any web page where substantial personal information is collected from the public. The memorandum also requires agencies to post privacy policies that clearly and concisely inform visitors to the websites what information the agency collects about individuals, why the agency collects it, and how the agency will use it. Finally, the memorandum requires that privacy policies are clearly labeled and easily accessed when someone visits a website.

In early 2000, GAO reviewed 70 agencies' principal websites and found that 69 had privacy policies posted on their principal websites and one did not. In addition, of the 69 agency websites, two had privacy policies that GAO determined were not clearly labeled and easily accessed. Thus, 67 of the 70 agencies' principal websites reviewed had privacy policies that were clearly labeled and easily accessed. This appears to be considerable progress from a 1999 survey of selected Federal websites by a public interest group.[13]

Agency Use of Internet Cookies

While Internet cookies help to enable e-government and other web applications, agency use of some types of cookies pose privacy risks. Federal agencies are using cookies to enable electronic transactions and track visitors on their websites. Cookies may be classified as either session cookies or persistent cookies. Session cookies are short-lived, used only during a one-time on-line session, and expire when the user exits the browser. For example, session cookies could be used to support an interactive opinion survey. Persistent cookies remain stored on the user's computer until a specified expiration date; these cookies can be used by a website to track — through potential linkage to other data — a user's browsing behavior whenever the user returns to a site.

Agency use of persistent cookies poses privacy risks. Even if these cookies do not gather personally identifiable information, the data contained in them may be linked to a user after the website is left. For example, links may be established when users accessing the website give out personal information, such as their names or e-mail addresses; this information can uniquely identify them to the organization operating the website, even if that was not the original intent of the operating website. Once a persistent cookie is linked to personally identifiable information, it is relatively easy to learn users' browsing habits and keep track of viewed or downloaded web pages. This practice raises concerns about the privacy of users on Federal websites.

OMB's guidance (Memorandum 99-18) indicated that persistent cookies would generally not be used on Federal websites. Persistent cookies could be used only when agencies (1) provide clear and conspicuous notice of their use, (2) have a compelling need to gather the data on-site, (3) have appropriate and publicly disclosed privacy safeguards for handling information derived from cookies, and (4) have personal approval by the head of the agency.

In early 2001, GAO found that most of the websites it reviewed were following OMB's guidance on the use of cookies.[14] Of the 65 sites reviewed, 57 did not use persistent cookies on their websites. However, of the eight sites that were using persistent cookies, four did not disclose such use in their privacy policies, as required by OMB. The remaining four sites using persistent cookies did provide disclosure, but did not meet OMB's other conditions for using cookies. In addition, four other sites that did not use cookies did not post privacy policies on their home pages. When GAO brought these issues to the attention of each of the agencies, all of them took corrective action or stated that they were planning to take such action. The GAO also reported that although OMB's guidance has proved useful in ensuring that Federal websites address privacy issues, the guidance remains fragmented, with multiple documents addressing various aspects of website privacy and cookie issues. In addition, the guidance does not provide clear direction on the disclosure of session cookies.

FTC's Fair Information Principles

The web requires the collection of certain data — such as an Internet address — from a website user in order for the site to operate properly. However, collection of even this most basic data can be controversial because of citizens' apprehension about what information is collected and how it could be used. Concerned about the capacity of companies that conduct business over the web to collect, store, and analyze vast amounts of data about users on commercial websites, the FTC developed four fair information principles that it believes are widely accepted:

- **Notice.** Data collectors must disclose their information practices before collecting personal information from consumers.
- **Choice.** Consumers must be given options with respect to whether and how personal information collected from them may be used for purposes beyond those for which the information was provided.
- **Access.** Consumers should be able to view and contest the accuracy and completeness of data collected about them.
- **Security.** Data collectors must take reasonable steps to ensure that information collected from consumers is accurate and secure from unauthorized use.

While the FTC's fair information principles address Internet privacy issues in the commercial sector, specific laws (e.g., Privacy Act of 1974) are designed to protect citizens' privacy when agencies collect personal information. However, because the FTC's fair information principles are specifically designed for websites, the GAO used them to evaluate agency compliance with generally accepted practices in the commercial sector. According to the GAO, in mid-2000, all 65 Federal agencies' websites surveyed collected personal identifying information from users; 85 percent of the sites also posted a privacy notice. A majority of these Federal sites (69 percent) met FTC's criteria for the Notice principle.[15] However, a much smaller number of sites implemented the three remaining principles — Choice (45 percent), Access (17 percent), and Security (23 percent). Few of the Federal sites (3 percent) implemented elements of all four of FTC's fair information principles. Finally, a number of sites (22 percent) said they may allow third-party cookies, but fewer (14 percent) actually did.

Personal Privacy Issues and Solutions

As discussed above, the government's role in making its privacy policies transparent to citizens is an important one, especially in cases where individuals may not have the option of controlling the uses of their personal information. Another major issue associated with the development of electronic government is how individuals can control their information in an era where data on them can be linked or obtained without their knowledge. Various approaches can afford individuals greater control and could reduce concerns over inappropriate use by government of their information. These approaches include using traditional instruments (e.g., consent forms used in surveys) to give individuals greater choice; to using special data collection techniques or applying technological tools.

A special case relates to Federal research and statistical programs, where the results are often made available on agency webpages through public use data sets.[16] The GAO's record linkage and privacy study illuminates two key factors related to personal privacy and suggested solutions. The first personal privacy factor relates to sensitivity of information about individuals. For example, certain stigmatized or illegal behaviors, such as drinking, delinquency and sexual behavior, clearly qualify as sensitive information. When research is conducted, individuals may be concerned that others will obtain very sensitive information about them, and they therefore become reluctant to provide important survey information. Therefore, when sensitive information is needed from survey respondents, such as their immigration status, it may be appropriate to use special data collection techniques (e.g., indirect estimation techniques such as randomized response or item-counts) that are designed to reduce sensitivity but still allow estimation of the sensitive answer category.

The second personal privacy factor discussed in GAO's study is whether the individual has control over information being shared with anyone else. Consent is derived from a core concept of personal privacy — the notion that individuals should have the ability to control personal information about them. When consent to linkage for research or statistical purposes is not obtained, data subjects might not know that their records are being linked. Asking survey respondents, for example, whether they consent to linkage allows them to maintain some degree of control over the use of their records — because linkage is not performed for those who withhold consent. One approach, used in a health and retirement study, is use of an explicit consent form that asks the respondent's permission for specific records to be transferred from a government agency to a university for the purpose of linkage. The consent form explains in clear language which records will be transferred and linked, why linkage is needed, and conditions of release.

If citizens are concerned about controlling their personal information on government or other websites, they can find technological solutions commercially available to meet their privacy preferences. An example of a technological tool to protect privacy is the Platform for Privacy Preferences Project (P3P), developed by the World Wide Web Consortium. P3P is advertised to provide a simple, automated way for users to gain control of personal information.[17] In P3P, a standardized set of multiple-choice questions, covering all the major aspects of a site's privacy policies, presents information on how a site handles personal information. P3P-enabled websites make this information available in a standard, machine-readable format. P3P enabled browsers can "read" this formatted information automatically, compare it with the user's privacy preferences, and enable the users to act on what is seen.

ENSURING CONFIDENTIALITY

Confidentiality is a status, accorded to information, based on a decision, agreement, obligation or duty. This status requires that the recipient of personal data must control disclosure. Confidentiality may be based on one or more of the following:

- Promises, explicit or implicit, made to whomever provides information,[18]
- A legal requirement, or
- A duty to avoid disclosure of personal information, especially if the disclosure of the information would be harmful to the data provider.[19]

This last point is particularly important if the data provider differs from the data subject (e.g., when a family member or employer provides information about the data subject)[20] or if the data subject is a member of a vulnerable population. Along with the duty to avoid harming the data subject through disclosing personal information, this duty might also extend to others in a personal relationship to the data subject, such as family members.

Confidentiality and privacy issues can also arise when (1) data is shared among agencies or (2) in a government-to-citizen exchange (e.g., public use data files disseminated via the Internet or other means). GAO discussed many of these concerns in a recent report on record linkage for research and statistical purposes.[21] To provide new kinds of information, linkage projects tap survey data, existing records on individuals, and contextual data, such as geographic location of residence or work. For example, Internal Revenue Service and the Social Security Administration data are shared and linked by the Census Bureau to help produce intercensal estimates of the population. An example of a government to citizen exchange through public use data files is the Department of Health and Human Services (HHS) survey project (Add Health) that links individual teens' survey responses to those of their best friends, thus providing new information on peer influences. Teens' survey responses are also linked to test scores, parent surveys, and geographic data regarding their homes and schools.

There are several confidentiality issues, briefly discussed below, that may arise with respect to record linkage for research and statistical purposes:

Consent to linkage. In some instances, data subjects' initial consent to linkage is obtained. In other instances, however, data subjects may be unaware that, in essence, new information about them is being created when the data they have already provided to an agency is linked to other data. Issues of personal privacy and confidentiality may be intertwined in many linkage situations. Some linkages require data sharing between agencies; when this occurs, certain laws and policies concerning disclosure and consent are relevant. For example, the Privacy Act generally requires consent for disclosure from one agency to another, but there are exceptions.

Data sharing. In order to compile the information needed for record linkage and make the link, agencies must often share identifiable individual citizen-specific data. However, traditionally data have been kept separately, and various statutes have been enacted to prohibit or control certain kinds of data sharing. For example, confidentiality laws govern sharing statistical data, and there are legal controls on sharing income tax records with other agencies. Security risks, discussed below, could also arise during data sharing with another agency.

Reidentification risks. Some data sets are linked through a code-number procedure or stripped of explicit identifiers as soon after the linkage as possible; nevertheless, reidentification of at least some data subjects may be possible through a deductive process, so only controlled use would be appropriate. To facilitate broader access to statistical and research data, agencies have created more fully "deidentified" public-use data sets. Although many linked data sets are not made available for public use, some are — and concerns about the reidentification risks associated with these data sets are increasing.

Potential sensitivity. Potential sensitivity (risk of harm to data subjects if the data is released) cuts across confidentiality as well as privacy concerns. This is true for linked data as well as for single-source data sets. However, linkage may heighten the sensitivity of data that appear to be relatively innocuous. When sensitivity is increased, there is also a need for greater caution in releasing identifiable linked data to researchers outside the linking organization(s).

Each of these confidentiality issues can potentially be addressed through a toolbox of techniques and procedures, as well as through relevant strategies for effective data stewardship[22] that Federal agencies should use to protect the rights of citizens regarding the use of their data.

A useful privacy-protection toolbox, according to GAO, would contain a variety of tools for protecting the privacy of data subjects or otherwise building in confidentiality and security.[23] Among the tools specifically related to confidentiality would be the following:

- **Techniques for masked data sharing.** Third-party models for masked data sharing include a three-way linkage procedure to ensure that no one — not even the third party or the agencies supplying the data — will ever have access to both personal identifiers and linked data.

- **Procedures for lessening reidentification risks (including safer data and safer settings).** Most tools or techniques for lessening reidentification risks can be categorized in one of the following groups: (1) traditional safer data techniques, notably data-altering techniques developed by statisticians at the Census Bureau and the federal interagency Confidentiality and Data Access Committee; (2) more radical synthetic or simulated data techniques; and (3) "safer settings," such as the data centers or "data enclaves" pioneered at Census, National Center for Health Statistics (NCHS), and some other agencies.

- **Techniques to reduce the sensitivity of the data.** If techniques such as those proposed earlier in this chapter are not adopted, then stronger confidentiality procedures may become necessary in order to protect information of heightened sensitivity due to the linkage.

GAO described the techniques discussed above and others in hopes of stimulating increased efforts to build an effective privacy protection toolbox. Although presented in the context of using these techniques for record linkage in research and statistics, they may also be relevant for other e-government operations for which the privacy of individual respondents needs to be protected. Given the potential advantages and disadvantages, these techniques should be evaluated, selected and applied with care. Federal agencies have designed several strategies to address the issues discussed above. Some of the techniques are uniquely relevant to specific computer operations (e.g., statistical programs or record linkage), while others have a more general application. Some of these techniques are now in use at some agencies (e.g., the Census Bureau and National Center for Health Statistics) and would rightly be termed currently available tools. Others are procedural and may require some feasibility assessment.

IMPLEMENTING APPROPRIATE SECURITY CONTROLS

Security refers to safeguards for data and related systems. Safeguards against unauthorized access, unauthorized disclosure and misuse by internal or external parties may include

- Physical controls (e.g., locks, guards),
- System hardware, software, and system access controls (such as passwords), and accountability controls (such as audit trails),
- Special procedures for data transfer (e.g., encryption), and
- Rules and regulations for handling information.

Security may also include personnel policies (such as background checks), emergency preparedness and other kinds of measures. Security has been described by GAO as one of the toughest challenges to extending the reach of electronic government. Even with privacy policies and procedures, information can be compromised if the security of web servers, operating systems, and software applications involved is inadequate.

GAO designated information security as a government-wide high-risk area starting in 1997, because growing evidence indicated that controls over computerized Federal operations were not effective and the related risks were escalating. While GAO reported that many actions have been taken, current activity is not keeping pace with the growing threat. Consequently, critical operations, assets and sensitive information — gathered from the public and other sources — continue to be vulnerable to disruptions, data tampering, fraud, and inappropriate disclosure. Various agency inspectors general have also made many recommendations to agencies regarding specific steps needed to make their security programs more effective. Most agencies have heeded these recommendations and taken at least some corrective actions.

Security program management, however, continues to be a widespread and fundamental weakness. To address this concern, GAO issued a guide to provide a road map for managing risks through an ongoing cycle of activities coordinated by a central focal point.[24] The concepts contained in the guide have become widely adopted throughout the Federal government. Provisions of the FY 2001 Defense Authorization Act require agencies to adopt these risk management practices along with annual management evaluations and independent audits of agency security programs. Effective implementation of these legislative reforms would significantly lessen agencies' vulnerability. In order to improve IT performance government-wide and effectively address the remaining challenges, sustained and focused central leadership is also essential. Accordingly, GAO has stated that a Federal Chief Information Officer (CIO) is needed. Such a position could provide strong focus and attention to the full range of government-wide information resources management and technology issues.[25]

Besides the need to improve IT security management practices, technological solutions to information security concerns are being implemented throughout government agencies. For example, Public Key Infrastructure (PKI) technology, discussed below, is a system of computers, software and data that relies on certain sophisticated cryptographic techniques to secure on-line messages or transactions. PKI is recognized by government agencies as being an important piece of the solution to the Internet-based security problem.

The potential for improvements in service delivery and productivity that come with e-government also include many of the security risks faced by commercial systems as well as new ones. In some cases, the sensitive information and communications that may be involved in these activities will require greater security assurances than can be provided by simple security measures, such as requiring passwords to gain access to a system. As a result, the Federal government is increasingly promoting PKI technology for many electronic government applications. A PKI is a system of hardware, software, policies, and people that, when fully and properly implemented, can provide security assurances that are important in protecting sensitive communications and transactions.

Some e-government functions — for example, the dissemination of public informa-tion — probably do not need such rigorous PKI measures. However, many important communications and transactions that involve sensitive personal and financial data cannot safely be conducted through purely electronic means until critical security features, such as those provided by PKI, are enabled. The Chief Information Officer Council's Federal PKI Steering Committee (FPKISC) and the General Services Adminis-tration (GSA) have been the chief promoters of PKI technology in the Federal govern-ment. The committee and GSA have made progress in promoting the adoption of PKI by individual agencies and in laying the groundwork for the future development of a broader governmentwide PKI. The committee has developed a mechanism, called the Federal Bridge Certification Authority (FBCA), to connect disparate agency PKI applications into a broad system. In addition, GSA is sponsoring a program designed to develop and provide some of the elements of an off-the-shelf PKI to individual agencies to promote wider adoption of the technology.[26] Although progress has been made in seeding PKI technology throughout the government, designing and implementing large-scale sys-tems that use PKI technology remains a daunting task.

GAO found that full-featured PKI implementation — those that offer all of the security assurances needed for sensitive communications and transactions — is not yet commonplace in either the government or the private sector; a number of substantial challenges must be overcome before the technology can be widely and effectively deployed.[27] GAO noted that in order to develop an interoperable government-wide system, agency PKIs would have to work seamlessly with each other. However, current PKI products and implementation suffer from interoperability problems. Full-featured PKIs are rare, and those that exist are in the early stages of implementation and use. It is not yet known how well this technology will truly scale and interoperate as use grows. In addition, adoption of the technology may be impeded by the high cost associated with building a PKI and enabling software applications to use it. These costs can easily add up to millions of dollars. GAO concluded that an effective PKI — at any level within the government — would require well-defined policies and procedures for ensuring that an appropriate level of security is maintained on an ongoing basis. Establishing such policies will require resolution of a number of sensitive issues in areas such as privacy protection, encryption key recovery and employee identification, based on electronic keys. As with any security technology, the success of a PKI implementation will depend on how well people interact with the system and how well the system is implemented. Thus, Federal agencies will be faced with the challenge of training and involving both users and system administrators in the adoption of a technology that many find complex and difficult to understand.

THE NEED FOR DATA STEWARDSHIP

"Data stewardship" is an organizational commitment to ensure that identifiable information is collected, maintained, used, and disseminated in a way that:

- Respects privacy,
- Ensures confidentiality and security,
- Reduces reporting burden, and
- Promotes access to data for public policy.[28]

The concept of data stewardship covers all three concepts of privacy, confidentiality and security, and is an important element for protecting individual citizens' privacy rights. Stewardship is a particularly important concept when it comes to what is now being called "e-trust." Individuals entrust information about themselves to agencies or research organizations that then assume the stewardship role. This is critical since it carries responsibility for data subjects' personal privacy, confidentiality of data, and data security. To deal appropriately with these privacy issues, several management strategies may enhance agencies' or research units' efforts. Stewardship involves compliance with relevant laws and data stewards may draw on the tools described above. In addition, stewardship involves the coordination of project-by-project decisions, which may include (1) whether or not to conduct a data project, (2) whether to release data, (3) systems for accountability, and (4) organizational culture.

CONCLUSIONS

New information technologies offer many possibilities for the government to improve the quality and efficiency of its service to the American people. Websites are powerful tools for conveying information on topics relating to Federal activities, objectives, policies, and programs. Websites provide a simple and quick way for accessing information about the government and what it is doing on the people's behalf. Congressional interest in the benefits of electronic and Internet-based operations has resulted in the passage of laws designed to encourage the deployment of e-government functions, while also protecting individual citizens' privacy. Increasingly, Federal agencies are using the World Wide Web and other Internet-based applications to provide on-line public access to information and services, as well as to improve internal business operations. These developments have naturally resulted in concerns about protecting the privacy of individuals for whom information is electronically available.

The three concepts discussed in this chapter — personal privacy, confidentiality, and security — are closely interrelated. Notably, if a breach in data confidentiality were to occur, this might affect personal privacy. In addition, a breach in security could potentially affect both confidentiality and personal privacy. Similarly, protecting confidentiality helps protect personal privacy; and through various security measures, confidential information can be shielded, thus protecting the privacy of individual citizens who are the subjects of the stored data. The concepts and practices discussed in this chapter are important for Federal agencies to understand in their stewardship role of protecting individual citizens' data. A loss of confidence in Federal agencies' ability to protect individual citizens' data would have serious consequences for citizens' trust and participation in government programs.

ENDNOTES

[1]   Hart-Teeter poll (February 2001). This was a nationally representative survey among 1,017 American adults for the Council conducted January 4-6, 2001. The survey findings have a margin of error of 3.1 percent.

[2]   In this chapter, we do not focus on noncitizens.

[3]   The survey defined interactive service delivery as two-way communications in which a website visitor can submit information or payment, as well as receive information.

[4]   U.S. General Accounting Office (July 11, 2001).

[5]   Senate Report 104-8 on P.L. 104-13, p. 6.

[6]   Public Law 93-579, Section 2.

[7]   U.S. Office of Management and Budget (February, 1996). See the Basic Considerations and Assumptions section: (e.) The nation can benefit from government information disseminated both by Federal agencies and by diverse non-Federal parties, including State and local government agencies, educational and other not-for-profit institutions, and for-profit organizations. (f.) Because the public disclosure of government information is essential to the operation of a democracy, the management of Federal information resources should protect the public's right of access to government information. (g.) The individual's right to privacy must be protected in Federal government information activities involving personal information.

[8]   The information stored in a cookie includes, the cookie name, the unique identification number, the expiration date, and the domain. In general, most cookies are placed by the visited website. However, Some websites also allow the placement of a third-party cookie — that is, a cookie placed on a user's computer by a domain other than the site being visited.

[9]   These concepts have been variously defined. See Boruch and Cecil (1979); Duncan, Jabine and de Wolf (1993); Fanning (1999); and Lowrance (1997). The relationships between these concepts were discussed in U.S. General Accounting Office (April, 2001), 116-118.

[10]   Record linkage refers to a computer-based process that combines multiple sources of existing data.

[11]   In drafting the Privacy Act, Congress developed eight principles regarding the government's treatment of a person's information, of which openness is first. Each of these principles is manifest in one or more of the Privacy Act's specific requirements, and in their application they all require a balancing of individual, organizational, and societal interests.

[12]   The Privacy Act defines a "system of records" as any group of records under the control of an agency from which information is retrieved by the name of an individual or other particular identifier for an individual. In addition, the Privacy

Act authorizes 12 exceptions under which an agency may disclose information in its records without the subject's consent.

[13]   See Center for Democracy and Technology (April 1999). The results of the survey indicated that just over one-third of 46 Federal agencies had privacy policies linked from their home pages; eight agencies had privacy policies that were not on their home pages; and 22 agencies did not have privacy policies.

[14]   U.S. General Accounting Office (April 2001).

[15]   U.S. General Accounting Office (October 11, 2000).

[16]   Data on individuals gathered for research and statistical purposes can be originally collected through surveys, or from other sources, such as administrative records obtained to operate benefit and other programs.

[17]   See website at http://www.w3.org/P3P/. It should also be noted that P3P has been criticized as needing more development. See the Electronic Privacy Information Center website at http://www.epic.org/reports/prettypoorprivacy.html.

[18]   A data provider is the person who supplies information on a data subject; the data subject is the person or unit (e.g., family) described in recorded data. The data provider and the data subject may or may not be the same.

[19]   Duncan, Jabine and de Wolf (1993). Included here, for example, would be the obligation to honor pledges made in eliciting consent. See also Lowrance (1997), citing Penslar and Porter (1993).

[20]   Some believe that data should not be obtained from a data provider (e.g., physician) when the data provider has not received the consent of the data subject (e.g., patient) to transfer data for research purposes.

[21]   Record linkage is defined as combining (1) existing individual citizen-specific data with (2) additional data that refer to the same citizens, their family and friends, school or employer, area of residence or geographic environment. See U.S. General Accounting Office (April 2001).

[22]   A steward manages another's property, affairs, or, in this case, data. For agencies, stewardship includes functions of officials and staff, such as privacy officers and advocates, disclosure officials, and survey managers. Stewardship carries responsibility for data subjects' personal privacy, and data confidentiality and security.

[23]   U.S. General Accounting Office (April 2001).

[24]   U.S. General Accounting Office (May 1998).

[25]   U.S. General Accounting Office (July 11, 2001). This report contains a comprehensive listing of GAO reports on electronic government, privacy and IT security.

[26]   For example, the Department of Defense (DOD), the Department of Energy (DOE), the Federal Deposit Insurance Corporation (FDIC), the National Aeronautics and Space Administration (NASA), and the U.S. Patent and Trademark Office (PTO) have already implemented or are in the process of implementing PKI systems.

[27]   U.S. General Accounting Office (February 26, 2001).

[28]   Defined by Gerald W. Gates in a presentation by the U.S. Census Bureau.

REFERENCES

Boruch, R. F. & Cecil, J. S. (1979). *Assuring the confidentiality of social research data.* Philadelphia, PA: University of Pennsylvania Press.

Center for Democracy and Technology. (1999, April). *Policy vs. practice: A progress report on Federal government privacy notices on the World Wide Web.*

Council for Excellence in Government. (2001, February). *The next American revolution,* (Hart-Teeter poll reported in e-government).

Duncan, G. T., Jabine, T. B. & de Wolf, V. A. (1993). *Private lives and public policies: Confidentiality and accessibility of government statistics.* Washington, D.C.: National Academy Press.

Information Infrastructure Task Force. (1995, June 6). *Principles for providing and using personal information.*

Lowrance, W. W. (1997). *Privacy and health research: A report to the U.S. secretary of health and human services.* Washington, D.C.

Penslar, R. L. & Porter, J. P. (1993). *Institutional review board guidebook.* HHS Office for Human Research Protections. Available at: http://ohrp.osophs.dhhs.gov/irb/irb_guidebook.htm

U.S. Department of Health and Human Services. *Federal policy for the protection of human subjects.* Codified at title 45, part 46, subpart A of the *Code of Federal Regulations.*

U.S. Department of Health, Education and Welfare. (1993, July). *Report of the secretary's advisory committee on automated personal data systems, records, computers and the rights of citizens.*

U. S. General Accounting Office (GAO reports are available on the Web at www.gao.gov)
   Computer security: Weaknesses continue to place critical Federal operations and assets at risk (GAO-01-600T, April 5, 2001).
   Electronic government: Challenges must be addressed with effective leadership and management, Statement for the Record by David L. McClure, Director, Information Technology Management Issues (GAO-01-959T, July 11, 2001).
   Executive guide: Information security management — learning from leading organizations (GAO/AIMD-98-68, May 1998).
   Information security: Serious and widespread weaknesses persist at Federal agencies (GAO/AIMD-00-295, September 6, 2000).
   Internet privacy: Agencies' efforts to implement OMB's privacy policy (GAO-GGD-00-191, September 2000).
   Internet privacy: Comparison of Federal agency practices with FTC's fair information principles (GAO-01-113T, October 11, 2000).
   Internet privacy: Implementation of Federal guidance for agency use of "cookies" (GAO-01-424, April 2001).
   Information security: Advances and remaining challenges to adoption of public key infrastructure technology (GAO-01-277, February 26, 2001).
   Record linkage and privacy: Issues in creating new Federal research and statistical information (GAO-01-126SP, April 2001).
   U.S. postal service: Update on e-commerce activities and privacy protections (GAO-02-79, December 2001).

U.S. Office of Management and Budget. (1996, February). *Management of Federal information resources.* Circular No. A-130.

Chapter X

E-Procurement: State Government Learns from the Private Sector

Mark K. Krysiak
Maryland Department of General Services, USA

Carla Tucker
eMaryland Marketplace, USA

David Spitzer
eMaryland Marketplace, USA

Kevin Holland
eMaryland Marketplace, USA

ABSTRACT

This essay is a careful examination of the effect of leveraging and integrating the power of the Internet as a tool in the total procurement process and its relationship to the supply and demand for goods and services. This work will be of interest to both informed and uninformed readers who wish to broaden their understanding and the effect of e-Procurement within the process of government purchasing. The chapter begins with a discussion of legacy systems and past practice purchasing methods. This is followed by sections on public sector versus private sector business practices, business models for e-Procurement, culture changes, legislative changes allowing for adoption of e-Procurement and advisory committees. There are also sections addressing the benefits of e-Procurement versus paper-based procurement, vendor retention and training. A case study of eMaryland Marketplace, the State of Maryland's e-Procurement Portal, is discussed with particular attention given to theoretical use versus "real life" experience associated with implementing an e-Procurement system. Statistics are cited comparing savings achieved in user efficiency and direct cost between e-Procurement versus "paper" purchasing methods. A discussion is presented outlining added modules to the initial eMaryland Marketplace program. This discussion will include the future implementation of regular and reverse-auctions conducted online through the eMaryland Marketplace portal. In addition, a discussion ensues on how the capital project solicitations were brought onto eMaryland Marketplace. These include all construction, architectural, and engineering contracts let through the eMaryland Marketplace. Finally, recommendations are made for other state or local jurisdictions that are considering implementation of e-Procurement.

INTRODUCTION

There is a major move throughout government to streamline the procurement process. Most are incorporating technology into the equation with the expectation of saving time and reducing costs so that more can be accomplished with the same amount of funding. The Federal government led the initiative and began moving its services to the Internet long ago. Maryland followed suit in moving more of its services to the Internet. A major part of providing services online is Maryland's *eMaryland Marketplace* Procurement System (*eMM*). Maryland was the first State to implement a functional, full spectrum, e-Procurement system on the Internet, comprised of an interactive bid module and an e-Catalog module for contract implementation. *eMM* came out of the pilot period and became the procurement system of choice on March 8, 2000. The intent of this essay is to explain our former procurement system and its methods and compare it to our chosen method for current and future procurements.

LEGACY SYSTEMS

Maryland, like many other states, had a computerized procurement and finance system in place prior to e-commerce. In Maryland's case, that system is the Financial and Management Information System (FMIS), a software system for fixed asset accounting, tracking, and management. Within FMIS, Maryland uses the Advance Purchasing and Inventory Control System (ADPICS) which ties into R*STARS, the accounting system. ADPICs has subsystems that allow for requisition processing, bid processing, purchase orders and contracts, receiving, inventory control, and payables processing. Though it fulfills its stated objectives, ADPICs has proven to be cumbersome and not user-friendly.

PAST PRACTICE PROCUREMENT

Government, though often touted to be a leader in promoting new programs, has been slow to incorporate new technology in the workplace. Past practice, especially in procurement of goods and services, relied heavily upon paper-based transactions. The process started when prospective suppliers would fill out and submit a Bidder's Application as a paper document to the Department of General Services (DGS), Office of

Procurement and Contracting. This document contained company information and three-digit category codes of the company's field of interest. Procurement department staff would then review the document for correctness. In all cases, the document was returned to the sender for further action. The prospective bidder then had to make any necessary corrections or, at a minimum, covert the approved three-digit codes to five-digit commodity codes within the categories. The prospective bidder would then return the document to DGS where the process of entering the information into the computer would begin. Up to four staff people would spend most of their work day entering information into the legacy computer system. Further, no requirement for a company contact person was present in the legacy system. Once suppliers had been approved and entered into the legacy system, the legacy system could create a supplier list for a given Invitation to Bid created within ADPICs when created by a procurement officer. To finally be added to the vendor list required much time, effort and money for both the supplier and the State.

One additional problem with a vendor being placed on the vendor list was duplication of the company name. For example, one staff member may enter International Business Machines™(IBM™) to the vendor list. Should IBM send in a request to change something about their company information and a different staff member makes the correction or update, duplication could occur if the company name is not entered exactly as it was the first time. Therefore, International Business Machines could have a second listing as IBM and possibly have a third entry as I.B.M. The result would be a vendor list being bloated with entries for the same company with no easy way of correcting the mistake. Secondly, when a procurement officer prints a list of the prospective bidders on a project, often the same company would show up with multiple names listed. Unless the person in charge of printing, copying, addressing, and mailing out copies of the solicitation to interested parties was alert, time and money were wasted in producing bid packages for distribution.

Typically, using paper-based procurement, a requisition was created by a department wishing to solicit goods or services and was forwarded along with specifications, etc. to a procurement officer. Once received, the procurement officer would check the documents to insure they met with procurement regulations. Any discrepancy, such as a specification that limited competition, would be noted, marked-up on the hard copy, and sent back to the requisitioner via in-house mail or by postal service delivery for correction and re-submittal. Often, it took more than one revision before the solicitation could be generated and made available for bid by vendors or contractors. The cost for procurement increased as revisions were made and paperwork passed back and forth. Also, where the need to purchase goods or services was time sensitive, moving paper back and forth often created an atmosphere of finger pointing and passing blame for not meeting timelines. In some cases it led to unavailability of a product or having to pay an increased cost due to a shortened delivery time.

With small procurements (those under $25,000), DGS requires that the procurement be completed within ten days. For large procurements (those over $25, 000), there is a 45-day requirement. For solicitations requiring Board of Public Works approval, all must be completed in 90 days. Finally, for Architectural and Engineering solicitations, there is a 120-day completion requirement. All of these time frames included the delivery of documents from one party to another, regardless of the mode of delivery. Consequently, small procurements requiring completion within ten days generally ended up being phone or fax bids in order to have any chance of meeting the deadline. The other procurement periods were also difficult to achieve if anything went wrong during the process.

Another failure of the paper-based method of procurement is the persistent issue that has plagued government procurement for ages. The rising costs of paper, postage, duplication and access to information make open competition an expensive prospect and tend to discourage competition particularly in the small procurement arena. Time lost in reproducing documents and waiting for mail to arrive deals a crushing blow to any attempt to take advantage of "just-in-time" supply chain management. Money lost in traveling to different agency sites to pick up solicitations works against vendors and procurement officials.

Further, paper-based procurement perpetuates the use of antiquated documentation. This becomes evident when reading specifications that are out of date and reference products and features no longer in existence. This leads to vendor inquiries and protests that extend the procurement process even longer. Procurement officers and requisitioners must then spend time assessing and updating collateral material to the solicitation rather than focusing on retaining goods and services in a timely manner.

Though these and other problems are present in a paper-based procurement system, the most important may be the inability to communicate effectively and in a timely manner. The inability to communicate does not limit itself to public sector participants in the procurement process; it also affects private sector suppliers trying to conduct business with the State.

Past practice meant providing time for vendors to contact a State agency to request a bid package. This could be done by coming to the agency to purchase bid packages or by sending in a company check for documents. The check had to clear prior to a bid package being sent out. In and of itself, this would require an additional five days be added to the standard 20-day large procurement posting for clearance of the check and postal service delivery. However, should questions be raised by the supplier community requiring answers or resulting in change orders to the original solicitation, all interested parties were notified via postal delivery. This added an additional three days to the procurement process.

Paper bid documents had to be received and "clocked-in" by DGS staff members in the Bid Room and could only be received during normal business hours. Bid documents could be mailed in, brought in via paid courier, or brought in by a company employee. All of these options cost the supplier money. In addition, should the company choose to have an employee hand deliver the documents, other expenses were incurred. There was the cost of the employee's time in transit and on-site, the cost of wear and tear on a vehicle, the cost of fuel for the vehicle, and the cost of parking. In addition, there was the cost to the State to produce paper-based bid packages. There was the cost of printing the original documents, having someone create copies of the documents, the cost of envelopes or packaging, and the cost of the postage to mail the document package. Further, an estimate was made as to how many packages should be produced. Not only were they sending out bid packages, but copies were kept in the Bid Room for people to pick up. Many were not picked up and had to be recycled; many were also returned as undeliverable.

What is the result of paper-based procurement? Inefficiency, wasted time, money and effort create a breakdown in what should otherwise be a straightforward process.

THE PUBLIC SECTOR VS.
THE PRIVATE SECTOR

There are distinct differences in financing and budgeting between the public and private sectors. The public sector concentrates upon the total amount of money available for appropriation. Any savings achieved through the implementation of an *e-Procurement* system increases the funding available by decreasing the amount encumbered with each procurement.

The private sector relies on creating and maintaining a competitive advantage over its rivals. In addition, private sector companies must maintain profitability. These two creeds are what drive private sector operational efficiency. Within the public sector, efficiency is mollified by the Constitutional requirement to distribute authority among the various branches of government. The public sector must perform its budgeting, spending and accounting in accordance with legislative requirements mandating allocation of funds.

There are also vast differences between "business models" used in the public and private sectors. Specifically in procurement, government must serve needs that are not present in the private sector. Government must create open markets where all suppliers, especially small and minority businesses, can compete on a level playing field. Government must also try to combine local and state agencies into one buying organization to establish aggregate buying power, leading to dynamic pricing of goods and services. While working toward these goals, government must strive to improve procurement efficiency, meet legislative mandates, and comply with procurement regulations. By establishing an e-Procurement system that fulfills the needs of government while still satisfying legislative mandates and regulations, government can also increase the speed of procurement, leverage its buying power and increase compliance with established contracts while reducing "maverick" buying.

Electronic procurement creates a means of establishing real savings by reducing the direct and indirect costs associated with procurement. Direct cost savings are realized from receiving better pricing on actual goods and services. Indirect cost savings result from streamlining the requisition, approval, receiving, and pay processes. This may be accomplished by reassigning employees to other task assignments, reducing postal costs associated with sending out bid packages, reducing the usage of copy and fax machines, and the time savings associated with employees conducting business "the old fashioned way."

Further, having statewide and agency contracts online, available in e-Catalog format, provides an effective way to manage existing contracts. Electronic catalogs provide a means of overseeing the purchasing process, maintaining budget controls, automating payments, and ensuring compliance with purchasing policies, including reducing off-contract purchasing, and assigning responsibility to buyers doing the purchasing on behalf of their agency.

CHOOSING THE BEST PATH TO REDUCE INEFFICIENCY

In 1997, Governor Parris N. Glendening's Task Force on Procurement recognized a need for the State to take advantage of the latest technologies to create a more efficient and effective means of providing Maryland government entities with necessary goods and services. Maryland's growing Web presence and the latest technologies afforded the State a unique opportunity to assess its procurement process from a more e-centric perspective. To meet that goal, the DGS answered the challenge with a vision. The vision outlined an Internet-based procurement system containing the functionality required to maintain registered business rules and security standards while remaining flexible enough to be used by all public sector procurement agencies in Maryland. This new procurement system was to become an important part of the State's eMaryland initiative. Toward that end, all agencies were given legislative mandated process conversion goals: at least 50% of services by 2002, 65% by 2003, and 80% by 2004 will be available online. By being available to all State agencies, the proposed e-Procurement system would contribute to meeting this aggressive schedule.

The selected solution was to include online bid tabulation, e-mail enhanced approval processing, purchasing card payments and electronic purchase orders. The solution was to offer an electronic bid lockbox, vendor self-registration, solicitation e-mail notification, and vendor maintained catalogs. This solution was to be supplied by a single prime contractor at no cost to the State (a self-funded/subscription based business model). With these basic guidelines, DGS created a Request for Proposal (RFP) and asked interested IT companies to outline a solution to the request. The solution would be known as the *eMaryland Marketplace*.

WHY SELF-FUNDED

There were other business models available when Maryland began its search for an Internet-based e-Procurement system. DGS could have opted to pay a yearly fee to the IT provider for creating and maintaining the e-Procurement system. Another option would have been to pay a percentage or flat fee per transaction conducted through the service. After much thought, the self-funded model seemed to serve in the best interest of the State.

A self-funded model requires that suppliers wishing to sell to the State subscribe to the e-Procurement system. In the case of *eMaryland Marketplace*, the supplier community pays an annual subscription. The fee provides them with full access to all solicitations posted on the system for a 12-month period from the date of their registration.

Questions have arisen from some in the supplier community as to whether charging a subscription fee was legal and, for that matter, moral. The Annotated Code of Maryland Regulation 21.05.02.04: ".04 Public Notice.

A.   ***Distribution.*** Invitations for bids or notices of the availability of invitations for bids shall be mailed or otherwise furnished to a sufficient number of bidders for the purpose of securing competition. Notices of availability shall indicate where, when, and for how long invitations for bids may be obtained, generally describe the supply, service, or construction desired, and may contain other appropriate information. A fee or deposit may be charged for the invitation for bids documents."

As referenced, Maryland has the ability to charge a fee to suppliers wishing to sell to the State. Suppliers should look at the subscription fee as just another "cost of doing business" and treat it as such. Shipping, handling, stocking, and subscription fees are all legitimate fees that can be recouped by working them into the bid, whether incrementally or all at once.

CULTURE CHANGE

Organizations and their employees form "corporate cultures" over time. This holds true for both public and private sector organizations. It takes years to build a corporate culture. The private sector reacts to economic factors much more quickly than do public sector agencies in most cases. Private industry must stay current or face the consequence of a failed bottom line.

Government, on the other hand, reacts more slowly to market influences. There are several reasons why government is slow to react. Due to technological changes, government must be brought up to speed in the world of e-commerce. In some cases, government agencies do not have computers, e-mail and/or Internet service. This creates a need for training on modern equipment. There are also the typical reasons voiced by some employees. Long-time employees say, "I've been doing it this way for 30 years." Others say they are not comfortable using computers or that they do not appreciate the idea that computer software allows tracking of individual usage and production, ultimately giving supervisory personnel the ability to track and assign responsibility to individuals rather than groups or unknown entities. Resistance by employees sometimes encompasses the belief that technology may ultimately eliminate their job function. Culture change may be the most daunting task facing the move to e-Procurement within government.

LEGISLATIVE ACTION TO ALLOW E-COMMERCE

All government entities will have to foster legislative change to procurement law before moving toward e-commerce. Only a few short years ago there was no such thing as e-commerce, let alone laws, regulation, or guidelines pointing the way toward transition to conducting business over the Internet.

The Federal government assumed a leadership role in the initial stages of the electronic commerce movement. The single most important legislative measure adopted on the Federal level, which propelled the move to electronic commerce, is the Uniform Electronic Transaction Act (UETA).

"The Uniform Law Commissioners promulgated the Uniform Electronic Transactions Act (UETA) in 1999. It is the first comprehensive effort to prepare state law for the electronic commerce era. UETA represented the first national effort at providing some uniform rules to govern transactions

in electronic commerce that should serve in every state. The objective of UETA is to make sure that transactions in the electronic marketplace are as enforceable as transactions memorialized on paper and with manual signatures, but without changing any of the substantive rules of law that apply. This is a very limited objective — that an electronic record of a transaction is the equivalent of a paper record, and that an electronic signature will be given the same legal effect, whatever that might be, as a manual signature. The basic rules in UETA serve this single purpose." (National Conference of Commissioners, 2001)

LEGAL CHANGES WITHIN MARYLAND

Maryland has adopted legislation specific to the transition to electronic commerce. Among those bills allowing for e-commerce are Senate Bill 3 (UETA), Senate Bill 70 and House Bill 730.

Senate Bill 3, entitled Commercial Law — The Maryland Uniform Electronic Trans-actions Act, was adopted June 1, 2000, and is Maryland's accepted version of the Federal UETA. Maryland Senate Bill 70, entitled State Procurement — Electronic Transactions, was adopted on June 1, 2001. Senate Bill 70 authorized primary procurement units of State government to conduct the solicitation, bidding, award, execution and administration of a contract by electronic means. However, bidding on a contract solicited by electronic means constituted consent to conduct all elements of the procurement of that contract by electronic means; authorizing the charge of reasonable fees for using electronic means to conduct procurement.

House Bill 779, entitled Department of General Services — Procurements on Behalf of Private Schools, was adopted in March of 2002 and became effective October 1, 2002. The bill authorizes the Department of General Services to purchase materials, supplies, and equipment on behalf of specified private elementary and secondary schools; clarifying that the Department may purchase materials, supplies, and equipment for specified nonpublic institutions of higher education; and prohibiting the Department from purchasing religious materials on behalf of a private elementary or secondary school or non-public institutions of higher education.

Finally, House Bill 730, entitled State Procurement – Public Notice of Procurement, was adopted in March of 2002 and became effective October 1, 2002. House Bill 730 altered the methods of publication of notice of specified invitations for bids by specified units of State government by requiring notice to be given in an Internet-based version of the Maryland Contract Weekly and authorizing notice in the Internet-based *eMaryland Marketplace* procurement system managed by the Department of General Services; defining specified terms; etc.

DOING BUSINESS WITH
MARYLAND — ONLINE

Recognized nationally as a leader in e-Procurement, *eMaryland Marketplace* is an important element in the State of Maryland's e-Gov portfolio. Maryland's electronic business efforts have been ranked number one in the nation by the Center for Digital Government in its 2001 Digital State Survey. The research group says that no other state government has as comprehensive a suite of online services as Maryland. The 2001 survey ranked Maryland fourth, up from ninth the previous year, in providing online services to citizens and businesses.

eMaryland Marketplace and an extensive array of online services have helped Maryland to move forward on one of Governor Parris N. Glendening's top priorities: to make Maryland the national leader in delivering government services over the Internet. Toward that end, all agencies have been given legislative mandated process conversion goals: at least 50% of services by 2002, 65% by 2003, and 80% by 2004 will be available online.

Available to all State agencies, *eMM* contributes to meeting this aggressive schedule.

Maryland began moving its $8 billion in annual State purchasing to the Internet with an innovative G2B/B2G no-cost project that was launched March 8, 2000. Conceived and launched by the Maryland Department of General Services (DGS) procurement division, *eMaryland Marketplace* allows government agency buyers to establish real time communications and business transactions with vendors in a paperless environment, producing savings for both the State and local government agencies and their vendors.

Since its inception, *eMM* has posted more than $300 million in procurements on its Web site. The system has grown to include more than 100 State and local government agencies and more than 2,400 bidding vendors. State commodity contracts are loaded as catalogs and are available to public buyers in an "amazon.com™"manner. In addition to being the first fully functional state procurement platform to move beyond the develop-ment phase, *eMM* was also the first to use a self-funding model. This strategy alone saved the State millions in the development costs incurred by other states. A creative procurement included a proof-of-concept phase and commercial off-the-shelf software to ensure a real, not "virtual," launch in March 2000.

Additionally, *eMaryland Marketplace* broke ground as the first state-sponsored e-Procurement vehicle to include local governments from its inception, offering the advantages of intergovernmental aggregation from the outset. One of the goals of *eMM* is, in fact, to build and strengthen the "marketplace" of Maryland vendors. *eMM* makes government contracts more available and levels the playing field for participating vendors, regardless of their location or company size. It can be especially helpful for small businesses by providing access to significantly more bid opportunities while increasing efficiency and decreasing expense. All vendors experience efficiencies by accessing a single portal to conduct business with government buyers. Rather than allocating sales representatives to pick up bid solicitations at each agency, companies can now have immediate electronic access to the State business opportunities of interest to them.

On the government side, *eMM* has saved time and taxpayer dollars. Using *eMM*, procurement officers can purchase or solicit bids for goods and services in minutes, rather than days or weeks. Invoicing and payment are accelerated, even immediate when purchasing cards are used for payment. Significant benefits to Maryland's government procurement organizations are realized by reducing the average administrative cost per order by an estimated $100. The system reduces "maverick" buying, increases purchas-ing power through intergovernmental cooperative procurement and heightens compe-tition among a wider spectrum of suppliers.

For bid solicitations, vendors have two options: they can either log in regularly to view solicitations within their specified field or interest that have migrated to their desktop page or they may subscribe to e-mail notification that a bid solicitation has been posted matching their business profile and then log in to the site to view the solicitation. Bids submitted online can also be awarded through the *eMM* procurement system. Bids that have been awarded are listed as public information on the system, including bid amounts by responsive vendors.

e-Procurement allows suppliers to compete for contracts they might not have otherwise been aware of and reduces paper usage. Possible even more importantly, e-Procurement allows access to bids 24 hours per day, seven days per week, a 76% increase in accessibility compared to a normal 40-hour workweek at a State facility.

In moving more and more services online, Maryland is adding value to the services we provide to businesses and we are leveraging the potential of the Internet to meet the needs of all of our citizens and customers. This is the real benefit of being the Digital State.

THE E-CORE ADVISORY COMMITTEE

Although there are many commonalities, each buying agency has its own requirements and process variations. The rollout of *eMaryland Marketplace* was designed for voluntary adoption of the initial phase. To direct the evolution of the system and to facilitate cross-agency implementation, a core advisory committee was formed with key senior procurement officers. This advisory committee is called e-Core. It meets monthly to address "stovepipe" and implementation issues and provides important input to the *eMM* project team.

The e-Core Steering Committee includes representatives from the Comptroller's Office, the Treasurer's Office, Maryland's primary procurement agencies, senior management officials of major State agencies, and the heads of agencies responsible for accounting, auditing, and information technology. Because *eMM* is available to other public sector organizations, e-Core also includes representatives from higher education and local government.

COMMITTEE RESPONSIBILITIES

The Steering Committee is responsible for monitoring the progress of *eMaryland Marketplace* to ensure that milestones are met and agency needs are considered. While not involved in the day-to-day management of the project, e-Core provides input regarding major functionality issues and decisions.

In addition, it provides cross-agency communication and guidance as *eMM* is rolled out to the various agencies. The group identifies alternative methods for resolving policy questions and recommends solutions that are most advantageous to the State.

Agency-specific requirements are handled by the responsible agency and the *eMM* project office. Any intra-agency differences are addressed by e-Core. As necessary, e-Core will document cross-agency issues in writing with supporting analysis to submit to the appropriate designees of the Constitutional or statutory officers for resolution.

e-Core is responsible for working with agencies to define required changes in the agencies' structure or financial management processes. The group focuses more on long-term changes that implementation may require, rather than solely current policy issues. The result is improved communication, shared ownership and more successful rollout of this revolutionary new system.

Moving Forward

As members of the *eMaryland Marketplace* team and others involved in Maryland's key e-Government initiatives tackle new responsibilities, it is critically important that we remain focused on long-term goals. We face rapid change; advancement and tremendous opportunity as advancing technologies influence every aspect of business and service delivery. Now, the initiative moves forward to meet our long-term goal to bring design and construction contracts onto *eMM*. To lay the groundwork for this move, we are in the process of addressing certain issues specific to the construction and architecture and engineering industry, such as bonding, the transfer of large documents, and electronic job costing. Our ultimate goal is to provide citizens (individuals and businesses) with access to government information and services, as they are needed. We are working to provide expanded access to bid opportunities from various government agencies, boards and commissions through one point of entry enabling citizens to tap into resources available through State and local government based on areas of interest and need. As we begin our fourth year of operation, you can expect to see a continuing effort to broaden the scope and nature of the *eMaryland Marketplace*. In addition, we will continue efforts to streamline the purchasing process not just for government buyers, but for our private sector suppliers as well. As we continue the enormous task of transforming government business processes through technology, we will face tough questions, issues and challenges.

We believe that a big-picture perspective will serve the citizens of Maryland well as we address infrastructure, policy and operational issues in the move to improve service delivery through e-Procurement.

CONSTRUCTION, ARCHITECTURAL AND ENGINEERING ONLINE

Bringing construction, architectural, and engineering contracts online has been the focus of *eMM* for the past few months and has presented us the most challenge. In part, this is due to the nature of construction, architectural, and engineering contracts. They usually contain large specification files, bid and performance bonds, and generally require blueprints. The specifications (even if 500 or more pages long) do not hinder the process of making the documents available online. Large size documents can be transmitted electronically by various means. They may be attached in their original form, saved and attached in portable document format (.pdf using Adobe Acrobat Reader™, or saved and attached as an executable zip file. From a practical standpoint, executable zip files provide the easiest mode of transmitting documents in that they are compressed and can be downloaded quickly, can be opened by merely clicking on them, and can be saved for future use. Portable document format files (.pdf) are also a good venue for transmitting documents in that Adobe Acrobat Reader™is a free resource to everyone in the form of a download. Documents saved and attached in .pdf cannot be altered by the end user, making them an attractive solution to contract documents being transmitted between interested parties.

Blueprints present another challenge. Blueprints are graphic files and use up great amounts of computer hard drive space. There are options, however, to be considered in transmitting or receiving blueprints. Blueprints can be "pushed" through the Internet using a standard browser and computer, but require an extensive download time. Large businesses may have the equipment to receive and/or transmit blueprints, i.e.,a high-speed Internet connection, state of the art computer equipment and a plotter. Even so, large blueprints may take hours to download.

To maintain a level playing field and not inhibit trade and bid opportunities by smaller companies, blueprints must be available without the need of specialized, expensive equipment or software. Formerly, contractors could come to our office complex and purchase specification and plan packages or could send in a check and wait for the package to be mailed to them. Some contractors had to drive several hours to pick up a package.

Now, with the implementation of e-Procurement, other options must be considered as a means of making plans available to the contracting community. We will no longer make blueprints and plan packages available for pick up at our facility. Rather, we sought the means of making bid packages and blueprints available to the public without the need for DGS personnel to dipense the documents.

Several options were reviewed. The first option considered was to split the State into regions and solicit print houses in each region provide blueprinting services for our projects. This option would require an open bid competition among suppliers within each group.

The second option considered would require that blueprints be transmitted over the Internet or "burned" onto a CD and mailed to print houses. The CD or Internet transmission would have to be initiated by the State or by our appointed agent, such as the architect or engineer allotted the task. Using this option, we feel we can achieve cost savings to the contracting community, promote regionalized business, and allow the contractor to get plans locally rather than a centralized state building. The contractor could pick up blueprints at the print house or have them printed and sent directly to the business.

A third possibility would be to allow contractors to designate a particular print house. This, too, would require blueprints to be "pushed" via the Internet or "burned" onto a CD and sent to the contractor's print house of choice. This would provide the contractor the opportunity to deal with a printer that they are both familiar and comfortable with and would promote business at the local level. Again, the CD or Internet transmission would be initiated by the State or by our appointed agent.

The problem with options two and three, however, is that rather than simplifying the process, more work and expense would be involved in disseminating the information to a greater number of print houses. Also, the more print houses supplying the service, the less business each can expect from any particular project.

The final option, and the one we have chosen as our solution, is to implement a "virtual plan room." Several companies have now created plan room solutions wherby the procurement office submits either hard copy or electronic documents. Those documents, whether blueprints or detailed specifications, are then scanned onto the Plan Room Server in portable document format (.pdf). Once uploaded, a contractor can log in, review a list of available projects, choose a particular project, open the project and see thumbnail skethces of the blueprints, order a specific number of blueprints and bid packages, and specifiy how and where to deliver them. This method uses but one supplier of the virtual plan room to provide service, thus the process is simplified. Also, getting reports on usage of the plan room are more easily generated with but one provider of the service. The use of a virtual plan room seems to provide the best solution for making plans and blueprints available through the use of eProcurement.

THE REVERSE AUCTION AS AN AIDE TO THE PROCUREMENT PROCESS

Reverse auctions are becoming an attractive tool to support the procurement process. In a reverse auction, buyers specify the product they wish to purchase while Sellers of the product compete to offer the best price for the product over a predetermined timeframe. It should be noted that the laws and government regulations that apply to ordinary acquisitions also apply to reverse auctions. Maryland expects to implement the reverse auction process as an adjunct to *eMaryland Marketplace* in the fall of 2003. The path to implementation was cleared for reverse auctions by Senate Bill 86, adopted in March of 2002 and effective July 1, 2002. Senate Bill 86 authorizes auctions for the procurement of supplies with estimated contract value of $1,000,000 or more by specified State procurement units under specified conditions. These conditions require: a procurement officer to seek bids by issuing an invitation for auction bids under specified circumstances; establishing procedures for conducting procurement auctions and awarding procurement contracts by the use of an invitation for auction bids andnotice of specified awards.

Some of the more popular reasons for reverse auctions in e-Procurement are:

- Online auctions are small and minority business friendly. Vendors need only have an Internet connection with a computer and browser to access bid opportunities, often from government agencies the suppliers never knew of previously.

- By automating the procurement process, online auctions result in a reduction of paper-based processes and manual activities that were once necessary in the traditional procurement model.

- The bidding history for an auction is captured in a report that can provide procurement officers with information that can be used in future auctions.

- Reverse auctions promote reduced acquisition time by the bid process being conducted in real-time over the Internet. Competitive bids are received in minutes instead of days or weeks.

REGULAR AUCTIONS AS A COST SAVING MEASURE

Internet auctions are open markets. Sellers generally offer one item at a time, but sometimes offer multiple lots of the same item. The auction web sites often refer to auctions of multiple items as "Dutch" or "English" auctions. At some sites, the seller may sell all items at the price of the lowest successful bid. At other sites, the seller is entitled to the prices bid by each of the highest bidders.

Occasionally, Internet auction sellers set a "reserve price," which is the lowest price they will accept for an item. Some sites disclose the reserve price during the auction. The bidding for each auction closes at a scheduled time, when the highest bidder "wins." In the case of sales of multiple lots, the participants with the highest bids at the close of the auction are obligated to buy the items. If no one bids at or above the reserve price, the auction closes without a "winner." At the close of a successful auction, the buyer and seller communicate — usually by e-mail — to arrange for payment and delivery of the goods.

The *eMaryland Marketplace* will use regular auctions to dispose of surplus property and other goods no longer in public service for the State. Just as with the rest of the *eMM* system, local government can use the regular auction module for their own needs.

TRAINING THE USERS OF EMARYLAND MARKETPLACE

The *eMaryland Marketplace* team continues to provide training to those buyers and procurement officers wishing to learn how to post solicitations and purchase from e-Catalogs. Half-day courses are offered at no cost to the agency. If a State or Local agency has a training facility and enough interest among its purchasing agents, a member of the *eMM* team will teach the class at the agency. The eMM team arranges to hold training at a centralized training when there are small numbers of people coming from several different agencies. Users of the system may access online support at any time. Telephone support is available during normal business hours by contacting the helpline or via e-mail.

To address the issue of some small businesses that may not have Internet activity, DGS is installing computers in the Multi-Service Centers (MSCs) throughout the state. In addition, if a vendor is a member of their local Chamber of Commerce, they may have access to computers. In addition, every public library has computer terminals and Internet connections. People may use the library's computers at no charge to access the Internet and in most cases may download to disk. There is a per page charge for printing using the library's resources. In other words, if the Internet is available, *eMaryland Marketplace* is available anytime and anywhere.

VENDOR PARTICIPATION

The vendor list in our legacy system does not reflect an accurate account of the vendors available to bid on State and local contracts. After scrubbing the original list of over 26,000 vendors listed in the system, it was found that only about 5,000 were real vendors and were still in business. Closer investigation revealed that some State and quasi-State agencies used the legacy system to issue purchase orders for many things other than purchases of goods and services. Some used the system for "payroll." Other similar uses were found. Consequently, the vendor list contained a large list of names, many of which were not active vendors, suppliers or contractors. Using *eMM* allows us to have an accurate vendor list in that only paid subscribers are on the vendor list. The

Figure 1: Figure example of the eMaryland Marketplace eProcurement system statistics indicating total number of vendors and the total number of certified minority business enterprises registered to bid on State projects.

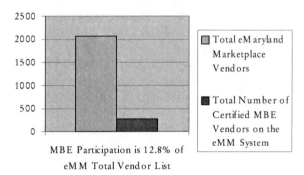

MBE Participation is 12.8% of
eMM Total Vendor List

subscriber also maintains his or her own vendor profile. If personnel changes take place at the company, the company is responsible for providing updated information within their profile. The same holds true for specifying their area of interest, phone numbers or e-mail addresses. DGS does review each vendor's profile to insure each is completed, but there are significant time and energy savings in not having a State employee continually having to update, remove, restore, or add vendors within the legacy system vendor list.

MINORITY AND SMALL BUSINESS PARTICIPATION

Contrary to popular belief, there has been a significant increase by Minority and Small Businesses participating in *eMM* over those listed in our legacy system. Over 12% of the subscribed vendors in *eMM* (Figure 2) are Maryland State Certified Minority

Figure 2: Figure example of legacy system statistics indicating total number of vendors, total number of vendors after the list was adjusted for accuracy, and the total number of certified minority business enterprises registered to bid on State projects.

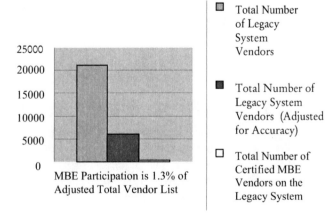

MBE Participation is 1.3% of
Adjusted Total Vendor List

Business Enterprises compared to only 1.3% of the total vendor base in our legacy system (Figure 1). There were those at the State and local level who voiced concern that small and minority businesses would not be able to participate in the bid process because *eMM* was online. It was also said that small and minority businesses did not have computers, Internet access or the wherewithal to retrieve and submit bids through an online e-Procurement system. This has not proved to be the case. Our experience has been that there is little to no difference in the percentage of small and/or minority business having computers and Internet access compared to other businesses.

In all cases, State contract holders are required to issue quarterly usage reports. We know of no vendors that use a typewriter to create reports and submit them as per their contract agreement. Issuance of reports, etc. is also required of contractors providing services to the State. Again, we know of no contractors using typewriters to generate reports, proposals, quotes or bids. Further, as we have discussed previously, other means of access are available to companies that do not have Internet access, namely libraries, Chamber of Commerce offices and our DGS Multi-Service Centers.

THE EFFECTIVE USE OF E-PROCUREMENT

Maryland implemented the first fully functional, Internet-based e-Procurement system at the State level. There were no predefined procedures or e-commerce systems available for Maryland from which to learn. Therefore, the *eMaryland Marketplace* system began as an idea, an idea that would require the system to be a work in progress. The only real constraints upon *eMM* were that it be user-friendly and meet all the Code of Maryland Regulations (COMAR) with respect to procurement issues. If COMAR limited or had no reference to e-Procurement, legislation would be introduced to smooth and promote the transition to e-Procurement.

For any process to succeed, including e-Procurement, it must meet the needs of its users. To insure the process is effective, efficient, and remains "cutting-edge," each user of the system has a responsibility to analyze and review how well the process works and what can be done to make it better.

Based upon user input, the evolution of technology and legislative action, the *eMM* system looks very little like the first edition. The end users' of the system have been the focal point of the *eMM* system from its inception. Users of the *eMM* system have been encouraged from the outset to weigh in with their thoughts on what works well and where improvements are needed. Each recommendation is taken seriously and is analyzed on merit. This approach works well in that it allows the actual users of *eMM* to determine how the system best meets their needs and promotes creative, forward thinking on their part.

STEPS TO E-PROCUREMENT SUCCESS

Over the past two and one-half years, we have found that there are certain steps that effectively promoted the move to e-Procurement. Each of these steps came about through trial and error. Each has withstood challenge.

1.   *Find Receivers, not a champion:* When we first began marketing *eMM* as the new way to conduct business, we looked for a single individual to champion the cause.

It did not take long to realize that a single champion was not the answer. It is often difficult for a single individual to effect change in a government agency unless that individual is the agency head. Rather, it is more effective to instill the idea in the procurement staff and mid-level managers who are receptive to changes that make their job easier. They, in turn, will pitch the change within their own agency. By having several "receivers" within the agency structure, a peer group is established. The peer group lends support to each member and helps to promote, encourage, and "talk up" new ideas within the agency.

2.   *Partnership means equal investment:* Each entity involved with the development and promotion of an e-Procurement system must make an equal investment. The developer of the system must make their staff available to address any issue with respect to the operation of or changes to the system. It is also imperative that they make themselves available for answering questions at outreach and training seminars for government users and the supplier community. State employees who staff the e-Procurement unit must take an equal stake in knowing the system and being available to answer help desk questions from State and supplier users efficiently and effectively. They must also be available to attend and promote the system at seminars throughout the state, as needed. End users, whether government or private sector users, must also invest in the operation and promotion of the system. They have a responsibility to assist each other in easing the transition to e-Procurement, sharing information in usage of the system and making recommendations for upgrades to the system.

3.   *The term "internal customer" is not an oxymoron:* All users of the system are your customers. Whether the users of the system are within your own agency or another state or local governmental agency, you must treat them as a customer and strive to make customer service a priority. Treat each user of the system just as you would like to be treated. Doing so promotes trust among your peers. Use each recommendation, comment or criticism as a stepping-stone to making the system better for all.

4.   *Implement locally, design globally:* Experience has shown that promoting and implementing e-Procurement in-house creates and promotes trust and understanding among the users and administrators. However, any e-Procurement system should be designed with enough flexibility to be used on a statewide, or global basis. It is important to remember that cities, counties, or school systems that may want to use the system may not use and adhere to the same procurement regulations governing the State.

5.   *Train locally, promote globally:* The premise for this action is similar to Item 4 above. In-house training offers an opportunity for first hand experience with examining the system for user-friendliness and developing straight-forward, easy to understand method of training. Promote the e-Procurement system on a more global basis using flyers, outreach events and word of mouth. Keep in mind that procurement professionals know and speak to other procurement officers in State service as well as local government agencies.

6.   *Create a team and hold scheduled briefing meetings:* Form a steering committee of individuals to discuss marketing strategies, system administration, training requirements Begin in-house and expand the team membership as user ship grows. It is important to hold regular progress meetings. Include the system developers,

in-house administrative personnel and normal users of the system at all meetings. Follow the same basic agenda for each meeting for continuity and include additional or unusual agenda items when they crop up. Delegate responsibility for agenda items to each member to promote and maintain interest in forwarding the project.

7.   ***There are no failures, only challenges and opportunities:*** When entering into a new process that had not been tested, DGS decided early on that there are no failures, only opportunities to find ways of meeting the challenges and overcoming them. Meet each head on and encourage creative thinking among team members to overcome each challenge as it arises. Each impediment should be treated as a learning experience and used to find ways of furthering the project.

8.   ***Remember the 80/20 rule:*** From a practical standpoint, the 80/20 rule holds true for e-Procurement applications and usage just as it does in standard business practice. Examples of the 80/20 rule are as follows:

- 80% of a problem can be solved by identifying the correct 20% of the issues;
- 80% of an instructor's time is taken up by 20% of the students;
- 80% of customer complaints are about the same 20% of your services;
- 80% of your time is spent on 20% of your customers, whether internal or external;
- 80% of your innovation comes from 20% of your co-workers or customers.

In nearly every case, the management team overseeing the implementation of an e-Procurement can increase their effective and efficient use of resources by analyzing the inputs required to produce the outputs they desire. The management team's challenge is to distinguish the right 20% from the trivial many in establishing policy, modifying the system, assigning personnel for training, and any other issue that may arise in conjunction with the system.

9.   ***Outreach to suppliers and procurement staff simultaneously:*** Experience has shown that procurement staff is hesitant to use a new system if suppliers are not available to bid on the solicitations they post. Likewise, suppliers are hesitant to join a system when there are not enough solicitations on which they can bid. To minimize hesitation among both segments of the user group, market to both simultaneously. Hold vendor outreach seminars and invite procurement officers to attend. In this manner, lines of communication and mutual understanding can be established. They may smooth the transition to e-Procurement for both user groups.

10. ***Manage momentum:*** Be prepared to adjust marketing plans to manage momentum of the transition to e-Procurement. It is better to market to a specific agency procurement staff and insure that they are using the new system effectively and efficiently to meet their needs rather than spreading your resources to thin in approaching numerous procurement staffs and not being able to promote and insure maximized usage.

11. ***Keep score:*** It is not enough to rely solely upon financial statements generated from procurement to measure an e-Procurement system. Statistics need to be keeping of every facet of system usage. Examples are: Who is using the system? What local or state agency they represent? Do they accept online bid submittal? Do they piggyback on statewide contracts? What statewide contracts are used the most?

How much money was spent by State and local government entities on statewide contracts? What percentage of their total allocation was spent through the e-Procurement system? How many vendors/suppliers are participating in the e-Procurement system? What percentage re-subscribes after the initial subscription period? What percent are minority business enterprises? What percent are small business enterprises? How much money was saved using e-Procurement? Remember that savings occur when the accepted bid price is less than previous procurement methods for the same goods and services. In addition, savings also occur when time is saved in the posting of solicitations using electronic means, copying costs, mailing costs, paper costs, and employee wages while performing the previously listed costing. These and any other pertinent information should be tracked in an ongoing manner so that success or the lack thereof may be measured. Current data must always be available for use in reporting functions and when preparing arguments to enhance and/or further system usage. Should the need arise for legislative action by State and/or local government to expand the e-Procurement system, current factual data must be available for formulating or explaining program changes.

12.   ***Redesign the system regularly:*** The *eMM* is currently in its third year of operation. To date, the *eMM* system has worked admirably. However, it barely resembles the first production rollout of the e-Procurement system put in place in at inception. Procurement officers, suppliers and administrative staff all suggest modifications to the system. Create a priority list of items suggested by the using community that will enhance the system's performance. Do not expect the system to ever be perfect or completely designed. It is far worse to allow the system to stagnate than to continue looking at ways to upgrade and intensify usage.

MISTAKES TO AVOID IN ANY E-PROCUREMENT ENDEAVOR

1.   ***Do not reinvent software:*** It is far better to use off-the-shelf (COTS) software whenever possible. The cost of COTS software will always be less than paying for a custom application that has not been tried and tested.

2.   ***Do not concentrate on buyers (or suppliers):*** As previously described, promote usage simultaneously to promote e-Procurement or any other facet of the system.

3.   ***Do not build a dedicated IT project team:*** IT staff generally concentrates solely on the intricacies of the e-Procurement system, not how well the system meets the needs of the user community. *Do* create a project team. Try to insure that every user and administrative group is represented on the team. This will promote a better understanding by all members of the team of the expectations and needs for everyone, including changes to the software.

4.   ***Do not build inflexible rules:*** Local and State governments usually operate under different procurement and other regulations. Do not build or implement an e-Procurement system that requires everyone to use it exactly the same way. Rather, build in the flexibility for every using group of procurement specialists to use the system in a manner consistent with their needs.

5. ***Do not expect buyers or vendors to understand e-Procurement:*** The purpose of an e-Procurement system is to provide a user-friendly, effective, efficient means of posting bid offerings for the public to respond to. Using "buzz" words and detailed schematics to explain how e-Procurement works will only serve to confuse most users. Focus on explaining the system simply, using normal procurement terminology when teaching procurement staff to use the system. For the supplier community, do the same. Communicate simply, succinctly and in terms common to the industry.

6. ***Do not be discouraged:*** People are creatures of habit as a rule. Any time that a new process, system or change is proposed, cynics will voice their concern. Some will express only negativity over any change to their old way of doing business. Others will voice any number of objections to changes to any system or process. Regardless of what obstacle you are confronted by, do not get discouraged. View each obstacle as a challenge to be overcome; use each victory as a benchmark of success. Change is inevitable. See change as an opportunity to accentuate all the positive things that e-Procurement offers to users of the system. Remain focused and move the project forward for the good of everyone using the system.

CONCLUSION

Private industry and the Federal government are far ahead of State and local government in all aspects of electronic business models. In order to meet the challenges of the electronic age, State and local government entities must commit to an increased presence in establishing and implementing electronic business processes. Any move toward e-commerce allows the using entity to analyze their business model and make changes to the process as needed. Antiquated means of communication and procurement must be addressed, updated and transitioned into a system that works within the parameters of the current business world. Procedures may need to be changed internally. Other issues may have to be addressed through legislative action. Many of the issues relating to e-commerce/e-Procurement have already been addressed at the federal level and/or by states such as Maryland that have already adopted electronic initiatives. State and local governments wishing to update their business processes would be wise to look at previously established programs as models for their own initiatives.

Change is inevitable. Be a part of it. Form a team of good people that are receptive to change. Support and promote innovation. Be tenacious in promoting, encouraging, and adopting changes and implementing programs that meet today's standards but are also user-friendly. Most importantly, never get discouraged.

REFERENCES

2001 National Conference of Commissioners on Uniform State Laws, (nd). Section Title: Annotated Code of Maryland Regulation 21.05.02.04

Introductions and Adoptions of Uniform Acts. Retrieved on July 8, 2002, from the World Wide Web: http://www.nccusl.org/nccusl/uniformact_summaries/uniformacts-s-ueta.asp)

Chapter XI

Issues in E-Commerce and E-Government Service Delivery

Genie N.L. Stowers
San Francisco State University, USA

ABSTRACT

This chapter examines three issues emerging in the fields of e-government service delivery and e-commerce — the need for and a potential structure for performance measures, the heightened need for security awareness around e-government and e-commerce, and the need for e-government web design centered around usability. Beginning these discussions are some basic definitions, a review of the current literature on e-government and a discussion of the stages of e-government development. The chapter concludes with a discussion of a future research agenda in e-service delivery and e-commerce.

Electronic government, or e-government, can be defined as the "use of technology, particularly web-based Internet applications, to enhance the access to and delivery of government information and service to citizens, business partners, employees, other agencies, and government entities" (McClure, 2000). As will be discussed later, e-commerce applications are a subset of e-government applications, and can be easily defined as "Business transactions conducted by electronic means other than conventional telephone service, e.g., facsimile or electronic mail (e-mail)" (National Telecommunications and Information Administration, 2002).

E-GOVERNMENT AND
E-SERVICE DELIVERY

In the short period in which research has been taking place on e-government, there has been a rapidly growing body of descriptive research concerning what is taking place at the international, federal, state and local levels. However, there has been virtually no research on the impacts of the fledgling e-government movement.

The forgotten ancestor of e-government and e-service delivery are the freenets, or community networks, that began in the 1980s as computerized bulletin board systems (BBSs) (Rheingold, 1993). These efforts were online discussion communities backed by government information and information about community events — they were early grassroots efforts to apply technology to the democratic process and neighborhood services. These efforts predated the wide diffusion of the World Wide Web and other graphical interfaces and were largely based upon text conferencing and Gopher data access systems. Their importance as ancestors is acknowledged by recognizing that several touted government websites are built directly on the backbones of previous freenets — Cleveland, Ohio Freenet (the very first of these online communities), Blacksburg, Virginia (Blacksburg Electronic Village or BEV), Santa Monica, California's Public Electronic Network (PEN), and Charlotte's Web in Charlottesville, North Carolina.

Throughout the history of the United States, scholars, activists, and democrats have been concerned with the ability of the everyday citizen to more actively participate in their governments and so, to improve the democratic potential of this representative democracy and society (Pool, 1983). As certain technological changes have occurred in American society, these changes have often been touted as the route to improve access and communication and so, to enhance democracy (Pool, 1983) — and the early freenets were no exception. In retrospect, some of these changes have improved access (telephone) and some have reduced it (television [Ranney, 1985]). The freenets encouraged participation, but then were swamped by the commercialization of the growing World Wide Web.

These community networks, or freenets, organized around virtual communities (Rheingold, 1993). Probably one of the most famous online communities was the Santa Monica, California Public Electronic Network (PEN). PEN was the first urban electronic communications network sponsored by the local government to offer free accounts to city residents. Established in 1989, its purpose was to increase citizen access to public information and increase citizen access to public officials through city-sponsored e-mail and discussion forums. PEN offered searchable information on a broad range of city services such as homeless shelters, consumer affairs, planning and building services, city council meetings, and an online connection to the city library catalog. Notable discussions occurred between residents and their elected officials — many of them quite heated and eventually driving off the officials. However, some community organizing projects were also created through PEN, like the SHWASHLOCK project. This grew out of a discussion on homelessness and led to the conversion of an old facility into SHowers, clothes WASHing, and LOCKers for the homeless.

As technology shifted from text-based communication tools that facilitated community discussion to graphics -based technology that allowed business to better make their case, and then e-commerce where business and business tools really flourished, individually based democratically sound communication floundered. Today, even the renowned Well, once the site of numerous online conversations and communities, has declined in usage and membership.

Beyond Community Networks to E-Government

By 1995, the World Wide Web was emerging as a graphical information provider, backed by the early Mosaic web browser. The graphical interface changed the dynamics of using technology for the provision of information since it eventually allowed business to take greater advantage of the medium for advertising and commercializing the information. When the tools were just text-based, business interests had not shown interest in using the tools for their own purposes and the technology had been left to community technology activists.

Thus began the push towards the use of the World Wide Web for both government and business usage. The research on these early efforts, as befits research in any new field, is largely descriptive and typically case study in nature, often just focusing on counting the number of jurisdictions taking advantage of any one technology or application.

In September 1995, early research had tracked the numbers of websites from six to 600 just 15 months later (Kanfer and Kolar, 1997). Survey research in 1995 (Moulder and Huffman, 1996) confirmed this extensive growth in the use of online services by local governments. By December 1996, Kanfer (1997) had found nearly 1,000 cities with websites while USA CityLink tracked over 1,300 by the summer of 1997.

Beyond tracking the level of activity, much of the research was anecdotal (Schooley, 1996; Greenberg, 1996) or survey research (Bimber, 1997; Fisher, Margolis, and Resnick, 1996) and focused upon how governments (Schooley, 1996), particularly state legislatures (Bourquard, 1994), and citizens (Rheingold, 1993), used the technology for changing pluralism and the political culture and discourse (Bimber, 1996). Since then, work on e-government has moved in two directions — that of democratic and political efforts online, which has blossomed, and that of the provision of government services in an online environment.

Efforts in the area of the e-service delivery have focused upon the description and validation of work at the local (Ho, 2002; Moon, 2002; Norris, Fletcher and Holden, 2001; West, 2001a, 2001b; Stowers, 1999; Moulder and Huffman, 1996), state (Gant and Gant, 2001; West, 2001; West, 2000; Stowers, 1999), federal (Cohen and Eimecke, 2001; West, 2001a; Stowers, 2002), and international (United Nations and American Society for Public Administration, 2001) levels. This work has also examined the presence or absence of basic e-government activity and subsequently, the existence of various features on e-government sites.

Researchers have also focused upon descriptions of web-based activity in various functional areas and utilizing various types of technologies. Research in functional areas has included much recent work on e-procurement (Moon, 2002), on web-based budgeting (Beckett, 2002, Stowers, 1998), and on how the courts are using the Internet (Kamal, 2002), among other areas. Researchers on electronic service delivery in general (Cohen and Eimecke, 2001, Stowers, 1995) have worked to describe the general efforts of governments moving towards an electronic service delivery future. Researchers have also examined the use of electronic commerce for government service delivery (Stowers, 2001) and, very recently, the use of intranets as an e-government tool (Mahler and Regan, 2001).

Using a variety of technologies, e-government service delivery has employed the following modes of service delivery (Stowers, 2001, 1995) on either the Internet to external audiences or to internal audiences via intranets (Mahler and Regan, 2002):

- Information access and delivery
- Document access and download
- Online databases
- Communication with officials
  - E-mail
  - Conferencing
  - Chat
  - Videoconferencing
- Online forms
- Interactive discussions
- Multimedia-streaming and Playback
- Online mapping/GIS applications
- E-commerce applications
- E-permitting
- Wireless applications

Today, 30.9 percent of all users over the age of three have used the Internet to access some government information. While this is a high proportion of users, only 12 percent used the Web to renew their drivers' licenses, seven percent to renew a professional license, and 4 percent to receive a recreational license (Pew Internet and American Life Project, 2002).

Stages of E-Service Delivery

The development of these technologies and services into some coherent form of e-government service delivery has followed several stages of development (Table 1), identified by four sets of researchers but following essentially the same themes. Stowers (1999) identified the stages as Virtual Bulletin Board, the Web Reaching Out, and 24/7 Service Delivery. Layne and Lee (2001) defined these stages as those of Cataloguing, Transaction, Vertical Integration, and Horizontal Integration, where integration referred either to integration of services vertically across various levels of government or horizontally across various fields of service. Sood (2000) defined the stages as presence, interaction, transaction, and transformation and the New Jersey Center for Governmental Studies defined the stages as static, interactive, transactional and transformational. But essentially, Sood's assessment is correct — the direction of e-government development began with only a presence and basic information where the technology was treated as simply another site on which to post information. Sites then moved to a stage where interaction and communication, between citizens, businesses, and government officials, was developed and was the focus. Next was where real e-service delivery was provided, as transactional efforts were the focus and citizens were able to accomplish largely simple, routine tasks online. Finally, some organizations are beginning to see real transformational possibilities occur, with the possibility of creating new and different ways for governments to serve their citizens.

Table 1: Comparative stages of e-government development

Stowers (1999)	Sood (2000)	Layne and Lee (2001)	CGS (2001)
Virtual Bulletin Board	Presence	Cataloguing	Static
Web Reaching Out	Interaction	Transaction	Interactive
24/7 Service Delivery	Transaction	Vertical Integration	Transactional
	Transformation	Horizontal Integration	Transformational

These developmental stages are cumulative — to achieve the transformational stage, any jurisdiction would have to work through and develop expertise and experience through all of other stages. No jurisdiction would just go straight to the transformational stage.   Each of the four stages would have included services like those presented as examples in Table 2. The types of technological applications used in each of these stages

Table 2: Delivery of e-services: Technologies and examples by stages of e-government development

Stages of E-Government Development (Revision of Sood, 2000)	Service Delivery Modes	Examples of E-Government Services- Internet or Intranet
Presence	• Information access and delivery • Document access and download • Online Mapping/GIS Applications	Providing names and phone numbers of government officials Allow access to government documents
Interaction and Communication	• Communication with officials • Multimedia–Streaming and Playback • Interactive discussions	Email forms to allow citizens to send requests for services to government officials Multimedia Presentations
Transaction	• Online databases • Online forms • E-Commerce Applications	E-commerce transactions like the purchase of hunting or fishing licenses, renewal of drivers' licenses and the purchase of government data or documents
Transformation	• Online Mapping/GIS Applications • E-Permitting/Wireless Applications	Smart permitting involving online request submissions, GIS, document management, 3D modeling of proposed projects, wireless applications

of e-service delivery are also presented in Table 2. For instance, documents are provided in the presence stage while e-commerce applications are part of the transactions stage.

PERFORMANCE MEASUREMENT FOR E-SERVICE DELIVERY

Since governments are rapidly moving through these developmental stages, it is far past time to begin with a concentrated effort at measuring the effects of these activities and ensure accountability for the citizens whose tax dollars are funding these efforts. The effects that would be examined involve cost efficiency, perceived cost efficiency, trust that citizens had in their government that could be attributed to their city's e-government efforts, sense of efficacy for citizens, satisfaction that citizens had in their government's efforts, and the ability of citizens to participate. What is working and, what is not?

How well are governments doing to provide these services? Although McClure, Sprehe and Eschenfelder (2000) have worked on performance measures for federal websites, there has been very little other work on proposed performance measures for e-government or e-service delivery. Thus, the very basics of performance measure development must be accomplished. Table 3 presents some initial proposed input, output and outcome measures proposed for e-service delivery, organized according to the mode of e-service delivery.

SECURITY ISSUES

Another crucial and growing issue for the near future of e-service delivery and e-commerce is the security of our information infrastructure and government information applications. Given the increased reliance of our economy and our entire society upon computers, information, e-government applications and other technologies, attacks on the infrastructure, computer systems and computer networks presents an appealing target to many criminals and terrorists (as well as to other nations interested in cyber warfare). As recently as October 22, 2002, the Internet sustained a denial of service attack against nine of the Internet's 13 root servers (please see Table 3).

As recognized in the Clinton Administration's Executive Order 13010, "Certain national infrastructures are so vital that their incapacity or destruction would have a debilitating impact on the defense or economic security of the United States. These critical infrastructures include telecommunications, electrical power systems, gas and oil storage and transportation, banking and finance, transportation, water supply systems, emergency services (including medical, police, fire and rescue), and continuity of government. Threats to these critical infrastructures fall into two categories: physical threats to tangible property ("physical threats") and threats of electronic, radio frequency, or computer-based attacks on the information or communications components that control critical infrastructures ("cyber-threats"). Because many of these critical infrastructures are owned and operated by the private sector, it is essential that the government and private sector work together to develop a strategy for protecting them and assuring their continued operation" (Cordesman and Cordesman, 2002, p. 56).

Table 3: Potential performance measures for e-service delivery and e-commerce

Mode of E-Service Delivery	Input Measures	Output Measures	Outcome Measures
Information access and delivery	- Amount of staff time to develop	- Number of hits on site/user contact sessions - Number of downloads - Amount of time spent on site	- Level of citizen satisfaction with government
Document access and download	- Amount of staff costs	- Number of hits on site/user contact sessions - Number of downloads	- Level of citizen satisfaction with government services
Communication with officials and agency	- Amount of other costs to develop - Amount of vendor time - Amount of vendor costs	- Number of hits on site/user contact sessions - Number of emails sent to agency and/or officials - Number of emails returned - Amount of time required for response back to citizens - Number of email requests successfully resolved	- Level of citizen trust in government
Multimedia– Streaming and Playback	- Total cost per user session - Staff time to maintain and update	- Number of hits on site/user contact sessions - Number of times presentations are played - Feedback on presentations	
Interactive discussions		- Number of hits on site/user contact sessions - Number of different topics discussed - Length of discussion - Resolution of discussion—number of problems resolved	- Costs saved by e-service provision
Online databases		- Number of hits on site/user contact sessions - Number of times databases are accessed - Information accessed most frequently	
Online forms		- Number of hits on site/user contact sessions - Number of times forms completed - Form requested most frequently	- Staff time saved by e-service provision
Online Mapping/GIS Applications		- Number of hits on site/user contact sessions - Application requested most frequently - Number of different types of maps requested	- % Site downtime
E-Commerce Applications		- Number of hits on site/user contact sessions - Number of e-commerce applications accessed - Number of applications processed - Dollar amount processed through sites	
E-Permitting		- Number of hits on site/user contact sessions - Number of permits processed	
Wireless Applications		- Number of hits on site/user contact sessions - Number of applications processed	

This critical information and technology infrastructure is now vulnerable to information warfare attacks from, to quote Director of Central Intelligence George Tenet, "national intelligence and military organizations, terrorists, criminals, industrial competitors, hackers and disgruntled or disloyal insiders" (Cordesman and Cordesman, 2002, p. 25). Cyber crimes have grown at an enormous pace, although there is a wide range in these attacks between the most serious and those which do not have much effect, i.e., low level hacker attacks. The range of these attacks can be perpetrated by anyone from those creating havoc for fun to state terrorists trying to bring down defense systems or entire economies.

Jordan (2002) illustrates the significance of the threat from cyber-crime, cyber-terrorism and information warfare:

"All of these computers and computer-dependent systems are vulnerable to physical and electronic ["cyber"] attack — from the computers on which individuals store and process classified information, privileged attorney-client information, or proprietary data, to our nationwide telecommunication and banking systems. Indeed the year 2000 {"Y2K"} problem demonstrates that we are even vulnerable to our own misfeasance and poor planning. A single non-nuclear, electromagnetic pulse can destroy or degrade circuit boards and chips, or erase all electronic media on Wall Street, in the Pentagon, or your local bank. The loss of a single satellite can terminate service for over 90 percent of the 45 million pages in the United States, as well as interrupt thousands of cable television stations and credit card transactions. GPS signals can be spoofed or degraded, or used as part of highly accurate targeting systems. Advanced computer technology can help build nuclear weapons. Internet and computer crime is so simple that two teenagers in Cloverdale, California, with a mentor in Israel can break into sensitive national security systems at the Department of Defense. Information warfare experts can use global television to selectively influence political and economic decisions or produce epileptic-like spasms in viewers. Cyber warfare of the 21st century could significantly impact the daily lives of every man, woman, and child in America" (Jordan, 2002).

In 1997, President Clinton's Commission on Critical Infrastructure Protection identified five types of potential attacks. These are cyber-attacks:
1. On a specific database of a specific owner
2. With the purpose of accessing a network
3. For espionage purposes
4. In order to shut down service (a "denial of service" attack)
5. In order to introduce harmful instructions to a computer system (Cordesman and Cordesman, 2002)

Given the types of databases, networks, and computer systems in use today for electronic service delivery, disruption of these systems by any of these means could be inconvenient to extremely damaging. Types of attacks particularly crucial to e-service delivery would be those on the specific database of an agency, on an agency's network, a denial of service attack, or the introduction of harmful instructions to a system (anything from a virus to the defacing of a government website).

The types of cyber-weapons include:

- Reconnaissance attempts, or sensitive intrusions into systems, are attempts by hackers to break into and explore a site with an eye to future intrusions and attacks. While not damaging themselves, the knowledge gained during these reconnaissance events is often used later to damage systems.

- Root compromise attempts are when hackers obtain access to the core (top directory) of a system, including administrator authorities and passwords. This allows them to move throughout a system and gives great power and control over a system. A hacker with root authority can cause enormous damage to a system since they essentially control it.

- Malicious codes (viruses, worms, Trojan horses) are pieces of computer code which are inserted into computer systems without the owner's knowledge; depending on their construction, they can wreak havoc on those systems, either taking up available memory, writing over existing programming, attaching themselves to other programs, or accomplishing other damaging tasks. Worms are types of viruses that can replicate themselves while Trojan horses are dangerous pieces of code that appear to be harmless. Viruses and other malicious codes can cause a great deal of monetary damage to companies and to governments by destroying and damaging systems and software.

- Denial of service (DOS) attacks are those brought about by repeated requests for service to a website in order to overwhelm the site and shut it down or prevent other users from accessing the site. In recent years, several denial of service attacks have caused commercial sites to shut down with resulting loss of millions of dollars, including the October 2002 attack.

- User compromise, when an individual user password or account is compromised and the attacker works their way into the system.

- Website defacement is the result of hackers breaking into government agency or private firm web servers and changing their appearance or content. Several U.S. federal government websites (U.S. Senate pages, FBI page, and others) have been recent targets of these types of attacks.

- Attacks on physical information infrastructure, i.e., cell towers, Internet infrastructure, can unleash untold damage upon the entire system.

Figure 1 describes the types of cyber-crime incidents that occurred in 2000, 2001 and estimated for 2002. Clearly, the types of attacks have changed over the years and differ according to some specific attacks that occurred during this period. Estimates for 2002 are for 414,345 reconnaissance attacks and 215 attacks involving malicious code of some sort (viruses, worms, etc.). Most common cyber crimes were attempts to check out systems (reconnaissance) (37 percent) and attempts to gain root, or administrator access, which can be used to manipulate the system (18 percent). Those receiving the most publicity, viruses (5 percent) and denial of service attacks (5 percent), together comprise ten percent of the incidents although at one point, the Defense Department alone was experiencing up to 100 hacker attacks every day (Cordesman and Cordesman, 2002, p. 16)

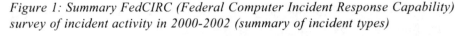

Figure 1: Summary FedCIRC (Federal Computer Incident Response Capability) survey of incident activity in 2000-2002 (summary of incident types)

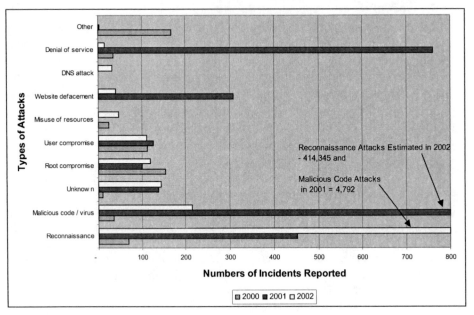

Source: Derived from FEDCIRC Activity Statistics, 2002. Federal Computer Incident Response Center, General Services Administration. Available at http:// www.fedcirc.gov/stats.html.

Clearly, after the September 11th attacks, all government web managers had to consider another issue — what information was being posted on their websites, in the interest of openness and providing information to the public, that could be used by terrorists against the United States or jurisdictions within it.

After the attacks, Federal web managers in particular, but also those of state and local government, had to reassess the content on their sites — and to remove that information which could be used by terrorists to harm the United States. In fact, even in 2000, the U.S. General Accounting Office (2000) was pointing out the potential harm in providing one site where users with damage in mind could easily access information. But those concerns have, of course, been severely heightened in light of the terrorist attacks.

It is particularly important for e-government managers to protect the privacy of the data in databases and other information about citizens that they possess. With e-government growing in acceptability and credibility, citizens must be assured that their information is protected. Government data posted online in databases is often more sensitive than credit card information, whose security is always a critical issue. For example, governments provide and use online data in the e-filing of taxes, in providing financial status information when applying for student financial aid, applying for a government job, and replacing a Medicare or Medicaid card.

All of these applications — and many more — require privacy and the ability to conduct secure transactions. It is crucial that websites provide privacy and do not include sensitive information about private citizens, government employees, or contractors — in order to continue to enjoy the public's confidence. In 2000, the U.S. Office of Management and Budget promulgated specific guidelines on the use of "cookies" (Government Accounting Office, 2001) on the part of Federal agencies to protect the privacy of individual users. Additional policies must be established in order to ensure that privacy and security is protected.

WEB USABILITY

A last critical issue to be discussed here is the importance of website and service usability for public sector websites. Government sites have to be accessible in every sense of the term to individuals with varying understanding of government, of computers and of the Internet — as well as accessible to individuals with disabilities. The digital divide in terms of access to computers and the Internet still exists even if it is diminishing (U.S. Department of Commerce, 2001). However, one digital divide has yet to be addressed — that of individuals who, even if they get to the Internet sites run by the public sector, cannot effectively find what they need. Due to lack of training and experience with government and lack of knowledge about how government agencies are organized, many users cannot find the information they need even if they have the computers and the Internet access. The design of the websites themselves can either help or hinder in this regard, depending on whether or not they are designed with the informed user in mind.

Working class individuals, those who already contact government least often for assistance with services, are also those who know the least about government, how government is organized, how to find information about and from government, and how to seek the correct services from government. If sites are designed so that *only* those who really understand governments and how they work can successfully navigate through them, another important barrier has been raised, the "other digital divide."

Bridging the "digital divide" therefore does not mean just making computers themselves accessible but also making websites themselves more user-friendly and easy to use. Designers and developers of public sector websites must assume that those using their sites have limited training and experience and will need sites that are easy to use and designed with usability and effective information architecture in mind.

Removing usability barriers includes designing for important elements of public sector website use (Nielsen, 2000; Reiss, 2000; Rosenfeld and Morville, 1998). These features include:
1.   Delivery of effective online information and services is crucial to any site.
2.   Effective information architecture, defined as how the information of a website is structured or organized or how the information is first presented to the user on the website. Incorporated into this concept is the organization of the content and structure of the site, organized so that those who are unfamiliar with government can find the services and information they need.
3.   Usability and help features — making sure users can get around the site, find what they want and what they need.

4.   Accessibility features must be included to ensure individuals with disabilities can use the sites.
5.   Legitimacy features — ensuring users' confidence in the sites and the content and services found on them.

The presence or absence of these features on public sector websites can greatly affect the ability of a user to find information and services that might be available on the site and to effectively use those services.

User Help Features. In addition to the basic services provided online by governments, it is essential that governments provide effective help to users visiting their sites, even assuming that they have limited experience with government, government services, and finding information on websites. Usability features include those that assist the user in finding information, finding services, and in finding their way around the website — like the usefulness of the search engines and visible help features, the existence of a help page, frequently asked questions (FAQs) about the site, site maps and tutorials on using the site. Ten user help features identified and found on public sector websites are listed in Table 4.

Table 4: User help features

Feature	Explanation
About the site	Link to information about the site
Email us	Email us for more information or for help with the site
FAQs	Frequently Asked Questions about the site
Feedback	Give us feedback about how the site works
Help	Agency-provided help with using the site
Index	Index of information, data and agencies available on the site
Search	Facility to allow users to search the site
Sitemap	Visual representation of sections of the website
User Tips	Helpful hints on how users can use the site
Other	Other user help features, including the use of other languages

Service Navigation Features. Designing a web site for effective use also means thinking about the services, information and content with the user in mind — in the case of public sector sites, citizens without in-depth knowledge of government and how it works. Web designers must design features that can lead users right to the services they are seeking and most want in addition to helping them move around the site most efficiently. Twenty-two possible features to assist users in finding services are listed in Table 5.

Accessibility Features. Accessibility features, those enabling individuals with disabilities to access the sites, are also crucial for websites. This is particularly true for public sector websites, which must ensure accessibility to all citizens. Some of these features include having alternative versions of the site written in just text (and accessible with text browsers like Lynx), having all graphics labeled with alternate text titles, having each frame clearly labeled with text names, reducing animations, and limiting other

Table 5: Service navigation aid features

Feature	Explanation
About	About the services available on the site
Answers a to z	Alphabetized listings of answers to questions
Calendars	Calendars of government events
Do you know/how do I..?	List of questions organized according to major service areas from the citizen's point of view, stating "how do I do x or y?"
E-government services	Direct link from home page to all e-government services
Events	Link to information on major events
Facilities locator	Direct linkage to way to locate government offices
Featured link/spotlight	Many sites have featured programs or linkages
FOIA	Many federal sites have direct linkages to Freedom of Information Act information on their site
Hot topics	Link to information on what are considered currently important issues
In the news/news online/ press room	News items about the agency
Just for students/kids	Collection of links or information about the agency designed for use by children
Link to all agencies	Linkages to listings of all agencies
Link to contact information	Linkages to direct contact information
Maps	Link to maps relevant to agencies
Online public notice	Public notices are posted online
Most visited/frequently requested site	Links to or listings of the most frequently visited sites, indicating the importance of that information
Popular services/major programs	Links to popular services or major programs
Special initiatives	Current, new or special initiatives from the agency
Welcome	Welcoming statement from the director
What's new	Listing of new items posted on the site

features that would make it difficult for someone to read information from a site to a user with limited vision.   Section 508 of the Rehabilitation Act of 1973, amended in 1998, required that all federal electronic and information technology be accessible to individuals with disabilities (with a focus upon new additions to those sites) by June 25, 2001.

Features Adding to the Legitimacy of the Site. Finally, there are several features that lead to added legitimacy for government websites along with reduction of individual fears (Gant and Gant, 2001).   These include:

- Endorsements of the site by outside, third parties
- The presence of a visible security policy for the site
- Privacy policies that can be read by users and which inform users of the degree to which their privacy will be respected
- Disclaimer statements, which inform the user of the exact nature of the information available on the site — which information is the product of the agency involved and what other information is available, through linkages
- Contact information so users know exactly how to reach the agency if there are additional questions
- Information on the date the site was last updated, which provides vital information to the user about the currency of the information

Information Architecture Features. The information architecture for a website focuses on the information is organized and labeled — particularly on the home page, or splash page. For government agencies, this is important since not all citizens have a good working knowledge of how government agencies are organized. So often, a traditional organization centered on listing the agencies in a department is not useful. Eleven types of information architecture have been identified — these vary from being organized like a newspaper to being organized according to the services provided by the agency to being organized according to the needs of individual audiences and clienteles of the particular agency. Table 6 presents these types and briefly defines each.

Table 6: Types of information architecture

Type of Information Architecture	Description... Site is Organized Around:
Audience/Market	The needs of particular audiences or markets. For example, Firstgov.gov has information organized around Online Services for Citizens, for Businesses, and for Governments
Agencies/Departments	Listings of agencies or departments
Branch of government	The various branches of government represented
Events	Events occurring in the life cycle of the agency
Metaphor	According to some metaphor
Officials	The main officials in the agency
Services/Tasks/Functions/ Processes	The services, tasks, or functions offered by the agency – like Living in, Working in, Visiting Jurisdiction
Topics/Issues	Various topics, often just miscellaneous listings of topics
Personalized/Customizable	Customizable site; user can organize the site according to their own preferences, within certain limits
Newspaper listing	Listings of news items; newspaper - like in appearance
Hybrid site	Combinations of all of the above

RESEARCH AGENDA FOR THE FUTURE

As the field of e-service delivery continues to grow and develop, much research should be done to fully understand the activity and its outcomes. This is made difficult by the speed in which the services are always growing and changing, a speed that matches the technologies on which they are based. As pointed out in the beginning of this chapter, the research in recent years has begun to keep pace with these changes but much still needs to be done. That agenda of needed research includes the following:

- **Cases of innovative service delivery.** There are many innovative jurisdictions that are always ahead of the curve in e-service delivery — San Carlos, CA, and the State of Washington are two of them. Why and how do they manage to keep up with the rate of change that they are perpetrating?

- **Performance measures.** This chapter includes suggestions for performance measures to be used as accountability for performance develops in e-service delivery. What is already being done, and what are the measurements showing? What is working, and what is not?

- **Relationship of e-government strategic plans to implementation.** Many jurisdictions have done extensive strategic planning for their e-government and e-service delivery efforts — what have those strategic plans contained and how must of those plans were actually implemented? What have been the issues involved in getting those plans implemented?

- **Use of e-government tools by courts.** As pointed out in this chapter, there has been extensive work on e-service delivery by the executive branch and agencies under its purview. There has also been extensive work on the use of the Internet by the legislature, but little work to date on how courts have been utilizing this technology. One study cited here (Kamal, 2002) has outlined several cases and the types of applications being used but there is much that needs to be done on this "other" branch of government.

- **Digital signatures.** The importance of digital signatures for the future development of e-service delivery needs to be underscored by research on its adoption by states and then, on their actual usage for implementing services.

- **E-mail, Internet and other internal policies.** How are e-mail, Internet and other internal policies being used by agencies? Are there problems with their implementation? How are the policies being policed? Are they effective at stopping or preventing abuses of these technologies?

- **What difference has e-service delivery made to the lives of citizens?** It is crucial that research begin on the effects of e-service delivery and what differences it is making in the lives of citizens and of the governments taking advantage of the technologies. Is the early promise of lower costs, more effective government and more satisfied citizens being met? Are citizens finding it too difficult to use? Is putting government services on the Internet creating even more of a digital divide? There are enough jurisdictions with years of experience now in this area that evaluation research on the effects of e-service delivery and e-government need to begin.

This chapter has highlighted several pending and emerging issues in the area of e-service delivery and e-government. This field is changing rapidly and these issues need to be addressed — performance of these services, security issues, and web usability. The lack of attention to these issues has the potential for creating additional problems for citizens and service providers alike. Attention to these issues has the potential to improve and protect services and enhance their effectiveness.

REFERENCES

Beckett, J. (2002). Trust but Verify: Availability of Local Government Budget Information on the Internet. Presented at the 2002 Meeting of the American Society for Public Administration, Phoenix, AZ.

Bimber, B. (1997). The Demographics of Internet Access. Available at: http://www.sscf.edu/~survey1/access.html.

Bourquard, J. (1994). Legislatures hit cyberspace. *State Legislatures,* (August), 31-33.

Center for Government Services. (2001). *New Jersey State Government: Online Services.* Unpublished report. Newark, NJ: Center for Government Services.

Cohen, S. & Eimicke, W. (2001). *The use of the Internet in government service delivery.* PricewaterhouseCoopers Endowment for the Business of Government. Available at http://endowment.pwcglobal.com/publications_grantreports.asp.

Cordesman, A. H. & Cordesman, J. G. (2002). *Cyber-Threats, Information Warfare, and Critical Infrastructure Protection: Defending the U.S. Homeland.* Westport, CT: Praeger.

Fisher, B., Margolis, M., & Resnick, D. (1996). Breaking Ground on the Virtual Frontier: Surveying Civic Life on the Internet. *The American Sociologist* (Spring), 11-29.

Gant, D. B. & Gant, J. P. (2002). Endowment for the Business of Government. *State Web Portals: Delivering and Financing E-Service.* Arlington, VA: PricewaterhouseCoopers. Available at http://www.businessof government.org./pdfs/Johnson.Report.pdf.

Greenberg, P. (1996). On the Net: Political possibilities. *State Legislatures* (March), 19-23.

Ho, A.T. (2002). Reinventing local governments and the e-government initiative. *Public Administration Review, 62*(4), 434-444.

Jordan, Lt. Col. Information Operations. Air War College, U.S. Department of Defense. Available at http://www.au.af.mil/au/awc/awcgate/army/jaoac-io.pdf (undated).

Kanfer, A. (1997). Ghost Towns in Cyberspace. Available at http://www.ncsa.uiuc.edu/edu/trg/ghosttown/slides/slide1.html.

Kanfer, A. & Kolar, C. (1997). What are Communities Doing On-Line? Presented at *Supercomputing '95,* (December 7, 1995). Available at http://www.ncsa.uiuc.edu/People/alaina/com_online/.

Layne, K. & Lee, J. (2001). Developing fully functional e-government: A four-stage model. *Government Information Quarterly, 18*, 122-136.

Mahler, J. & Regan, P. (2002). *Federal Intranet Work Sites: An Interim Assessment. Endowment for the Business of Government.* PricewaterhouseCoopers Endowment for the Business of Government. Available at http://endowment.pwcglobal.com/pdfs/MahlerReport.pdf.

McClure, C. R., Sprehe, J. T., & Eschenfelder, K. (2000). *Performance Measures for Federal Agency Websites.* Defense Technical Information Center and Energy Information Administration. U.S. Government Printing Office.

Moon, J. (2002). The evolution of e-government among municipalities' rhetoric or reality. *Public Administration Review, 62*(4), 424-433.

Moon, J. (2001). *State Government E-Procurement in the Information Age: Issues, Practices, and Trends.* PricewaterhouseCoopers Endowment for the Business of Government. Available at http://endowment.pwcglobal.com/publications.asp.

Moulder, E. R. & Huffman, L. A. (1996). Connecting to the future: Local governments on line. *Municipal Year Book 1996.* Washington, D.C.: International City Management Association.

National Telecommunications and Information Administration (2002). Telecommunications: Glossary of Telecommunications Terms. Available online at: http://www.its.bldrdoc.gov/fs-1037/dir-001/_0065.htm.

Nielsen, J. (2000). *Designing Web Usability: The Practice of Simplicity*. Indianapolis, IN: New Riders Publishing.

Norris, D. F., Fletcher, P. D., & Holden, S. H. (2001). *Is Your Local Government Plugged In? Highlights of the 2000 Electronic Government Survey*. Washington, D.C.: International City/County Management Association.

O'Looney, J. (2002). *Wiring Governments*. Westport, CT: Quorum Books.

Pew Internet and American Life Project. (2002). *Rise of the E-Citizen: How People Use Government Agencies' Web Sites*. Pew Internet and American Life Project. Available at http://www.pewinternet.org/reports/toc.asp?Report=57.

Pool, I. (1983). *Technologies of Freedom*. Cambridge, MA: Belknap Press.

Ranney, A. (1985). *Channels of Power: The Impact of Television on American Politics*. New York: Basic Books.

Reiss, E. L. (2000). *Practical Information Architecture*. New York: Addison Wesley.

Rheingold, H. (1993). *The Virtual Community: Homesteading on the Electronic Frontier*. Reading, MA: Addison-Wesley.

Rosenfeld, L. & Morville, P. (1998). *Information Architecture for the World Wide Web*. Sebastopol, CA: O'Reilly and Associates.

Schooley, D. (1996). Local governments go on the World Wide Web. *FPR (ForumFor Policy Research) News*. Camden, NJ: State University of New Jersey, 1-3, 15.

Sood, R. (2000). *The Four Phases of E-Government in the Public Sector Market*. The Gartner Group. Resource ID: 308459.

Stowers, G. N. L. (1995). Citizen service and the information superhighway. *The Public Manager*, 24(3), 15-19.

Stowers, G. N. L. (1999). Becoming cyberactive: State and local governments on the World Wide Web. *Government Information Quarterly*, 16, 111-127.

Stowers, G. N. L. (2002). *The State of Federal Websites*. PricewaterhouseCoopers Endowment for the Business of Government, E-Government Series. Available at http://www.endowment.pwcglobal.com/pdfs/StowersReport0802.pdf.

United Nations & American Society for Public Administration. (2001). Global Survey of E-government. Available at http://www.unpan.org/egovernment2.asp.

U.S. Department of Commerce. (2001). *A Nation Online*. Washington, D.C.: U.S. Government Printing Office.

U.S. General Accounting Office (2000). Electronic Government: Opportunities and Challenges Facing the FirstGov Web Gateway. (GAO-01-087T). Available at http://www.gao.gov.

U.S. General Accounting Office (2001). Internet Privacy: Implementation of Federal Guidelines for Agency Use of "Cookies". (GAO-01-424). Available at http://www.gao.gov.

West, D. (2000). *Assessing E-Government: The Internet, Democracy and Service Delivery. By State and Federal Governments*. Available at http://www.insidepolitics.org/policyreports.html.

West, D. (2001a). *State and Federal E-Government in the United States, 2001*. Available at http://www.insidepolitics.org/policyreports.html.

West, D. (2001b). *Urban E-Government: An Assessment of City Government Websites*. Available at http://www.insidepolitics.org/policyreports.html.

Chapter XII

Digital Government and Criminal Justice

J. William Holland
Georgia Bureau of Investigation, USA

ABSTRACT

This chapter outlines the history of digital government in criminal justice, starting with the Johnson Administration's findings concerning automation in its report, "The Challenge of Crime in a Free Society," the development of the national criminal justice network, and the creation of SEARCH Group, a consortium of states that led the effort to create computerized criminal histories of individual offenders. A brief discussion of the issues these efforts attempted to solve will be developed.

The narrative will describe how these initial activities created the basic parameters for all subsequent developments in the area of criminal justice automation. Several major problems and controversies of criminal justice automation will be described and placed in their historical context. Examples of criminal justice initiatives will be provided and their success in solving some of the problems discussed will be described. The chapter concludes that it is time to rethink the older criminal justice digital government paradigm from the 1960s and create a new model more in tune with today's developments in a highly mobile, digital and integrated society. Questions about the impact of this new model on traditional constitutional safeguards, including individual liberty and privacy will be raised.

DIGITAL GOVERNMENT AND CRIMINAL JUSTICE

Criminal justice has been one of the public sectors in the forefront of the move toward automation and digital government. By digital government, it is implied that the use of automated systems assists governmental entities to perform their legally mandated duties and responsibilities. The current e-government focus on citizen access is a vital part, but only a part of the larger digital government story within criminal justice. The effect of computerization on American criminal justice has been profound and it has transformed the criminal justice process in many fundamental ways. The major literature tracking this entire process is mainly found in task force reports, government publications, reports from state initiatives, and a few secondary source books mainly related to legal issues. Perhaps the best sources for information on the large-scale trends in this field are the various reports and analyses developed by SEARCH Group for the U.S. Department of Justice. A major factor in criminal justice systems since the beginning, SEARCH through its documents addresses the entire range of criminal justice systems and issues. Rereading many of these documents reminds one of the many miles we have traveled since 1967. This chapter is designed to cover those miles; to relate how criminal justice automation began, how it has evolved, its major controversies, problems, and issues, how solutions for these difficulties were devised and implemented, and what problems remain today. The chapter concludes with a brief set of suggestions for the future development of digital government in criminal justice.

To understand the current state of digital government in American criminal justice, we have to go back in time. Back beyond the Internet, local area networks, even back beyond the advent of personal computers in the 1980s. We must seek the origins of our current justice systems in a world of a few massive and costly computer systems of limited capacity with primitive networking capabilities. This world did not know of Bill Gates, Microsoft or CNN. Television, dominated by the big three networks, carried nightly vistas of death and destruction from far off Vietnam and from the streets of America's major cities. The assassination of President John Kennedy was still a recent scar, Lyndon Johnson was President and many Americans still hoped that Robert Kennedy would soon occupy the Oval Office.

Clearly, this era, known to historians as the Sixties, was one of turmoil and violence. It was also, however, an era of many sweeping reforms. The Civil Rights Movement, War on Poverty, and the Great Society shared the stage with emerging issues of feminism and environmentalism. Many Americans still believed that large-scale governmental intervention could solve the nation's social problems. Chief among those social problems was the issue of urban violence and crime. Therefore, it was natural that the Johnson Administration turned to a national solution for what had traditionally been seen as a local problem; the prevalence of crime and violence in the American society (Dallek, 1998, pp. 405-407, 409-411).

The Johnson answer was a large government commission with numerous task forces, charged with ascertaining the causes and nature of crime, the state of the American criminal justice system, and the needed reforms, programs, and policies required to meet the threat. The commission's recommendations were contained in a lengthy series of reports listed under the long official title of *The Challenge of Crime in a Free Society: A Report by the President's Commission on Law Enforcement and the Administration of Justice.* A major component of this effort was a separate task force report focused on science and technology, specifically on the information needs of the criminal justice system and the computer systems to meet those demands. At a time when computerization was minimal throughout the criminal justice system, these task force members developed the blueprint for today's multilayered automated criminal justice environment. Remarkably, their recommendations still govern developments within criminal justice information systems today. It is, therefore, critical that we understand what they recommended and how their vision happened. For it is in large measure true that the very success of this early effort contains the germs for today's problems and difficulties in criminal justice systems (Dallek, 1998, pp. 405-407, 409-411; *Challenge of Crime in a Free Society*, 1967, pp. 268-271).

Among the major recommendations of the commission were the creation of a national directory of offenders' criminal records, what came to be known as Computerized Criminal History (CCH) and the development of similar directories at the state level. The commission also called for the creation of national assistance programs for research and development to assist states, and Federal coordination of standards for criminal justice information and sharing. Finally, the report urged that a study of fingerprint classification techniques be undertaken with a view to automating much of the fingerprint search and identification effort and that work be intensified to create a national linkage of files on wanted persons and stolen vehicles under the name of the National Crime Information Center (NCIC) (*Challenge of Crime in a Free Society*, 1967, pp. 255, 268-271; *Task Force Report on Science and Technology*, 1967, p. 69).

Structurally, the report and the associated task force report envisioned a nationwide system organized around a state-Federal nexus. The Federal componenet would contain summaries of the states' detailed information on individual offenders and their criminal records. This decentralized approach took advantage of the distributed nature of criminal justice and the Federal structure of the American system of government. While the concept revealed a clear preference for some decentralization of data, it still relied heavily upon a hierarchical organization of systems wherein local jurisdictions were linked through their respective state entities to the national center. Moreover, despite the focus on state and local development, the report clearly set aside a significant command and control function for the national level (Task *Force Report*, 1967, p. 70).

Still for its day, the report was visionary. The description of an integrated justice system written in 1967 could well have been penned in 2002:

> *Since the administration of criminal justice is primarily a local and state function, a national criminal justice information system must be geared to their requirements. Fundamentally, the information system must be directly accessible to them and they must specify the information they need from other jurisdictions. This leads to a concept of a hierarchy of information interchange and information files. This approach leaves with the local implementing agencies the greatest amount of design flexibility in tailoring their own system to their unique requirements. Information to be exchanged with other jurisdictions must, however, meet minimum standards of content and format. Furthermore, reporting jurisdictions must be responsible for updating their portion of a common information pool. Only that way can the*

files be kept current and complete and the system not saturated with useless information (Task Force Report, *1967, p. 70).*

The authors of the report also recognized the difficulty of developing such systems from a cost standpoint. The computer industry was still in its infancy; development and support costs for systems were high. With large private sector markets coalescing, there was little incentive for computer firms to move aggressively into what was widely regarded as a fragmented and marginal public market in criminal justice. In addition, the available pool of skilled computer systems personnel was fairly small and expensive to retain; too expensive for criminal justice agencies facing significant funding constraints. Even if adequate funds had been available, the structure of public budgeting with its emphasis on yearly budgets, individual generic budgetary line items and little means of allocating monies to long term multiyear funding initiatives dampened political support. The only viable solution, they concluded, was to assign to the Federal government the dominant role in funding and research efforts to assist the state and local governments with these initiatives (*Task Force Report*, 1967, p. 1; *Use and Management of Criminal History Record Information: A Comprehensive Report, 2001 Update*, 2001, p. 26).

One of the earliest responses to this report was the creation of the Law Enforcement Assistance Administration (LEAA) within the United States Department of Justice (DOJ). An organization devoted to the award and administration of Federal grant monies for state and local law enforcement agencies, LEAA was the forerunner of the multi-faceted justice grant program of today's Department of Justice. In 1969, LEAA funded Project SEARCH to create a nationwide computerized criminal history system. From this initial effort, SEARCH quickly evolved into an independent consortium of states with the mission of demonstrating a computerized system for the electronic exchange of criminal history information. On the national level, the United States Attorney General assigned management responsibility for the interstate and national portion of this system to the Federal Bureau of Investigation. The states also formed the National Law Enforcement Telecommunications System (NLETS) electronically linking the states as well as the FBI and the Royal Canadian Mounted Police. In 1972, LEAA created the Comprehensive Data Systems (CDS) program to provide funds to states to develop criminal justice systems meeting state and national needs. By 1976, 26 states had used CDS funding to create state level central repositories for computerized criminal history information. With these developments, the major groups involved in automated criminal justice had emerged. DOJ grant programs were created to fund development, SEARCH was created to serve as the clearinghouse for development of model systems and policies, the FBI was the manager of the interstate component of the system, state level repositories began to support state development of criminal justice information systems, and NLETS to provide the telecommunications linkage among the states (*Use and Management of Criminal History*, 2001, p. 26).

It became apparent during the last half of the 1970s, however, that greater decentralization of the nation's criminal history systems was urgently needed. The Federal file was incomplete, missing many arrests and reports of final dispositions and it was generally recognized that state criminal histories were more complete and accurate. Furthermore, in the post-Watergate era, there were concerns about threats to personal liberties posed by a national file of criminal histories managed by the FBI. To respond to these issues and concerns, the various states, FBI and SEARCH created the Interstate Identification Index or Triple I (III) concept in 1980 (*Use and Management of Criminal History*, 2001, pp. 26-27, 76-82, 88).

Designed to replace a centralized national criminal history file, III was an index of criminal offenders that pointed to the state or states where detailed criminal history information could be found. Offenders were listed as either single state, meaning their criminal offenses occurred in one state, or multi-state, meaning their criminal offenses occurred in multiple states. The goal was to free the FBI from maintaining detailed criminal histories on all offenders, allowing it to focus on maintaining this fingerprint based national index of offenders. There was widespread acceptance of III for criminal justice purposes. By 2001, 43 states participated. Legal restrictions and concerns, however, limited use of III for noncriminal justice use and weakened any effort to achieve a truly decentralized criminal history system. Consequently, the FBI continued to maintain criminal histories on individuals to meet interstate noncriminal justice needs (*Use and Management of Criminal History*, 2001, pp. 76-82).

Issues surrounding release of criminal history information, its security and privacy, had been entangled with the development of criminal justice information systems since the 1960s. Initially, in an atmosphere of government mistrust fueled by the Vietnam War and climaxed by the furor surrounding the Watergate scandal and its aftermath in the 1970s, the American public viewed the government as the primary threat to its liberties. To redress this fear, lawmakers placed greater restrictions on the release of an individual's criminal history information, making it difficult to obtain such information for employment, licensing and public service purposes. In the 1980s, as memories of the 60's and 70's faded and "horror" stories about child molesters teaching children, violent criminals obtaining firearms, and drunken drivers driving school buses emerged in the media; an angry public demanded greater availability of criminal history information. As a result, noncriminal justice access to this information was broadened. Some states, such as Florida, adopted open record laws that allowed the states, upon payment of a fee, to give all criminal history information to anyone requesting it. Many states only made felony convictions available to the public and others remained very restrictive in their access policies (*Public Attitudes Toward Uses of Criminal History Information*, 2001, p. 7; *National Task Force on Privacy*, 2001, pp. 1, 53-54).

As the states liberalized their access to criminal histories, the demand among noncriminal justice users intensified. But this growth hid a major problem. Disparities among various states' laws and regulations on release of criminal histories for noncriminal justice purposes hampered the interstate sharing of this information. To rectify this gap, Federal and state representatives in the late 90's crafted an interstate compact governing noncriminal justice access to criminal history information through the FBI's III system. Signatories to the compact agreed to provide criminal history data not legally sealed by law to all authorized interstate requestors. Under the terms of the compact, the requesting state's laws and regulations on dissemination of criminal history data determined release of the information to the requestor. A council of signatories to the compact was created to oversee its terms and conditions. Many states, however, objected to release of their information being controlled by the laws of another state and refused to ratify the compact (*Use and Management of Criminal History*, 2001, p. 90; *Task Force on Privacy*, 2001, pp. 53-54).

Another factor that prevented the decentralization of criminal history information was the vast effort required in the time-consuming fingerprint identification process. Since an individual's criminal history file was based upon identification of the individual by fingerprints, this problem had to be solved. The first initiative to address this issue, the National Fingerprint File (NFF) program of 1990, outlined a system where the first arrest fingerprint card of an individual within a state would be sent to the FBI's national fingerprint file. All subsequent arrest fingerprint cards for that individual would be retained at the state level and the state would assume the burden of providing criminal history information on the individual to any authorized requestor. Full implementation proved difficult. One of the main obstacles was the lack of automation in the fingerprint identification process (*Use and Management of Criminal History*, 2001, pp. 84-85, 88-89).

Before the late 80's, fingerprint capture, classification, and identification was a labor-intensive, time consuming, tedious, error prone, and costly process. Paper bound, it relied upon manual efforts and painstaking searching and comparing of large manual files of prints. The time involved to identify a current arrestee with a previous arrest event and confirm an identity often took weeks or even months in large state and national files. This, of course, delayed the addition of current criminal arrest information to criminal history files, reducing the completeness and accuracy of those files. Furthermore, the long time involved to identify arrestees meant that serious felons or wanted persons were often released before their identity could be determined   The situation was even worse for comparisons of fingerprints left at crime scenes; latent fingerprints to the law enforcement community. These prints, typically individual partial or smudged finger-prints, did not contain enough data to reduce the fingerprint search for any given print. Consequently, a search of prints of unknown suspects against a large, manual, finger-print card file was virtually impossible. Only after a suspect was determined could a true comparison of latent prints to the suspect's prints be conducted.

The problem was that the technology was not available to automate the fingerprint processing and identification effort. Without such automation, a truly decentralized fingerprint and criminal history file was unrealistic. In the original *Challenge of Crime in a Free Society*, its authors had recognized this weakness and advocated some sort of semi-automated classification and search scheme for fingerprints. The result, a new classification system called the NCIC classification, was simpler to learn and lent itself to use as a semi-automated screening device to reduce the number of prints an individual fingerprint expert had to compare. It was, however, not very selective in the number of potential match candidates it produced and it did nothing to speed up the actual identification process (*Challenge of Crime in a Free Society*, 1967, p. 255; *Task Force Report*, 1967, p. 16; Ms. Shirley Andrews, personal communication, September 9, 2002).

During the mid 1980s, new technological solutions for fingerprint processing and identification emerged on the market. These systems, called automated fingerprint identification systems (AFIS), significantly reduced the manual tasks needed to search a fingerprint and made true searching of latent crime scene fingerprints possible. By the close of the 1980s, many states and a few local agencies had purchased these systems. Most were stand-alone systems dedicated to the fingerprint input, search and presen-tation of potential candidates for human comparison. As such, they increased the speed of fingerprint identification but did little to reduce the overall delays in criminal history processing. A few states attempted to expand the capabilities of these systems and link them to other criminal history processes. For example, in 1989, the state of Georgia implemented an AFIS to improve statewide identification efforts. In addition to supporting the standard fingerprint and latent fingerprint searching, Georgia's system also linked the AFIS on-line to its state criminal history system for automatic updates of the criminal history files. Results of this system were dramatic; overall, criminal history processing time was reduced from two months to eight hours. When combined with the proven effectiveness of the AFIS latent search capability, the new technology contained the potential to transform criminal justice systems (*Task Force on Privacy*, 2001, pp. 43-44; *Use and Management of Criminal History*, 2001, pp. 61-63).

Such improvements, however, were limited to the state central processing centers or repositories. Interaction with arresting agencies still relied upon use of the U.S. Mail. This, at a minimum, added three days to the initial receipt of the arrest card, one day for processing, and another three days for the return of the response to the arresting agency. In total, it took seven days from the date of arrest until the arresting agency received a response to the arrest and this was the ideal situation. If a state experienced backlogs in processing or still maintained an extensive manual criminal history file, the actual end-to-end processing time was far greater. Moreover, this did not include the additional weeks required to obtain a response from the national file at the FBI. Of course, by the time an arresting agency received a response the arrested individual had usually been released. In essence, the overall processing time was still too long to aid local jurisdictions booking offenders into jails and confronting vital decisions on bail and release (*Use and Management of Criminal History*, 2001, p. 62).

To eliminate this critical bottleneck in the development of a national criminal justice system, an electronic means of capturing and transmitting fingerprint, personal descriptor, and arrest data had to be developed. A small number of electronic fingerprint capture devices, called live scan machines, were already available. These machines, however, were primarily designed to electronically print fingerprint cards at the booking site, reducing the need for repeated ink based printing of individuals. They had no capability for electronic transmission of fingerprint images and data over telecommunications lines. Even worse, there was no agreed upon standard for electronic transmission of fingerprint, descriptor and arrest data.

In the early 1990s, efforts were made through the National Institute of Standards and Technology (NIST) to devise such a national standard; an effort spearheaded by the FBI. Deeply involved in a massive effort to streamline its own fingerprint identification process called the Integrated Automated Fingerprint Identification project, the Bureau recognized that electronic submission of fingerprints offered the only viable solution to its problem of long processing delays. In 1993, a national standard for the electronic interchange of fingerprint information was approved by NIST that became the basis for the electronic linkage of local jurisdictions to state criminal history bureaus and the FBI. Subsequently updated in 1997 and 2000 to include standards for transmission of photographs of faces, scars, marks and tattoos, it formed the basis for the emerging national network of real-time identification and criminal history systems. By 2000, for example, Georgia received over 75 percent of its criminal fingerprint cards electronically, identified the individual, updated the individual's criminal history, electronically notified the submitting agency and transmitted the electronic fingerprint to the FBI for national searches within 30 minutes of booking of the arrestee. Further, at the national level, the

FBI processed all electronic submissions and returned responses on a national finger-print search within two hours of receipt of the record. (See *Data Format for the Interchange of Fingerprint, Facial, and SMT Information,* originally issued in 1993, amended in 1997 and further amended in 2000; *Use and Management of Criminal History,* 2001, pp. 61-63.)

In conjunction with these activities in fingerprint and criminal history automation, emphasis within state and national criminal justice circles shifted to the need to share information, what came to be known as integrated criminal justice. Before this, funds and efforts had been diverted to creating individual criminal justice systems designed to serve specific functions. With the rare exception of efforts such as Georgia's to integrate AFIS and criminal history information, most initiatives created single function systems or "stovepipes" with little or no linkage to other systems. With the explosion of the Internet and simultaneous cost limitations on criminal justice system development, both Federal and state funding entities in the late 90's began requiring that new criminal justice system developments build in the concept of information sharing, realignment of processing functions, and greater involvement of all criminal justice parties in individual systems development. The goal of this new focus was to eliminate duplicate entry of the same information and increase the overall completeness and accuracy of criminal justice information (*Use and Management of Criminal History,* 2001, pp. 63-65; Harris, 2000, pp. 7, 14, 18-20, 41; *Task Force on Privacy,* 2001, pp. 47-48, 50; *Planning the Integration of Justice Information Systems,* 2002, pp. 2-3).

Two separate approaches to integration of criminal justice information emerged. The first, based upon merger of the various data bases into a super data base or data warehouse, required extensive rewrite of existing systems, abandonment of essential operational systems in favor of a large new super system, and raised serious concern among various agencies about the security and confidentiality of highly sensitive agency specific data. Furthermore, it became apparent that any effort to merge all kinds of data into one database posed specific technical and definitional problems because various criminal justice agencies defined specific information and relationships differ-ently. The second approach, transmission of specified information among the various criminal justice systems at key decision points appeared to be more plausible. It had the advantage of minimizing the disruption to mission critical criminal justice systems, eliminating concerns about confidentiality of agency-specific data and allowing separate information systems to exchange data already shared in a manual environment. At the same time, through this sharing of data, duplicate entry of information would be eliminated and the various criminal justice agencies could tie their systems into an integrated criminal justice process. With the advent of new software tools and capabili-ties for information sharing, the cost of linking these systems would also be reduced. As a result, this second approach quickly became the favored method for developing integrated justice applications (Harris, 2000, pp. 7-11; *Use and Management of Criminal History,* 2001, pp. 67-68; *Task Force on Privacy,* 2001, p. 49).

Yet, there were also problems with this approach. Integral to this strategy was the need to create a governance method that crossed agency and constitutional separation-of-powers boundaries. Integration of justice systems and sharing of data demanded that agencies work more closely together, sharing objectives and plans, than had been done in the past. To make this happen meant criminal justice executives had to become involved in the planning and governance of these complex integration activities. Plans for such involvement assumed that all involved agency leaders had realized that sharing of critical information was a key management responsibility. Obviously, some criminal justice executives were quicker to adopt this concept than others, a fact that hampered these initiatives. A true integrated justice governance model also required the involvement of management from various levels of government: local, state and Federal. While there were many groups with representation from these three levels of government, integration was not always their primary focus (Harris, 2000, pp. 12-13, 21-25; *Task Force on Privacy*, 2001, pp. 1, 49; *Use and Management of Criminal History*, 2001, pp. 71-72).

Integrated justice efforts also resurrected older worries about privacy of such information and merged them with new concerns about greater linkage of criminal justice and noncriminal justice information on individuals. Questions about release of integrated information were linked to serious questions about the accuracy of the information released. These fears were intensified as private companies began to demand access to criminal history information, gathered at public expense, to market to customers for profit. In many jurisdictions, the old line between public and private responsibilities and authority began to fade as private companies assumed many of the traditional criminal justice information systems functions (*Task Force on Privacy*, 2001, pp. 2-3, 27-28, 50; *Public Attitudes Toward Uses of Criminal History*, 2001, pp. 8, 12; *Planning the Integration of Justice Information Systems*, 2002, p. 5).

Still, despite these concerns and the obvious weaknesses in criminal justice automation, the initiatives of the last 34 years have transformed the landscape of American criminal justice. Thirty-four years ago, it would have been inconceivable that offenders could be booked into local facilities and within minutes have the local agency receive notification of their identity and criminal history. The idea of wanted person, drivers license, stolen vehicle and other roadside checks has become so routine that it is impossible for today's law enforcement to remember a time without them. Even today's television crime shows routinely have their actors talk about NCIC and AFIS. Citizens of today are beginning to take for granted that people in a position of trust have been checked on a nationwide basis to ensure that they pose no threat to the community. Web pages with public access to prisoner information, sex offender status, criminal histories and other public safety and justice information are coming into existence. To gain a better understanding of how such events have happened, following are two brief case studies of specific initiatives in states that transformed the way criminal justice did business.

In 1980, the state of Georgia faced a crisis in its criminal justice information system. An earlier string of murders of elderly women in Columbus, Georgia had left the state's Bureau of Investigation frustrated at its inability to identify fingerprints left at the crime scenes of the murders. At the same time, the failure of the state's Crime Information Center, a division of the Bureau of Investigation, to maintain a complete and accurate fingerprint and criminal history system called into question the viability of the state's efforts since 1972 to create such a system. Backlogs were in excess of four months and the accuracy levels of the old manual fingerprint identification system were unacceptable. To rectify this situation, agency leadership in 1985 embarked upon a plan to modernize and enhance the center's operations in fingerprint and criminal history processing.

By 1987, the Georgia Bureau of Investigation (GBI) issued a competitive Request for Proposal for the development and implementation of an automated fingerprint identification system (AFIS). Unlike other such procurements, GBI specified that the

AFIS be integrated with the state's criminal history system and that the vast majority of the then current manual functions be automated. Also included in the requirements were a complete crime scene fingerprint search capability and a capability to search arrest and applicant fingerprints against those crime scene prints that were not matched to suspects on the original search. In 1989, this system came on-line and immediately proved its value by solving the murder of a relative of the governor of Georgia; a case with no known suspects and totally reliant upon the matching of crime scene prints against a large database of known offenders.

To achieve the system's stated goal of identifying offenders and updating the criminal history file for all submitted criminal fingerprint cards within eight hours of receipt of the card, GBI had to completely redesign its internal processes and eliminate its old manual criminal history files. This "reengineering" effort allowed it to meet its goal in 1989. As mentioned earlier, however, this decrease in internal processing time did not provide any critical improvement in response times to local arresting agencies. In 1995, using the recently released national standard on electronic transmission of fingerprint information, the GBI initiated an upgrade project to accept electronic fingerprints for processing, return electronic responses to the arresting agency, and submit these electronic prints to the national FBI file when it became available. This capability was prototyped with an Atlanta area county sheriff's office in 1996. The benefits were immediately apparent; fingerprint cards electronically submitted were processed, identified, criminal history files updated, and responses returned to the submitting agency within two hours of the actual booking of the individual. Over the next three years, this capability was expanded to include over 50 percent of all criminal fingerprints received by the GBI and the electronic link to the FBI was implemented. Furthermore, the GBI instituted a skeleton round-the-clock operation to support this new service.

Still not satisfied with the response time or usage levels of electronic fingerprint transmission, the GBI, as part of it year 2000 upgrade efforts, further upgraded its AFIS allowing it to make basic booking identification decisions on over 80 percent of received prints without human intervention. At the same time, it expanded its support to a fully staffed around the clock operation. In 2002, the GBI received over 80 percent of its criminal fingerprint cards electronically, processed, identified, updated its criminal history files and responded to the local agency and the FBI within 15 minutes of the booking of the arrested individual. Moreover, it had developed a capability for noncriminal fingerprint checks to be done electronically within 10 minutes of transmission of the card. Utilizing a phased approach, the state of Georgia reduced its processing and response time from months with labor intensive processing and backlogs to minutes with extremely high levels of automation and no backlogs. The result was a more complete and accurate criminal history file with much greater use by the criminal justice community and the public.

Like Georgia, Colorado faced difficulties with its criminal justice systems. Those systems contained a high level of duplicate entry of information, little standardization, heavy reliance upon paper transfers of information among agencies, no linkage of criminal incidents and offenders, and no capability to obtain information from the system without numerous separate inquiries. In May 1995, the Colorado legislature passed legislation calling for the creation of an integrated approach to the criminal justice systems of the five major components of the state's criminal justice community; Public Safety, Judiciary, District Attorneys, Corrections, and Youth Corrections. These components would share only their most serious offenses and the sharing and transfer of such information would only involve common information and crucial data required to ensure officer safety. In May of 1998, the first phase of the system involving common sharing of vital information became operational. In June 1999, the second phase using a common inquiry format began testing (*Toward Improved Criminal Justice Information Sharing*, 2000, pp. 97-98, 102, 104, 108).

The operating concept for this system relied upon sharing of critical information among agency systems without major changes to these existing systems. Similarly, the inquiry function rested upon access to the same systems. To achieve these goals, extensive redesign of business processes or reengineering was required. Manual processing tasks and paper transfers of information had to be eliminated and new automated functions created. The actual linkage and integration was accomplished through use of an index specifying which databases contained information on the requested individual as well as middleware that networked these systems together. Due to the scope of the project and potential cost impacts, access to the shared information was restricted to the five participating components. This, of course hampered the usefulness of the integrated system (*Toward Improved Criminal Justice Information Sharing*, 2000, pp. 98, 101-102, 104-107, 109-110).

To increase the usefulness of its system and expand access to the Colorado criminal history component of the integrated system, the state launched an Internet-based service called Colorado Criminal History Internet Check on May 28, 2002. The state engaged the services of a specialized contractor to develop and manage this system. Funding for the system relied upon the e-gov financial model wherein users of the system were assessed an access fee for each criminal history check performed. These funds went to pay the cost for the contractor to maintain and operate the system. Colorado provided copies of the public portion of their database to the contractor on an event driven basis and the contractor made that portion available through a web page module. In addition to increasing public access to vital criminal history information, this approach also eliminated five positions formerly involved in the processing of public requests for this information. (See *The ICHC System: An Internet Based Criminal History Check System*, 2002.)

The successful examples from Georgia and Colorado share several common traits. These characteristics form a type of best practices guide for development of criminal justice systems and applications. First, both states clearly specified the problem, requirements and issues they sought to address. Second, both remained focused on their goals and avoided the urge to expand the project's scope well beyond what was achievable. Third, both states used a phased approach that allowed staff to implement the overall initiative in concrete clearly measurable steps with targeted funding. This approach also allowed the projects to have successful components in operation before moving to the next upgrade or enhancement. Consequently, the criminal justice community and the public saw early successes, maintaining strong support for the overall initiatives. Finally, both states involved cross sections of the criminal justice community and used prototype testing to validate new capabilities. This ensured broad support and allowed for customer participation in the final development of the systems.

As these studies demonstrate, the American criminal justice community can take pride in its achievements in the use of computer systems to transform the way it does business. That community, however, cannot rest on its laurels. As we have seen, much remains to be done. Automation, while widespread, contains glaring gaps and lapses. Criminal history files are incomplete, missing many final dispositions of individual criminal charges. Too many active criminal histories still reside in inaccessible paper files. Missing dispositions and paper criminal records keep these systems from providing proper notification of individuals prohibited from purchasing a firearm, driving a school bus, or working in a position of high trust. These incomplete records also prevent convicted repeat offenders from receiving the proper punishment for their crimes. In addition, many localities throughout the nation still lack automated information and do not have the infrastructure to obtain access to larger automated files on a timely basis. With highly mobile criminals and the heightened awareness of terrorist activity within the nation, areas of disconnected and lightly automated criminal justice agencies present a clear public safety danger as the nation moves deeper into the new century (*Survey of State Criminal History Information Systems*, 1999, p. 2; *Use and Management of Criminal History*, 2001, p. 3).

At the same time, the overall increase in access to criminal justice information over the Internet and the expansion of its availability from non- criminal justice sectors has pushed renewed privacy concerns to the forefront. Even with the events of September 11, 2001 as a backdrop, American citizens remain worried over identity theft, availability of incorrect information about themselves or their family members, and the potential privacy invasions inherent in growing use of newer technologies such as DNA. Numerous and conflicting state laws governing access to criminal history information have only compounded these fears. Finally, there is a mushrooming awareness of the dangers posed by sophisticated criminals and terrorists to the nation's criminal justice system infrastructure and information systems. Without adequate security of criminal justice assets and information, it is possible for these individuals to eliminate wanted persons checks, terrorist alerts, and records of felony convictions, to dispatch first responders to the wrong address or area, and to eavesdrop on security and public safety planning (*Public Attitudes Toward Uses of Criminal History*, 2001, pp. 4, 12; *Task Force on Privacy*, 2001, pp. 5-7, 45-48, 51-52).

Many of these difficulties are shared by other sectors of the digital society, but solutions to these problems are complicated for criminal justice agencies by the basic concept underlying most criminal justice systems. Specifically, nearly all of the systems and databases developed up to the present time have occurred within the original design parameters and relationship roles specified in the *Challenge of Crime in a Free Society*. Those parameters were developed in a command hierarchy set of network relationships linking local jurisdictions to state and Federal systems. Given the state of telecommunications technology at the time, such structures were essential to transmit and access information in a rapid manner. This was particularly true in the area most affected by rapid communications; wanted person and stolen vehicle checks by roadside officers. Since the explosion of the Internet and the World Wide Web in the 1990s, however, these types of separate telecommunications systems have become increasingly hard to justify in terms of cost and overall access to critical information. At the same time, the belief that separate criminal justice networks provided ample security delayed the installation of the advanced system security measures needed in the new digital environment. Even now, as current criminal justice telecommunications structures struggle to adopt the newer security standards and Internet based capabilities, questions must be raised about the viability of maintaining costly separate telecommunications entities in an increasingly wired world.

This clamor grows even louder when the issue of data duplication and completeness is added to the agenda. Developed in an era of large expensive mainframe computers with very high storage costs and limited processing power, criminal justice systems relied upon redundant information bases at the state and national level. While many of the larger local criminal justice agencies also developed their own systems, the major focus remained on state development of large repository systems linked to the FBI and to each other through restricted criminal justice telecommunications links. This type of development presented two problems. First, some states were unable to support such systems and were forced to join regional entities such as the Western Identification Network (WIN) to gain access to sufficient computer processing power to support their information needs. Second, states were one step removed from the actual daily operations of the criminal justice system. The vast majority of the arrests, trials and disposition of cases in American criminal justice occur at the local jurisdictional level. Moreover, the first response to crime is nearly always at the local jurisdiction. All too often, local agencies are required to complete additional paperwork to submit copies of arrests and disposition of cases to state level criminal history files. The result, as noted earlier, is that many state criminal history files are incomplete and national files are even worse. Even with large-scale automation of submission, many local agencies retain paper files and processes for their daily work.

The recent initiatives to create integrated justice systems are designed to address some of these problems. Unfortunately, most of these initiatives are state-centric while the greatest need is at the local jurisdictional level. Under the current criminal justice system environment, with its heavy emphasis on state and national large-scale systems, such focus is unavoidable. These state and national systems have provided much value to the nation's criminal justice system. Nevertheless, a large state and national superstructure is resting on a very weak foundation of local jurisdiction automation. The danger of system collapse is becoming more apparent to criminal justice professionals. Hints can be seen in newspaper accounts of court case backlogs, horror stories of individuals left in local jails and "lost" for weeks or months, accidental release of convicted offenders, and inadequate supervision of released offenders.

The answer cannot be found in further improvement based upon concepts created in the 1960s. What is urgently needed is to rethink the approach to criminal justice automation and digital government. This new vision must place local criminal justice agencies at the center of new initiatives while retaining the current state and national systems. It must move more aggressively into the Internet world of web-hosted systems with multi-level linkages to other agencies. The new era of criminal justice digital government must be multi-dimensional and information must be shared and accessed in a simple and uniform manner. New technologies must be seamlessly interwoven into the system and a completely new outreach to users of the information must be developed. As part of this outreach, new stronger national security and privacy safeguards to protect the information, its access, and use must be enacted. The current fragmented and piecemeal approach to security of and access to this vital information must be discarded.

In 1967, a national commission developed *The Challenge of Crime in a Free Society*, the roadmap for today's highly automated but incomplete criminal justice system. This report has served the nation well but it is time to move beyond its confining vistas, time to recognize that dramatic developments in computer technology and digital government demand new answers to old questions and the formulation of entirely new questions. The events of September 11, 2001 have raised anew questions about lack of information on potential threats to society and posed new questions on how we as a nation can weave together governmental and private computerized information to detect dangerous individuals intent on mass murder without compromising constitutional safeguards and individual liberties. It is time to convene a new national task force charged with the duty to assess the challenge of crime and terror in a free digital society. Only then can criminal justice automation and digital government move forward in a planned and comprehensive way.

REFERENCES

Challenge of Crime in a Free Society: A Report by the President's Commission on Law Enforcement and Administration of Justice. (1967). Washington, D.C.: U.S. Government Printing Office.

Dallek, R. (1998). *Flawed Giant: Lyndon Johnson and His Times, 1961-1973.* New York: Oxford University Press.

Data Format for the Interchange of Fingerprint, Facial, and SMT Information. (2000). Washington, D.C.: U.S. Government Printing Office.

Harris, K. J. (2000, September). *Integrated Justice Information Systems: Governance Structures, Roles and Responsibilities.* Retrieved on July 10, 2002 from SEARCH Group, Inc. website: http://www.search.org/images/pdf/governance.pdf/.

ICHIC System: An Internet-Based Criminal History Check System. (2002, August). Presentation at the Georgia Bureau of Investigation, Decatur, GA.

Planning the Integration of Justice Information Systems: Developing the Justice Information Exchange Model. Retrieved July 10, 2002 from SEARCH Group, Inc. website: http://search.org/integration/pdf/JIEM.pdf.

*Task Force Report: Science and Technology. (1967). Washington, D.C.: U.S. Government Printing Office.

Toward Improved Criminal Justice Information Sharing: An Information Integration Planning Model. (2000, April). Available from the International Association of Chiefs of Police, 515 North Washington Street, Alexandria, VA. 22314-2357.

U.S. Department of Justice. (2001). *Public Attitudes Toward Uses of Criminal History Information: A Privacy, Technology and Criminal Justice Information Report* (NCJ187663). Washington, D.C.

U.S. Department of Justice. (2000). *Survey of State Criminal History Information Systems, 1999: A Criminal Justice Information Policy Report* (NCJ184793). Washington, D.C.

U.S. Department of Justice. (2001). *Report of the National Task Force on Privacy, Technology, and Criminal Justice Information* (NCJ187669). Washington, D.C.

U.S. Department of Justice. (2001). *Use and Management of Criminal History Record Information: A Comprehensive Report, 2001 Update* (NCJ187670). Washington, D.C.

(References marked with a * indicate reports included in the Commission report.)

Chapter XIII

Digital Government: Balancing Risk and Reward through Public/ Private Partnerships

Carole Richardson
American University, USA

ABSTRACT

The modern focus on the application of business principles to the running of government is unique due to an escalated emphasis on divesting the public sector of as many service provision responsibilities as possible. This divestiture is being accomplished through an array of arrangements alternatively described as privatization, contracting out, outsourcing and public/private partnerships. There are three fundamental challenges to this process: (1) defining those responsibilities which cannot and should not be turned over to the private sector, (2) ensuring that such arrangements balance both the risks and rewards between the parties involved, and (3) getting the best deal for the public. This chapter focuses on the second point: achieving a reasonable balance that should, if implemented successfully, result in that elusive "best deal."

INTRODUCTION

An intense drive currently exists in the U.S. to make government more like business. This is not an altogether new idea. U.S. history is filled with periods when scholars and practitioners believed that government could be made more efficient through adopting business "best practices." In modern times, the "businessification" of government gained popularity during the Clinton Administration's focus on the reinvention of government. This became formalized with the Government Performance and Results Act (GPRA) of 1993. The GPRA has been vigorously implemented during the Bush era's commitment to the President's Management Agenda.

U.S. Government Contracting

The Office of Management and Budget within the Executive Office of the President of the United States issued Circular Number A-76 in 1983, and revised it in 1999. The purpose of A-76 is to define procedures for determining when government can or should contract with commercial entities for products or services. A-76 states that "certain functions are inherently governmental in nature, being so intimately related to the public interest as to mandate performance only by Federal employees." According to A-76, functions that are inherently governmental in nature fall into one of two categories:

1.   The *act of governing* — i.e., the discretionary exercise of Government authority. Examples include criminal investigations, prosecutions and other judicial functions; management of Government programs requiring value judgments, as in direction of the national defense; management and direction of the Armed Services; activities performed exclusively by military personnel who are subject to deployment in a combat, combat support or combat service support role; conduct of foreign relations; selection of program priorities; direction of Federal employees; regulation of the use of space, oceans, navigable rivers and other natural resources; direction of intelligence and counter-intelligence operations; and regulation of industry and commerce, including food and drugs.
2.   *Monetary transactions and entitlements* — such as tax collection and revenue disbursements; control of the Treasury accounts and money supply; and the administration of public trusts (Office of Management and Budget).

Specific examples of such functions are absent from this circular. Subsequent attempts by various agencies to define precisely which functions are eligible to be commissioned through "commercially available sources" and which are reserved to government have failed to totally resolve this lack of specificity.

Nevertheless, functions related to computerization, management of information resources, telecommunications and Internet connectivity are rather commonly outsourced. The general consensus of government appears to indicate that these information and communications technology (ICT) support functions are distinct from those "intimately related to the public interest." Electronic government (e-Government) clearly stands upon an ICT foundation; therefore, activities, resources and staff necessary for any e-Government endeavor are likely candidates for outsourcing. Thus, e-Government, in all its many guises, relies on the involvement of the commercial sector for its development, implementation and maintenance.

Leon deLoof, in his book, *Information Systems Outsourcing Decision Making*, defines information system (IS) outsourcing as "…the commissioning of part or all of the IS activities an organization needs, and/or transferring the associated human and other IS resources, to one or more external IS suppliers" (p. 30). In other words, government might contract with external entities for all its IS needs (privatization), or it might select only certain functions as eligible for outsourcing (server management, for example), or it might engage in a carefully structured partnership as a means to benefit from talent and skills which are internally absent.

The Pressure to Outsource E-Government

Various factors have brought about the current push toward government IS outsourcing. The Federal Activities Inventory Reform (FAIR) Act of 1998 requires government agencies to assess the extent to which their activities are subject to competition from private or non-profit sector competition. Agencies must prepare an inventory for submission to Office of Management and Budget (OMB) review. The established goal for 2002 was to off-load at least 5% of the staff positions which support functions determined to be subject to private competition. This goal increased to 10% in 2003. Agencies are encouraged either to develop public/private partnerships or to completely privatize such functions to meet these goals.

In addition to traditional IS functions related to data gathering, storage, retrieval and manipulation, public sector managers are strongly motivated to expand IS to support full-scale deployment of e-Government initiatives. "Expanded electronic government" is one of the five government-wide initiatives included in the President's Management Agenda, with which all Federal agencies must comply. OMB will use the infamous Executive Branch Management scorecard to assess the extent that Federal agencies meet these goals. Those agencies and programs that receive the dreaded "red" mark of failure risk losing their funding. The United States Senate unanimously passed Bill 803 of the 107th Congress on July 8, 2002.

Commonly referred to as the "E-Government Act of 2002," Bill 803 establishes an Office of Electronic Government within the Office of Management and Budget. This bill is currently sitting in committee at the Office of Government Reform in the House of Representatives. Its eventual passage will send a clear signal that the U.S. places a high priority on e-Government.

Public/Private Partnership as a Unique Form of Outsourcing

The term "public/private partnership" (or P3) is often loosely used to describe any number of government outsourcing arrangements. However, as described by the National Council for Public-Private Partnerships, a P3 is actually "… a contractual agreement between a public agency (Federal, state or local) and a for-profit corporation. Through this agreement, the skills and assets of each sector (public and private) are shared in delivering a service or facility for the use of the public. In addition to the sharing of resources, each party shares in the risks and rewards potential in the delivery of the service and/or facility" (NCPPP, 2000).

The United States government is the world's largest consumer of ICT products and services, having spent more than $15 billion in 2002. It is imperative that this money be spent wisely and in the public interest. Increasingly, governments at all levels are focusing their efforts on designing public/private partnerships as a way to merge the skills of both internal and external talent in building systems that support the complex needs of the public sector. According to Mark Forman, Associate Director for IT and e-Government in OMB, some of those complex needs include:

- 5,600 government-to-business (G2B), government-to-government (G2G) and government-to-citizen (G2C) transactions to be put online,
- About 1,000 transactions to be put online,
- Over 33 million web pages must be made operational across 22,000 Federal government websites.

Given the magnitude of these e-Government needs, public/private partnerships can be considered reasonable alternative methods for meeting these needs in an expeditious manner. Government simply lacks the capacity to do it using strictly in-house staff. A partnership with business may provide access to important skills and resources that are in short supply in many government agencies and departments. If crafted carefully, a P3 has the ability to build in incentives to ensure the private partner understands the precise needs of government, and creates systems that meet them.

The General Accounting Office states that in a public/private partnership:

"...sometimes referred to as a joint venture, a contractual arrangement is formed between public- and private-sector partners that can include a variety of activities that involve the private sector in the development, financing, ownership, and operation of a public facility or service. It typically includes infrastructure projects and/or facilities. In such a partnership, public and private resources are pooled and responsibilities divided so that the partners' efforts complement one another. Typically, each partner shares in income resulting from the partnership in direct proportion to the partner's investment. Such a venture, while a contractual arrangement, differs from typical service contracting in that the private-sector partner usually makes substantial cash, at-risk, equity investment in the project, and the public sector gains access to new revenue or service delivery capacity without having to pay the private-sector partner. Leasing arrangements can be used to facilitate public-private partnerships (from http://www.gao.gov/special.pubs/gg97121.htm#PAGE23)."

The relationship described in the next section is a clear example of a public/private partnership that exhibits many of these characteristics.

VIRGINIA DEPARTMENT OF TAXATION AND AMERICAN MANAGEMENT SYSTEMS

The State of Virginia took an extraordinarily innovative approach to public/private partnership when it forged an agreement with American Management Systems (AMS) to re-engineer the Department of Taxation's (TAX) business processes. The agreement included a plan to replace the aging legacy computer system that was used to manage the state's revenues.

Together, TAX and AMS developed a self-funded project that is the largest and most comprehensive public/private partnership ever undertaken by a state revenue agency thus far. This $153 million contract, spanning six years, was authorized by the Virginia legislature in 1996 and signed in 1998. The partnership is unique for more reasons than just the size and scope of the project; it is unique because of the nature of the relationship between the partners. This project won the 2001 NASCIO (National Association of State Chief Information Officers) Recognition Award in the public/private partnership category. It is a vivid example of performance-based procurement and benefits-driven funding on a large scale (NASCIO, 2001).

The agreement between TAX and AMS takes an innovative approach to the sharing of risks and rewards. American Management Systems would not be paid until the Department of Taxation uses the new application successfully to increase tax collections. In many ways, the partnership operates like a fixed price contract, i.e., AMS performs services, TAX accepts deliverables, AMS invoices TAX, and TAX pays invoices from money previously deposited into a Technology Fund established as part of the project. The difference is that invoices are paid only if there is money available in the fund. The Technology Fund is derived from the difference between projected baseline revenues based on historical collections and the actual collections. Collections over or under that baseline are netted and deposited into the fund. The incremental revenue split is then 90% AMS and 10% TAX, until AMS is paid or the term of the contract expires. There is no benefit sharing; AMS is only paid for specified deliverables.

Those directly involved in the process consider this project to be a resounding success. Farley Beaton, chief information officer for the Virginia Department of Taxation says:

> The benefits-funded aspect provided a lot of incentive for our private partner to understand our needs, expectations and how we do business. This is critical, because the new tools have to be effective to generate the revenue to pay for the project. In addition, AMS needs us to be comfortable and capable of using the new tools effectively (remember AMS can't do audits for example — our auditors must be able to do audits faster using the new tools). So there is lots of focus on training and change management activities (Beaton, 2002).

The taxpayers are excited about the results of the project as well. They now have a "one-stop-shopping" web portal that provides access to policy information, forms and support for remote filing. This award-winning P3, with its customer-service focus, allowed TAX to undertake mission-critical improvements when appropriated funds were not available. Enhanced services to the public have been provided using e-Government technology, while costs to the public have been minimized through the partnership's unique benefits-funded payment method.

In addition to the money, there is other reward potential for the business partner. AMS and TAX are developing innovative and unique tools that AMS will subsequently have the ability to market to other states. Given the success of the Virginia model, it is inevitable that other fiscally strapped state governments will look favorably upon a similar opportunity to collaborate with AMS.

It would seem this P3 is a win-win situation for all involved.

E-GOVERNMENT P3 RISKS

When typical government contracts with business are negotiated, there is much discussion to determine how the risks will be distributed. In fixed-fee contracts, business assumes all the risk. In cost-reimbursement contracts, the risk shifts to government. However, such risk analyses are fundamentally financial in nature. They reference the fact that either the government or the business is more or less likely to lose money on the deal. Not to belittle this focus, but there are other risks that are just as important and they must be evaluated before government enters into a partnership agreement with the private sector. Government's charge to obtain the best value for the public must be balanced with its obligation to protect the public good. Public/private partnerships must be carefully negotiated to ensure government minimizes its exposure to financial risk. At the same time, one must consider other risks that threaten the public well being.

Individual Privacy

When governments partner with private entities for provision of public services, there should always be assurances that exposure to confidential records and citizen data will be protected. This issue becomes especially critical when the service being provided controls, manipulates and/or extracts the data itself.

Christopher Corbett (2002), director of the E-Government Forum at the Centre for Public Sector Studies at the University of Victoria in British Columbia, uses the term "data monopolies" to describe entities that own certain types of data to which others have no access. U.S. governments typically keep personal identification data about individual citizen compliance with tax regulations, criminal statues, entitlement programs, etc. confidential. They only publicly release such information collectively. Ownership of this data can be regarded as a government-run data monopoly. Yet, the public generally regards such a monopoly, designed to protect citizen privacy, as a good thing. What happens to the ownership of that data when government collaborates with business to develop e-Government applications? There are risks to the public when data traditionally controlled by public agencies and public employees, sworn to protect the public good, become input for private sector IS partnerships. If records acquired, stored, and maintained by government about its citizens are public goods, and many believe they are exactly that, then those records must be protected from commercial exploitation. Such data are shared resources owned by the public as a whole.

When public/private partnerships are created, a virtual monopoly results because the activities of government are unique and competitors are absent. For example, departments of taxation do not compete for their "market" with other organizations. Their private sector business partners participate in that monopoly. Information about the taxpayers, which is a necessary part of the e-Government system, must be protected from potential for-profit use by the business partner. That protection needs to be built into the contract and understood by all involved in the project.

Data Security

Closely tied to the notion of citizen privacy is the necessity of developing appropriate systems to protect collected data from unauthorized access and use. Often, government collaborates with the private sector to provide the required secure environment. A key component of any security system is the establishment of rules to determine who has what level of access to what type of data. The IS security manager, whatever his or her title, is responsible for implementing these rules. A P3 must address this issue in the contract negotiation phase by specifying precisely how the private-sector partner and its employees will work within an environment where data security is of utmost importance.

The events of September 11, 2001, resulted in a long overdue interest in U.S. "Homeland Security." Under the umbrella of a multitude of initiatives designed to protect the country and its citizens from terrorism in general, issues related to data security have moved to the forefront. The President's Critical Infrastructure Protection Board is developing a report entitled the "National Strategy to Secure Cyberspace" which was originally due to be released on September 8, 2002 (Fisher & Carlson). Instead of a final release, that report has been presented as a working draft to industry executives and government officials with requests for more input. Securing data, especially data that is transmitted by way of the public Internet, is an enormous challenge. Complicating the issue is the fact that the technology itself is a moving target.

Among the early recommendations in the report was the establishment of a federal Network Operations Center that would monitor the Internet for purposes of national security, and for which the government would seek a private sector partner. The technology industry, not surprisingly, is lobbying to limit the liability risks involved in sharing citizen data for the purposes of national security. Their concerns are legitimate. Data cannot be guaranteed to be 100% secure; at least not given the technology available today. Still, it would be unreasonable to shift all data security risks to government. The systems provider will need to bear responsibility for delivering what the contract specifies, and be willing to deal with the consequences when e-Government failure results in legal action.

Legal Liability

Should the unthinkable happen and citizens' data becomes compromised, made public and its unauthorized use becomes the source of business profit, who is ultimately held liable for the breach of security? Governments commonly require that their employees sign confidentiality agreements prohibiting them from revealing personal information from the public records that they work with on a daily basis. At the same time, specific penalties are attached to any violation of the agreement. Penalties range from disciplinary action to job loss to criminal charges, depending on the severity of the infraction. The frightening thing is that data loss, corruption and unauthorized dissemination can often occur without anyone noticing until long after the responsible employee has moved on. Thus, while it is important to have specific policies and penalties that hold individuals responsible for security breaches, inevitably government is ultimately liable for these mishaps.

Liability issues become more complex when government collaborates with business for the development and delivery of services that handle citizen records. In many cases, government insists on the same confidentiality agreements with its business partners that it requires from its own employees. Still, employee turnover, especially in the information technology field, is even more rapid in the private sector than in government. What happens if a private sector partner has a disgruntled employee who decides to destroy records of all public assistance recipients in a given jurisdiction? By the time it is discovered that the records are missing, and possibly millions of people have failed to receive their food stamps, that employee may have moved on. Government must then repair its public image, assist those people who have been shorted, investigate the matter, assess penalties for the disaster to its private sector partner, find the individual responsible and press criminal charges against that person. If any of those families affected suffer irreversible losses and seek legal counsel, government will be held primarily liable. The original rationale for the public/private partnership - achieving cost efficiencies — becomes an impossible goal at that point.

Government Accountability

Not surprisingly, public employee unions are adamantly opposed to public/private partnerships, as well as to other forms of outsourcing and privatization. While many of their arguments express concern about the loss of jobs and the economic impact of those losses on local communities, they also describe the risks to government accountability posed by such arrangements. The American Federation of State, County and Municipal Employees, for example, states in its report entitled, *Government for Sale,* that "the most efficient and effective use of public resources can be achieved through true partnership between front-line workers and managers without subjecting state and local governments and citizens to the risks associated with contracting out" (AFSCME, 2001). Leaders of this association emphasize the dangers of losing government capacity to provide public services through the dependency that results from contracting out. If the private partner fails to meet designated performance measures, government remains responsible for the service and may face legal liability by not providing it. They feel this risk is too great to justify the wide-scale privatization efforts currently underway.

The National Education Association (NEA) could not agree more. This group insists, "after years of study the alleged economic benefits of privatization are still unproven" (NEA, 2001). The association lists the following as risks posed by privatization:
- Lower Quality Services
- Accountability Problems
- Dependency
- Hidden Costs

The NEA is particularly concerned that "private companies cannot be held to the same standard of public scrutiny as school districts because they are not subject to the same requirements for open meetings, public information, and public input."

These and other public employee collective bargaining association concerns are often dismissed as being self-serving and motivated solely by a desire to save jobs, benefits and unreasonably high salaries and wages. Whether the risk to their personal standard of living is the primary motivation for pubic employee union opposition to P3s or not, their accountability concerns should not be dismissed. The risk is real.

E-Government Failure

According to many experts, 60% of e-Government initiatives are expected to fail or fall short of their goals. Judith Carr (2002) describes an environment in which the failure rate is extraordinarily high. She says, "The governance structures of many governments are not designed to support multi-department initiatives such as e-government. To complicate matters, some still view them as information technology projects rather than business initiatives. E-government can require new legislation, new procurement processes and new civil service rules — which are all difficult to change." There is no way to argue that e-Government public/private partnerships are simple matters. Government is complex. Technology is complex. Partnerships are never easy. At the intersection of these three concepts is the enormously challenging e-Government P3. Many believe overcoming those challenges is worth the effort. It is imperative, however, that such partnerships be approached with caution. Technology projects are expensive; when they involve Web-based applications (as most e-Government projects do), they become very public embarrassments when failure occurs.

One can certainly argue that there is much to be learned from e-Government project failure. Still, it is to be vigorously avoided since taxpayers are loath to discover that public dollars have been spent with little or nothing to show for the expense. Public/private partnerships are more complex than other forms of outsourcing. Their success is dependent upon the building of relationships between the contract partners and their employees, who are ultimately responsible for managing and monitoring the project. This relationship building is no easy accomplishment when the entities have such different value systems. There must be a balance struck that sets appropriate boundaries between these two realms, while allowing innovation and creativity to flourish. In many ways, this is unexplored territory and not every e-Government public/private partnership is an immediate success.

Threat of Market Enclosure

As David Bollier so eloquently argues in his book *Silent Theft*, unbridled privatization of the commons leads to market enclosures that threaten the very foundations of democracy. He defines "commons" as resources that the public collectively owns. As public/private partnerships are forged, and those agreements are cemented, public contract managers have a responsibility to ensure that ownership of public assets is not inadvertently (or intentionally) transferred into private hands. For example, the issue of data ownership mentioned previously described threats to citizen privacy through access to personal information. This is a very real concern and one that must be carefully considered. Perhaps even more important is the protection of ownership of data that are commonly held public resources, such as geospacial data, voter demographics or records of scientific discoveries. It is the nature of private companies to attempt to create boundaries around public resources to build monopoly markets for themselves. That is a tendency to be expected. It is the responsibility of government to restrict their ability to do so. This is a responsibility, as Bollier points out, which government rarely takes seriously. Inattention to the protection of our shared resources has led to such travesties as the plunder of public lands by mining and oil companies. The extraction of valuable resources from public land has often left in its wake dangerous chemical by products for which the minor fines assessed to business are insignificant compared to the billions in profits they realize. It is imperative that similar mistakes are not made as government partners with business to develop e-Government applications which provide expedited access to the greatest shared resource of all — information.

According to Bollier, enclosure can "impose new limits on citizen rights and public accountability, as private decision-making supplants the open procedures of our democratic polity" (p. 7). An interesting example of this risk can be seen in the U.S. Government handing off its right to control Internet domain name registration to a private company, Network Solutions, Inc. in 1993. NSI used this monopoly to charge exorbitant rates for some domain names, particularly with the .com suffix, and it lobbied Congress to ensure there were no competing domain name registration companies allowed to enter the market (Bollier, p. 115). This is a particularly egregious example of privatization resulting in the loss of a public resource. Public/private partnerships, for the most part, do at least ensure some form of continued government oversight and involvement. Still, technical complexities often make it difficult to see insidious market enclosure threats. An important first step for public managers is to ensure that all public/private partnership contracts cede sole ownership of all data, whether project input or output, to the public, under the stewardship of the government partner. Another safeguard is to insist that any code or software produced by the business partner as part of the agreement be non-proprietary and that it adhere to open-source standards.

E-GOVERNMENT P3 REWARDS

Federal information technology contracting amounted to $32 billion in 2001. In 2002, Federal IT contracts are projected to top $45 billion by 2002. Despite all the risks described in the previous section, there are clearly huge monetary rewards available to business for forming these relationships. In addition, there must be rewards to government as well, or this trend would not be on the increase.

Bruce Cahan discusses public/private partnerships as a type of public purpose partnership (PPP) uniquely positioned to find optimal solutions to problems by combining the resources of multiple players. He describes public purpose partnership arrangements as "dynamic mechanisms for locally-aware, situational governance and management of rapid change" (p. 1). Cahan argues that the historical growth and expansion of the United States would have been impossible without strategically leveraging the interests of the business community through careful use of PPPs in the service of the public good. He provides the example of the U.S. transcontinental highway system as one substantial public reward that resulted from the strategic use of PPPs in the twentieth century. He goes on to cite an array of rewards available to the public through these partnerships. First on the list, of course, is cost savings. In addition, he lists flexibility and less red tape, speedy implementation, increased innovation, and high quality service as the positive by products of PPPs (p. 8). These are obvious advantages to government and to the public. What, however, are the rewards to the non-governmental entity that decides to partner? Are there more than just financial rewards?

Here is where there are opportunities for unique and innovative partnerships to evolve. This issue of reward is also one that brings into sharpest focus the distinction between the values of public sector vs. private sector vs. non-profit sector organizations. A reward will only be perceived as such when it conforms to the value system of the organization for which it is intended.

Accelerated Research

Government partnerships with business, industry and academic institutions can provide essential resources dedicated to the solution of problems that threaten our health, welfare and way of life. For example, the federal government has played a leading role in the development of the Internet, the protocols of which support the e-Government ventures of today. Research funded by the Department of Defense led to the development of ARPANET, the precursor to the Internet. Even as early as 1969, when the first ARPANET node was established at UCLA, government partnered with other entities to achieve its information system and technology goals. In 1989, Tim Berners-Lee, a CERN (European Organization for Nuclear Research) computer scientist, invented the World Wide Web with its innovative use of hypertext for associating information. In 1993, Mosaic was developed by a team of 40 programmers at the National Center for Supercomputing Applications (NCSA) at the University of Illinois in Urbana-Champaign. This revolutionary graphical user interface allowed for browsing of the World Wide Web in a visually exciting format. Marc Andreessen, who helped form Mosaic Communications Corporation in 1994, was one of those programmers. This company slightly re-wrote Mosaic and brought it to market as Netscape Navigator. So government-developed software was appropriated by a private company and made available to a wider public. Clearly, this was not a true public/private partnership. Yet, the explosive growth of the World Wide Web demonstrates the positive results possible when government-funded research is partnered with private-sector marketing.

Public/private partnerships of all types are essential to the advancement of innovations in e-Government. Left to its own devices, the private sector is so focused on short-term profits that creative research and development is often discouraged. However, bring in government as a partner, and the intellectual capital produced by the two together can be incredible. The Internet has produced a global revolution that has rapidly changed the way we live, work and govern. As we learn to exploit its advantages for bringing us together, while controlling the chaos that occurs when we get too close, the need for continued research is imperative. The potential benefits to partnerships in this area include rewards for the public at large and profit-making applications for the private sector. These partnerships must be managed to avoid the market enclosure risks that might lead to private sector monopolies.

Open Source

Tim Berners-Lee is still very much involved with his creation. He leads the World Wide Web Consortium (W3C), which is an industry consortium, headed by the Laboratory for Computer Science at the Massachusetts Institute of Technology. The Internet and the World Wide Web were created in an open source environment. Programmers from all over the world participated in modifying and improving the code, developing standards, and designing protocols that allowed for cross-platform, non-proprietary tools to support time-and-place-independent collaboration, communication and research. The W3C believes that this open source approach is necessary for the continued evolution of the Web. Initially created in 1994 with the help of funding from the Defense Advanced Research Project Agency (DARPA), this group has as its focus the development of interoperable technologies.

The W3C is an example of a P3 that is composed of a large number of partners including government, business and higher education. The goal of interoperability requires adherence to open source tenets, but it does not preclude the ability to develop marketable products from the innovations fostered through the partnership. The open source movement, which for years was passionately supported by researchers and academicians, is beginning to be embraced by the private sector as well. Here is a force for innovation based on long-range planning, which acknowledges the role of the market in the dissemination of products developed through use of its standards.

Emergency Management and Disaster Recovery

On September 11, 2001, most U.S. citizens became aware, perhaps for the first time, that our emergency preparedness systems were poorly equipped to handle a large-scale disaster. Intergovernmental and inter-jurisdictional data 'fiefdoms' led to a situation where public safety departments at every level were unable to share information in a timely way. In New York, much of the recovery in those first few days following the attack was the result of public and private sector cooperation and collaboration. Utility companies came together to stabilize power and telecommunications systems. Within 48 hours, the Emergency Mapping & Data Center was established to provide spatial data to law enforcement, the military and rescue crews. Engineers and architects worked with government agencies to analyze the events leading to the destruction of the World Trade Center. The partnerships formed because of this horrible terrorist attack were unprecedented in the level of information sharing and goal communication. Such public/private cooperation for the public good will most certainly continue. Public/private partnerships which focus on the development of information systems that share essential data, while protecting proprietary business secrets and citizen privacy, are necessary to the improvement of the U.S. emergency management and disaster recovery process.

Cybersecurity

As discussed previously, public/private partnerships present unique risks to the security of public data. At the same time, there is a pervasive sense that the protection of the United States' technological infrastructure from terrorism is dependent upon the involvement of both government and business in cybersecurity efforts. NASCIO (National Association of State Chief Information Officers) has signed a memorandum of understanding with the multi-agency National Infrastructure Protection Center (NIPC) that will allow participating states to receive alerts concerning cyber and physical terrorism threats. This is believed to be the first step toward a full-featured Interstate Information Sharing and Analysis Center (ISAC). Neither the NIPC nor the ISAC will be truly effective without the involvement of private sector partners. One of NIPC's partners is the Financial Services Information Sharing and Analysis Center, which is designed for and by professionals in the banking, securities and insurance industries. The FS/ISAC is a resource that fosters trust among its members in the interest of sharing information regarding cybersecurity threats and solutions. While the federal government is not and cannot be a member of FS/ISAC, the two have collaborated to ensure that vital cybersecurity information moves smoothly between them.

The information sharing that is essential to protecting the nation's technological infrastructure is clearly a valuable result of the public/private partnership philosophy.

The rewards to the private sector are far more meaningful than the profits generated by the typical government contract. If cybersecurity partnerships work well, they will produce rewards shared by all in the form of a safer and more stable national information and telecommunications network.

Electronic Citizenry

Many believe that new digital technologies will enable widespread citizen participation in democratic government. Pippa Norris (2001) refers to those who see only positive results from the use of information and communications technology as *cyber-optimists*. These folks are convinced that ICT and the Internet will expand public knowledge and thus lead to citizen engagement with political leaders, ultimately resulting in a more representative democracy. On the other hand, she states that *cyber-skeptics* believe that digital technology will only exacerbate the existing divide between the haves and have-nots. She stated that "the global and social divides in Internet access mean that technological resources remain far from equally distributed and online politics may thereby amplify the voice of the affluent and well educated, with the prior interest, cognitive skills, and technical ability to utilize new forms of communication, but it may also further marginalize the apathetic and underprivileged" (p. 98). Clearly, the verdict is still out on whether technology and its use as a foundation for e-Government and e-Democracy will ultimately bridge the gap between the information rich and the information poor.

One of the most fundamental means of involvement in the democratic process is the act of voting. Technology use as an aid in elections is nothing new. However, its insertion into the most critical part of the process, the act of voting itself, is quite new. Following the 2000 Presidential election fiasco, local governments found themselves under greatly intensified pressure to develop stable and accurate election systems. Many of these jurisdictions, lacking the capacity and resources to build digital solutions themselves, have contracted with commercial entities to develop these systems. They have not been overwhelmingly successful.

The September 10, 2002 primary election in Florida presents an interesting case study. Election Systems & Software Inc. (ES&S) based in Omaha, Nebraska, supplied 22,440 of its iVotronic machines for use in 32 of Florida's 67 counties at a cost of $30 million. This was handled as a standard procurement contract with ES&S supplying the deliverables, and Florida then paying the bill. The use of this touch screen technology proved to be disastrous in some areas, including Miami-Dade and Broward counties. In many cases, the polls did not open because workers failed to pick up the devices needed to run the machines the night before the election. Other issues included precinct workers struggling to determine how to change the batteries in the machines, as well as the inability to download the votes from the machines once the votes were cast. Some reports state that at least 600 voters were turned away at the polls.

One often cited cause of these problems is inadequate training of the volunteers who work at the polling places. John Harrell (2002) at Kiosk Marketplace.com wrote, "the company was not contracted to train poll workers, according to Todd Urosevich (ES&S spokesman), though that service is available. Instead, ES&S trained county staff members, who then led poll worker training." However, Rebecca Mercuri (2002),

Computer Science faculty member at Bryn Mawr College and highly regarded expert on electronic voting issues, describes other serious flaws as well:

> *"A thorough inspection of the machines...was denied by the court, on the grounds that the purchase contract with Election Supervisor Teresa LaPore made it a felony violation (for her) of the vendor's trade secret clause if any devices were provided ... for an internal examination. This trade secrecy also apparently prevents disclosure of the program code files and testing reports maintained by the state of Florida as part of their certification process.... Sadly, many U.S. communities seem to feel that it is necessary to rush ahead with voting equipment procurements, while reliable systems, appropriate testing, usability, security, and auditability procedures, and other safeguards, are years away."*

Mercuri goes on to emphasize the need to verify that the ballot was properly cast, perhaps in the form of a paper printout or receipt that voters carry away with them. She also stresses the need for full-scale testing in an offline environment where verification of accuracy can be determined before Election Day.

Perhaps if government and business had worked together in a public\private partnership arrangement, many of these problems could have been circumvented. P3s require the negotiation of risks and rewards in an environment where the partners acquire an understanding of the goals of their respective organizations. Electronic government and e-Voting are too important to be left to the confines of traditional contract agreements. Had ES&S known more about the functions of the polling place, understood the nature of the workers, the comfort level of the voters, and the tolerance-level of both for a sudden introduction to new technology, the company may have been in a position to strongly recommend a focus on training and testing. Likewise, had government a better understanding of the necessary boundaries which protect business secrets, they may have been better able to negotiate a means of verifying the functionality of the voting system that would have respected those bounds.

After experiencing the national embarrassment of the primary election fiasco, Florida and ES&S came together to plan a strategy for the October 2, 2002 municipal elections which included "stationing three county employees and a representative of the voting machine manufacturer at every polling location to help the volunteer poll workers" (Robinson et. al., 2002). This Election Day came and went without controversy in large measure because government and business worked together as partners to ensure its success. The beauty of public/private partnerships, and the potential for rewards that enrich the private sector and serve the public well, lie at the intersection of the values that both sectors share. To the extent that public/private partnerships designed to support the development of an electronic citizenry carefully weigh the risks, and work to acquire a multitude of possible rewards, the public will be well served.

CONCLUSION

The Center for Technology in Government (http://www.ctg.albany.edu/) published a report in July 2002 entitled, *Making a Case for Local E-Government.* In that document, the authors declare the four dimensions of e-Government to be: e-Services, e-Management, e-Democracy, and e-Commerce (p. 3). From the simplest website which displays office addresses and phone numbers, through customizable portals providing the ability to pay taxes online, e-Government works only to the extent that it meets the needs of the public it serves. Like all government decision-making, the task of making discriminating technology-related choices is complex. Government managers must satisfy elected officials, political appointees, interest groups and the public at large. Often, the stated wishes of these various groups are in conflict. Nowhere is this more evident than when technology is involved.

There are some areas of convergence these days, however. With the advent of the terrorist attacks on September 11, 2001, there is now consensus on the issue of the need to protect the nation's technological resources. Most of us nod our heads vigorously when asked if we support research and development in support of technology innovation. Combine this with the present administration's intense focus on service provision through public/private partnerships, and we have an environment that is rich with creative ideas and innovative solutions. This is clearly a good thing.

There have been some incredible benefits derived from public/private partnerships, including the development of the Federal government's web portal, FirstGov.

"The Federal Search Foundation's pioneering 18-month PPP to initiate and populate a ubiquitous architecture for searching government Web pages and documents led to indexing over 50 million pages at 26,000 separate sites. The next generation of FirstGov will be based on an international partnership to search an anticipated 200 million indexed pages in less than half of a second. By not locking itself into a long-term arrangement and retaining rights to content and other intellectual property generated through the use by Fed Search of Inktomi technology, FirstGov was a successful experiment in interoperability. It also furthered the goals of e-Government and electronic freedom of information statutes" (Cahan, p. 19).

The rewards are many. But we must be ever vigilant to guard against the risks involved in these arrangements, including threats to citizen privacy and data security; legal liability and government accountability issues; the high chance of e-Government failure; and the dangers of market enclosure.

Answering the following questions could help public sector managers to evaluate potential e-Government public and private partnership projects (adapted from Wilson, p. 358):

1. What baseline capacity must the government agency or department retain? Will the partnership affect this capacity?
2. Does a private sector capacity exist? Is it adequate for government requirements?
3. What are the total costs of completing the project using internal resources versus collaborating with a commercial entity?
4. Can both internal and external partners provide data of adequate quality for project needs?
5. Can both internal and external partners complete the project within established deadlines?
6. How do internal and external partners impact legal requirements and regulatory action? What are the impacts on chain-of-custody and record retention?
7. Are the partners stable and reliable enough to fulfill contractual obligations?

8.   How will the partnership affect freedom of information and/or confidentiality concerns?
9.   Does the partner have the technical capacity to meet needs? Do they have the capability to meet needs using required protocols?
10. How does the partner assure the comparability of data it generates?
11. How will the government agency or department complete the project in the event of the failure of the partner?

That last question is an important one. If the e-Government partnership fails, government will inevitably be responsible for continuing the project anyway. It is extremely important to design the partnership in such a way that the risks and rewards, both monetary and non-monetary, are balanced. To the extent that both government and its business partner feel invested in the success of an e-Government project, the partnership is likely to thrive. Only through such a balance are the goals of all four dimensions of e-Government likely to be achieved. Public/private partnerships have proven themselves strong incubators for innovative solutions to e-Government problems.

REFERENCES

AFSCME. (2001). *Government for sale: An examination of the contracting out of state and local government services.* Retrieved 9/10/02 from the World Wide Web: http://www.afscme.org/wrkplace/saletc.htm.

Andersen, D.F. & Dawes, S.S. (1991). *Government information management.* Englewood Cliffs, NJ: Prentice Hall.

Beaton, F. (2002) E-mail and telephone correspondence. 9/10/02 through 10/02/02.

Bollier, D. (2002). *Silent theft: The private plunder of our common wealth.* New York: Routledge.

Cahan, B. B. (2002). *United states experience with public private partnerships.* Retrieved on 9/20/02 from the World Wide Web: http://www.fgipc.org/presentations/020531_OECDPublicPrivatePshipPaperFinal.pdf.

Carr, J. (2002). *GartnerEXP says a majority of e-government initiatives fail or fall short of expectations.* Retrieved on 9/28/02 from the World Wide Web: http://www4.gartner.com/5_about/press_releases/2002_04/pr20020430b.jsp.

Center for Technology in Government. (2002). *Making a case for local e-government.* Retrieved on 9/16/02 from the World Wide Web: http://www.ctg.albany.edu/egov/making_a_case.pdf.

Cooper, P.J. (2002). *Governing by contract: Challenges and opportunities for public managers.* Washington, D.C.: CQ Press.

Corbett, C. (2002). Are partnerships the right tool to manage privacy risks? Privacy and E-Government Conference presentation (February).

Dawes, S.S., et al. (2002). Four realities of it innovation in government. In Kobrak, P. (Ed.) *The political environment of public management.* New York: Longman (272-280).

DeLooff, L. (1997). *Information systems outsourcing decision-making: A managerial approach.* Hershey, PA: Idea Group Publishing.

Federal CIO Council. (2002). *The president's management agenda: Fiscal year 2002.*

Retrieved on 9/25/02 from the World Wide Web: http://www.fgipc.org/
  02_Federal_CIO_Council/Resource/48_Presidents_Management_Agenda.htm.
Fisher, D. & Carlson, C. (2002, September 23). Critics take on new fed plan. *E-Week* (p.
  1).
Forman, M. (2002, April 8). *Digital government: Emerging issues for the next six months.*
  NASCIO Presentation. Retrieved on 9/29/02 from the World Wide Web: http://
  www.iaconline.org/pptfiles/020409_Mark_Forman.ppt.
General Accounting Office. (2001). *Definition of public private partnership.* Retrieved
  on 9/18/01 from the World Wide Web: http://www.gao.gov/special.pubs/
  gg97121.htm.
Gronlund, A. (2002). *Electronic government: Design, applications & management.*
  Hershey, PA: Idea Group Publishing.
Hamlett, P.W. (1992). *Understanding technological politics: A decision-making
  approach.* Englewood Cliffs, NJ: Prentice Hall.
Harrell, J. (2002, September 19). *A touchscreen election saga.* Kioskmarketplace.com.
  Retrieved on 10/8/02 from the World Wide Web: http://www.kioskmarketplace.com/
  news_story.htm?i=13614.
Johnson, M. & Radcliff, D. (2001, November 9). *Cybersecurity czar: Protect IT infra-
  structure.* CNN.com. Retrieved on 09/16/02 from the World Wide Web: http://
  www.cnn.com/2001/TECH/internet/11/09/infrastructure.protection.idg/?related.
Kettl, D.F. (1993). *Sharing power: Public governance and private markets.* Washington, D.C.: Brookings.
Mercuri, R. (2002, September 11). Florida primary 2002: Back to the future. *Risks journal.*
  Retrieved on 10/02/02 from the World Wide Web: http://catless.ncl.ac.uk/Risks/
  22.24.html#subj1.
National Association of State Chief Information Officers (2001). *2001 NASCIO recognition award winners.* Retrieved on 9/10/02 from the World Wide Web: https://
  www.nascio.org/awards/2001awards.
National Council for Public-Private Partnerships. (2000). *How partnerships work.* Retrieved on 9/28/02 from the World Wide Web: http://ncppp.org/howpart/index.html.
National Education Association. (2001). *The case against privatization of educational
  support services.* Retrieved on 9/14/02 from the World Wide Web: http://
  www.nea.org/esp/privatization/privcase.html.
Norris, P. (2001). *Digital divide: Civic engagement, information poverty, and the
  internet worldwide.* New York: Cambridge University Press.
Office of Management and Budget. *Circular A-76.* Retrieved on 9/28/02 from the World
  Wide Web: http://www.whitehouse.gov/omb/circulars/a076/a076.html.
Robinson, A., Spangler, N. & Ross, K. (October 2, 2002). Palmetto Bay, North Miami see
  glitch-free votes. *Election Systems and Software.* Retrieved on 10/8/02: http://
  www.essvote.com/index.php?section=news_item&news_id=65.
Watson, R.P. (2002). To privatize or not to privatize? A city prepares to contract out
  services. In Watson, R.P. (Ed.), *Public administration: Cases in managerial role
  playing.* New York: Longman (142-145).
West, D. M. (2002). State and federal e-government in the united states. *Center for Public
  Policy.* Retrieved on 9/15/02 from the World Wide Web: http://
  www.insidepolitics.org/Egovt02us.html.

Wilson, J.Q. (1991). *Bureaucracy: What government agencies do and why they do it.* New York: Basic Books.

Chapter XIV

Ethics and Digital Government

Ronald E. Anderson
University of Minnesota, USA

ABSTRACT

After considering the high costs to digital government of inadequate ethical choices, the role of ethics in government generally is reviewed. While codes of ethics may not go far toward resolving ethical challenges, they provide bases for ethical discourses and embody key ethical principles. Selected principles from the Code of Ethics of the Association for Computing Machinery (ACM) are applied to contemporary ethical issues in the context of digital government. In the rapidly evolving environments of digital technology, it is impossible to anticipate the leading-edge ethical issues. However, there are solid ethical or moral imperatives to use these principles for resolution of the issues.

ETHICS AND THE COST OF DIGITAL GOVERNMENT

Inadequate ethical decision-making results in major cost implications for digital government. One cost area is unauthorized system access, particularly for producing damage, e.g., from computer code commonly called viruses. The other problem area is that of poor system design, particularly software failing to meet professional standards of quality. The former generally results from persons with an ethically defective intent to produce harm to the systems and their users. The latter generally results from the neglect of professional ethical standards requiring the implementation of a quality development process that yields quality products.

Security Failures

In the 1970s, when researchers first began to study the impact of information technology (IT) upon municipal and federal governments, their discourse rarely contained the terminology of risks, vulnerability or even unauthorized access (Kraemer, 1976). Even 20 years later, as the Internet began to play major roles in business and government, security breaches in IT systems generally were not seen as grave problems. Now, despite the regular practice of anti-virus screening and related procedures, security problems are expected and treated with utmost seriousness. Solutions are no longer seen as solely technical but social and ethical as well. Typically the IT (information technology) or IS (information system) departments in government agencies establish complex procedures allowing access to different system resources only by specific categories of employees. In addition, these agencies typically establish codes of conduct and require employees to sign an acceptable use policy (AUP).

Despite these ethics-related measures to contain malicious attempts to violating information systems, there are millions of destructive agents circulating the Internet at any given moment. In the year 2000, *InformationWeek* Research and PricewaterhouseCoopers LLP jointly conducted a global survey of 4,900 IT professionals across 30 nations to help estimate the cost of viruses and computer hacking.[1] The study estimated that the one-year cost amounted to more than 2.5% of the United States' Gross Domestic Product (GDP). Furthermore, the estimate cost worldwide was $1.6 trillion for the year 2000.

Quality Control Failures

Breakdowns in hardware are well known but software malfunctions are far more elusive. System failures are inherent to large software systems due to their complexity. Malfunctions also occur from design and programming mistakes, from errors in data input, and from user errors. Peter Neumann (1995) has devoted much of his professional career over the past two decades to documenting system risks and has found that a large share of them are due to failures in quality control. He continues to manage an Internet forum "The Risks Digest — Forum on Risks to the Public in Computers and Related Systems."[2] Many of his collected stories reveal the huge cost of system malfunctions that could have been avoided if professional standards of quality control had been followed. The ethical standards of the Software Engineering Society (Gotterbarn, 1991) as well as the Association for Computing Machinery (ACM) specify professional responsibility to follow quality processes and ensure quality systems.[3] Digital government systems, especially in the areas of revenue management and tax collection, with inherent weaknesses due to poor construction quality may yield huge financial costs.

Non-Monetary Costs

Failure to comply with IT-related ethical standards may result in major non-monetary losses such as the loss of personal privacy. Digital government systems for criminal justice are particularly problematic as breakdowns in arrest management and unintended releases from incarceration may eventually lead to loss of life due to criminal misconduct.

Solutions to System Failures

Technical solutions are critical to immediate or short-term reduction in risk due to system failures. (The degree of system risk is generally measured in terms of some combination of threat, vulnerability, and cost of recovery.) However, longer-term, strategic reductions in risk must include social, ethical and legal approaches. The more serious the general public, and stakeholder groups in particular, views violations of computer laws and computer ethics, the greater will be the pressure upon potential security violators to avoid or desist from destructive actions. However, the public is not likely to take these problems seriously unless IT-related professional societies and educational institutions take the lead. Furthermore, there are actions that governments themselves can take.

ETHICS AND GOVERNMENT

It is generally considered best practice for every government and every government agency to have a code of ethics or conduct. The American Society for Public Administration (ASPA)[4] recommends and gives specific guidelines for implementation of such codes. The United Nations and OECD also offer guidelines for national and local governments in developing codes of ethics. A compilation of government (both national and local) codes of ethics can be found at the web site of the Center for the Study of Ethics in the Professions (CSEP) at the Illinois Institute of Technology.[5]

Almost all states and most large cities have web sites with their codes of ethical conduct. However, very few of these ethical codes address issues specific to IT.

The American Society for Public Administration (ASPA) Code of Ethics is summarized in Table 1. The complete code further qualifies each of the five main imperatives with seven specific principles. The main imperatives of this Code are similar to those of most similar professional associations with the exception of inclusion of imperatives on "serving the public" (I) and on building organizational ethical capacity (IV).

Table 1: Summary of Code of Ethics of the American Society for Public Administration

Ethical Imperatives	Clarification of Imperatives
I. Serve the Public Interest	Serve the public, beyond serving oneself.
II. Respect the Constitution and the Law	Respect, support, and study government constitutions and laws that define responsibilities of public agencies, employees, and all citizens.
III. Demonstrate Personal Integrity	Demonstrate the highest standards in all activities to inspire public confidence and trust in public service.
IV. Promote Ethical Organizations	Strengthen organizational capabilities to apply ethics, efficiency and effectiveness in serving the public.
V. Strive for Professional Excellence	Strengthen individual capabilities and encourage the professional development of others.

The Association of Government Accountants (AGA) has established a much larger Code because not only does it include standards for ethical behavior, but also it incorporates a guide for making ethical decisions.[6] It even goes a step further and specifies minimum expected levels of behavior. The ASPA and the AGA are professional associations of persons primarily working in government, and their Codes of Ethics should not be confused with government codes of conduct.

The predominant emphasis in government codes of conduct or ethics tends to be conflicts of interest. These conflicts range from the general ones derived from an employee having both a public and private role to those conflicts arising from political campaigning and from contracting for services. In addition to these conflicts of interest, the ethical codes of governments and government agencies tend to specify a variety of rules addressing such issues as stealing, punctuality, honesty and quality of relations with the public.

Typical codes of ethics of public agencies reveal the political character of the implementation of ethical standards. The ethical codes of organizations attempt to control and constrain the behavior of employees or similar subservient groups, such as students. Compared with the ethical codes of professional associations, they are much more regulatory than normative. When codes of professional ethics first emerged, they tended to be regulatory, if not authoritarian, in character. The obligations of members were explicitly stated so that there could be a basis for judging compliance and sanctioning noncompliance. Contemporary codes of professional ethics recognize the role of social norms and tend to minimize issues of enforcement. They implicitly recognize that codes of professional ethics are only a partial representation of the ethical standards of the members of the professional group (Parker, Swope, and Baker, 1990). In this way, they reinforce the fact that professional's participation in an association is voluntary. Professionals are expected to apply standards autonomously.

It is generally accepted that employee roles are less autonomous and that employees must abide by the directions and rules of the organizational hierarchy in which they work. Perhaps because of the traditions of power that government organizations have over their employees, the ethical codes of these organizations tend to overlap with and become confused with non-ethical rules such as punctuality. The implicit message to employees is that moral obligations are on par with "company" rules.

This undermining of individual moral responsibility is reinforced by the fact that most codes of ethics of government organizations were designed for their employees rather than the organization itself or the organization's leaders. This implicitly suggests to the government worker that ethics are a matter of power and control rather than personal and moral responsibility.

Professional groups and government agencies are both technical and moral communities because the members have shared goals and need to specify appropriate ways to achieve them (Camenisch, 1983; Frankel, 1989). In order to specify appropriate actions it is necessary to detail what types of behavior are ethically acceptable or not, and codes of ethics serve that function. Neither every agency nor professional group has established a code of ethics, however. The Computer Professionals for Social Responsibility (CPSR) rejected a code of ethics because it was seen as an excuse for avoiding personal and collective action (Chapman, 1990). Because ethical codes on specific issues often leave the interpretation up to the individual, they are sometimes viewed by political activists as a failure to take action.

ETHICS FOR DIGITAL GOVERNMENT

As the digital government movement is recent and relatively uninstitutionalized, it is not surprising that there have been few attempts to write ethical principles specific to IT applications in government. One exception is an "e-gov ethics code" written by a partnership between govWorks Inc., Arthur Andersen and American Management Systems, Inc.[7] Their five principles are: (1) to prohibit use and resale of consumer data, (2) disclose all fees and costs associated with e-government services, (3) accurately represent the number and scope of e-government services offered, (4) accurately represent affiliate relationships relevant to vendor selection, and (5) help bridge the digital divide. With the exception of the latter principle, all of them are intended to establish fairness among those involved in the process of government procurement of digital products and services. This is consistent with the earlier argument that ethics is often used as a political tool. In this instance it is not intended so much as an alternative to policy but as an interim measure until the field expands and matures.

In order to analyze ethics for digital government, we use the ethical standards of the ACM (Association for Computing Machinery) Code of Ethics and Professional Conduct. The full code appears as an appendix to this article. The ACM Code was chosen because of its generic character. While it is already over ten years old, it still addresses the underlying ethical considerations behind new technical and organization issues arising from recent developments in new technology. With a membership of over 75,000, the ACM is the largest, oldest and most influential association of computer scientists and IT professionals.

In the decade since the ACM Code was established, the Internet has grown at an extremely fast pace, but the institutional structures have not outgrown those of the older IT industry. Thus, there has not been a lot of progress in the development of ethical codes for the Internet and its culture. One typical exception is the Ethics Code of the Association of Ethical Internet Professionals (AEIP).[8] Some specifics of this Code will be mentioned below, but with the exception of a few points regarding web site management and SPAM, a lot of work remains to be done.

The ACM Code is divided into four sections with the first section giving a set of general moral considerations, the second identifying additional ethical principles applying to computing professionals, the third section pertaining to organizational leaders, and the final dealing with issues of general compliance with the code. (See Appendix A.) There is an important consideration embedded within this structure. The first section contains general moral imperatives that on the surface do not have anything to do with issues unique to IT. One purpose of incorporating these general moral imperatives is to implicitly demonstrate how specific professional issues are grounded in the general moral principles found in every ethical code. Too often, the imperatives of an ethical code appear to be arbitrary rules rather than interpretations of how to apply general ethical principles (Luegenbiehl, 1992). One significant feature of this approach is that it demonstrates how individual members can apply the general moral principles to new problems or dilemmas. With a rapidly evolving technology that often raises new moral dilemmas, it is critical that the individuals be given the 'tools' to make their own decisions in the face of novel ethical situations (Christensen, 1986).

The first seven imperatives, numbered from 1.1 to 1.7, all are generic in that they do not specify any to technology-specific issues. The second set, which is numbered from

2.1 to 2.8, is written implicitly from the point of view of an IT professional. In addition, some deal explicitly with information technology.

Human Well-Being

1.1 Contribute to Society and Human Well-Being

This imperative should be given highest priority because it is fundamental to many of the other moral imperatives that follow. It implies that the quality of life of all people is a critical value and that respect for the interests and rights of human beings, no matter what race or culture, is important. In their review of 31 codes of ethics of IT associations, Berleur and Ewbank de Wespin (2002) found this principle to be a common thread throughout all of the codes.

1.2 Avoid Harm to Others

This principle on the surface seems to be a rephrasing of the first principle. Both point to beneficence as a key ethical principle, which Spinello (2000) argues is consistent with most ethical theories. This principle is particularly important in the context of digital government because (1) it suggests that systems are ethically inappropriate if they produce harm and (2) such harm applies to people in all relevant roles including users, employers, employees, as well as the general public.

Honesty and Integrity

1.3 Be Honest and Trustworthy

Honesty and integrity are another part of another principle found in the majority of IT-related codes of ethics (Berleur and Ewbank de Wespin, 2002). As mentioned earlier, a major preoccupation of ethical codes in government is conflict of interest. Honesty and openness is a principal step to reconcile the conflicts. Of course, honesty cannot always resolve the problems and other steps may be necessary.

Fairness

1.4 Be Fair and Take Action Not to Discriminate

This imperative prohibits "discrimination on the basis of race, sex, religion, age, disability, national origin, or other such factors." Issues of fairness and discrimination have consolidated since 1995 around the rhetoric of the "digital divide" movement. To facilitate access to e-government resources, a major initial challenge is in building Internet access to very low-income homes, but several exemplary programs have demonstrated that it is feasible.[9]

Intellectual Property

1.5/1.6 Honor Property Rights Including Copyrights and Patents, and Give Proper Credit for Intellectual Property

Rights to digital artifacts such as software and multimedia materials have become considerably more complex and challenging in an era of rapidly expanding Internet technology. For instance, ownership of domain names and the right to link to valuable web-based resources have become valuable commodities. Even the right to use specific words or names in web page content, or to use those words as metatags, can sometimes have considerable commercial value. When these information commodities are perceived to have serious value, any unauthorized use may result in a lawsuit. As new information commodities emerge from new technologies, initially neither conventional legal precedents nor ethical standards are likely to satisfy the parties involved. This process will continue in the future such that it is unlikely that current interpretations of ethical principles regarding intellectual property will resolve the questions within the short-run.

Privacy

1.7/1.8 Respect the Privacy of Others, and Honor Confidentiality

These principles specify an explicit obligation to protect data about individuals "from unauthorized access or accidental disclosure to inappropriate individuals." The ACM Code Guidelines also specify that "organizational leaders" have obligations to "verify that systems are designed and implemented to protect personal privacy." Privacy is the ethical area in which there is the greatest divergence of opinion across national cultures. Whereas in the United States, privacy is generally thought to be an ethical issue, outside the United States, privacy is not so often justified with a moral foundation. Nevertheless, in some European and Asian countries, the privacy laws and norms are more stringent than in the United States.

Internet technology and associated services continue to raise new concerns over the ways in which personal information is readily collected, transferred, sold and misused. For instance, whenever one accesses a web page or interacts with a web page, information about one's personal interests is left behind. That information often has commercial value and so, despite popular objections to the loss of such personal information, there is considerable pressure to allow for its collection and use. Some of the strategies to deal with these conflicts of interest include implementation of the ethical principle of informed consent, and this is generally applied by allowing one to clearly opt-out of any planned use for one's personal data or to opt-in, that is to explicitly choose to release the data. It is likely that both government- and self-regulation will be useful strategies for dealing with these challenges.

Quality of Work

2.1 Strive to Achieve the Highest Quality, Effectiveness and Dignity in Both the Process and Products of Professional Work

The ACM Code contains numerous references to quality. Principle 2.1 stipulates quality as a goal for professional work and 3.2 stipulates enhancement of the quality of life as a criterion for evaluating information systems. Principle 2.4 specifies that one must accept and provide appropriate professional review, in part to assure quality of work products. "Professional review" here suggests a class of review commonly called peer review. While this is institutionalized among independent professionals, when professionals work on projects intended to produce propriety products, then an open review process is unlikely to be feasible. The Code provides for such situations by stating that peer review is necessary "whenever appropriate." Principle 2.5 specifies that professionals should conduct thorough evaluation of systems for possible problems and risks. The elaboration of this principle goes one step further and spells out that such details suggesting risks should be reported to appropriate authorities.

Respect for Existing Law

2.3 Know and Respect Existing Laws Pertaining to Professional Work

This imperative is interpreted by the Code as saying that one should obey laws (pertaining to one's professional work) "unless there is a compelling ethical basis not to do so." It also states that if a law is considered inappropriate, then it "must be challenged," but individuals must accept full responsibility for any violation of such laws.

Unauthorized Access

2.8 Access Computing and Communication Resources Only When Authorized to Do So

This principle arose from the growing concern about controlling the rising variety of computer viruses and other intrusions that threatened computer and communications systems in the early 1990s. Now more than ever, such intrusions are producing widespread damage and need to be contained. While some argued that unauthorized accesses were sometimes a desirable intrusion because system vulnerabilities were identified, this argument has become less compelling.

Freedom of Speech

The main issue of contemporary cyber ethics not addressed by these principles drawn from the ACM Code is that of free speech and content control. To some extent, free speech issues overlap with privacy issues. For example, spam (e.g., unsolicited e-mail advertising) senders claim to justify their actions by the principle of freedom of speech. It is also argued that it consists of a violation of the privacy of the individual recipient.

Probably the most controversial free speech issues in cyberspace are those having to do with filtering web sites, that is, using software that steers web browsers away from web sites with particular types of content. Two types of content that are most often found objectionable are pornography and "hate speech." It is not personal use of filters that has become controversial, but public use. For instance, it is argued that schools that use filters keep students from accessing desirable educational materials, and libraries that use filters take away the access rights of those who wish to view or read the material. It is challenging, if not impossible, to project the new forms of speech that will arise in the evolving digital age.

CONCLUSION

Ethical responsibilities increase, as the potential for harm increases from a single unethical decision due to technological development (Kidder, 1992). Law enforcement cannot keep pace with such rapid technological change. It is impossible to write a definitive ethical code for digital government because of the rapidly changing nature of the field. Although it is only part of the solution, creating and applying an effective code of ethics can be an extremely important process.

New technological risks and dilemmas cause us to re-think how to apply fundamental moral imperatives to our everyday lives. Thus, computing serves as a mirror for society to reflect upon its moral standards and ethical performance. Many ongoing ethical issues that have been raised by the evolution of computing technology point to the significance of this reflective experience for society. We should not forget that ultimately our hope for survival in the face of computer-based risks depends largely on the ethical standards of individuals working with computers.

While the ethical controversies in digital government may seem prominent, the ethical consensus may be far more significant. In examining the values of the cyberspace freedom advocates or the promoters of media control, we find a remarkable degree of ethical consensus. The vast majority still deeply believes in integrity, fairness, human well-being, respect for privacy, professional responsibility, and even respect for intellectual property. We need to remember these solid areas of agreement while discussing or debating the controversial topics. We also should attempt to coordinate action on the divisive issues, such as intellectual property and privacy that underlie specific ethical disagreements.

ENDNOTES

[1]   The results of this study were reported widely on the Internet and can still be found on such URLs as http://www.vnunet.com/News/1106282.

[2]   The Risks Digest is located at http://catless.ncl.ac.uk/Risks.

[3]   The ACM Code of Ethics is appended to this chapter. It also can be found at http://www.acm.org/constitution/code.html. The Software Engineering Code of Ethics and Professional Practice is given in full at http://www.acm.org/serving/se/code.htm.

[4]   The APSA guidelines and Code of Ethics are at their web site: http://www.aspanet.org/ethics/.

[5]   The large list of links to government codes of ethics is found at CSEP's web site: http://www.iit.edu/departments/csep/PublicWWW/codes/gov.html.

[6]   The AGA Code of Ethics can be downloaded from http://www.agacgfm.org.

[7]   See article by Daniel Keegan, June 26, 2000 in the *Federal Computer Week* and reprinted at http://www.fcw.com/fcw/articles/2000/0626/tec-ethics-06-26-00.asp.

[8]   The code is located at http://www.aeip.com/ethics-f.html.

[9]   See the Benton Foundation's report "The Digital Beat," Vol. 1, No. 8 (July, 1999) at http://www.benton.org/DigitalBeat/db070899.html.

REFERENCES

Anderson, R., et al. (1992). Using the new acm code of ethics. *Communications of the ACM, 35*(5), 94-99.

Berleur, J. & Ewbank de Wespin, T. (2002). Self-regulation: Content, legitimacy and efficiency - governance and ethics (pp. 89-108). In *Human Choice and Computers: Issues of Choice and Quality of Life in the Information Society*. Boston, MA: Kluwer Academic Publishers.

Camenisch, P. F. (1983). *Grounding Professional Ethics In a Pluralistic Society*. New York: Haven Publications.

Chapman, G. (1990). Presentation at the ACM/SIGCAS conference on computers and the quality of life. Washington, D.C.: The George Washington University.

Christensen, K. E. (1986). Ethics of information technology. In Geiss, G. and Viswanathan, N. (Eds.), *The Human Edge: Information Technology and Helping People.* New York: Haworth Press.

Clark, D. (1990). *Computers at Risk: Safe Computing in the Information Age.* National Research Council, National Academy Press.

Forester, T. & Morrison, P. (1990). *Computer Ethics: Cautionary Tales and Ethical Dilemmas in Computing.* Cambridge, MA: MIT Press.

Frankel, M. S. (1989). Professional Codes: Why, How, and with What Impact? *Journal of Business Ethics, 8*(2 & 3), 109-116.

Gotterbarn, D. (1991). Computer ethics: Responsibility regained. *National Forum: the Phi Kappa Phi Journal,* LXXI(3).

Johnson, D. (1985). *Computer Ethics.* Englewood Cliffs: Prentice Hall.

Kidder, R. M. (1992). Ethics: A matter of survival. *The Futurist,* (March/April), 10-12.

Kraemer, K. (1976). A future cities survey research design for policy analysis. *Socio-Economic Planning Sciences, 10*(11), 199-211.

Luegenbiehl, H. C. (1992). Computer professionals: Moral autonomy and a code of ethics. *Journal of Systems Software, 17,* 61-68.

Martin, C. D. & Martin, D. H. (1990). Comparison of ethics codes of computer professionals. *Social Science Computer Review, 9*(1), 96-108.

Neumann, P. G. (1995). *Computer-Related Risks.* Reading, MA: Addison-Wesley.

Parker, D., Swope, S. & Baker, B. (1990). *Ethical Conflicts in Information and Computer Science, Technology and Business.* Wellesley, MA: QED Information Sciences.

Spineollo, R. (2000). *Cyber Ethics.* Sudbury, MA: Jones and Bartlett.

APPENDIX A
ACM Code of Ethics and Professional Conduct*

Preamble. Commitment to ethical professional conduct is expected of every member (voting members, associate members and student members) of the Association for Computing Machinery (ACM).

This Code, consisting of 24 imperatives formulated as statements of personal responsibility, identifies the elements of such a commitment. It contains many, but not all, issues that professionals are likely to face. Section 1 outlines fundamental ethical considerations, while Section 2 addresses additional, more specific considerations of professional conduct. Statements in Section 3 pertain more specifically to individuals who have a leadership role, whether in the workplace or in a volunteer capacity such as with organizations like ACM. Principles involving compliance with this Code are given in Section 4.

The Code shall be supplemented by a set of Guidelines, which provide explanation to assist members in dealing with the various issues contained in the Code. It is expected that the Guidelines will be changed more frequently than the Code.

The Code and its supplemented Guidelines are intended to serve as a basis for ethical decision making in the conduct of professional work. Secondarily, they may serve as a basis for judging the merit of a formal complaint pertaining to violation of professional ethical standards.

It should be noted that although computing is not mentioned in the imperatives of Section 1.0, the Code is concerned with how these fundamental imperatives apply to one's conduct as a computing professional. These imperatives are expressed in a general form to emphasize that ethical principles that apply to computer ethics are derived from more general ethical principles.

It is understood that some words and phrases in a code of ethics are subject to varying interpretations, and that any ethical principle may conflict with other ethical principles in specific situations. Questions related to ethical conflicts can best be answered by thoughtful consideration of fundamental principles, rather than reliance on detailed regulations.

1.   GENERAL MORAL IMPERATIVES. As an ACM member, I will …
1.1   Contribute to society and human well-being.
1.2   Avoid harm to others.
1.3   Be honest and trustworthy.
1.4   Be fair and take action not to discriminate.
1.5   Honor property rights including copyrights and patents.
1.6   Give proper credit for intellectual property.
1.7   Respect the privacy of others.
1.8   Honor confidentiality.

2.   MORE SPECIFIC PROFESSIONAL RESPONSIBILITIES. As an ACM computing professional, I will …
2.1   Strive to achieve the highest quality, effectiveness and dignity in both the process and products of professional work.
2.2   Acquire and maintain professional competence.
2.3   Know and respect existing laws pertaining to professional work.
2.4   Accept and provide appropriate professional review.
2.5   Give comprehensive and thorough evaluations of computer systems and their impacts, including analysis of possible risks.
2.6   Honor contracts, agreements, and assigned responsibilities.
2.7   Improve public understanding of computing and its consequences
2.8   Access computing and communication resources only when authorized to do so.

3.   ORGANIZATIONAL LEADERSHIP IMPERATIVES. As an ACM member and an organizational leader, I will …
3.1   Articulate social responsibilities of members of an organizational unit and encourage full acceptance of those responsibilities.
3.2   Manage personnel and resources to design and build information systems that enhance the quality of working life.
3.3   Acknowledge and support proper and authorized uses of an organization's computing and communication resources.
3.4   Ensure that users and those who will be affected by a system have their needs clearly articulated during the assessment and design of requirements; later the system must be validated to meet requirements.
3.5   Articulate and support policies that protect the dignity of users and others affected by a computing system.

3.6   Create opportunities for members of the organization to learn the principles and limitations of computer systems.

4.   COMPLIANCE WITH THE CODE. As an ACM member, I will..
4.1   Uphold and promote the principles of this Code.
4.2   Treat violations of this code as inconsistent with membership in the ACM.

Guidelines
1.   GENERAL MORAL IMPERATIVES. As an ACM member I will..
1.1   Contribute to society and human well-being.

This principle concerning the quality of life of all people affirms an obligation to protect fundamental human rights and to respect the diversity of all cultures. An essential aim of computing professionals is to minimize negative consequences of computing systems, including threats to health and safety. When designing or implementing systems, computing professionals must attempt to ensure that the products of their efforts will be used in socially responsible ways, will meet social needs, and will avoid harmful effects to health and welfare.

In addition to a safe social environment, human well-being includes a safe natural environment. Therefore, computing professionals who design and develop systems must be alert to, and make others aware of, any potential damage to the local or global environment.

1.2   Avoid harm to others.

"Harm" means injury or negative consequences, such as undesirable loss of information, loss of property, property damage or unwanted environmental impacts. This principle prohibits use of computing technology in ways that result in harm to any of the following: users, the public, employees, employers. Harmful actions include intentional destruction or modification of files and programs leading to serious loss of resources or unnecessary expenditure of human resources such as the time and effort required to purge systems of "computer viruses."

Well-intended actions, including those that accomplish assigned duties, may lead to harm unexpectedly. In such an event, the responsible person or persons are obligated to undo or mitigate the negative consequences as much as possible. One way to avoid unintentional harm is to carefully consider potential impacts on all those affected by decisions made during design and implementation.

To minimize the possibility of indirectly harming others, computing professionals must minimize malfunctions by following generally accepted standards for system design and testing. Furthermore, it is often necessary to assess the social consequences of systems to project the likelihood of any serious harm to others. If system features are misrepresented to users, co-workers or supervisors, the individual computing professional is responsible for any resulting injury.

In the work environment, the computing professional has the additional obligation to report any signs of system dangers that might result in serious personal or social damage. If one's superiors do not act to curtail or mitigate such dangers, it may be necessary to "blow the whistle" to help correct the problem or reduce the risk. However, capricious or misguided reporting of violations can be in itself harmful. Before reporting violations, all relevant aspects of the incident must be thoroughly assessed. In particular, the assessment of risk and responsibility must be credible. It is suggested that advice be sought from other computing professionals. See principle 2.5 regarding thorough evaluations.

1.3   Be honest and trustworthy.

Honesty is an essential component of trust. Without trust, an organization cannot function effectively. The honest computing professional will not make deliberately false or deceptive claims about a system or system design, but will instead provide full disclosure of all pertinent system limitations and problems.

A computer professional has a duty to be honest about his or her own qualifications, and about any circumstances that might lead to conflicts of interest.

Membership in volunteer organizations such as ACM may at times place individuals in situations where their statements or actions could be interpreted as carrying the "weight" of a larger group of professionals. An ACM member will exercise care to not misrepresent ACM or positions and policies of ACM or any ACM units.

1.4   Be fair and take action not to discriminate.

The values of equality, tolerance, respect for others, and the principles of equal justice govern this imperative. Discrimination based on race, sex, religion, age, disability, national origin or other such factors is an explicit violation of ACM policy and will not be tolerated.

Inequities between different groups of people may result from the use or misuse of information and technology. In a fair society, all individuals would have equal opportunity to participate in, or benefit from, the use of computer resources regardless of race, sex, religion, age, disability, national origin or other such similar factors. However, these ideals do not justify unauthorized use of computer resources nor do they provide an adequate basis for violation of any other ethical imperatives of this code.

1.5   Honor property rights including copyrights and patents.

Violation of copyrights, patents, trade secrets and the terms of license agreements is prohibited by law in most circumstances. Even when software is not so protected, such violations are contrary to professional behavior. Copies of software should be made only with proper authorization. Unauthorized duplication of materials must not be condoned.

1.6   Give proper credit for intellectual property.

Computing professionals are obligated to protect the integrity of intellectual property. Specifically, one must not take credit for other's ideas or work, even in cases where the work has not been explicitly protected by copyright, patent, etc.

1.7   Respect the privacy of others.

Computing and communication technology enables the collection and exchange of personal information on a scale unprecedented in the history of civilization. Thus, there is increased potential for violating the privacy of individuals and groups. It is the responsibility of professionals to maintain the privacy and integrity of data describing individuals. This includes taking precautions to ensure the accuracy of data, as well as protecting it from unauthorized access or accidental disclosure to inappropriate individuals. Furthermore, procedures must be established to allow individuals to review their records and correct inaccuracies.

This imperative implies that only the necessary amount of personal information be collected in a system, that retention and disposal periods for that information be clearly defined and enforced, and that personal information gathered for a specific purpose not be used for other purposes without consent of the individual(s). These principles apply to electronic communications, including electronic mail, and prohibit procedures that capture or monitor electronic user data, including messages, without the permission of users or bona fide authorization related to system operation and maintenance. User data observed during the normal duties of system operation and maintenance must be treated with strictest confidentiality, except in cases where it is evidence for the violation of law, organizational regulations, or this Code. In these cases, the nature or contents of that information must be disclosed only to proper authorities (see 1.9).

1.8   Honor confidentiality.

The principle of honesty extends to issues of confidentiality of information whenever one has made an explicit promise to honor confidentiality or, implicitly, when private information not directly related to the performance of one's duties becomes available. The ethical concern is to respect all obligations of confidentiality to employers, clients and users unless discharged from such obligations by requirements of the law or other principles of this Code.

2.   MORE SPECIFIC PROFESSIONAL RESPONSIBILITIES. As an ACM comput-
        ing professional, I will . . .
*2.1   Strive to achieve the highest quality, effectiveness and dignity in both the process
        and products of professional work.*

Excellence is perhaps the most important obligation of a professional. The comput-
ing professional must strive to achieve quality and to be cognizant of the serious negative consequences that may result from poor quality in a system.

2.2   Acquire and maintain professional competence.

Excellence depends on individuals who take responsibility for acquiring and maintaining professional competence. A professional must participate in setting standards for appropriate levels of competence, and strive to achieve those standards. Upgrading technical knowledge and competence can be achieved in several ways: doing independent study; attending seminars, conferences, or courses; and being involved in professional organizations.

2.3   Know and respect existing laws pertaining to professional work.

ACM members must obey existing local, state, province, national and international laws unless there is a compelling ethical basis not to do so. Policies and procedures of the organizations in which one participates must also be obeyed. However, compliance must be balanced with the recognition that sometimes existing laws and rules may be immoral or inappropriate and, therefore, must be challenged. Violation of a law or regulation may be ethical when that law or rule has inadequate moral basis or when it conflicts with another law judged more important. If one decides to violate a law or rule because it is viewed as unethical, or for any other reason, one must fully accept responsibility for one's actions and for the consequences.

2.4   Accept and provide appropriate professional review.

Quality professional work, especially in the computing profession, depends on professional reviewing. Whenever appropriate, individual members should seek and utilize peer review as well as provide critical review of the work of others.

2.5   Give comprehensive and thorough evaluations of computer systems and their impacts, including analysis of possible risks.

Computer professionals must strive to be perceptive, thorough and objective when evaluating, recommending and presenting system descriptions and alternatives. Computer professionals are in a position of special trust, and therefore have a special responsibility to provide objective, credible evaluations to employers, clients, users and the public. When providing evaluations, the professional must also identify any relevant conflicts of interest, as stated in imperative 1.3.

As noted in the discussion of principle 1.2 on avoiding harm, any signs of danger from systems must be reported to those who have opportunity and/or responsibility to resolve them. See the guidelines for imperative 1.2 for more details concerning harm, including the reporting of professional violations.

2.6   Honor contracts, agreements, and assigned responsibilities.

Honoring one's commitments is a matter of integrity and honesty. For the computer professional this includes ensuring that system elements perform as intended. Also, when one contracts for work with another party, one has an obligation to keep that party properly informed about progress toward completing that work. A computing professional has a responsibility to request a change in any assignment that he or she feels cannot be completed as defined. Only after serious consideration and with full disclosure of risks and concerns to the employer or client, should one accept the assignment. The major underlying principle here is the obligation to accept personal accountability for professional work. On some occasions, other ethical principles may take greater priority.

A judgment that a specific assignment should not be performed may not be accepted. Having clearly identified one's concerns and reasons for that judgment, but failing to procure a change in that assignment, one may yet be obligated, by contract or by law, to proceed as directed. The computing professional's ethical judgment should be the final guide in deciding whether or not to proceed. Regardless of the decision, one must accept the responsibility for the consequences.

However, performing assignments "against one's own judgment" does not relieve the professional of responsibility for any negative consequences.

2.7   Improve public understanding of computing and its consequences.

Computing professionals have a responsibility to share technical knowledge with the public by encouraging understanding of computing, including the impacts of computer systems and their limitations. This imperative implies an obligation to counter any false views related to computing.

2.8   Access computing and communication resources only when authorized to do so.
    Theft or destruction of tangible and electronic property is prohibited by imperative 1.2 — "Avoid harm to others." Trespassing and unauthorized use of a computer or communication system is addressed by this imperative. Trespassing includes accessing communication networks and computer systems, or accounts and/or files associated with those systems, without explicit authorization to do so. Individuals and organizations have the right to restrict access to their systems so long as they do not violate the discrimination principle (see 1.4). No one should enter or use another's computer system, software or data files without permission. One must always have appropriate approval before using system resources, including .rm57 communication ports, file space, other system peripherals, and computer time.

3. ORGANIZATIONAL LEADERSHIP IMPERATIVES. As an ACM member and an
    organizational leader, I will . . . . .

BACKGROUND NOTE: This section draws extensively from the draft IFIP Code of Ethics, especially its sections on organizational ethics and international concerns. The ethical obligations of organizations tend to be neglected in most codes of professional conduct, perhaps because these codes are written from the perspective of the individual member. This dilemma is addressed by stating these imperatives from the perspective of the organizational leader. In this context, "leader" is viewed as any organizational member who has leadership or educational responsibilities. These imperatives generally may apply to organizations as well as their leaders. In this context, "organizations" are corporations, government agencies and other "employers," as well as volunteer professional organizations.

*3.1   Articulate social responsibilities of members of an organizational unit and
    encourage full acceptance of those responsibilities.*
    Because organizations of all kinds have impacts on the public, they must accept responsibilities to society. Organizational procedures and attitudes oriented toward quality and the welfare of society will reduce harm to members of the public, thereby serving public interest and fulfilling social responsibility. Therefore, organizational leaders must encourage full participation in meeting social responsibilities as well as quality performance.

*3.2   Manage personnel and resources to design and build information systems that
    enhance the quality of working life.*
    Organizational leaders are responsible for ensuring that computer systems enhance, not degrade, the quality of working life. When implementing a computer system, organizations must consider the personal and professional development, physical safety and human dignity of all workers. Appropriate human-computer ergonomic standards should be considered in system design and in the workplace.

*3.3   Acknowledge and support proper and authorized uses of an organization's
    computing and communication resources.*
    Because computer systems can become tools to harm as well as to benefit an organization, the leadership has the responsibility to clearly define appropriate and

inappropriate uses of organizational computing resources. While the number and scope of such rules should be minimal, they should be fully enforced when established.

3.4   Ensure that users and those who will be affected by a system have their needs clearly articulated during the assessment and design of requirements; later the system must be validated to meet requirements.

Current system users, potential users and other persons whose lives may be affected by a system must have their needs assessed and incorporated in the statement of requirements. System validation should ensure compliance with those requirements.

3.5   Articulate and support policies that protect the dignity of users and others affected by a computing system.

Designing or implementing systems that deliberately or inadvertently demean individuals or groups is ethically unacceptable. Computer professionals who are in decision-making positions should verify that systems are designed and implemented to protect personal privacy and enhance personal dignity.

3.6   Create opportunities for members of the organization to learn the principles and limitations of computer systems.

This complements the imperative on public understanding (2.7). Educational opportunities are essential to facilitate optimal participation of all organizational members. Opportunities must be available to all members to help them improve their knowledge and skills in computing, including courses that familiarize them with the consequences and limitations of particular types of systems. In particular, professionals must be made aware of the dangers of building systems around oversimplified models, the improbability of anticipating and designing for every possible operating condition, and other issues related to the complexity of this profession.

4.   COMPLIANCE WITH THE CODE. As an ACM member, I will ...

4.1   Uphold and promote the principles of this Code.

The future of the computing profession depends on both technical and ethical excellence. Not only is it important for ACM computing professionals to adhere to the principles expressed in this Code, each member should encourage and support adherence by other members.

4.2   Treat violations of this code as inconsistent with membership in the ACM.

Adherence of professionals to a code of ethics is largely a voluntary matter. However, if a member does not follow this code by engaging in gross misconduct, membership in ACM may be terminated.

Section IV

Preparing for Digital Government

Chapter XV

Data Warehousing and the Organization of Governmental Databases

Franklin Maxwell Harper
National Civic League, USA

ABSTRACT

Data warehousing is a technology architecture designed to organize disparate data sources into a single repository of information. As such, it represents a strategy for creating the architecture necessary to support the vision of e-government. Data warehousing enables a new type of "decision intelligence" by providing access to historical trend data, typically difficult to retrieve through operational database systems. Government data warehousing is complex, expensive, and often fraught with data privacy and security issues. E-government goals may be met through a successful data-warehousing project, be it in the form of a more efficient, informed government or as a result of increased public access to information. But given the substantial barriers to success, a thorough planning and investigation process is necessary.

INTRODUCTION

Governments today are inundated by rapidly increasing volumes of data. The source of this data explosion lies in the proliferation of data sources (Hoss, 2001), largely stemming from the recent rise in e-government initiatives (Norris, Fletcher, & Holden, 2001). This could turn out to be either a boon to decision makers or a bane, as the ever-growing store of data holds the potential to improve government decision making, but could just as easily stagnate and continue to add cost to governmental operations. It is important, therefore, to somehow intelligently manage this data and create an environment where it may be analyzed quickly and cheaply. Optimally, the relevant portions of data could be shared with the public through the Internet. One potential technological approach to this situation, and the approach that this chapter will concern itself with, is known as data warehousing. Data warehousing is a technology architecture designed to organize disparate data sources into a single repository of information. It is intended to leverage data to promote organizational knowledge. For government agencies that are "drowning in data and dying for information," a data warehouse can provide an environment where powerful information comes cheaply and quickly (Singh, 1998).

More specifically, data warehousing is the practice of intelligently managing historical "secondhand" data (Simon, 1997) by periodically copying data from multiple sources into a large database optimized for the extraction of information. A data warehouse enables its users to retrieve useful data regardless of "platform, application, organizational, and other barriers" (Simon, 1997).

To understand more clearly the uniqueness of data warehousing, one must understand the distinction between an *operational* database and an *informational* database (Singh, 1998). Operational databases are far more common — they are read/write sources of current data, and are typically used to support online systems. Informational databases, on the other hand, are typically read-only and contain historical, subject-oriented data optimized for information gathering and analysis. A data warehouse is a type of informational database, intended to enable a discovery-oriented approach to database querying (Inmon, 2002). In this way, data warehousing enables a new type of "decision intelligence" by providing access to historical trend data, typically difficult to retrieve through operational database systems. It can serve as an "unambiguous source of informational truth within the organization" (Poe, 1998).

Data warehouses can be put online via the World Wide Web to enable public access to government information stores. Certainly, some government agencies will have a strong interest in releasing their data to the public in this way. In a survey conducted by the International City/County Management Association (Norris & Demeter, 1999), over 70 percent of all governments responded that they use their web sites for the purpose of information dissemination or citizen education. Citizens most commonly visit government web sites for the purpose of retrieving information, often searching through online databases (Larsen & Rainie, 2002). They believe that the most important potential benefits of e-government have to do with government accountability and greater public access to information (Hart-Teeter, 2000). Government data warehouses provide a service in line with this demand, and extend the potential availability of information well beyond that provided in conventional web-enabled databases.

This chapter is an examination of the practical considerations relevant to government data warehousing, as they relate to improving decision-making, accountability, and public access to information. It will begin with a discussion of some applications of data warehousing relevant to the government sector, along with several warnings about potential impediments to project success. This will be followed be a review of how best practices in the evaluation, planning, implementation, and growth phases of a project can positively impact the success of a project. The chapter will then examine Iowa State's recent data warehousing project as a model for successful implementation through agency collaboration.

ENHANCING E-GOVERNMENT: OPPORTUNITIES AND BARRIERS

There are compelling reasons for governments to adopt a data warehousing architecture. By providing high quality information, this technology has the potential to improve the quality of government services and policy decisions. However, prohibitive factors such as high costs and security and privacy issues can make data warehousing success in the government sector difficult. This section will look at these factors in an attempt to elucidate the reasons for and against governmental adoption of this technology.

Governmental Decision Support

A data warehouse is often written about in terms of a technology designed specifically for decision support (Sakaguchi & Frolick, 1996). Typically, the architecture is designed to help users "to understand the business, to make decisions, and to solve problems" (Singh, 1998). The uniqueness of the integrated, historical nature of the warehouse architecture may be used to answer questions that would be difficult or expensive to answer using operational or legacy systems.

Governmental agencies may leverage this aspect of the technology to gain insight into the efficacy of programs or initiatives. There are primarily two underlying concepts that support this potential. First, a data warehouse provides an aggregated or integrated information environment. By bringing together several related but physically separate data sources, queries and reports have more potential breadth. Such advantages have made data integration a top priority in some U.S. governmental agencies (Hammer, 2002).

Integration of data sources may be useful, for example, in cases where there are operational databases distributed statewide. The data could be cleaned, validated, and integrated into a data warehouse to enable the government to analyze statewide trends. Such a use would have profound implications not only for the quality and completeness of potential information, but for the cost of retrieving it.

Second, the historical nature of data warehousing presents an opportunity to assess variations in data over time. This can in turn lend depth to the users' view of the data, and is a powerful way to reveal trends. By definition, data warehousing is time-variant and nonvolatile (Inmon, 2002), accomplished by storing data periodically with a time stamp rather than overwriting previous data. Contrast this with operational data sources, which often contain only a snapshot of the current data. It is useful to have a historical view of data, for example, in examining changes in success or quality of initiatives over time.

Coupling integration and history can provide a complete view of governmental data sources. In this way, policy analysis may be performed with an eye for widespread trends across agency boundaries, geography, or time. An integrated, historical view of government data can provide solid grounds on which to base performance analysis and policymaking.

Public Access to Government Databases

Community members, businesses, and non-governmental organizations all benefit from better access to government data. They are not, however, concerned with the possibility that this data may be spread across multiple agencies, stored in multiple incompatible databases, or otherwise (Public Access, 2002). Data warehouses that are made public through the Internet hold the potential to meet some of these demands. These public stores of information can increase government accountability through visibility of results.

Public access to data warehouses is a subject less discussed in data warehousing literature, due to the typically industry-oriented nature of the available information (Sakaguchi & Frolick, 1996). Regardless, publicly accessible data warehouses may be quite similar in design and implementation to standard business intelligence warehouses from a technical perspective. Fundamentally, they differ most in terms of their heightened security and privacy requirements and their data models which may be oriented toward facilitating a different type of research.

Data warehouses built for public access, like those built for decision support, provide a great breadth and depth of information. Where a typical online governmental database might provide answers to a specific question or type of inquiry, data warehouses are designed for exploration and discovery (Inmon, 2002). While both types of database are useful to the public, they each meet a different need.

A Hart-Teeter poll (2000) shows that a majority of Americans feel that the most significant benefits of e-government have to do with allowing citizens to become better informed and more involved. It determined that respondents were nearly twice as likely to rank public access to information as the top e-government priority than they were to rank government services first. Providing public access to data warehousing, then, may be seen as providing an important service to the public; not just a luxury item.

The Environmental Protection Agency's "EnviroFacts" data warehouse (http://www.epa.gov/enviro/) is an example of a data warehouse that is used for the purpose of public access to government data. EnviroFacts provides access to a spectrum of environmental data that is easily accessible through a web browser.

EnviroFacts provides an integrated view of environmental data, not only in terms of data sources (Garvey, 1997), but also in terms of issue area. In this way, the user's view of the data is very complete. Largely, the data organization is focused on providing current data on a wide variety of environmental issues, but there is some access to historical data to lend depth to queries. The popularity of the site is indisputable — it has grown from receiving about 100,000 page hits per month in 1997 to regularly receiving between 350,000 and 450,000 page hits per month in mid/late 2002 (Top 20, 2002).

In several ways, EnviroFacts serves as a model for data warehousing as a tool for public access to government information. Access to the data is controlled by an easy to use web site interface, which provides accessibility to anyone with a modern web browser. Also, the data model is easy to understand from the perspective of the user, and the quantity and breadth of the data is impressive. These elements come together to provide an environment for discovery, investigation, and fact-finding.

Privacy and Security Issues

It is interesting to note that in early 2002, direct query access to EnviroFacts was shut off, citing concerns over homeland security issues (EPA, 2002). The web interface to the database was not affected by this change. But this access method is more easily controlled and less flexible than direct SQL access.

This change in policy demonstrates that data security issues are inherent and relevant to this field of information technology. Government data warehousing projects are more susceptible to the emergence of security and privacy issues than those in the private sector (Bieber, 1998), largely due to the content and visibility of the data contained within. This problem is relevant considering the current push for e-government measures, as there are many information security deficiencies within United States government agencies (Public Access, 2002).

Privacy issues in e-government can arise from a database containing personal information that has been made public, or in a data integration scenario where sensitive data is incorrectly made available internally. In some cases, the law regulates the sharing of information, as is the case with some U.S. agencies that are legally prevented from sharing information (Hammer, 2002). As government agencies process increasing amounts of public information through their information systems, the privacy issues continue to grow (Public Access, 2002).

The United States' E-Government Act of 2002 is making a formal attempt to address privacy issues by introducing the concept of a "privacy impact assessment" into government technology initiatives (Lieberman, 2002). This document would be required to describe the information in question, the necessity for the information, the intended use, and the security measures that will be taken to protect the information (S. 803, 2002). This provision of the E-Government Act would be highly relevant to data warehouse implementers in the United States, but issues of privacy should be considered at all times regardless of the law in any situation where private information could be released to the public domain.

Security in data warehousing is a separate, but related issue. Without good security, private data cannot be kept private. A data warehouse, like any networked information system, is vulnerable to information loss or theft at the hands of crackers. Through 2005, 80 percent of enterprises will have not adequately planned their data warehouse security, increasing significantly their chances of a security breach (Strange, 2002).

The U.S. public is very concerned about security and privacy issues in adopting e-government, and a strong majority advocates a measured approach to developing governmental information systems to ensure that these issues are not overlooked (Hart-Teeter, 2000). To address these concerns, governments should refocus their efforts on architecture-wide security plans to help prevent information loss or theft. While a data warehouse can never be totally safe from privacy or security risks, attention to the issue can substantially decrease the odds of information misuse or damage.

Cost Issues

Data warehousing projects are very expensive, which is a prime concern for governmental entities. Spending on governmental information technology has been increasing over the past several years (Public Access, 2002), but implementing a data warehousing strategy may go well beyond the current levels of expenditure. Some methods are starting to emerge that can mitigate costs without sacrificing project scope or quality.

One such method is probably unique to the government sector. Governments may approach warehousing in a collaborative manner to spread hardware and programming costs across several agencies, thus reducing the per-agency cost. As an example of this approach, the Iowa State government's data warehouse was planned and built by a consortium of separate agencies (Sarkar, 2001). The collaboration is intended to minimize the long-term costs of support and training (State of Iowa, 2000). It has the additional benefit of drastically lowering the barriers for subsequent agencies joining the project (Sarkar, 2001), as the hardware, architecture, and user tools are already in place.

Such a collaborative approach is intelligent in a variety of situations. The collaboration possibilities are not limited to just intergovernment agencies, but could extend to collaboration between local and state governments. Clearly, such an approach carries real advantages in data breadth over a more traditional single department data warehousing solution as well.

Outsourcing a data warehouse to a Business Intelligence Service Provider (BISP) is an approach that can reduce a governmental agency's expenditures on infrastructure, free capacity on in-house systems, and result in better quality software and equipment (Thornton, 2002). As such, outsourcing may provide a way for smaller governmental entities to access data warehousing solutions (Hicks, 1999). Outsourcing is an area that is growing in more traditional government database applications. In 2001, 27.5 percent of local governments were outsourcing the work of integrating databases with their web site, while 72.5 percent were planning to outsource this work in the future (Norris et al., 2001). Similar movement is likely in the data warehousing sector given the high costs and complexity associated with the activity.

Another possibility is to take advantage of the relatively recent boom of open source software, which has started to become a significant actor in the realm of data warehousing (Lindquist, 2002). Largely, mainstream adoption of open source technology is a result of the successes of Linux as a stable, cheap server operating system. The partnering of Linux distributions with major database vendors such as Oracle will help to lower costs for small- or mid-size warehouse projects. Additionally, open source database packages such as MySQL and PostgreSQL have matured, and are now in some cases viable alternatives to pricey packages like Oracle, although governments must consider development time, integration of add-on tools, and ease of setup when determining the potential cost savings.

FACTORS FOR
DATA WAREHOUSING SUCCESS

Due to its typical scale and complexity, data warehousing is a technology prone to implementation failure. By some estimates, data warehousing projects fail to meet their goals from 60 to 80 percent of the time (Nguyen, 1999). For a government IT department on an already tight budget, this is probably an unacceptable failure rate. This section deals with some of the most fundamental issues in ensuring the success of a data warehouse project.

Evaluation of Need

We have seen some of the benefits that data warehousing can produce for governments and citizens. But due to the complexity and expense related to these projects (Sakaguchi & Frolick, 1996) it is important that there are solid grounds for project justification before several million dollars are committed.

The process of justification begins with the determination of real need by the user community. A data warehouse cannot be built because other people have done it and experienced benefits, or because of vendor sales pitches. Anecdotal evidence predicts that projects that start from roots like these can easily end in failure (Paul, 1997). Instead, it would be advisable to listen to the thoughts of local community of information systems users, developers, and administrators.

These users are often able to enumerate the advantages that an integrated system of databases could provide, although their reasons may be intuitive and require further research (Inmon, 1999). Nevertheless, these anecdotal statements may form the basis of a useful investigation into the benefits that warehousing could provide. This bottom-up approach is superior to a vendor- or technology-driven approach where supposed generic benefits are projected onto a non-generic environment (McKnight, 1999; Bieber, 1998).

The next step in project evaluation involves relating the core needs as expressed by the users to the benefits of the data warehouse in terms of return on investment (ROI) (McKnight, 1999). This step is often prerequisite for governments to receive funding, in the form of some sort of ROI report.

Unfortunately, unlike many IT projects, quantifying the benefits of data warehousing is difficult (Inmon, 1999; McKnight, 1999). The feasibility of generating a strong ROI argument for a warehouse may vary substantially based upon the data in question. For example, it may be easy to demonstrate cost-savings in the case of a data warehouse containing tax data, but more difficult in the case of one that contains data on environmental hazard sites. Additionally, many of the ROI benefits may not manifest themselves until the warehouse is built and in production (Inmon, 1999).

Further complicating the calculation is the fact that in many cases the data warehouse fundamentally changes the way that business is conducted. In such a case it is extremely difficult to try and predict future ROI, as there may be many potential outcomes (McKnight, 1999).

In these cases and others, some benefits associated with a data warehouse are difficult or impossible to measure. For example, this will often be true with a public access data warehouse, which may save time and money for citizens and businesses, but may not have much of an effect upon government expenditures. In some cases, it may be possible to include these savings in the calculation of ROI (State of Iowa, 2000). In other cases, the project may have more difficulties getting funding.

Planning

The phase of a data-warehousing project that occurs after the determination of need and before the process of implementation is critical to the project's eventual success. Several objectives must be accomplished during this phase relating to planning the warehouse architecture and readying the end users for the new technology. These will probably include choosing an implementation team, establishing a long-term warehousing strategy, choosing a technology vendor, evaluating outsourcing options, writing documentation, collecting input from users, and establishing the initial data sources and a data model.

Of these tasks, most will directly affect a warehouse project's chances of success. However, it seems that two areas of the planning process in particular are the most important: those relating to long-term flexibility of the database technology, and those relating to user acceptance of the technology.

Long-term data warehouse flexibility means the ability of the architecture to grow in size and change directions over time. This characteristic is determined largely by the quality of the sources of data and the data model (Singh, 1998). A poorly devised data model can greatly shorten the useful lifetime of the data warehouse (Manning, n.d.), but one that is properly devised will provide the data warehouse the opportunity to grow. A common approach to increase long-term flexibility is to plan for the presence of data marts, a method of subdividing a data warehouse into smaller chunks pertinent to certain departments.

The scalability of the chosen vendor's technology is also important to the long-term viability of the data warehouse. It is important that the technology not only supports the data model preferred by the project planners, but that it is capable of supporting both a startup warehouse and an advanced implementation (Singh, 1998).

The "technology hype" that surrounds data warehousing can overshadow relevant business needs, which should always provide the basis for vendor tool evaluation (Poe, 1998). Technology is often, unfortunately, the easy place to start the planning process, due to departmental preferences or existing contracts (Bieber, 1998). While the planning process does not need to be vendor-agnostic, it should never allow technology to dictate the development plan, as technical solutions should always be chosen in response to e-government goals (Poe, 1998).

Another determining characteristic of the planning process is user acceptance, a concept less about technology than internal marketing. Because implementation of a data warehouse for decision support could present a significant shift in business practices, government agencies should include internal marketing to users in the planning stage of the project and beyond. The marketing should simultaneously foster acceptance, encourage use, and manage expectations (Poe, 1998).

User acceptance may be augmented through internal feedback. To stimulate user knowledge of the project, documentation should be released (Inmon, 2002). Also, the project managers should solicit feedback from eventual end-users through surveys, interviews, or meetings.

Development and Maintenance

Data warehousing projects are never complete, but rather are continually evolving (Sakaguchi & Frolick, 1996). Partially as a result of this quality, the approach to development that is advocated by Inmon (2002) and others in the field is iterative and incremental. Data warehousing projects occupy such a large scale that to try and tackle an entire project at once can drive a project over budget and over schedule. Inmon (2002, p. 41) goes so far as to claim that this "big bang" approach is "simply an invitation to disaster and is never an appropriate alternative."

Developing a data warehouse by iterations emphasizes smaller, more manageable goals, with focus on quality and efficiency in meeting them. Inmon (2002) visualizes this process happening in a sort of evolutionary pattern, where as each iteration is finished, the acceptance of the warehouse in the user community grows, leading to more sub-projects in other departments.

The first of these iterations of development may come in the form of a pilot project, intended to demonstrate the potential usefulness of the warehouse technology. Then, based on the success of the pilot, the project can be reevaluated. Some advocate that the pilot should be "fast and safe" in order to minimize risk if it is unsuccessful (Singh, 1998). While running a pilot project may or may not be the course of action appropriate for a given project, Inmon (2002, p. 65) offers, "the first iteration of the data warehouse should be small enough to be built and large enough to be meaningful."

Throughout the development process, there should be a focus on data quality. Collecting, cleaning, and reformatting the data from existing operational and legacy systems is time-consuming, and may account for 60 to 80 percent of the total cost of the warehouse (Manning, n.d.). Much of the success of the data warehouse depends on the completeness and reliability of its information.

Finally, for a data warehouse to succeed it must have an understandable user interface. The database should be made accessible to users without advanced knowledge of database systems through graphical, self-explanatory query tools (Singh, 1998). In the case of a data warehouse that has been designed for public access, the interface should be web enabled to allow widespread use.

CASE STUDY: IOWA STATE

The Iowa state government, starting in the late 1990s, has been in the process of building a data warehouse to support the Criminal and Juvenile Justice Planning (CJJP) Department, the Department of Human Services (DHS), and the Department of Revenue and Finance (DRF) (Enterprise, n.d.). The project was designed to improve decision making by providing quality information to the state's 20,000 employees, and to analyze the efficacy of statewide spending (Implementing Enterprise, n.d.).

There are several aspects of this project that demonstrate effective practices in data warehouse planning and implementation. Most impressive, however, is the way in which several agencies within the government were able to join together to collectively plan and implement the system (State of Iowa, 2000). Since the initial collaboration, about 30 additional state agencies have agreed to participate or provide data sources (Sarkar, 2001).

Iowa's data warehouse was built based on several of the principles discussed earlier in this chapter. It was a project based on solid business needs, which were written out clearly in state project evaluation forms (State of Iowa, 2000). These forms also contained detailed breakdown of costs in terms of ROI and security and privacy policies.

The development process has been based on iterations (Sarkar, 2001), beginning by addressing core issues, then expanding outward. The process was begun with the creation of several pilot projects, which formed the basis for subsequent additions to the architecture (State of Iowa, 2000). With a view on future expandability and architectural flexibility, the project has been built on the concept of a central data warehouse feeding smaller data marts with information.

Security issues were addressed in the development of the warehouse (Implementing Enterprise, n.d.) through attention to user access policies and the security of the data sources (Enterprise, n.d.). Access to the public has been limited so far to select reports published on the Iowa State web site, although there is a possibility of expanding in the future to allow public access to select databases within the warehouse (Dizard, 2002).

Internal access to the data is currently provided via a range of access methods, including web-based and vendor-based tools (Enterprise, n.d.).

Iowa's project was strongly focused on achieving certain goals that were known to be attainable through the implementation of a data warehousing architecture. The project continues to be forward-looking, and has managed to sustain growth through several iterations of development. The successes are numerous, ranging from improved access to information and diminished reporting time in the criminal justice branch (Justice, n.d.) to real cost savings in the human resources branch (Enterprise, n.d.).

CONCLUSION

This chapter has discussed the concept of data warehousing as a tool for governments. There are several compelling reasons to employ this technology architecture. It can integrate disparate data sources to support governmental decision-making. Or it can be made public, and improve citizen access to government information.

But government data warehousing is complex, expensive, and often fraught with data privacy and security issues. These barriers to implementation can be overcome given sufficient resources, but they must be heeded. Therefore, best practices must be employed in planning and building a data warehouse.

Ultimately, the goal of e-government initiatives must be to provide substantial benefit to the public. This goal may be met with a successful data-warehousing project, be it in the form of a more efficient, informed government or as a result of increased public access to information. But given the substantial barriers to success, a thorough planning and investigation process is necessary to determine the feasibility of such a project.

REFERENCES

Bieber, M. (1998). Data Warehousing in Government. *DM Review*. (May). Retrieved from the World Wide Web on June 10, 2002, from: http://www.dmreview.com

Byers, J. (2002). Government Web Sites: Do They Meet a Need? *County News*, *34*(11), 14.

Dizard, W. P. III (2002). Iowa Eyes an Identity Clearinghouse [Electronic Version]. *Government Computer News*, *21*(5).

Dykstra D. V. (n.d.). *Identity Security Study Findings*. Retrieved August 5, 2002, from the Iowa State Government, Information Technology Department web site: http://www.itd.state.ia.us/Identity_Findings_v1_5.htm

Enterprise Data Warehouse. (n.d.). Retrieved August 26, 2002, from the Iowa State Government, Information Technology Department web site: http://www.iowaccess.org/government/its/data_warehouse/

EPA Announces Plans to Restrict Access to Envirofacts. *OMB Watcher*. (2002). Retrieved September 20, 2002, from http://www.ombwatch.org

Garvey, P. (1997). Mapping the Environment on the Web. *Government Technology*. Retrieved October 9, 2002, from http://www.govtech.net

Hammer, K. (2002). Another View: Can government integrate all its databases? *Government Computer News*, *21*(13).

Hart-Teeter (2000). *E-Government: The Next American Revolution.* (September). Retrieved October 9, 2002, from http://www.excelgov.org/egovpoll/index.htm

Hicks, J. D. (1999). WebWorks: Outsourcing the Data Warehouse. *DM Review.* (October). Retrieved October 2, 2002 from the World Wide Web: http://www.dmreview.com

Hoss, D. (2001, October). Top Ten Trends in Data Warehousing. *DM Review.* Retrieved June 10, 2002, from the World Wide Web: http://www.dmreview.com

IACP Technology Clearinghouse. (2002). Retrieved August 25, 2002 from the Iowa Department of Public Safety section: http://www.iacptechnology.org/Programs/iowa.htm

Implementing Enterprise Strategy Leading Edge Programs. (n.d.). Retrieved August 5, 2002 from the National Governors' Association Center for Best Practices web site: http://www.nga.org/center/egovernment/enterpriselep/

Inmon, W. H. (1999). *Cost Justification In The Data Warehouse.* Retrieved August 1, 2002 from the World Wide Web: http://www.billinmon.com/library/articles/article2.asp

Inmon, W. H. (2002). *Building the Data Warehouse* (3rd ed.). New York: John Wiley & Sons.

Insider's Guide to Using Information in Government. (n.d.). Retrieved June 20, 2002 from the University at Albany, SUNY, Center for Technology in Government web site: http://www.ctg.albany.edu/guides/usinginfo/index.htm

Justice Data Warehouse. (n.d.). Retrieved August 5, 2002 from the Iowa State Government, Division of Criminal and Juvenile Justice Planning web site: http://www.state.ia.us/government/dhr/cjjp/JDW.html

Larsen, E. & Rainie, L. (2002, April 3). *The Rise of the E-Citizen: How People Use Government Agencies' Web Sites.* Retrieved September 9, 2002 from http://www.pewinternet.org/reports/toc.asp?Report=57

Lieberman, J. I. (2002). *E-Government Act of 2002* [Electronic Version]. Retrieved October 10, 2002, from the World Wide Web: http://www.senate.gov/~gov_affairs/leginfo.htm

Lindquist, C. (2002, June 10). *New Dawn for Databases? Open Source May Open Possibilities for Data Warehousing.* Retrieved August 26, 2002 from the World Wide Web: http://www.cio.com/online/techtact_061002.html

Manning, I. T. (n.d.). *Data Warehousing – Adopting an Architectural View, and Maximizing Cost Benefits.* Retrieved August 1, 2002 from the World Wide Web: http://www.ittoolbox.com/peer/dwarticle.htm

Matthews, W. (2002, June 3). FBI to build data warehouse. *Federal Computer Week.* Retrieved August 5, 2002 from the World Wide Web: http://www.fcw.com

McKnight, W. (1999, November). Data Warehouse Justification and ROI. *DM Review.* Retrieved August 1, 2002 from the World Wide Web: http://www.dmreview.com

Nguyen, B. T. (1999, October 4). AF officer: Warehouse only good data [Electronic Version]. *Government Computer News, 18*(33).

Norris, D. F. & Demeter, L. A. (1999). Information Technology and City Governments. In *The Municipal Year Book* (Vol. 66, pp. 10-18). Washington, DC: International City/County Management Association.

Norris, D. F., Fletcher, P. D., Holden, S. H. (2001, February 27). *Is Your Local Government*

Plugged In? [Electronic Version]. Retrieved August 1, 2002 from the World Wide
   Web: http://www.icma.org/download/cat15/grp120/sgp224/E-Gov2000.pdf

Overview of Data Warehousing. (n.d.). Retrieved August 5, 2002 from the Iowa State
   Government, Information Technology Department web site: http://
   www.iowaccess.org/government/its/mission_and_goals.htm

Paul, L. G. (1997, November 15). *Anatomy of a Failure.* Retrieved August 26, 2002 from
   the World Wide Web: http://www.cio.com/archive/enterprise/111597_data.html

Poe, V., Klauer, P., & Brobst, S. (1998). *Building a Data Warehouse for Decision Support*
   (2nd ed.). NJ: Prentice Hall.

Public Access Key to E-Government. *OMB Watcher.* (2002, March 20). Retrieved
   August 26, 2002 from the World Wide Web: http://www.ombwatch.org

Reimers, B. D. (1999, March 22). Data warehousing unites agency data. *Federal
   Computer Week.* Retrieved August 5, 2002 the World Wide Web: from http://
   www.fcw.com

S. 803, E-Government Act of 2002, as Amended, Section by Section Description
   [Electronic Version]. (2002). Retrieved October 10, 2002 from the Center for
   Democracy and Technology Website: http://www.cdt.org/legislation/107th/e-gov/

Sakaguchi, T. & Frolick, M. N. (1996, January). *A Review of the Data Warehousing
   Literature.* Retrieved July 15, 2002 from http://www.nku.edu/~sakaguch/dw-
   web.htm

Sarkar, D. (2001, January 25). Breaking ground in data warehousing. *Federal Computer
   Week.* Retrieved August 5, 2002 from the World Wide Web: http://www.fcw.com

Simon, A. R. (1997). *Data Warehousing for Dummies.* California: IDG Books Worldwide.

Singh, H. S. (1998). *Data Warehousing: Concepts, Technologies, Implementations, and
   Management.* NJ: Prentice Hall.

State of Iowa - Return on Investment Program / IT Project Evaluation. (2000). Retrieved
   October 1, 2002 from the Iowa State Information Technology Department web site:
   http://www.infoweb.state.ia.us/keydocuments/cdforitd/index.html

Strange, K. (2002, August 29). *Data warehouses: A security disaster.* Retrieved October
   10, 2002 from the World Wide Web: http://techupdate.zdnet.com/techupdate/
   stories/main/0,14179,2878609-1,00.html

Thornton, M. (2002, March). What About Security? The Most Common, but Unwarranted, Objection to Hosted Data Warehouses. *DM Review.* Retrieved June 10,
   2002 from the World Wide Web: http://www.dmreview.com

Top 20 Sites. (2002, September). Retrieved October 9, 2002, from the Environmental
   Protection Agency web site: http://www.epa.gov/reports/top20s/

Walker, R. W. (1999, February 22). Patience is a virtue when building data warehouses
   [Electronic Version]. *Government Computer News, 18*(4), 46.

Williams, T. (2000, November 6). E-Government Push Bolsters Data Warehousing
   Demand [Electronic Version]. *Washington Technology, 15*(16), 28-29.

Chapter XVI

Digital Government and Geographic Information Systems

Jon Gant
Syracuse University, USA

Donald S. Ijams
Tucson Police Department, USA

ABSTRACT

The focus of this chapter is to examine how government agencies are deploying geographic information systems (GIS) to enhance the delivery of digital government. We will explain how critical technological advances are enabling government agencies to use GIS in web-based applications In addition, we will illustrate the approaches that state and local governments in the United States are taking to deploy GIS for e-government applications using examples from Indianapolis, Indiana, Tucson, Arizona, Washington D.C. and the State of Oregon's Department of Environmental Protection. While these examples greatly improve service delivery performance and enhance public decision-making, we raise the issue that e-government GIS applications may be more broadly deployed in organizations that are better adept at dealing with the managerial and technical issues related to using GIS.

INTRODUCTION[1]

Government agencies worldwide are increasingly deploying digital government strategies to provide citizens and businesses with greater access to services and information through highly innovative integrated service delivery applications. It is, for example, now commonplace for citizens to file taxes, renew professional licenses, and track legislation through web applications available on Internet gateways or portals for each state. These applications offer numerous possibilities to use the Internet and web-based technologies to extend government services online, allow citizens to interact more directly with government, employ citizen-centric services, and transform operational and bureaucratic procedures.

Emerging as a critical component of digital government are geographic information system (GIS) applications that provide computerized mapping capabilities to citizens, businesses, and governments. GIS uses information and communication technology tools to store, analyze, query, manipulate, distribute and display data that has been spatially-referenced using addresses, political and administrative boundaries, or earth bound coordinate systems. GIS is used in a broad range of public sector applications including, for example, land use and urban growth planning, legislative redistricting, crime tracking and law enforcement, benchmarking human services, emergency management, environmental monitoring, and public information services (O'Looney, 2000).

GIS greatly enhances the business of government by making it easier to integrate data based on geographic location, particularly as GIS is increasingly embedded with decision support models, artificial intelligence tools, advanced database technologies, and Internet communication protocols. As Dangermond (2002, p. 57) notes, "[t]he integration of Web services with GIS is appealing within complex organizations like local governments that have many entities or departments and integrate many layers of independently collected and managed data, such as roads, pipes, surveys, land records, and administrative boundaries." Marrying GIS with e-government applications empowers citizens with user-controlled maps served over the Internet while viewing a government web page using a personal computer or personal digital assistant (Greene, 2002). Citizens can quickly see, for example, what streets are being snowplowed, when the garbage will be picked up, where the closest polling place is and what neighborhoods have higher incidence of crime.

The focus of this chapter is to examine how government agencies are deploying geographic information systems to enhance the delivery of electronic government services. We will explain how critical technological advances are enabling government agencies to use GIS in web-based applications. In addition, we will illustrate the approaches that state and local governments in the United States are taking to deploy GIS for e-government applications using examples from Indianapolis, Indiana, Tucson, Arizona, Washington D.C., and the State of Oregon's Department of Environmental Protection. We will present two cases to further examine the managerial, technical and policy related barriers limiting the broader adoption of geographic information system (GIS) applications for e-government. These cases include: "Snow Fighter," a GIS application used by the City of Indianapolis to manage snow removal; and, "CityScan," the first project sponsored by the City of Tucson GIS Cooperative where web-enabled GIS applications assist citizens to achieve the Livable Tucson Vision. While these examples greatly improve service delivery performance and enhance public decision-making, we raise the issue that GIS-enabled e-government applications may be more broadly deployed in organizations that are better adept at dealing with the managerial and technical issues related to using GIS.

HOW CAN GIS ENABLE DIGITAL GOVERNMENT?

The convergence of communication, database, and GIS technologies is moving GIS applications far beyond basic map-making and opening opportunities for GIS-enabled E-government applications. Today's GIS applications now have the capability to integrate easy to use software and hardware technologies that allow users to perform such complex tasks as modeling patterns and trends, forecasting the impact of planning, policy, or strategy initiatives, and streamlining internal business and operation processes. More advanced GIS applications also include such capabilities as statistical analysis, operation research modeling and automated spatial modeling, mobile computing features using real time or near real time data (e.g., global position systems data), enterprise-wide database integration, user-controlled customization of analytical and modeling tools, and deployment of expert systems and artificial intelligence agents.

The challenge for digital government architects is to figure out how to deploy GIS to improve the ways that government agencies deliver services to citizens, businesses and governments. E-government refers to the broad spectrum of information and communication technology-enabled processes that predominately use web-based technologies to deliver government services. These applications offer numerous possibilities to use the Internet to extend government service online, and allow citizens to interact more directly with government. We consider e-government to be an information technology-enabled process innovation (Davenport & Short, 1990) as the new e-government systems depend on information and communication technologies. E-government applications involves congruently developing information and communication technology applications and making associated changes in agency service delivery practices to develop more responsive, efficient and accountable government operations (National Research Council, 2002).

Integrating GIS functions with e-government applications should greatly improve the delivery of government services because they, among other factors, will:
* Allow greater access and integration of enterprise-wide data
* Improve the availability of spatial data
* Improve coordination within and across job duties, departments and agencies
* Promote organizational learning and enhance organizational/managerial controls
* Speed-up decision-making, especially if integrating real-time data
* Improve accountability and citizen access, especially when output or applications are available via the Internet
* Place better organized information in the hands of day-to-day decision-makers and empower workers providing the services
* Enable task and operational reengineering and streamlining.

Figure 1 illustrates how a GIS-enabled e-government application improves the City of Pittsburgh Planning Department's ability to provide parcel and land use information. This prototype was developed under the direction of Dr. Danny Fernandes of Carnegie Mellon University. Figure 1 shows significant improvements in service delivery by allowing various planning department customers to acquire their maps and land use data through a web-based GIS application. Before using the web-based GIS application, customers would either have to make an in-person visit to the planning department or get permission to use a dial-up modem to access the text data. If the customer made an in-person visit, the clerk would then perform the query and provide the customer with text data. Regardless of the method for retrieving the text data, the customer would then have to use their own GIS software to perform subsequent analyses, queries and manipulations.

The redesigned process deploys GIS through an e-government application. Customers access the data that they need from the planning department through a GIS powered application residing seamlessly on an Internet portal page. While the first generation version of Internet-based GIS applications delivered static maps to users, contemporary applications dynamically deliver maps to the desktop (Harder, 1998). Using client/server architecture, processing of the user request is split between the middleware, the database backend and a map generation server. The data is queried from the database, which is typically running on a database server that is responsible for database storage, access and processing. The middleware provides an application program interface link to the relational database. In addition, the middleware allows the GIS software to interoperate with the database software in a fashion that is transparent to the user. The resulting table is then joined with the map layer in a GIS software application running on a file server and sent back to the Internet browser. The user can typically zoom, pan, turn map layers on and off and control the design, color, and symbolization of the map.

Figure 1: Illustration of GIS-enabled redesign of local government services

Figure 1: Illustration of GIS-enabled redesign of local government services (continued)

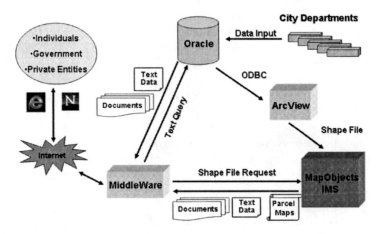

Several emerging technological advances promise to expand the possible use of GIS for e-government. All of the major GIS software vendors now include software links to enterprise-wide database architectures including enterprise resource (ERP) systems and data warehouses that support operations and decision-making across the organization. In addition, because GIS integrates data based on its spatial references, GIS can be used to create e-government applications that cut across functional areas within and between agencies and with all levels of government. A second important trend is that GIS software vendors are beginning to deploy GIS using web services architecture. Web services is the next generation of client/server architecture designed to support distributed computing using software components comprised a series of servers, desktops, and lightweight pervasive clients interconnected over the Internet or Intranet using the TCP/IP or HTTP protocol. As Dangermond (2002, p. 57) notes, "the integration of GIS and web services will simply mean that GIS can be more extensively implemented, and people will be able to take mapping, data, and geoprocessing services from many servers, and integrate them in a common environment." The architecture will allow, for example, users to visit a state government web portal and use online applications that directly integrate maps and data published by a state agency.

EXAMPLES OF GIS AND DIGITAL GOVERNMENT IN PRACTICE

GIS-enabled e-government applications are growing in use across the Internet landscape. The GIS software vendor MapInfo has collaborated with various government agencies to develop such GIS-enabled e-government solutions as:

*   A live accident map of the Tulsa region that allows users to view traffic and accident data distributed through the City of Tulsa's Computer Aided Dispatch system.

- A portal developed for the U.S. Department of Commerce's International Trade Administration that allows users to track worldwide export information on maps; and maps tracking cancer mortality in the U.S. for the U.S. National Institute of Health's National Cancer Institute[2]. ESRI also has developed solutions for Kentucky's Geographic Explorer, Afghanistan Interactive GIS and Visualization Service, Los Angeles County, the City of Tucson, and HUD's e-Maps[3].

Washington D.C. introduced "DC Atlas" (see Figure 2) in June 2002 to allow users to directly access pools of demographic, service, and geographic data produced by all of the District's agencies. Among a long list of functions, DC Atlas features information that will help users review the District's emergency preparedness plans, examine public safety initiatives, and lodge citizen complaints. DC Atlas also includes information about fire, schools, elections, zoning and cultural landmarks. DC Atlas also makes it easy for users to do basic data analyses and view the output on a map. Users can map where school and police districts overlap and examine the average age and education level of the population in those areas (District of Columbia, 2002). Users can also orthographic photos and digital video of the District. DC Atlas is comprised of interagency information that is available to District employees only through secure intranet server. The police department, for example, used 3D GIS modeling tools to prepare for the International Monetary fund protests. Adam Rubinson, Deputy Director of Washington D.C.'s Office of the Chief Technology Officer, says, "We made this available to the police department so that they could run simulations and simulate traffic flows in various scenarios to plan the IMF protests" (Francica, 2002, p. 2).

The State of Oregon's Department of Environmental Quality is using GIS to meet its strategic priorities. The agency has developed the Oregon DEQ Facility Profiler to assist users with locating the sites that are regulated or permitted to discharge air and water pollutants. The site also locates hazardous and solid waste sites, cleanup sites and leaking and underground storage tanks.

Figure 2

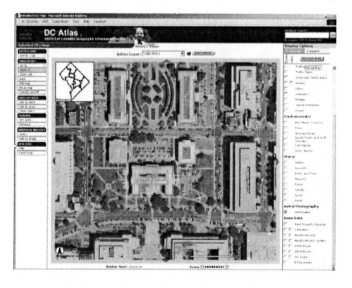

The following two cases will illustrate the potential for GIS in enhancing e-government, particularly for improving service delivery. The first case describes Snow Fighter, which is a GIS application used by the Department of Public Works in Indianapolis, Indiana, to manage snow removal during winter emergencies. The second is CityScan, a GIS-enabled e-government designed to provide citizens with greater access to the City of Tucson, Arizona services.

Snow Fighter

Snow removal is a critical local government service that can be very costly to manage[4]. In general, managing snow removal is a slow process due to operational burdens, namely the time it takes to clear the snow, and, because of the administrative burdens. Obviously, because of the unpredictable nature of winter storms from year to year, managing snow removal is a great challenge for most local governments. Local decision-makers are often uncertain about the timing of winter storms and snow fall amounts, making it difficult for public works managers to determine the best snow removal strategy and how much equipment, material and people is needed. Finally, if the area affected by the storm is declared an emergency officially, local governments apply to Federal and state emergency management agencies once the snow is removed to recover portions of the money spent on snow removal.

Snow removal in Indianapolis, Indiana, is very similar to most other cities. The city is divided into four districts based on the current location of three garages. The garage are the staging locations for snow removal trucks and serves as a place where the drivers get their snow removal instructions, and where the trucks are loaded down with salt and other traction management materials. The city has 611 snow routes that were created over a decade ago. Each route is assigned one of three priority levels including, priority snow routes that are major streets and thoroughfares, priority residential routes, and all other streets. Key information that is collected and tracked during the snow removal process includes information about the drivers, contractors, trucks, equipment status, number of actual hours worked, amount of salt and chemicals used, etc. Additionally, managers consult with weather experts, track the number of citizen calls for snow removal services, and communicate with the drivers for information about each route.

Figure 3

In order to keep snow removal costs manageable, such local governments as the City of Indianapolis, are using GIS tools along with new operation processes to make better decisions and plans for clearing the city streets of snow and ice (see Figure 3). Since 1996, the City of Indianapolis has been using an innovative advanced GIS application called "Snow Fighter" that helps the Department of Public Works manage snow removal during winter emergencies. Indianapolis is on the forefront of deploying GIS for e-government as users of the city's web portal, Indygov[5], can view storm damage, zoning boundaries, law enforcement incidents, wells, bus routes, and polling place locations online.

Snow Fighter is an application that superimposes information about the snow removal activities on a map of the street network of Indianapolis. Therefore, managers and supervisors from the Department of Public Works are able to visualize the amount of snow on the roads, the location of the snow trucks, and the amount of snow removed from the routes. Snow Fighter integrates a combination of software modules. The user interface and application management software is written in Visual Basic. This module also is used to interface with the Oracle database that allows the module to store and retrieve data that are collected from work orders and snow management forms during the project. The GIS functions for the application use ESRI's Map Objects. Internet map server (IMS) application updates information about the snow removal process on map themes originally created using ArcInfo. The IMS also enables the application to be shared to all authorized users who are located in disparate office and garage locations throughout the city. The application uses real time data radioed in from the drivers as a key input into a networking algorithm to determine the snow routes that need to be plowed. The algorithm helps the managers to compute the optimal route for each truck plowing snow. The city is experimenting with using GPS and an automated data reporting system to track the real-time location and other attributes of each truck.

This application has greatly improved snow removal services in Indianapolis. Snow Fighter allows managers in the department to develop a strategy for removing snow from the city streets and spreading traction enhancing materials (e.g., salt, sand, and chemicals), manage and track the actual snow removal, communicate with the public about snow removal progress, and submit information and forms to Federal and state departments of emergency management for cost recovery. The Department of Public Works can remove snow more quickly, calculate the snow-removal costs quickly and transparently, and estimate the needs and costs of supplies and equipment more accurately.

CityScan

CityScan is a GIS-enabled e-government application used in the City of Tucson, Arizona designed to provide user access to a variety of information from a variety of sources using maps and other GIS and non-GIS based methods to display the information in a usable and readily understandable format. The City of Tucson has an award-winning GIS e-government site located at http://www.ci.tucson.az.us/ed/ed.htm. Tucson is located in Pima County, Arizona, a 9,184 square mile area in the Southwestern United States that borders Mexico. Tucson, the county seat and largest city in Pima County, had a 2000 U.S. Census population of 486,699, while the County's 2000 population was 843,746.

Early GIS efforts facilitated the planning, development and implementation of CityScan. GIS development in Pima County started in earnest with a public bond

Figure 4: City of Tucson e-government site

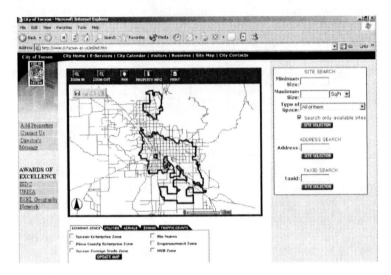

referendum in 1986, providing $5,000,000 for the development and installation of base data sets and the building of GIS capacity. Housed in several Pima County departments over the intervening years, the GIS development effort came to reside in the Department of Transportation and Flood Control District in 1995. The years since 1986 produced over 500 thematic GIS layers, orthophotos of the metropolitan area and other spatial data that is widely used by a variety of government users through the Pima County GIS Library. The layers use a common NAD83 State Plane Feet coordinate system.

This rich GIS base came about through significant government-to-government cooperation over several decades. In the early 1990s, the City of Tucson Planning Department's base maps were found to be the most current and carefully maintained source for establishing a base parcel layer for the City area. These maps were digitized by County technicians, enhanced in a number of ways and integrated with parcel data from the surrounding areas. The GIS parcel land base has served as the underlying base layer for much of the current GIS structure.

The long-standing good relationship between the City Transportation and County Transportation departments has been another foundation of local GIS success. The two departments promoted the adoption by their respective management staffs and elected officials of an intergovernmental agreement that established the basis for sharing GIS data, hardware and software costs and expertise. The agreement was renewed for another five years during 2001.

Another periodically renewed intergovernmental agreement between the City and the County assures that the County has the authority it needs to serve as the official addressing agent. One organizational entity, the Pima County Development Services Department, manages street naming for new subdivisions, street name changes, address number assignment and dispute resolution, and a myriad of related functions for the entire county.

The Pima Association of Governments (including Pima County and the City of Tucson) sponsored the acquisition of an extensive collection of digital orthophotographs of the Tucson metropolitan area in 1998. The Association contracted for aerial photography and related image processing and has managed the packaging and distribution of digital images to a wide variety of interested users. The orthophotography was extended in 2000 and refreshed in 2002. Pima County and City of Tucson employees access aerial photos and the GIS library through their desktop via a joint network connection over a shared server.

During the period covered by the base GIS development, a number of City employees met occasionally as a GIS users group. People from a number of City departments, including Planning, Transportation, Library, Water, Economic Development, Solid Waste Management, Fire and Police, were early adopters of GIS technology and met to share discussion and ideas on topics of mutual interest.

Following a significant effort to anticipate the Year 2000 changeover, the City's Information Technology Department saw several opportunities for focusing its staff in new directions. New technologies ripe for integration into City government included the digital government core areas of the Internet and GIS. The information technology department saw the need for guidance from end users in bringing GIS into central computing. They prompted the GIS Users Group to become something slightly more formal, which in 1999 became the Tucson GIS Cooperative.

Early on, the Cooperative decided to minimize its formal structure by having only an elected chairman. The Cooperative receives clerical and budget support from the City's Information Technology Department. During its third year of operation, the Cooperative had over 70 members from 17 City departments and offices, as well as members from Pima County and The University of Arizona.

The Cooperative has met monthly, except for a summer recesses, since its inception. The two hour meetings typically have speakers on topics of mutual interest, sharing of department level GIS projects and review of current GIS events. The Cooperative has sponsored on-site GIS training, conference attendances and has purchased GIS software for use throughout the City. The Cooperative has a web site for communication among its members and with others interested in GIS within the City of Tucson government.

A GIS Cooperative supported plan for integrating GIS into City business processes, including a flagship project called CityScan, was presented to City Management in January 2000. Associated with this plan was a budget request for $250,000 to support GIS infrastructure development, the CityScan project and GIS expansion throughout City government. The plan and budget request were accepted and GIS expansion began in the summer of 2000.

Conceived to be a web-based information portal using GIS technology, CityScan was the first project sponsored by the City of Tucson GIS Cooperative (see Figure 5). Based on the core concept that City information assets can and should be used to best advantage in assisting its citizens to achieve the Livable Tucson Vision, CityScan would use GIS and the World Wide Web as major technology components in achieving this end. As a municipal government, the City had a great deal of information linked to one geographic entity or another. Street addresses, neighborhoods, City Wards, census tracts and many local service area definitions were a mostly unused part of much of the data.

Figure 5

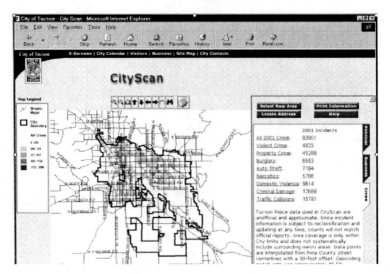

The CityScan project was developed to:
1. Provide easy citizen/business/city employee access to relevant, current data
2. Deliver coordinated, "seamless" access to data from throughout the City
3. Improve GIS skills of City employees
4. Improve Information Technology's ability to support GIS
5. Integrate with and enhance digital government initiatives
6. Deliver a flagship product that brings distinction to the City

As of mid-2002, CityScan has evolved through two generations of development. The early prototype deployed features that allowed users to retrieve information and display the services offered in the City of Tucson. It also allowed users to enter a specific location by providing an exact address, intersection or neighborhood name and generate maps centered on that specific location. A second-generation prototype is running on the City's intranet.

Several concurrent efforts are under way to prepare the infrastructure needed for rollout to the Internet. Standing behind the CityScan interface is an important data structure, the spatially enabled master address database. This structure, initiated by the GIS Cooperative and developed by City of Tucson's Information Technology department, was based on linking a wide variety of geographic areas, and their related data fields, to the official street addresses of Pima County. Maintained in a major commercial relational database system, frequent updates to the system come from many sources, including the Pima County maintained and geocoded official address file. Maintenance programs use point-in-polygon and related GIS functions to preprocess the database.

A computer interface to the master address database allows the end user to enter a street address and receive back answers (using text and maps as appropriate) to such questions as:
1. Who represents me?
2. Where do I vote?

3.   What are my garbage pickup days?
4.   What neighborhood am I in?
5.   What is the recent crime experience in my area?
6.   Can I build a second residence on my property?
7.   Are there upcoming property-related hearings or meetings that affect me?
8.   Are registered sex offenders living near me?
9.   Where is the nearest auto parts store?
10.   When is the pavement in front of my house due for resurfacing?
11.   Have I missed my bus?

The GIS Cooperative paid for several GIS Interns to work with County staff to enhance the official address source files and to assist in resolving questioned addresses. A good relationship between the Cooperative and the Information Technology department has existed from the start. For example, when City employees and their management express a need for financial support for GIS related software, the Cooperative forwards a short questionnaire regarding how the proposed use of the software will affect business objectives, whether the proposed user has training in its use, whether the proposed user's job will entail sufficient use of the GIS software to maintain skills and whether other sources of funding have been exhausted.

Given satisfactory answers to these questions and a review of past Cooperative expenditures and those planned in the budget, the purchase is usually authorized. The requesting department prepares a requisition that receives the Cooperative's signature as part of the review process. The GIS Cooperative's account number is used for the purchase process. The Cooperative has served as a sounding board for the Information Technology department when changes to policy regarding access to information over the Internet were considered. The balancing act between easy access to information and the need for concern about security has been a critical issue.

As the originating sponsor for the CityScan project, the Cooperative has served several roles when interacting with the information technology department. The Cooperative assisted in setting policies regarding needs assessment, project phasing, technology choices, data sourcing and system testing. Since a great deal of GIS learning and skill development were required by the in house staff, project schedules were hard to come by and implementation time lengthened. Platform changes, database licensing issues and web technology advances have all been subjects of the Cooperative-IT relationship.

After three years of operation, the Cooperative's focus is changing. As a volunteer organization, the chairperson's available time for Cooperative activities has been a critical element and a risk factor for the Cooperative's continued operation. Much of the original interest by City employees who participated as members of the Cooperative was due to personal curiosity about the GIS technology, the desire to share GIS experiences, and to find needs for GIS software and training. A significant amount of that GIS learning has taken place, as has the extension of GIS software and training into many City areas not having it at the start. At this writing, talks are underway about the transitions needed to assure the Cooperative's future operation and to determine what its evolving role should be as the City works toward full integration of the spatial aspects of data into ongoing governmental processes.

CHALLENGES OF IMPLEMENTING GIS FOR DIGITAL GOVERNMENT

At the heart of these GIS-enabled e-government applications are a number of management and technical issues that may limit the broader adoption of similar e-government services in the near future. The cases show to a varying degree that agencies are endowed with a range of capabilities for designing, planning and implementing GIS applications. Developing GIS-enabled e-government applications is challenging as resources and skills are needed to redesign or develop new government services and software applications, embed the GIS functions into the enterprise portal management schema, and integrate the GIS services with the database backend. Government agencies find that they are many times unable to use standard off-the-shelf solutions and must instead customize solutions to fit their particular structure, work methods and requirements (Somers, 1998).

Consequently, one of the key management challenges is for agencies to develop information technology (IT) capabilities. IT capabilities refer to the ability of an organization to leverage its assets to fulfill its information technology-related strategic objectives (Ross & Beath, 1996; Bharadwal, 1999). IT capabilities exists through contributions of IT-based assets and routines (Sambamurthy & Zmud, 2000) as organizations develop the capacity "for a team of resources to perform some task or activity ... [C]apabilities involve complex patterns of coordination between people and between people and other resources" (Choudhury & Xia, 1999, p. 62). IT capabilities include both the technical and managerial expertise required to provide reliable IT-enabled services (Broadbent & Weill, 1999). Ross and Beath. (1996) note that organizations must build and leverage a strong IT staff, a reusable technology base, and a partnership between the IT service functions and management in order to add value to the organization through information technology. Expanding on this, Feeny and Willcocks (1998) describe nine IS capabilities necessary to ensure successful adoption and implementation of "high-value-added" IT applications including: leadership; business systems thinking; relationship building; IT architecture planning; making technology work; informed buying; contract facilitation; contract monitoring; and, vendor development.

There are also many technical issues that may limit the broader use of GIS-enabled e-government applications. These applications need to operate in a networked environment and enable access by users from all corners of society. This is further complicated as more advanced applications also need to integrate data from disparate data sources and to distribute the information to not only desktop machines, but also other hand held devices. e-government architects and managers will need to resolve such issues as:

- What type of enabling communication infrastructure is needed?
- What special technical needs are required to implement wireless access?
- What types of security is needed given the communication infrastructure?
- How can the agency overcome the high short-term costs of developing web-based applications, especially where significant costs are derived from programming the web interface and presentation layer and the backend processing?
- What types of data standards need to be established to facilitate organization-wide sharing of data?

Table 1: IT capabilities (Feeny & Willcocks, 1998; Van der Heijden, 2001)

IT Capability	Description
IS/IT governance	*Integrating IS/IT effort with business purpose and activity*
Business systems thinking	*Envisioning the business process which technology makes possible*
Relationship building	*Getting the business constructively engaged in IS/IT issues*
Designing technical architecture	*Creating the coherent blueprint for a technical platform which responds to present and future business needs*
Making technology work	*Rapidly achieving technical progress – by one means or another*
Informed buying	*Managing the IS/IT sourcing strategy which meets the interests of the business*
Contract facilitation	*Ensuring the success of existing contracts for IS/IT services*
Contract monitoring	*Protecting the business' contractual position, current and future*
Vendor development	*Identifying the potential value of IS/IT service suppliers*

- How should the data be distributed through the agency?
- What should be done to integrate multiple systems including data from earlier systems that users may want?
- How will different supporting data protocols, affect the performance of advance GIS software applications?
- These three cases require using interorganizational databases. What strategies are most effective for enhancing interoperability across organizational boundaries? Where is the locus of control?
- What types of application design will ensure user friendliness and acceptance? How can the application design promote effective and efficient service delivery?

CONCLUSION

As technological advances enable government agencies to find new ways to deploy geographic information systems, GIS is emerging as a highly effective tool for bringing government closer to citizens through a number of exciting e-government applications. As the cases of Snow Fighter in Indianapolis and City Scan in Tucson show, GIS is being used in highly innovative ways to give users access to mapping tools. Users are able to use mapping tools online to examine demographic trends in their communities, review service delivery performance in their neighborhoods, and participate in policy decisions in their regions. The future is promising as GIS software vendors develop such technical solutions as web services and enterprise-wide database integration that will enable government agencies to develop high-functioning e-government applications using GIS. As government agencies move forward, they also need to make further investments into its information technology capabilities and overcome critical technical hurdles. GIS has truly come a long way.

ENDNOTES

1. The authors would like to thank Madlena Hakobyan, Olga Vassilieva, Danny Fernandes, Adam Rubinson, Doug Terra, Janine Salwasser, and members of the Tucson GIS Cooperative.
2. http://www.mapinfo.com/industry/government/egov_solutions.cfm
3. http://www.esri.com/software/internetmaps/visit_sites.html
4. Madlena Hakobyan and Olga Vassilieva, Master Thesis, May 2000, Indiana University, School of Public Environmental Affairs. The information was collected through interviews with Mr. David Mockert, GIS Director for the City of Indianapolis and review of project documents during March and April 2000. Other sources include: http://www.indygov.org/gis/projects/longrange/pdf/gis2001swpv.pdf, 2001 GIS Summary, http://www.indygov.org/gis/newsandevents/pdfs/yearend2001.pdf, and 2000 GIS Summary, http://www.indygov.org/gis/newsandevents/pdfs/yearend2000.pdf.
5. http://www.indygov.org/egov.htm

REFERENCES

Broadbent, M. & Weill, P. (1997). Management by maxim: How business and IT managers can create IT infrastructures. *Sloan Management Review, 38*(3), 77-93.

Choudhury, V. & Xia, W. (1999). A resource-based theory of network structures. J.C. Henderson & N. Venkatraman (Eds.), *Research in Strategic Management and Information Technology, 2*. Stamford, CT: JAI Press (55-85).

Dangermond, J. (2002). Web services and GIS. *Geospatial Solutions*, *12*(7), 56-57.

Davenport, T. & Short, J. (1990). The new industrial engineering: Information technology and business process redesign. *Sloan Management Review, 31*(4), 11-26.

Feeny, D. & Willcocks, L. (1998). Core IS capabilities for exploiting information technology. *Sloan Management Review, 39*(3), 9-22.

Francica, J. (2002). Debut of the DC Atlas. *Directions Magazine*. (June 2001). Available at: http://www.directionsmag.com/article.php?article_id=220

Green, R. (2002). *Open Access: GIS in e-Government*. Redlands, CA: ESRI Press.

Harder, C. (1998). *Serving Maps on the Internet: Geographic Information on the Web*. Redlands, CA: ESRI Press.

National Research Council. (2002). *Computer Science and Telecommunications Board Information Technology Research, Innovation and E-Government*. National Academy of Sciences, Washington, D.C.

Ross, J., & Beath, C. (1996). Develop long-term competitiveness through IT assets. *Sloan Management Review, 38*(1), 31-43.

Sambamurthy, V. & Zmud, R. (2000). Research commentary: The organizing logic for an enterprise's IT activities in the digital era – A prognosis of practice and a call for research. *Information Systems Research*, *11*(2), 105.

Somers, R. (1998). Developing GIS management strategies for an organization. *Journal of Housing Research*, *9*(1), 157-177.

Van der Heiden, H. (2001). Measuring IT core capabilities for electronic-commerce. *Journal of Information Technology, 16*, 13-22.

Chapter XVII

Training for
Digital Government

Shannon Howle Schelin
North Carolina State University, USA

ABSTRACT

The era of digital government is upon us. Are government officials and employees prepared for this paradigm shift? The use of digital government applications has increased exponentially in the past decade but the training that should accompany it has not. This article seeks to offer insight into the current need for and state of training for digital government, as well as to highlight key models at each level of government. Additionally, it attempts to outline a training methodology for Federal, state and local employees and officials in order to reduce the information asymmetry that occurs within the context of digital government.

INTRODUCTION AND OVERVIEW

As the information age advances, citizens expect a more responsive and accountable government. They demand government information and services to be available 24 hours a day, seven days a week. The use of digital government enables the people to have immediate access and responsiveness, while reducing the number of personal interactions with government employees. Often, this is translated into "citizens online instead of in line." With the era of digital government upon us, Federal, state and local governments need to prepare their elected officials and employees to handle the multitude of changes incorporated into digital government.

Digital government is the public sector component of the information technology revolution. Technology has been touted as a vehicle for enabling new methods of production, increasing the flow and accuracy of information, and even replacing traditional standard operating procedures (Landsbergen and Wolken, 2001). Information technology in government has long been acknowledged as a method for improving efficiency and communication (Kraemer and King, 1978; Norris and Kraemer, 1996). However, until the advent of the Internet, the use of technology in government primarily dealt with batch processing of mass transactions using mainframe computers. Now, IT developments such as electronic mail (e-mail) have changed interpersonal communications to eliminate the constraints of geography, space and time, with profound organizational consequences (Rahm, 1999). The newest phase of digital government moves far beyond back-office applications and engages citizens, businesses and other governments in collaborative, virtual experiences that traditionally existed in real time and space.

To adequately address the training issues associated with digital government, it is essential to understand its current and projected roles. The increasing importance and widespread application of digital government has been broadly examined over the past decade. Recent articles indicate that digital government applications and Web-based services are growing exponentially (Moon, 2002; Fountain, 2001). According to the 2002 International City/County Managers Association e-government survey, over 73 percent of municipalities with populations larger than 2,500 have web sites. The 2002 Pew Internet and American Life Project indicates that 58 percent (68 million people) of American Internet users have accessed at least one governmental web site (Larson and Rainie, 2002). Clearly, the citizen demand for and governmental usage of digital government indicates that digital government and its applications will only increase in importance over time. This further illustrates the need for assessing the current state of training for digital government, as well as offering prescriptive recommendations for additional training undertakings.

The importance of technology training for public administrators is highlighted by the studies and publications dealing with the topic; however, the primary focus of available literature is on the integration of technology training into collegiate public administration programs. The focus on information technology in schools of public administration began in 1988, when the National Association of Schools of Public Affairs and Administration (NASPAA) added computing as a skill set for accredited Masters of Public Administration (MPA) programs (Northrop, 2002). In 1993, Perry and Kraemer advocated for new educational practices to educate public sector employees on understanding and implementing information technology. In 1998, Brown and Brudney completed a comprehensive examination of 106 MPA programs to determine program efficacy in meeting the NASPAA requirements related to information technology education. They found that only about 30 percent of the schools included in the sample offered instruction on technology planning, policy development, and evaluation, despite the NASPAA recommendation to include these in the curriculum (Brown and Brudney, 1998). By 2001, Kim and Layne had conducted an empirical study of student perceptions of digital government and developed a straw man for future training, both in the schools of public administration as well as for the leaders of the public sector. Based on their recommendations, this article seeks to examine the need for training, the current state of training, the best practices in Federal, state, and local government, as well as offer prescriptive suggestions for new training initiatives.

DEMONSTRATING THE NEED:
EMPIRICAL ANALYSIS

In an attempt to underline the importance of high-quality training opportunities for Federal, state, and local government elected and appointed officials, a data set was analyzed with respect to the implementation and maintenance of digital government applications. The data examines the issues of staffing and training in local government units (counties and municipalities) by analyzing data obtained from the 2002 E-Government Survey conducted by the International City/County Management Association. The survey was conducted in order to evaluate the involvement of local governments in e-government activities, including web site development, electronic services, geographic information systems, changes associated with e-government adoption, and barriers preventing such adoption. The survey was sent to 7,844 municipal and county governments with populations over 2,500. Four thousand, one hundred and twenty three surveys were completed and returned, a response rate of 52.6 percent. Table 1 indicates the response rates by population size of the jurisdiction.

For the purposes of this analysis, the municipalities and counties have been divided into three population categories. Small jurisdictions contain less than 50,000 inhabitants. Medium jurisdictions contain 50,000 to 249,999 inhabitants and large jurisdictions contain 250,000 or more. The responding jurisdictions represent all four geographic regions, Northeast, North-Central, South and West, as defined by the ICMA. Table 2 demonstrates a slight over-representation of the West and a slight under-representation of the Northeast.

How Local Governments Implement Digital Government

Not only is digital government adoption important, the manner of application implementation is critical to understanding the nature of public sector information

Table 1: Response rate by jurisdiction population

	No. of municipalities/ counties surveyed	No. responding	
		No.	% of (A)
Total	7,844	4,123	52.6%
Population group			
Over 1,000,000	33	13	39.4%
500,000-1,000,000	63	20	31.7%
250,000-499,999	114	58	50.9%
100,000-249,999	331	198	59.8%
50,000-99,999	544	308	56.6%
25,000-49,999	923	502	54.4%
10,000-24,999	1,980	1,029	52.0%
5,000-9,999	1,899	960	50.6%
2,500-4,999	1,957	1,035	52.9%

Table 2: Response rate by geographic location

	No. of municipalities/ counties surveyed	No. responding	
		No.	% of (A)
Geographic region			
Northeast	1,996	871	43.6%
North-Central	2,242	1,280	57.1%
South	2,427	1,252	51.6%
West	1,179	720	61.1%

technology. In terms of the presence of information technology departments, there is a significant disparity between small and large jurisdictions. Only 28 percent of small municipalities have IT departments, while 84 percent of medium municipalities and 85.7 percent of large have such departments. In counties, 44.1 percent of small counties have IT departments, compared with 86.4 percent of medium and 98.4 percent of large counties. The increased establishment and formalization of the technology department, as well as its leadership counterpart, the Chief Information Officer (CIO), indicates the importance of high-quality technology staff and, subsequently, their training. As noted by various sources, staffing issues are one of the key factors in determining the success or failure of technology applications (Brown and Brudney, 1998; Standish Group, 1995). Therefore, proper training is a critical business issue for governments engaged in digital government.

One of the most notable differences based on population size occurs in the area of in-house versus outsourced web site applications. Chart 1 demonstrates the differences

Chart 1: Percentage of municipalities using in-house sources, by population

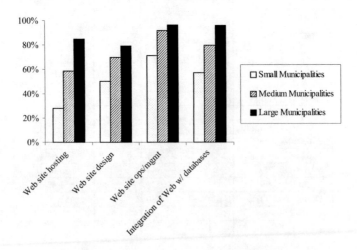

found between small, medium and large municipalities, with regard to web site hosting, design, operations/management and integration of databases.

The small municipalities use in-house sources for web site applications far less than the large municipalities. However, it is important to note that a majority of all sizes of municipalities uses in-house sources for web site design, operations and management, and database integration. Only small municipalities do not have majority performing in-house hosting services. The use of in-house staff for digital government applications is another key indicator as to the importance of high-level digital government training.

Similar findings occur with respect to the counties and their use of in-house sources for web site applications. Most counties, whether they are small, medium or large, have in-house sources for web site design, operations and management, and database integration. Only 35.9 percent of small counties have in-house web hosting, whereas 56.2 percent of medium and 71 percent of large counties have this application in-house. Chart 2 demonstrates the percentage of counties, grouped by size, that have in-house web site applications.

Barriers to E-Government

According to the data collected via the 2002 ICMA E-Government Survey, local governments face several barriers to successful implementation of e-government. The most common barriers across both types and all sizes of government are lack of technology/web staff, lack of financial resources and lack of technology/web expertise. Lack of technology/web staff, the issue with the highest frequency, is cited as a barrier by 45.4 percent of small, 47.8 percent of medium, and 44.8 percent of large municipalities, along with 40.7, 46.1, and 22.6 percent of small, medium, and large counties, respectively. Lack of financial resources was the second most common barrier, with 37.1, 54 and 58.6 percent of small, medium, and large municipalities, respectively, citing it. Over 40 percent of all sizes of counties also cite lack of financial resources as a barrier to implementing e-government. Finally, the lack of technology/web expertise is a barrier for 33.1, 28.6 and 24.1 percent of municipalities, small, medium and large respectively. It also is cited as a

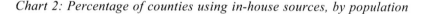

Chart 2: Percentage of counties using in-house sources, by population

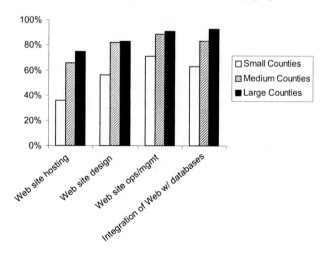

Table 3: Change resulting from e-government implementation, by size

Change Category	Small Municipalities	Medium Municipalities	Large Municipalities
Increased demands on staff	23.40%	34.50%	27.60%
Increased citizen contact with elected/appointed officials	22.40%	42.50%	51.70%
Changed role of staff	16.30%	35.10%	44.80%
	Small Counties	Medium Counties	Large Counties
Increased demands on staff	14.40%	26.90%	30.60%
Increased citizen contact with elected/appointed officials	13.40%	35.60%	51.60%
Changed role of staff	14.40%	31.10%	59.70%

barrier by 29.9, 25.1 and 19.4 percent of small, medium and large counties. Each of these limitations is concerning due to the proclivity of the local governments to rely on in-house development and administration of e-government and web-based applications. By increasing the training opportunities available to government employees and officials, the barriers to successful implementation can be significantly reduced.

Changes Resulting from E-Government

Organizational change is commonly associated with e-government initiatives. Table 3 demonstrates the most commonly noted changes according to local governments, based on size.

The most common change cited by small municipalities is the increased demand on staff. Small counties also cite this change, as well as a changed role of staff, as the largest change. Medium municipalities and counties view increased citizen contact with elected and appointed officials as the biggest change, as do large municipalities. Large counties note the changed role of staff as the largest change resulting from e-government implementation. In a follow-up survey, conducted by the author, with selected local governments who identified the changed role of staff as a change, the most common types of changed roles for staff include task expansion and task reorientation. Specific examples offered by local governments of task expansion include answering e-mails at a higher rate than previous channels of communication, such as face-to-face contact or telephone contact. Examples of task reorientation include changing employee positions from education and training to web masters. Again, the focus on the changing roles and increased demand on staff further heightens the need for quality digital government training. The data from the 2002 ICMA e-government survey demonstrates a viable need for digital government training; however, the reality of the situation indicates that very few opportunities are offered.

BEST PRACTICES

An informal examination of the state web sites indicates that most states offer some modicum of training, primarily technology-focused with the majority offering application, infrastructure, and software training. However, very few sites offer comprehensive digital government training with organizational, political and technological components. In lieu of examining the current offerings, or lack thereof, of each state and local government, this article posits three models of digital government training, one at each level of government.

The first model, at the Federal level, is the CIO University, spearheaded by the U.S. General Services Administration and the CIO Council. The CIO University is essential a consortium of graduate university programs within the greater Washington DC area (CIO University, 2002). These universities include Carnegie Mellon University, George Mason University, George Washington University and University of Maryland University College. The universities each offer specific courses related to the "core competencies" associated with the experiences and skill set required of CIOs and those who work within CIO frameworks.

Each individual participating in the CIO University has one of three options with respect to their coursework. The first option is a certificate program and closely mirrors other graduate certificate programs. The second option allows for a high-level overview of the core competencies, but does not require the same level of time commitment or detail orientation. The final option offers selected remedial work for those individuals seeking greater knowledge on specific topical areas. Each university in the consortium offers a variety of courses, as outlined in Table 4.

The CIO University offers a comprehensive, customizable training program for executive level Federal and non-Federal candidates. The offerings allow students to gain valuable knowledge about the various facets of digital government, including organizational, policy, and technological issues. For additional information about the CIO University, please visit the GSA's web site at www.gsa.gov.

The second model for digital government training, at the state level, is found in Washington. The Washington State Digital Government Applications Academy was formed in 1999 and focuses on application development and training related to digital government (Welsh, 2001). Some of the courses offered by the Academy include e-licensing, e-permitting and e-forms. The courses typically focus on the critical business issues associated with state government agencies. Additionally, the Academy focuses on collaborative agency ventures that produce standardized templates for digital government applications. The Digital Government Applications Academy also encourages local government participation in the training and application development sessions in order to foster quality digital government opportunities throughout the state of Washington. For additional information on the Washington State Digital Government Applications Academy, please visit their web site at www.wa.gov/dis.

Finally, at the local level, the third model for digital government training is Access eGovernment. Access eGovernment was created by the University of Minnesota Extension Service upon the request of the Association of Minnesota Counties (Access eGovernment, 2002). According to Rae Montgomery, project leader of Access eGovernment, "[it] explains the content, services, technology, politics, and issues

Table 4: General overview of CIO offerings by university

University	Courses/Degrees Offered
Carnegie Mellon University	Leadership
	Process and Performance
	Information Resources Strategy and Planning
	IT Acquisition and Program Management
	IT Management
	Information Assurance-Technical, Organizational, and Policy Issues
	E-Commerce and E-Government
	Key Technical Topics
George Mason University	M.S. in Technology Management (36 semester hours)
	Includes courses in: • Management Consulting • Negotiation and Conflict Resolution • Managing in a Global IT Environment • Accounting and Financial Information for Management Control • Several other offerings
George Washington University	Integrated M.S. in Information Systems Technology (10 courses)
	Includes courses in: • Principles of MIS • Project Management • Information Resource Management • Information Systems Development and Applications • Organization and Management • Several other offerings
University of Maryland University College	Strategic Issues in Managing Information Technology (nine graduate credits)
	IT Systems and Operations (nine graduate credits)
	CIO Processes (six graduate credits)

specific to e-government" (Montgomery, R. personal communication, July 31, 2002). It offers a free tutorial to any web user on the processes, benefits and implications of engaging in digital government.

The web-based tutorial follows a typical project lifecycle design. The first section in the training focuses on an overview of e-government. The second section centers on the Internet and methods for successful navigation. The third section concentrates on planning for e-government, included stakeholder identification and environmental scans. The fourth section focuses on designing for the user, including web sites and digital government applications. It also includes sections on accessibility and privacy. The final two sections highlight implementation and testing of the system, as well as its maintenance and updating. Access eGovernment is a valuable training tool that is available to all Internet users. For additional information on the program, please visit their web site at www.access-egov.info.

The importance of quality training for Federal, state, and local government employees and officials has been demonstrated by data collected in the 2002 ICMA e-government survey. The previous examples offer high-level examples of the "best practices" among such training opportunities. Although only three training models have been discussed, there are additional examples of high-level digital government training offerings found in a variety of organizations. However, such opportunities and offerings are limited and often do not address some of the key issues related to digital government implementation, such as organizational or political constraints.

PRESCRIPTIVE RECOMMENDATIONS

As outlined by Kim and Layne (2001), there are several core components to effective digital government training for public sector officials. Their model includes an understanding of e-government infrastructure, the political, economic, and legal contexts of e-government, best practices, conceptual issues such as portals and transactions, service-related issues pertaining to Internet-based offerings, and citizen-centric government (p. 238). The suggestions offered for possible training development in this article draw extensively on the best practice models previously identified, as well as Kim and Layne's research. Furthermore, the training focuses on the paradigmatic shift from traditional bureaucratic models of government to the newly emerging e-government model. According to Ho (2002), the e-government model, which emphasizes coordinated network building, external collaboration and customer services, is slowly replacing the traditional bureaucratic paradigm and its focus on standardization, hierarchy, departmentalization and operational cost-efficiency.

One of the most crucial components to understanding digital government is to gain familiarity with the e-government business model. This model is supported by the contention of many e-government proponents that e-government is more than just a shift in communication patterns or mediums (Foutain, 2001; Ho, 2002). Potentially, it involves a transformation of the organizational culture of the government. Recent authors argue that governments are mandated by citizen and business demands to operate within new structures and parameters precipitated by information technology (Osborne and Gaebler 1992; Heeks 1999; Ho 2002). In fact, as early as 1986, Bozeman and Bretschneider noted the transformational, progressive nature of technology adoption in the government sector. Others have concluded that e-government and associated information technology adoption lead to shifting paradigms, extending beyond the notion of simple progress (Reschenthaler and Thompson, 1996; Ho, 2002). Reschenthaler and Thompson (1996) contend that e-government offers a basis for reengineering the business of government, refocusing its work on the needs of the citizens, and returning government to its core functions (Reschenthaler and Thompson, 1996).

The first component of the proposed training methodology to understanding the power of the structural alterations associated with e-government is to engender understanding of the e-government business model. The use of this model has been touted by scholars, such as Fountain, as well as recently codified by the Office of Management and Budget (see The Business Reference Model Version 1.0, 2002). The OMB architecture creates a functional view of Federal government services in order to eliminate redundant technology investments and to maximize economies of scale. One of the key components of this new model is to work in collaborative, interagency and cross-departmental fashions. Current demands require crosscutting services, which in turn require government to improve communication and interaction across traditional bureaucratic lines (Alexander and Grubbs, 1998). These new requirements, which fundamentally alter the nature of government, are made possible through the strategic use of information technology. Therefore, in outlining an e-government training methodology, it is important to emphasize the conceptualization of the e-government business model.

A second training component focuses on learning the basic concepts of technology, which facilitates the understanding of, and communication with, the technical experts involved. A basic overview of information technology concepts, including hardware, software, and infrastructure, would engender a more holistic comprehension of digital government. Specifically, the concepts to be covered include input, output, and storage devices, the system unit, communication devices, operating systems, application software, networking designs, and key Internet terms, such as transmission mediums, protocols, transmission speeds, and service providers.

The third module highlights project management skills. Developing a digital government strategy involves internal and external education, leadership cultivation, partnership building and team designation. Kim and Layne (2001) note the benefit of including project management skills in e-government training. The fourth component of

Table 5: Summary of digital government training curriculum

Module	Title	Components
Module 1	Understanding the Concept of E-Government	• Definitions • Focus (internal and external) • Roles • Organizational assessment
Module 2	Basic Overview of Technology Components	• Hardware • Software • Infrastructure
Module 3	Project Management Skills	• Education (internal and external) • Leadership cultivation • Partnership building • Team designation
Module 4	Business Case Metrics	• Methodologies
Module 5	Organizational Transformation	• Information sharing • Citizen-centric focus • Policy and social issues
Module 6	Digital Civic Engagement	• Citizens • Businesses

the digital government curriculum involves developing business case metrics for assessing and generating strategic IT investments. An assortment of tools, including return-on-investment, net present value, and cost-benefit analysis, can be included in the training in order to develop the skill set of the student.

The impact of digital government on the organization and its members is another crucial component of the training curriculum. Dealing with the organizational mindset, fostering information sharing, and focusing on citizen-centric services are unique components of digital government and must be included in public sector training. Furthermore, issues such as privacy, accessibility, authentication and security are critical to the development of safe and equitable systems. The final module of the digital government curriculum involves digital civic engagement. Essentially, this section focuses on using technology to foster new relationships and improving existing one between the government unit and the citizens and businesses in its jurisdiction. This module is where the intangible value-add of digital government becomes palpable.

It should be noted that the following curriculum is just one approach to developing a holistic training effort for digital government. Other issues not addressed by this model should be incorporated as needed in order to continually expand and improve the state of digital government at the Federal, state and local levels. Table 5 offers a summary of the curriculum.

CONCLUSION

Information technology has fundamentally altered the way we interact in today's society. As connectivity becomes more readily available to disparate geographical and demographic sectors of the United States, the role of the Internet continues to increase in society. The changing information environment and the movement toward the knowledge economy, juxtaposed against citizen and business demands, mandates that government become involved in digital government initiatives (Ho, 2002). Furthermore, the success of existing e-government efforts provides increased legitimacy for further information technology adoption (Norris, 1999).

With the era of digital government upon us, Federal, state, and local governments need to prepare their elected officials and employees to handle the multitude of changes incorporated into digital government. However, the lack of training opportunities, as well as the lack of research dedicated to training for digital government, is ominous for successful digital government endeavors. This article attempts to outline a training methodology for Federal, state, and local employees and officials in order to reduce the information asymmetry that occurs within the context of digital government. Additionally, it seeks to offer insight into the current need for and state of training for digital government, as well as to highlight key models at each level of government.

REFERENCES

Access eGovernment. Retrieved on July 28, 2002 from http://www.access-egov.info/.
Alexander, J. H. and Grubbs, J. W. (1998). Wired Government: Information Technology, External Public Organizations and Cyberdemocracy. *Public Administration and Management: An Interactive Journal, 3*(1). Available at: http://www.pamij.com.

Bozeman, Barry and Stuart Bretschneider (1986). Public management information systems: Theory and prescription. *Public Administration Review*, 46 (special edition): 475-487.

Brown, M. M. and Brudney, J. L. (1998). Public Sector Information Technology Initiatives. *Administration and Society 30*(4), 421-443.

CIO University. Retrieved on September 5, 2002 from http://ciouniversity.cio.gov/.

Fountain, J. (2001). *Building the virtual state: Information technology and institutional change.* Washington, D.C.: Brookings Institution.

Fountain, J. (2001). The Virtual State: Transforming American Government? *National Civic Review, 90*(3), 241-252.

Heeks, R. (ed.) (1999). Reinventing government in the information age. In *Reinventing Government in the Information Age*, (pp. 9-21). New York: Routledge.

Ho, A. T.-K. (2002). Reinventing Local Government and the E-Government Initiative. *Public Administration Review, 62*(4), 434-444.

Kraemer, K. L., et al. (1978). *Local Government and Information Technology in the United States.* Paris: OECD Informatics Studies #12.

Landsbergen Jr., D. and Wolken Jr., G. (2001). Realizing the Promise: Government Information Systems and the Fourth Generation of Information Technology. *Public Administration Review, 61*(2), 206-220.

Larsen, E. and Rainie, L. (2002). The rise of the e-citizen: How people use government agencies' web sites. *Pew Internet and American Life Project.* Available at: http://www.pewinternet.org/reports/pdfs/PIP_Govt_Website_Rpt.pdf.

Montgomery, R. (2002). Personal communication. July 31.

Moon, M. J. (2002). The Evolution of E-government among Municipalities: Rhetoric or Reality? *Public Administration Review, 62*(4), 424-433.

Norris, D. and Kraemer, K. (1996). Mainframe and PC Computing in American Cities: Myths and Realities. *Public Administration Review, 56*(6), 568-576.

Norris, D. F. (1999). Leading Edge Information Technologies and their Adoption: Lessons from U.S. Cities. In Garson, D.G. (Ed.), *Information Technology and Computer Applications in Public Administration: Issues and Trends* (pp. 137-156). Hershey, PA: Idea Group Publishing.

Northrop, A. (2003). Information Technology and Public Administration: The View from the Profession. In Garson, G.D. (Ed.), *Public Information Technology*. Hershey, PA: Idea Group Publishing.

Office of Management and Budget. (2002). The Business Reference Model Version 1.0. Retrieved on October 20, 2002 from the World Wide Web: http://www.feapmo.gov/resources/fea_brm_release_document_rev_1.pdf.

Osborne, D. and Gaebler, T. (1992). *Reinventing Government: How Entrepreneurial Spirit is Transforming the Public Sector*. Reading, MA: Addison-Wesley.

Perry, J. L. and Kraemer, K. (1993). The Implications of Changing Information Technology. In Thompson, F.J. (Ed.), *Revitalizing State and Local Public Service: Strengthening Performance, Accountability and Citizen Confidence* (pp. 225-245). San Francisco, CA: Jossey-Bass Publishers.

Rahm, D. (1999). The Role of Information Technology in Building Public Administration. *Theory Knowledge, Technology, and Policy, 12*(1), 74-83.

Reschenthaler, G.B. and Thompson, F. (1996). The Information Revolution and the New Public Management. *Public Administration Research Theory, 6*(1), 125-143.

Welsh, W. (2001). Washington's Digital Academy Speeds E-Gov Revolution. Washington Technology, *15*(20). Retrieved on October 10, 2002 from http://www.washingtontechnology.com/news/15_2.

Chapter XVIII

The E-Government Challenge for Public Administration Education

Alexei Pavlichev
North Carolina State University, USA

ABSTRACT

As public sector agencies use the e-government model to improve delivery of their services, it is important that this model become integrated into education of future leaders of the public service. A fully scaled implementation of e-government requires more than simple automation of the existing processes. It can affect significantly the overall organizational structure of public agencies, their missions and goals, and the way they interact with customers and with each other. Because of its profound impact on the functions and even structure of government, implementing e-government involves significant challenges, including resistance to change and the problem of lack of information technology skills among public managers. To address these challenges, public affairs programs must include into their curricula courses that would prepare cadre qualified for the era of e-government. Survey results are presented outlining efforts of graduate public affairs programs to meeting demands related to the e-government model. Major components of the model are outlined and the extent to which these components are covered in graduate courses in leading public affairs programs is assessed.

INTRODUCTION

Today in public administration there is a new focus on the use of information and communication technologies (ICT) as a mechanism for improving public service. For government agencies, entering the new millennium was accompanied by a rapid increase in the use of various forms of ICT. The Internet is the most vivid example. Citizens can use Internet technology not only to obtain information about government services, download various documents and forms, but also to conduct their business with government through electronic transactions. Using ICT to facilitate government services has been called electronic or digital government. Descriptions of e-government in the literature indicate that it offers an extra value to both government and its customers (Kim & Layne, 2001; NECCC, 2000b; Zweers & Plangué, 2001).

The extra value of e-government is now possible because use of the Internet by citizens and businesses with which government conducts its business has been dramatically increasing. In 2000, the number of Internet users in the U.S. was estimated to be 110 million (GAO, 2000). Worldwide, more than one billion people will be using the Internet in the first decade of this century (Layne & Lee, 2001). Of all Internet users in the U.S., more than 60 percent interact with government web sites (OMB, 2002a). Those who are comfortable with using Internet technology can gain access to government services and information online through web portals any day of the week at any time of the day at their convenience. For government transferring services online also means savings in time and resources. It has been estimated that government can save up to 70 percent of its costs by moving its services online (NECCC, 2000a).

Overall, government agencies on all levels are embracing e-government and are increasing the number and the range of services provided online (West, 2000). The Federal government alone features 22,000 web sites and over 35 million web pages (OMB, 2002a). E-government is one of the key elements in the five-part President's Management Agenda for improving performance of Federal government. According to this agenda, the President's Budget proposes a $20 million e-government fund for 2002 and $100 million over the years 2002 through 2004 (OMB, 2002b). The Government Paperwork Elimination Act requires that by October 21, 2003, Federal agencies, when practicable, provide the public with the option of submitting, maintaining and disclosing required information electronically (GAO, 2001).

The notion prevails among government agencies and academia that implementing e-government will meet modern expectations of citizens and businesses regarding improvement of government services. According to this notion, full-scale e-government is much more customer-centric than is possible with the "traditional" way of conducting services over the counter. E-government features as "one-stop-shopping" to enable citizens and businesses to access to all government services and information through a singe web portal. In a fully implemented e-government model, citizens would no longer have to be concerned with organizational boundaries of government agencies or limited jurisdictions of different departments. Government web portals are supposed to be structured in a way that would allow a customer to pay for a parking ticket and apply for a Federal scholarship at the same portal. Portals featuring single touch-point entry should allow a person to input his or her information, such as change of address, just once, and software would automatically update all government databases that use this information.

E-government goes beyond simple automation of the existing processes. Layne and Lee (2001) point out that e-government initiatives should be accompanied by re-conceptualization of the nature of government service itself. The full benefit of e-government will be realized only if organizational changes accompany technological changes. All ICT and especially the Internet will significantly affect the organizational structure of public agencies and the way they interact with their customers and each other. Unlike the "traditional" channels of information dissemination in government, the Internet is fragmented, non-hierarchical, decentered and non-linear (Frissen, 1998). It contradicts the classic bureaucratic structure of government agencies (Atkinson & Ulevich, 2000; Fountain, 2001a; Frissen, 1998; OMB, 2002b). This means that e-government requires major changes in the way traditional government is operating. Tradition-ally, public agencies are bound by an institutional environment that discourages horizontal cross-agency initiative while encouraging competition of individual agencies for resources (Fountain, 2001a). Government has a multi-layered structure. Agencies of each layer operate in limited jurisdictions, such a state and municipality. As rule, funds are allocated to individual agencies for specific projects. Since other agencies are perceived as competitors, information sharing is often discouraged. This leads to various agencies asking their customers for the same information.

The e-government model, with its concepts such as one-stop shopping and single-touch point data entry, assumes vertical and horizontal integration across different agencies, functions and services (Bekkers, 1998; Frissen, 1998; Layne & Lee, 2001). For most agencies, transformation to e-government can lead to reconsidering missions, changing of internal and external boundaries, jurisdictions and accountability. To create fully functioning portals, government has to integrate services provided by local, state and Federal agencies and enable their information systems to share data to avoid duplicate entries. Inter-agency collaboration would require agencies to reconsider such fundamental principles as funding and accountability.

Many government agencies are experimenting with transition to the e-government model. According to the General Accounting Office, there are 1,371 e-government initiatives just at the Federal level (GAO, 2001). The situation is similar on other levels of government. Results of e-government survey jointly conducted by the International City/County Management Association and Public Technology Inc. indicate that 85.3 percent of municipal governments have their own web sites, and 57.4 percent have an intranet (Moon, 2002). There are, however, many findings that demonstrate that the transition to fully functional e-government has been slow and does not always produce desired results. According to a Center for Technology in Government report (1999), more than 80 percent of projects related to information systems implementation in organiza-tions fail to achieve their objectives or to be implemented at all. Despite government's escalating investments in ICT, new technologies have not always led to an increase in efficiency or improvements in service delivery. The President's Management Agenda (OMB, 2002b) expressed clear concern that the $45 billion that the U.S. government will spend on information technologies in 2002 may not be producing measurable gains in the productivity of public-sector agencies.

Recent studies have demonstrated that technology alone is not likely to affect efficiency or quality of services (Atkinson & Ulevich, 2000; Fountain, 2001b; Kling, 1996; Kling & Allen, 1996; Kraemer & Dedrick, 1997, OMB, 2002a; OMB, 2002b; Seneviratne, 1999). To make a successful transition to the e-government model, public agencies have to realize that this model in most cases requires significant changes in organizational structures and processes. Merely automating the pre-existing processes without changing them to fit the e-government model is unlikely to result in the desired improvement of agencies' functions. Currently, however, most agencies implement e-government initiatives without developing a comprehensive plan of how it will be incorporated with redesigned organizational processes and the overall mission of the agency (Kling, 1996; Kling & Allen, 1996; Moon, 2002).

Resistance to change is another important challenge to successful e-government implementation. This resistance results for the most part from the bureaucratic structure of government agencies with its highly institutionalized hierarchical relationships. Under the e-government model, bureaucratic divisions may become obsolete and have to be transformed or eliminated. Agencies may have perceived this option as a threat and make "wasteful and redundant investments in order to preserve chains of command that lost their purpose" (OMB, 2002b). According to Wilson (1989), to a certain point all organizations by design are enemies of change. However, it is especially true for government agencies because their objectives are typically broader and more general than those of private companies. Public agencies are destined to serve customers whose interests are often in conflict. Public agencies have to deal with more red tape than their private sector counterparts. They also must take into consideration a broad spectrum of procedural, political and legal accountabilities (Heeks & Bhatnagar, 1996; Kraemer & Dedrick, 1997).

The third challenge to e-government is related to the lack of ICT skills of public managers (Heeks & Davies, 1999; Seneviratne, 1999). For a long time, technology experts have been either outsourced or they were isolated in IT departments and, for the most part, were narrowly trained in technical issues and not concerned with the agency mission, objectives, and strategies. This situation was acceptable for the purpose of computerization of simple procedures of a single agency that do not affect its organizational structure and processes. However, the e-government model requires integration of the ICT function into management processes that include planning, decision-making, project implementation and evaluation. Such e-government components as one-stop shopping require vertical integration of information systems of different levels of government as well as horizontal integration across agencies of different functional areas (Layne & Lee, 2001). In fact, the influence of ICT on the organization structure of government agencies is so profound that this structure can no longer be characterized as bureaucracy. Instead, the term, *infocracy* has been proposed to distinguish the new structure that is emerging because of transition to e-government (Zuurmond, 1998). Just like bureaucracy, it is often said that infocracy is characterized by rational rules of formalization and standardization that regulate agencies processes. However, with infocracy, these rules are often not so easily distinguishable because they are no longer documented in the manuals and standard operating procedures, but are embedded into the software and hardware in the form of servers, networks, user interfaces, and programming codes (Fountain, 2001a; Frissen, 1998). It is therefore essential for public managers to have a certain level of ICT skill to be able to make sense out of the modified "infocratic" system of databases and standard operating procedures. If public managers do not have these skills, it will be difficult for them to manage agencies, or to understand agency processes. As Fountain (2001b) observed:

Public executives and managers can no longer afford the luxury of relegating technology matters to technical staff. Many issues that appear to be exclusively technical are also deeply political and strategic in nature...Information architecture, both hardware and software is more than a technical instrument; it is a powerful form of governance. As a consequence, outsourcing information architecture and operation is, effectively, outsourcing of policy making.

So far, according to the UN/ASPA report on benchmarking e-government in the UN member states, no country, including the U.S., has progressed in its e-government initiatives far enough to reach the fully integrated e-government stage that is character- ized by instant one-stop access to any services and demarcation of levels and functions of government in cyberspace (Ronaghan, 2002). However, the U.S. and other countries in Northern America and Europe have made substantial progress in implementing a full- scale e-government model. As this progress continues, an important question is whether education for the public service is keeping pace with the rise of the e-government model.

E-GOVERNMENT AND PUBLIC AFFAIRS PROGRAMS

For some time, researchers have been recommending that public affairs graduate programs focus on training public managers to acquire strong skills in the sphere of e- government, including ICT (Brown & Brudney, 1998; Brown et al., 2000; Brudney et al., 1998; Kim & Layne, 2001; Northrop, 1999). This literature also points out that the nation's graduate public affairs programs fall behind in adapting their curricula to the impacts of e-government on organizational structure and service delivery in the public sector. E- government is a relatively new concept, still in the process of evolving and change.

Training in e-government often requires teaching some concepts that are outside of the "traditional" curriculum of public affairs graduate programs. Though many e- government concepts are new for public affairs programs, not all of them are. Importance of including courses on ICT in the public affairs curricula was repeatedly brought up in the past. In 1986, the National Association of Schools of Public Affairs and Administra- tion (NASPAA) Ad Hoc Committee on Computers and Public Management Education recommended including courses on computers and information systems in the public administration curriculum. The courses were to include such topics as hardware, software, purposes and nature of programming languages, and uses of computers for management. These courses had to provide managers with three levels of computer literacy: (1) the ability to use technology in the course of their work, (2) the ability to use the technology of the organizations they manage, (3) the ability to develop policies for effective use and control of the technology for strategic and operational advantages. NASPAA expressed concern that the use of computers in public affairs program was only limited to statistical analysis. From the NASPAA point of view, our society needs more extensive training in ICT because the United States was "increasingly becoming an information society" and ICT skills were important for successful functioning of the government. In 1988, NASPAA included a requirement that public affairs graduate programs provide skills in computing as part of its formal standards for institutional accreditation (NASPAA, 1988).

However, not all public affairs programs followed the NASPAA recommendations and for the most part implementation was only partial. The computer-related courses that most public affairs programs have included in their curriculum are largely focused on such basic computer skills as word processing, spreadsheets and database management (Brudney et al., 1993; Brown & Brudney, 1998; Brown et al., 2000). In 1995, nine years after the NASPAA Ad Hoc Committee made its recommendations, only 18.8 percent of the public affairs program required at least some knowledge of computers for graduation.

Most of the problems which current literature outlines with regard to successful integration of ICT into the e-government model are the same that were raised in 1986. Most of the solutions proposed to overcome these issues are also similar. Should public affairs programs have followed the NASPAA recommendations more fully, perhaps the adoption of e-government model would be less problematic.

The following section discusses the efforts of graduate programs in public affairs in meeting demands posed by the reuse of the e-government model. The research outlines the major components of e-government model and evaluates the extent that these components are covered in the public affairs graduate courses.

METHODOLOGY AND DATA COLLECTION

To determine the degree to which graduate programs in public affairs provide students with skills related to e-government, the research outlined the major components of e-government model. These components are listed in Table 1.

The sample of the graduate programs in public affairs for the research was compiled from the *U.S. News and World Report Premium Online Edition* rating of the graduate schools in public affairs (http://www.usnews.com/usnews/edu/grad/rankings/pub/pre-mium/pubadm.php). The sample consists of the 20 schools that received the highest rating. The list of the schools is presented in Table 2.

First, the programs' web sites were examined to determine if and in what way the e-government model was included in the curricula of surveyed institutions. For this purpose, the following questions were considered:

* What types of degree does the school offer?
* Does the school offer e-government as an area of academic concentration?
* How many courses related to e-government does the school offer?
* Are courses in e-government included in the core curriculum of the school? If yes, how many?
* Does the school refer the students to other departments or schools for the e-government courses that it does not offer?

Next, courses related to e-government components offered by the schools were identified. The information about the e-government courses was extracted from the school web sites and online course catalogs. The syllabi for the e-government courses were obtained to evaluate which components of e-government are covered by the courses. Syllabi for some of the courses were available online. For those courses that did

Table 1

#	Component	Definition
E-government Components		
1	Theory of E-Government	Theoretical paradigm of e-government model. The place of e-government model in the public administration theory.
2	International/Global Issues of E-Government	E-government role in the globalization processes. Similarities and disparities between different countries in adopting e-government model.
3	Electronic Service Delivery	Use of ICT to provide services that were originally provided by "traditional" means; providing new types of services, specific to ICT.
4	E-Commerce	Use of ICT to conduct business transaction with government or private entities.
5	Privacy and Security in Cyberspace	Keeping information provided for specific purposes from being used for different purposes; protecting this information from unintended breaches.
6	E-government and Organizational Change	Changes in organizational structure and functions required for successful adoption of e-government model and integration of ICT into management processes.
7	Digital Divide	Gap in opportunities to benefit from e-government between socio-economic groups of people with different levels of accessibility to ICT.
8	Legal Issues Related to E-Government	Regulating e-government and the Internet. Influence of e-government model on civil rights and liberties of citizens.
9	Electronic Democracy	Using the Internet and other ICT to facilitate democratic processes, such as online voting, participating in democratic forums, and communicating with political representatives.
10	Database Management and Data Mining	Database design, construction, and maintenance; extracting necessary information out of vast amounts of data with specialized tools.
11	Geographic Information System	Using of computerized systems for collection, storage, analysis, and output of information related to government services that are spatially referenced.
12	Technology Issues	Use of programming languages; information systems design and management; technical aspects of web development.

not have the syllabi online, the instructors who teach these courses were contacted by e-mail if the school or university web sites provided their contact information. In the e-mail, the instructors were requested to send the syllabi for their courses. If the contact information for the instructors was not available online, the graduate schools were contacted with the request to provide contact information for the instructors who teach e-government courses. After the information was obtained, the instructors were contacted with the request to provide the syllabi.

The courses that involve learning of the programming languages, web development, and creation and maintenance of the information systems were combined under the "Technology Aspects" category (see Table 1 for definition). The courses in statistics, basic computer skills such as word processing, and spreadsheets were not considered for analysis. Courses differ concerning the scope of material they cover. Some of the

Table 2

Top Twenty Graduate Schools in Public Affairs
1   Harvard University (MA)
2   Syracuse University (NY)
3   Indiana University--Bloomington
4   Princeton University (NJ)
5   University of California--Berkeley
6   University of Georgia
7   Carnegie Mellon University (PA)
8   University of Michigan--Ann Arbor
9   University of Southern California
10   University of Texas--Austin
11   University of Wisconsin-Madison
12   American University (DC)
13   Columbia University (NY)
14   SUNY--Albany
15   University of Chicago
16   University of Kansas
17   University of Minnesota--Twin Cities
18   University of North Carolina--Chapel Hill
19   Duke University (NC)
20   George Washington University (DC)

Source: U.S. News and World Report Premium Online Edition. Available at http:// www.usnews.com/usnews/edu/grad/rankings/pub/premium/pubadm.php

courses cover specific topics, such as database creation and management or organizational change. On the other hand, there are courses that are more general and cover several topics. Courses of the latter category are introductory in nature.

Despite certain potential limitations, the approach restricted to the Internet and e-mail was chosen for several reasons. First, these methods of obtaining information are consistent with the e-government model, according to which the Internet is used as primary medium for providing most services. It would therefore be expected for programs that offer courses in e-government to utilize the methods of e-government model at least for elementary information dissemination purposes. The programs that do not use the Internet to provide comprehensive information about the areas of concentrations and the courses they offer potentially lose an entire segment of students who use the Internet to make decisions about applying for the programs or about courses they are going to take once they are in the program. This can result in a phenomenon of "reversed" digital divide, making the process of obtaining the program information longer and more

Table 3

Types of Degree Offered	Percentage
Public Administration/Management	30
Public Policy	15
Public Administration and Public Policy	40
Public Affairs	15

complicated for the people who are located at significant distance from universities, such as out-of-state or international students. By failing to provide the information via the Internet, these programs also put themselves at disadvantage because they narrow the pool of potential applicants.

Findings on How E-Government Fits into the Programs' Curricula

Table 3 provides a summary of the types of degrees offered by programs. Most of the programs (40 percent) offer degrees both in public administration and public policy. A degree in public administration alone is offered by 25 percent of schools. Degrees in public policy alone are offered by 15 percent of schools. Same percentage of schools offers degrees in and public affairs.

Table 4 demonstrates that 45 percent of programs offer e-government or information technology as a concentration area. This does not necessarily mean that the programs offer all or even any courses required to obtain the concentration. In fact, 50 percent of the public affairs programs refer their students to other schools, such as business schools or schools of information systems, for taking all or some of the courses related to e-government or information technology concentration. Only ten percent of programs incorporate e-government courses into their core curricula.

Findings on E-Government Components in the Programs' Courses

Combined, the sampled programs' web sites listed 91 courses related to e-government (Table 5). It is important to note that 32 of these courses, or 35.2 percent, were offered by one program. All other 19 programs combined offered 59 courses (64.8 percent). Table 6 presents the basic statistics for the distribution of courses, with and without the outlier. Four programs (20 percent) did not offer any courses related to e-government, and six

Table 4

E-Government and Schools' Curricula	Percentage
Programs with E-Government Concentration Area	45
Referral to other Departments	50
Programs with E-Government Core Courses	10

Table 5

E-Government Courses and Syllabi	N
Number of E-Government Courses	91
Number of E-Government Core Courses	3
Number of Syllabi	32

programs (30 percent) offered only one course. Request for the course syllabi yielded a response rate of 35.2 percent, or 32 syllabi.

Findings on E-Government Components

Based on the syllabi analysis, components of e-government are covered in the courses, as illustrated by the pie chart in Figure 1.

As Figure 1 demonstrates, the components that are covered the most extensively are "theory of e-government" and "e-government and organizational change." Each of these components is covered in 13 percent of courses. "Privacy and security" is the next popular component, which is covered in 11 percent. All other components are covered almost equally by the courses, with "Legal Issues" being the least widespread (five percent). It is noteworthy that only seven percent of the courses offered within public affairs programs address the "Technology Aspects" component of e-government.

CONCLUSION

As government is recognizing the benefits and potential of e-government, it is important that public affairs programs turn their attention to the research of theoretical foundations and practical applications of e-government model. It is important that public affairs students who express interest in pursuing careers in government receive sufficient exposure to the major components of the e-government model. There is evidence that currently public affairs programs fall behind in this respect.

Table 6

Statistics for E-Government Courses		
	With the Outlier (N = 20)	*Without the Outlier (N = 19)*
Mean	4.55	3.11
Median	1.50	1
Mode	1	1
Std. Deviation	7.49	3.90
Minimum	0	0
Maximum	32	14

Figure 1: E-Government components chart

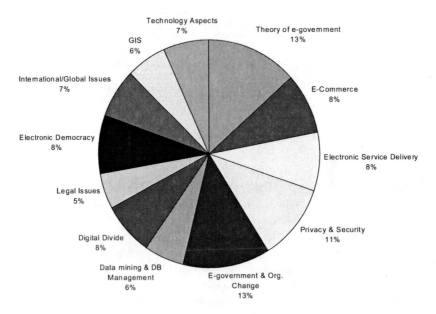

In some of the programs, students have an opportunity to take classes such as electronic commerce or information technology through a school of business or information technology. Though such referrals to different schools might be beneficial in the short run, it is important that public affairs schools develop their own courses in all of the major e-government components, including ICT management. The discussion of including such courses into the public affairs curricula is not new. In its 1986 recommendation, NASPAA Ad Hoc Committee on Computers in Public Management Education concluded that it is impractical to send public affairs students to other schools to take ICT courses because outside courses "offer some topics that would not be relevant for public management students," such as using ICT for profit-related activities. Alternatively, outside ICT courses "might not include topics that are especially relevant and important for public management students, such as government information systems, and public policy issues concerning computers and information systems in society" (NASPAA, 1986). These conclusions remain true today and, given the dramatic rise of the e-government model, now assume a new urgency.

REFERENCES

Atkinson, R.D. & Ulevich, J. (2000). *Digital government: The next step to reengineering the Federal government.* Washington, DC: Progressive Policy Institute. Available online at: http://www.dlcppi.org

Bekkers, V.J.J.M. (1998). Wiring public organizations and changing organizational jurisdictions. In I.Th.M. Snellen & W.B.H.J. van de Donk (Eds.), *Public Administration in an Information Age* (pp. 57-77). Amsterdam, The Netherlands: IOS Press.

Brown, M.M. & Brudney, J.L. (1998). Public sector information technology initiatives: Implications for programs of public administration. *Administration & Society*, *30*(4), 421-442.

Brown, M.M. & Brudney, J.L., Waugh, W.L., & Hy, R.J. (2000). Graduate education technology in the public sector: The need and response. In G.D. Garson (Ed.), *Handbook of Public Information Systems* (pp. 9-25). New York: Marcel Dekker, Inc.

Brudney, J.L., Hy, R.J., & Waugh, W.L. (1993). Building microcomputing skills in public administration graduate education: An assessment of MPA programs. *Administration & Society*, *25*(2), 183-203.

Center for Technology in Government. (1999). *Some assembly required: Building a digital government for the 21st century.* Accessed August 14, 2002 at: http://www.ctg.albany.edu/resources/abstract/abdgfinalreport.html

Fountain, J.E. (2001a). *Building the virtual state: Information technology and institutional change.* Washington, DC: Brookings Institution Press.

Fountain, J.E. (2001b). The virtual state: Transforming American Government? *National Civil Review*, *90*, 241-251.

Frederickson, J.H. (1996). Comparing the reinventing government movement with the new public administration. *Public Administration Review,* (56), 266-269.

Frissen, P.H.A. (1998). Public administration in cyberspace: A postmodern perspective. In I.Th.M. Snellen & W.B.H.J. van de Donk (Eds.), *Public Administration in an Information Age* (pp. 33-46). Amsterdam, The Netherlands: IOS Press.

General Accounting Office. (1994). *Executive guide: Improving mission performance through strategic information management technology.* (GAO/AIMD-94-115). Washington, DC: U.S. Government Printing Office.

General Accounting Office. (2000). *Electronic government. Federal initiatives are evolving rapidly but they face significant challenges.* (GAO/T-AIMD/GGD-00-179, May 2000). Washington, DC: U.S. Government Printing Office.

General Accounting Office. (2001). *Electronic government: Challenges must be addressed with effective leadership and management.* (GAO-01-959T, June 2001). Washington, DC: U.S. Government Printing Office.

Heeks, R. & Bhatnagar, S. (1999). Understanding success and failure in information age reform. In R. Heeks (Ed.), *Reinventing Government in the Information Age: International Practice in Public Sector Reform* (pp. 49-74). London: Routledge.

Heeks, R. & Davis, A. (1999). Different approaches to information age reform. In R. Heeks (Ed.), *Reinventing Government in the Information Age: International Practice in Public Sector Reform* (pp. 22-48). London: Routledge.

Kim, S. & Layne, K. (2001). Making the connection: E-government and public administration education. *Journal of Public Administration Education,* *7*(4), 229-240.

Kling, R. (1996). The centrality of organizations in the computerization of society. In R. Kling (Ed.), *Computerization and Controversy: Value conflicts and Social Choices* (pp. 108-132). San Diego, CA: Academic Press.

Kling, R & Allen J.P. (1996). Can computer science solve organizational problems? The case for organizational informatics. In R. Kling (Ed.), *Computerization and Controversy: Value Conflicts and Social Choices* (pp. 261-276). San Diego, CA: Academic Press.

Kraemer, K.L. & Dedrick, J. (1997). Computing and public organizations. *Journal of Public Administration Research and Theory*, *7*(1), 89-113.

Layne, K. & Lee, J. (2001). Developing fully functional e-government: A four stage model. *Government Information Quarterly, 18,* 122-136.

Lee, G. & Perry, K. L. (2002). Are computers boosting productivity? A test of the paradox in state governments. *Journal of Public Administration Research and Theory, 12*(1), 77-102.

Macintosh, A., Davenport, E., Malina, A., & Whyte, A. (2002). Technology to support participatory democracy. In Å. Grönlund (Ed.), *Electronic Government: Design, Applications and Management.* Hershey, PA: Idea Group Publishing.

Moon, M.J. (2002). The evolution of e-government among municipalities: Rhetoric or reality? *Public Administration Review, 62*(4), 424-433.

National Association of Schools of Public Affairs and Administration. (1988). *Standards for professional masters degree programs in public affairs and administration.* Washington, DC: NASPAA.

National Association of Schools of Public Affairs and Administration Ad Hoc Committee on Computers and Public Management Education. (1986). Curriculum recommendations for public management education in computing. *Public Administration Review, 46,* 595-602.

National Electronic Commerce Coordinating Council. (2000a). *Critical business issues in the transformation to electronic government.* NECCC Annual Conference, Las Vegas, NV. (December 13-15). Accessed online on August 16, 2002 at: http://www.ec3.org/InfoCenter/02_WorkGroups/2001_Workgroups/2001_White_Papers_&_EDs.htm

National Electronic Commerce Coordinating Council (2000b). *E-government strategic planning.* (white paper). NECCC Annual Conference, Las Vegas, NV. (December 13-15). Accessed online on August 21, 2002 at: http://www.ec3.org/InfoCenter/02_WorkGroups/2001_Workgroups/2001_White_Papers_&_EDs.htm

Northrop, A. (1999). The challenge of teaching information technology in public administration graduate programs. In G.D. Garson (Ed.), *Information Technology and Computer Applications in Public Administration: Issues and Trends* (pp. 7-22). Hershey, PA: Idea Group Publishing.

Office of Management and Budget. (2002a). *E-government strategy: Simplified delivery of services to citizens.* Retrieved on August 14, 2002 at: http://www.whitehouse.gov/omb/inforeg/egovstrategy.pdf

Office of Management and Budget. (2002b). *The President's management agenda.* Retrieved on August 17, 2002 at: http://www.whitehouse.gov/omb/budintegration/pma_index.html

Riera, A., Sànches, J. & Torras, L. (2002). Internet voting: Embracing technology in electoral processes. In Å. Grönlund (Ed.), *Electronic Government: Design, Applications and Management.* Hershey, PA: Idea Group Publishing.

Ronaghan, S.A. (2002). *Benchmarking e-government: A global perspective. Assessing the progress of the UN member states.* A UN-ASPA joint report. Retrieved on June 27, 2002 at: http://www.aspa.org.

Seneviratne, S. J. (1999). Information technology and organizational change in the public sector. In D. G. Garson (Ed.), *Information Technology and Computer Applications in Public Administration* (pp. 41-61). Hershey, PA: Idea Group Publishing.

Stark, A. (2002). What is new public management? *Journal of Public Administration Research and Theory, 12*(1), 137-151.

U.S. News and World Report. (2001). Best Graduate Schools in Public Affairs (Master). Premium Online Edition. Retrieved on September 17, 2002.

West, D.M. (2000). Assessing e-government: The Internet, democracy, and service delivery by state and Federal governments. Retrieved on August 20, 2002 at: http://www.insidepolitics.org/egovtreport00.html

Wilson, J.Q. (1989). *Bureaucracy: What government agencies do and why they do it.* Basic Books, Inc.

Zuurmond, A. (1998). From bureaucracy to infocracy: Are democratic institutions lagging behind? In I.Th.M. Snellen & W.B.H.J. van de Donk (Eds.), *Public Administration in an Information Age* (pp. 259-272). Amsterdam, The Netherlands: IOS Press.

Zweers, K. & Planqué, K. (2001). Electronic government. From an organization based perspective toward a client-oriented approach. In J.E.J Prince (Ed.), *Designing E-Government: On the Crossroads of Technological Innovation and Institutional Change.* The Hague, The Netherlands: Kluwer Law International.

Section V

The Future of Digital Government

Chapter XIX

Digital Government and the Digital Divide

Richard Groper
California State University, Fullerton, USA

ABSTRACT

There seems to be a consensus among scholars and pundits that the lack of access to the Internet among African-Americans and Latinos has created a digital divide in the United States. The digital divide has negatively affected the ability of minority groups to accumulate social capital . This study compares Internet access rates in California and the United States in order to test the premise that race is the primary influence upon Internet access. In California, the data explicitly depicts a stronger relationship between Internet access and education and income than it does with Internet access and race.[1] Across the United States, the results are not as stark. However, education and income are increasingly becoming important variables. The policy implications of this study are dramatic . Since most governmental and non-profit efforts in the United States have put resources and money into decreasing the racial divide, this study suggests that at least some of those resources should be shifted to alleviating the educational and economic discrepancies that exist among the American people.

WHAT IS THE DIGITAL DIVIDE AND WHY IS IT IMPORTANT?

In the last year alone, many surveys have been released that have confirmed the existence of a digital divide in this country. The General Accounting Office (2001) released a comprehensive survey stating that Internet users are more likely to be Caucasian and less likely (by a large margin) to be African-American or Hispanic.[2] Other recent surveys (Lenhart, 2000; U.S. Department of Commerce, 2000) have corroborated these findings.[3] Therefore, the Internet digital divide may prevent ethnically disadvantaged groups from reaping the advantages of the Internet because of their lack of access to the new technology (Wilhelm, 2001).[4]

The Lenhart/PEW study found that those who do not use the Internet are less "networked" in their social lives, less trusting of government, and politically less active. When people are less networked in their everyday lives, they lack the necessary social capital to participate in their communities. Whole communities of individuals, simply based upon the color of their skin, are being disenfranchised from the political process (Putnam, 2001). Social capital, as described below, can be looked upon as the "glue" which holds together societal interests and plays a large role in the progress of any community.

The Relationship Between the Digital Divide and Social Capital

The concept of social capital has evolved greatly over the last few years . In 1988, James Coleman brought the concept into the academic mainstream with his landmark work, "Social Capital in the Creation of Human Capital." It was postulated that social capital is realized through personal networks of communication (Coleman, 1988). Social capital is a by-product of these social interactions, which enhance individual civic capacity and expertise, thereby allowing individuals to become more fully engaged in politics (Ibid.).

A dominant influence in the writings of Coleman can be found in the works of Mark Granovetter. Granovetter (1985) stated that individual socialization is best seen within the context of continuous participation in particular patterns of social networks. Individuals who are joiners appear to develop skills that make them more likely to become politically engaged in a wider range of political activities (Coleman, 2000).

Robert Putnam is credited with the contemporary revival of the debate concerning social capital.[5] In his study about the production of social capital in modern Italy, Putnam (1993) found that communities which had high levels of social capital were also the ones that had the highest levels of political and social participation, as well as effective governance (Ibid.). The more citizens participate in their communities, the more they learn to trust each other (Brehm and Rahn, 1997).

Social capital is not an easy concept to define or measure. Perhaps the best way to display the power of social capital is by advancing its positive attributes more succinctly (Putnam, 2000). First, social capital allows citizens to resolve collective problems more easily by providing a routine and ritualized behavioral pattern based upon social norms and the networks that enforce them. Second, where people are trustworthy and subject to repeated interactions with fellow citizens, everyday business and social transactions are less costly. This basic trust between citizens mitigates the need to spend time and money making sure that others will uphold their end of the arrangement. Finally, when people lack connections with others, they are unable to test the veracity of their own views whether in the give-and-take of casual conversation or in more formal, deliberative patterns (Ibid.).

The relationship between the digital divide and social capital is a critical one. The digital divide prevents whole communities from realizing its political, economic and social potential. Scholars such as Robert Putnam, in his seminal study, "Bowling Alone," maintains that one of the largest obstacles which must be overcome when accumulating social capital is the "digital divide" (Ibid.). New communication technologies like the Internet provide the means by which individuals can stay connected to their government. Government and community websites provide invaluable resources to those who want to stay in touch with events, rallies and meetings in their cities and neighborhoods. The more information an individual has at their disposal, the greater their chance of participating politically. Political participation, in turn, holds elected officials more accountable.

Since ethnicity is one of the greatest determinants of civic engagement, it is critical that the digital divide is mitigated in minority neighborhoods. In fact, ethnic diversity often determines the differences in community involvement and political participation.[6] The implications of this fact are staggering: Many areas across the United States that have large ethnic populations lack the dense networks, and hence social capital, necessary to advance both economically and politically.

In addition to enhancing the likelihood of accumulating social capital, access to the Internet can provide people with the requisite research resources necessary to become productive members in their communities (Ibid.). That is why Putnam and others believe that access to the Internet is critical to the future of many U.S. communities, particularly those where minorities dominate.

THE DIGITAL DIVIDE IN CALIFORNIA

While the digital divide still exists in many parts of the United States, the statistics are a bit more complicated in California. In a March 2001 survey, the Public Policy Institute of California (PPIC) presented statistics that showed Latino Californians trail other ethnic groups in computer (65%) and Internet use (47%). Not all Latinos lag behind, however. Such demographic variables as education and income are mitigating factors in the digital divide. In a departure from nationwide statistics, African-Americans in California are similar to all Californians in computer (76%) and Internet use (62%). Like their nationwide counterparts, Caucasians and Asians are over-represented in computer and Internet use (Johnson, 2001).

Data and Measures

The research in this paper seeks to further examine the concept of the digital divide, and whether race is becoming a less important variable in the controversy surrounding the "digital divide." The CSUF survey was intended to test this possibility. While the CSUF survey had a robust sample of 604 respondents, the racial breakdown of the respondents was skewed. There was an overrepresentation of whites, while there was

Figure 1: The racial breakdown of the CSUF survey

Race/ Ethnicity

		Frequency	Percent	Valid Percent	Cumulative Percent
Valid	Asian	68	11.3	11.3	11.3
	Black or African American	37	6.2	6.2	17.5
	Hispanic or Latino	170	28.1	28.1	45.6
	Caucasian or White	309	51.1	51.1	96.7
	Other	20	3.3	3.3	100.0
	Total	604	100.0	100.0	

an under-representation of Asians, African-Americans and Hispanics.[7] To account for those differences, a weighted formula was applied to adjust the frequencies to the 2000 U.S. Census (U.S. Census, 2001). See Figure 1 for the weighted breakdown of the survey's race/ethnicities.

Is the Digital Divide Obsolete in California?

In California, the "digital divide" scenario is very complicated. Figure 2 finds that most of the relationships between the various races are not statistically significant with respect to Internet access. Only the relationship between African-Americans and Asians (at .012) are significant, where African-Americans are less likely than Asians to access

Figure 2: The relationship between race and Internet access

Multiple Comparisons

Dependent Variable: ACCESS
Tukey HSD

(I) Race/ Ethnicity	(J) Race/ Ethnicity	Mean Difference (I-J)	Std. Error	Sig.	95% Confidence Interval	
					Lower Bound	Upper Bound
Asian	Black or African American	.2771*	.08598	.012	.0418	.5123
	Hispanic or Latino	.1131	.06020	.330	-.0516	.2778
	Caucasian or White	.1154	.05610	.240	-.0381	.2689
	Other	.1551	.10674	.594	-.1370	.4471
Black or African American	Asian	-.2771*	.08598	.012	-.5123	-.0418
	Hispanic or Latino	-.1640	.07659	.204	-.3735	.0456
	Caucasian or White	-.1617	.07341	.180	-.3625	.0392
	Other	-.1220	.11677	.834	-.4415	.1975
Hispanic or Latino	Asian	-.1131	.06020	.330	-.2778	.0516
	Black or African American	.1640	.07659	.204	-.0456	.3735
	Caucasian or White	.0023	.04026	1.000	-.1079	.1125
	Other	.0420	.09933	.993	-.2298	.3137
Caucasian or White	Asian	-.1154	.05610	.240	-.2689	.0381
	Black or African American	.1617	.07341	.180	-.0392	.3625
	Hispanic or Latino	-.0023	.04026	1.000	-.1125	.1079
	Other	.0396	.09690	.994	-.2255	.3048
Other	Asian	-.1551	.10674	.594	-.4471	.1370
	Black or African American	.1220	.11677	.834	-.1975	.4415
	Hispanic or Latino	-.0420	.09933	.993	-.3137	.2298
	Caucasian or White	-.0396	.09690	.994	-.3048	.2255

*. The mean difference is significant at the .05 level.

*Note: The variables which have the * symbol attached are statistically significant. All other variables fall outside the .05 significance level.*

the Internet. Therefore, race is only a factor with Internet access when it comes to comparing African-Americans and Asians. All other comparisons between the races (i.e., Caucasian vs. Asian, Caucasian vs. African-American, etc.) are insignificant. The Asian/ African-American relationship is only one of many possible relationships in the data. This hardly constitutes the grounds for any definitive statement about the relationship between race and Internet access.

In addition, if we look at the means plot in Figure 3, there is no overall trend (either downwards or upwards) that depicts a definitive result that would indicate a racial digital divide. The data points are skewed and not in any discernible order. In other words, no conclusions about Internet access either between or among any given race can be derived from the data.

In contrast, education and income seem to be powerful indicators of Internet access. The means plot in Figure 4 indicates that the more education one attains, the greater the access to the Internet. Virtually every relationship between access and educational level is statistically significant. Starting from those with the least amount of education (*some high school or less*) to those who have the most education (*postgraduate degree*), there is a definitive upward trend that indicates greater Internet access. Therefore, there can be little doubt that education is a strong influence upon access.

The same can be said for the relationship between income and Internet access.

Figure 5 indicates a strong positive relationship between income and Internet access. Those who earn less money (particularly those under the annual household income of $36,000) have less Internet access than those with higher incomes.

If we look at Figure 5 again, people who earn less than $36,000 a year show a dramatic decline in Internet access. Since computers are considered luxury items that usually cost

Figure 3: Means plot graph of the relationship between race and Internet access

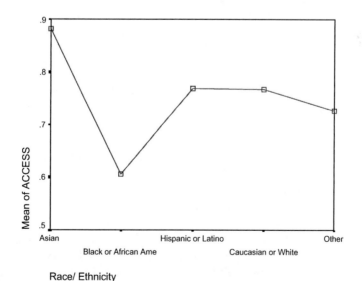

Note: The dependent variable is Internet access and the independent variable is race.

Figure 4: Means plot graph of the relationship between education and Internet access

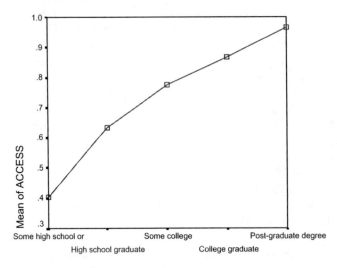

Last grade of school completed

Note: The dependent variable is Internet access and the independent variable is education.

more than $1,000; those that earn under $36,000 have to concentrate on those commodities (like food, shelter, etc.) that are absolute necessities. Therefore, it is easy to understand that the wealthier one becomes, the more likely one has Internet access.

In order to understand why education and income seem to be more powerful influences upon Internet access than race, we have to understand the dynamics of Internet socialization. There was a great movement during the 1990s to get every American wired to the Internet. The country's most powerful government and business leaders in this nation promoted this far-reaching effort (Margolis and Resnick, 2000). The campaign was focused upon two primary areas, education and business. First, it was a goal to get every school wired to the Internet. The Internet was seen as an important educational tool. Schools across the nations espoused the virtues of the Internet as a method toward scholastic success in the new century. Therefore, students were socialized to believe that access to the Internet was very important: The more education one attains, the greater the indoctrination.

Business and industry were similarly aided by government efforts to promote the Internet (Dutton, 1999; Noll, 1997). The National Information Infrastructure (NII) was created in part to help business connect to the Internet. The Internet was seen as a way to increase profits in the Information Age. Socialization was so successful that the diffusion of the Internet in the business sector is almost complete (Ibid.).

In summation, while education and income influences upon Internet access are on the rise in California, racial influences, however, are becoming increasingly insignificant in determining Internet access in California. The following figure highlights this sentiment: Latinos have the lowest access rates in California, but more than three in four Latinos with college degrees (79%) and incomes of at least $60,000 (83%) have access

Figure 5: Means plot graph of the relationship between income and Internet access

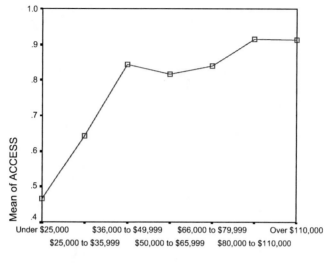

Household income

Note: The dependent variable is Internet access and the independent variable is income.

to the Internet, similar to all Californians with college degrees and higher incomes (Johnson, 2001). These well-educated middle class Latinos have been socialized to believe that Internet access is an essential commodity in the twenty-first century. Race is not a factor, but education and income certainly are.

THE DIGITAL DIVIDE ACROSS THE UNITED STATES

Like the state of California, the United States has seen an increase in Internet use across all demographic groups and geographic regions (Department of Commerce, 2002). Not only are many more Americans using the Internet and computers at home, they are using them at work, school and other locations for an expanding variety of purposes.

In particular, Internet use among all ethnic groups, particularly those groups, like African-Americans and Latinos, who have been traditionally left behind on the information superhighway, has increased dramatically. In fact, in the past year, Internet use rates increased faster for African-American and Latinos than for Whites, Asian Americans and Pacific Islanders (see Figure 6). From December 1998 to September 2001, Internet use among African-Americans grew at an annual rate of 31%. Internet use among Latinos grew at an annual rate of 26%. During that same period, Internet use continued to grow among Asian American and Pacific Islanders (21%), and Whites (19%), although not as rapidly as for African-Americans and Latinos. Although not as dramatic, African-Americans and Latinos also have had somewhat faster growth in computer use than Whites and Asian Americans (see Figure 6) (Ibid.).

Figure 6: Internet use anywhere by race/Hispanic origin, percent of persons age 3+

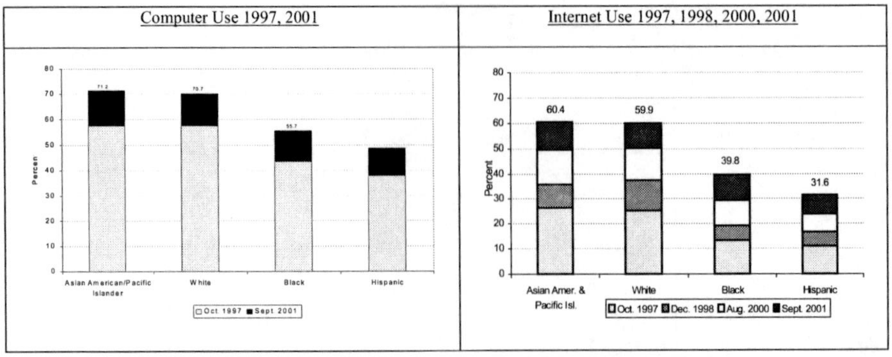

Source: NTIA and ESA, U.S. Department of Commerce, using U.S. Census Bureau Current Population Survey Supplements

Differences in computer and Internet use across these broad race categories persist, however. In each survey, Whites, Asian American and Pacific Islanders have higher rates of both computer and Internet use than do African-Americans and Latinos.

In September 2001, Internet use among Whites, and Asian American and Pacific Islanders hovered around 60%, while Internet use rates for African-Americans (39.8%) and Latinos (31.6%) trailed behind. There is still an apparent digital divide between the races, but upon closer inspection of the data, other intervening variables, such as education and income, may be able to provide a more definitive explanation of the phenomenon.

Family income remains a large indicator of whether a person uses a computer or the Internet. Individuals who live in high-income households are more likely to be connected compared to those who live in low-income households (see Figure 7). This relationship has held true in each survey of Internet use. Therefore, it can be argued that the cost of Internet access matters much more to households with lower incomes than to those with higher incomes. The Department of Commerce study (2002) asked households without Internet subscriptions the question, "What is the main reason that you don't have the Internet at home? The survey results indicated that the largest specific response was that the cost was "too expensive." In addition, Figure 7 shows the relationship between income and the adoption of home Internet connections (Ibid.). With successively higher income categories, fewer households report that cost is a barrier and more households are making their first connections to the Internet at home. Households with incomes below $15,000 volunteered cost as the barrier to home Internet subscriptions 34.7% of the time. Among households in that income category, the share of the population without home Internet subscriptions declined by only 6% between August 2000 and September 2001. At the other end of the spectrum, only 9.6% of households with incomes of at least $75,000 said that they were deterred by cost.

Educational achievement also factors into computer and Internet use. The higher a person's level of education, the more likely he or she will be a computer or Internet user. As shown in Figure 8, adults (age 25 and above) with education beyond college were most likely to be Internet users. Those with bachelor's degrees trailed closely behind those

Figure 7: Adoption rate and Internet "too expensive" by income percent of U.S. households without Internet

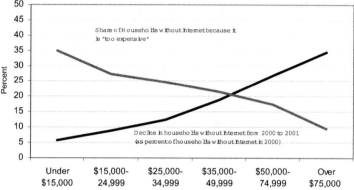

Source: NTIA and ESA, U.S. Department of Commerce, using U.S. Census Bureau Current Population Survey Supplements.

with postgraduate degrees. At the opposite end of the spectrum are those adults who have achieved less than a high school education. In September 2001, the computer use rate for those with levels less than a high school education was only 17.0% and the Internet use rate was 12.8%. Internet use for adults with an education level beyond a Bachelor's degree was approximately 88% and 83%. This shows a stark contrast in Internet access between those with higher education and those without.

In summary, while the racial digital divide still exists in many areas across the United States, it is important to note that these trends are definitely beginning to change. In the last couple of years, the rate of African-American and Latino Internet access has

Figure 8: Internet use anywhere by educational attainment, percent of persons age 25+

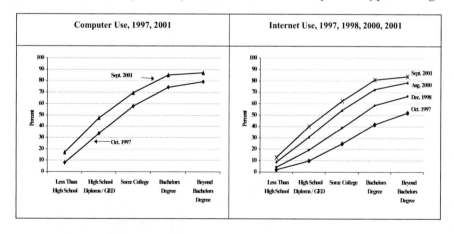

Source: NTIA and ESA, U.S. Department of Commerce, using U.S. Census Bureau Current Population Survey Supplements

increased dramatically, even higher than that of Caucasians and Asians. Other surveys corroborate this trend: 78% of Caucasians in U.S. households earning more than $75,000 are online; 79% of Latinos and 69% of African-Americans in similar economic circumstances are online (Lenhart, 2000). Another interesting statistic comes from demographic information concerning educational attainment: 68% of Internet users have college degrees in America, while only 24% of Americans have a college degree (U.S. General Accounting Office, 2001). Since African-Americans and Latinos tend to have less education and income than Caucasians and Asians (U.S. Department of Commerce, 2002), the racial discrepancies in Internet access in the United States may be explained according to income and education. The influence of the racial variable is becoming mitigated. If African-Americans and Latinos across the nation continue to make gains in education and income, they too will have greater levels of Internet access. There are many signs that these gains may be already underway (Ibid.).

POLICY IMPLICATIONS

In order to combat the growing disparity between the information haves and have-nots in the United States, in 1993, President Clinton created the National Information Infrastructure Advisory Council (NIIAC), chaired by Vice President Gore, to focus on the development of a national network of telecommunications services. The Council's final report in 1995 recommended, among other things, that a national goal be set to provide Internet access to all public schools and libraries by the year 2000. Within a year, Congress passed the Telecommunications Act of 1996, which led to the creation of the *E-Rate* program.

The Universal Service Fund program for Schools and Libraries — commonly known as the "E-Rate" — was created to provide discounts on the cost of telecommunications services and equipment to all public and private schools and libraries (Puma, 2002). Typically eligible services range from basic local and long-distance phone services and Internet access services, to the acquisition and installation of equipment that can provide network wiring within school and library buildings. Discounts range from 20% to 90%, depending on economic need and rural location (Ibid.).

Even though the United States leads the technological revolution, there are segments of American society that have had traditionally lower access. For many of those separated by this so-called "digital divide," the targeting of schools and libraries by the E-Rate program was important because these institutions are most influential in gaining access to what the new technology has to offer. In particular, they offer dramatic changes in the education of the nation's children (i.e., computer and Internet access to enhance a student's writing and researching abilities) (Ibid.).

For this reason, the U.S. government targeted the E-Rate funds to high-poverty and high-minority school districts. After an initial slow start in getting the program publicized to all eligible school districts, the E-Rate program, in the last couple of years has disproportionately gone to high poverty and high minority school districts. This suggests that these districts did generally apply for substantial funds and that, therefore, the program may be helping to reduce potential increases in social inequality caused by the digital divide (Ibid.).

Because E-Rate funding is related to poverty — and minority students tend to be concentrated in low-income areas — the total amount of E-Rate funding generally rises with increasing percentages of minority students. For example, total E-Rate commitments to public school districts ranged from $120 million for those with less than 5% minority students to more than $800 million for districts with 50% or more minority students. Similarly, average E-Rate funding per student ranged from $17-$21 for districts with less than 20% minority students to almost $67 per student for high-minority districts (Ibid.).

While this billion dollar program has successfully targeted the poor and minority communities in the first few years of its existence, should funding for E-Rate continue at its present level or should spending priorities change? The digital divide is decreasing, but the spending of E-Rate money remains the same.

The Future of the E-Rate Program

It is difficult to deny the success of the E-Rate program in getting schools connected to the Internet. Most scholars and pundits agree that the E-Rate program was a good investment in our nation's youth. More children than ever are being connected to the Internet, thanks in part to the success of this program.

However, every program must undergo some type of evaluation process. When the program started five years ago, there was a dramatic difference in the Internet connectivity rates between the races and between the wealthy and poor (Ibid.). However, at least in part to the success of the E-Rate program, this chasm has been dramatically mitigated. While the racial digital divide is still a factor, it is important only when income and educational are controlled. Until about two years ago, race was still an important factor in determining Internet access rates (Ibid.). Currently, the racial variable has become a lesser factor in determining access, while income and education have increased.

The E-Rate program has served its purpose well. Therefore, it should be continued; however, not at the same funding rate as previous years. There are still minority communities that need funding to help get access to the Internet, however, the need is not as great.

Therefore, the mission of the E-Rate program should be reformed. While the Internet does provide society with a useful communicative and research function, it does not necessarily bring one out of poverty or prevent racism. Since college-educated people are more likely to have access to the Internet, maybe more of an emphasis should be placed upon raising the level of education in this country, rather than just increasing access rates. Once in college, the necessity of connecting to the Internet becomes apparent. Students realize that the Internet provides a very useful role in their college career. They can use the Internet to perform research for their papers, to communicate with professors, and even to apply for jobs.

CONCLUSION

There has been much attention given to the digital divide issue. The research suggests that the accumulation of social capital in Latino and African-American communities is greatly influenced by the digital divide. The lack of access to the Internet can have dire consequences, including a dearth in the garnering of social capital, which fosters political participation (Putnam, 2000). In many academic circles, it is commonly perceived that Latinos and African-Americans have been left behind on the Information Superhighway, and therefore do not have access to as much social capital as do their

Caucasian and Asian counterparts. The E-Rate program is a testament to the generally understood notion that certain minority groups, most notably African-American and Latino, need governmental assistance to mitigate the divide.

This essay, in part, attempts to question this premise. It was ultimately found that education and income have at least as great an impact upon Internet access as does race or ethnicity. This fact should not be a surprise to those who have closely followed the developments of this controversy, for education and income have always had a considerable impact. Such scholars as Compaine (2001) maintain that costs have always been the number one factor in determining Internet access.

Since much of the focus of this essay is upon the state of California, many people might question the validity of this study and argue that California is an aberrant example. But demographically speaking, the nation seems to be moving toward California, not the opposite way (U.S. Department of Commerce, 2002). The facts seem to confirm this statement. All across the United States, race is becoming less of a factor when determining Internet access, and income and education are becoming more important (Ibid.).

Due to this shift, social capital priorities must change as well. No longer can the accumulation of social capital be solely attributed to the racial divides in this country. Other variables, such as education and income, must be considered important. If the E-Rate program is to continue to be effective in targeting its primary audience, it also needs to shift its priorities.

ENDNOTES

1   From February 3 to March 12, 2001, the Social Science Research Center (SSRC) and the Center for Public Policy (CPP) at California State University, Fullerton conducted an English language telephone survey resulting in completed interviews in 604 randomly selected households throughout California (average margin of error was 4%). The survey instrument was lengthy. Administration times ranged from nine to 45 minutes, with an average of 16.95 minutes. The population of inference is the head of household or his or her spouse or domestic partner, age 18 years or older, residing in households with telephones. I would personally like to thank Drs. Alan Saltzstein, Keith Boyum and Greg Robinson for all of their assistance in helping to get this project completed.

2   In the GAO study, Caucasians comprise 72% of America's population, but about 87% of the country's Internet population (this signals an over-representation of Internet users). African-Americans comprise 12% of the American population, but only 3% of the Internet population. Hispanics comprise 11% of America's population, but only 5% of the Internet population. Both these figures represent a severe under-representation of the Internet population. (Note: Asian Americans, Native Americans and other racial groups were statistically insignificant.)

3   The importance of the digital divide was exhibited in July 1999 by Assistant Secretary of Commerce, Larry Irving, when he stated that the digital divide is 'now one of America's leading economic and civil rights issues.' Business leaders such as America Online CEO, Steve Case, concurred, when "[he] stated that there was merit in viewing access to the Internet as a key civil rights issue in the coming years."

⁴   In the Department of Commerce study, among the largest racial groups, the biggest discrepancy in the digital divide is among Blacks and Hispanics. Note that 56.8% of Asians have Internet access, while only 23.5% of Blacks and 23.6% of Hispanics have access. The national average is 41.5%. In fact, the gap between Blacks (up three percentage points) and Hispanics (up 4.3 percentage points) and the national rate has actually increased since December 1998, thus signaling a greater digital divide.

⁵   Many scholars (such as Pippa Norris and Michael Schudson) criticize Putnam's postulation that the decline of social capital is negatively influencing civic life. They criticize him on both methodological and theoretical grounds.

⁶   Blacks and Hispanics were less than half as likely to trust their neighbors as whites (56% of Whites trusted people versus 21% for blacks and 19% for Hispanics). Residents of more diverse communities are more likely to be personally isolated, they claim fewer friends, spend less time socializing and have less sense of community. They are also less likely to vote, to participate in demonstrations, to sign petitions, and, in general, are more disengaged from politics. Overall, rates of political participation, social participation and social trust differ according to race.

⁷   In the CSUF survey, the percentage of Whites (66.4%), Asians (5.6%), African-Americans (6.5%) and Hispanics (13.1%) were all skewed when compared to the California ethnic breakdown in the 2000 Census. The remaining percentages (classified in the survey as 'other') were negligible. The 2000 Census data for people 18 years and older in California, had Whites at 51.1%, Asians at 11.3%, African-Americans at 6.2% and Hispanics at 28.1%. The CSUF survey data was weighted in order to account for the differences. Since the survey was done in English, some of the responses (mainly Spanish speakers) were left out of the sample. When looking at the post-survey comments, it should be noted that although there was a small proportion of respondents who did not answer due to language difficulties, it was a statistically insignificant percentage.

REFERENCES

Blanchard, A. and Horan, T. (1998). Virtual Communities and Social Capital. *Social Science Computer Review, 16*(3), 294-307.

Brehm, J. and Rahn, W. (1997). Individual-Level Evidence for the Causes and Consequences of Social Capital. *American Journal of Political Science, 41*(3), 999-1023.

Briggs, X. (1997). Social Capital and the Cities: Advice to change agents. *National Civic Review*, 86, 111-117.

Cawkell, T. (2001). Sociotechnology: The Digital Divide. *Journal of Information Science, 27*(1), 55-60.

Coleman, J. (1988). Social capital in the creation of human capital. *American Journal of Sociology, 94*(Supp), S95-S120.

Coleman, J. (2000). Social Capital in the Creation of Human Capital. In P. Dasgupta and I. Serageldin (Eds.), *Social Capital: A Multifacted Perspective*. Washington D.C.: The World Bank.

Compaine, B. (2001). Reexamining the Digital Divide. In B. Compaine (Ed.), *The Digital Divide: Facing a Crisis or Creating a Myth*. Cambridge, MA: MIT Press.

Cortes Jr., E. (1996). Community Organization and Social Capital. *National Civic Review*, *85*(3), 49-53.

Dutton, W. (1996). Network Rules of Order: Regulating Speech in Public Electronic Fora. *Media, Culture and Society*, 18, 269-290.

Dutton, W. (1999). *Society on the Line: Information Politics in the Digital Age.* Oxford: Oxford University Press.

Fukuyama, F. (2000). *Social Capital and Civil Society.* International Monetary Fund Working Paper. IMF Institute.

Granovetter, M. (1985). Economic Action and Social Structure: The Problem of Embeddness. *American Journal of Sociology*, 91, 481-510.

Horrigan, J. (2001). The Internet, Cities and Civil Society. *Information Impacts.* Available at http://www.cisp.org/imp/may_2001/05 01horrigon.htm

Johnson, H. (2001). *California's Digital Divide.* Public Policy Institute of California. Available at http://www.ppic.org/facts/digital.mar01.pdf

La Due L. and Huckfeldt, R. (1998). Social Capital, Social Networks, and Political Participation. *Political Psychology, 19* (3), 567-584.

Lenhart, A. (2000). Who's Not Online. *Pew Internet and American Life Project.* Washington D.C.: PEW. Available at http://www.pewinternet.org

Margolis, M. and Resnick, D. (2000). *Politics as Usual: The Cyberspace Revolution.* Thousand Oaks, CA: Sage.

Newton, K. (1999). Mass Media Effects: Mobilization or Media Malaise? *British Journal of Political Science*, 29, 577-599.

Noll, A. M. (1997). *Highway of Dreams: A Critical View Along the Information Superhighway.* Mahwah, NJ: Lawrence Erlbaum Associates.

Onyx, J. and Bullen, P. (2000). Measuring social capital in five communities. *The Journal of Applied Behavorial Science*, *36*(1), 23-42.

Orr, M. (1999). *Black Social Capital: The Politics of School Reform in Baltimore, 1986-1998.* Lawrence, KS: University of Kansas Press.

Ostrom, E. (2000). Social Capital: A Fad or a Fundamental Concept. In P. Dasgupta and I. Serageldin (Eds.), *Social Capital: A Multifacted Perspective.* Washington D.C.: The World Bank.

Puma, M. J., Chaplin, D.D. and Pape, A.D. (2002). *The E-Rate and Digital Divide.* Urban Institute.

Putnam, R. (1993). *Making Democracy Work: Civic Traditions in Modern Italy.* Princeton, NJ: Princeton University Press.

Putnam, R. (1995). Bowling Alone: America's Declining Social Capital. *Journal of Democracy*, *6*(1), 65-78.

Putnam, R. (2000). *Bowling Alone: The collapse and revival of American Community.* New York: Simon and Schuster.

Putnam, R. (2001). *Social Capital Community Benchmark Survey.* Cambridge, MA: Harvard University. Available at: http://www.cfsv.org/communitysurvey/results_pr.html

Ray, M. (1999). Technological Change and Associational Life. In T. Skocpol and M. Fiorina (Eds.), *Civic Engagement in American Democracy.* Washington D.C.: Brookings.

Rich, P. (1999). American Voluntarism, Social Capital and Political Culture. *Annals of the American Academy of Political and Social Science*, 565, 15-34.

Schuelfele, D. and Shah, D. (2000). Personality strength and social capital. *Communication Research, 27*(2), 107-131.

Skocpol, T. and Fiorina, M. (eds.) (1999). Making Sense of the Civic Engagement Debate. *Civic Engagement in American Democracy.* Washington D.C.: Brookings.

Sullivan, J.L. and Transue, J.E. (1999). The psychological underpinnings of democracy. *Annual Reviews Psychology, 50,* 625-650.

United States Department of Commerce (2000). *Falling Through the Net: Toward Digital Inclusion* (October). Washington D.C.: U.S. Department of Commerce. Available at http://www.commerce.gov/Statistics_and_Research/

United States Department of Commerce (2002). *A Nation Online: How Americans are Expanding Their Use of the Internet* (February). Washington D.C.: U.S. Department of Commerce. Available at: http://www.commerce.gov/Statistics_and_Research/

United States Department of Commerce, Bureau of the Census (2001). *California Quick Facts from the 2000 Census.* Washington D.C.: Department of Commerce. Available at http://quickfacts.census.gov/

United States Department of Education (2002). Formative Evaluation of the E-Rate (January). Washington D.C.: U.S. Department of Education. Available at http://www.commerce.gov/Statistics_and_Research/

United States General Accounting Office (2001). Characteristics and Choices of Internet Users. *Report to the Ranking Minority Member, Subcommittee on Telecommunications, Committee on Energy and Commerce, House of Representatives* (February). Washington D.C.: GAO.

Wilhelm, A. (2001). Access denied in the information age. In S. Lax (Ed.), *Access Denied in the Information Age.* New York: Palgrave.

Chapter XX

Digital Government and Citizen Participation in the United States

Marc Holzer
Rutgers University—Campus at Newark, USA

Lung-Teng Hu
Rutgers University—Campus at Newark, USA

Seok-Hwi Song
Rutgers University—Campus at Newark, USA

ABSTRACT

This chapter addresses the topic of citizen participation via digital government in several sections: first, we discuss the relationship between digital government and citizen participation from the academic literature. Second, we introduce some best practices of citizen participations through digital government in the United States; third, we offer some principles and implications from these best practices; and fourth, we discuss several potential problems of digitized citizen participation in terms of further research. The best practices described in this chapter include Minnesota's Department Results and Online Citizen Participation Opportunities, Santa Monica's Budget Suggestions, California's California Scorecard, Virginia Beach's EMS Customer Satisfaction Survey and others. We extract some common features from these best practices, such as citizen as customer, recognizing a citizen's capacity, and direct participation. Further, we recommend principles for designing digitized citizen participation: operationalize direct policy involvement, enable the citizen to influence policy priorities, enhance government accountability, encourage participatory deliberation and shape digital citizenship.

INTRODUCTION

Although digital government has evolved at varied rates worldwide, all countries are concerned with (1) the quality of the developing online services and (2) how digital government can contribute to public participation and competence as the basis for a more democratic administration or democratic society (Leigh and Atkinson, 2001).

These new concerns are raising fundamental questions as to a digital government strategy. What are the purposes of digital government's functions? How can digital government cultivate citizen participation and citizen competence for public affairs? How might digital government influence the structures or functions of the public organization? These questions stem from a more basic philosophical question as to how we set the relationship between the state and the citizen in the information age (Wyman, Beachboard, and McClure, 1997).

Efficiency-oriented applications of digital government in the public sector may have side effects. In brief, many public sector organizations focus only on their own immediate interests, rather than the public interest, in the formulation of their digital government system. Some may focus on the appearance of the digital government rather than substantial contributions that digital government may make — such as increasing citizen participation, citizen competence, responsibility or responsiveness, and transparency or openness (Dunleavy and Margetts, 2000; West and Berman, 2001; Cullen and Houghton, 2000; Relyea, 2002; Wyman, Beachboard, and McClure, 1997).

Superficial approaches to digital government that focus on the appearance of the website or simple online transactions fail to take advantage of, or address, fundamental opportunities. That is, most current government websites merely provide public information instead of allowing citizens to interact with governments (Leigh and Atkinson, 2001). Therefore, it is not surprising that new ways of thinking about digital government are emerging based on citizen participation and citizen competence for democratic administration of a democratic society (Relyea, 2002).

This chapter consists of four sections: First, we discuss the relationship between digital government and citizen participation from the academic literature. Second, we introduce some best practices of citizen participation through digital government in the United States. Third, we offer some principles and implications from these best practices. Finally, we discuss several potential problems of digitized citizen participation in terms of further research.

DIGITAL GOVERNMENT AND CITIZEN PARTICIPATION

Dunleavy and Margetts (2000), in their depiction of the Digital State Paradigm, hold that radical web-enabled change inside government has already replaced the New Public Management as a dominant public administration paradigm. In this "paradigm," the use of the Web has become "a part of a process of continual organizational learning," making incremental improvements and testing effects by asking for continual and rapid customer feedback, and the purposes of this improvement are to get close to customer's demands and to stimulate the reengineering of public services through feedback from customers. The creation of a genuinely and radically open government is an essential element of the digital state paradigm.

By getting closer to its customers, an open government allows its citizens to monitor agencies' performance, and hopes to re-imagine services by providing the most effective possible ways of delivering them seamlessly, and increasing policy transparency to the public.

However, some critics, such as Korac-Kakabadse and Korac-Kakabadse (2002), argue that "it is not certain that adding an electronic dimension to democracy will encourage participation by any but a small, motivated minority" if most people do not have enough desires, incentives, or even time, to pay attention to public issues (p. 218). They further warn that within the context of digital democracy, "citizens will be responsible for influencing the political agenda but will not be held accountable for their impact on policy implementation" (p. 219); in contrast, "elected representatives will be driven by an aggregation of electronically democratic demands and will be held account-able for policies for which they are not responsible and over which they have little influence" (p. 220). Moreover, Shi and Scavo (2000, p. 260) doubt the verification of citizen participation through the computer networks and raise the question of "how can anyone be sure that the person behind the keyboard or mouse is actually you and not somebody masquerading as you?"

Fountain (2001) claims that, through the connection of information networks, the "virtual state" could expand its social capital and attain the mutual benefits between social and informational capital as well. Moreover, based upon social capital, a decision maker could attain constructive information for improving decision quality. In this regard, electronic citizen participation systems could be seen not only as the facilitator for expanding a public agency's social capital, but could provide a decision maker with more comprehensive information as a consultant system.

Reviewing the progress of digital government in the United States, a growing number of governments are employing network techniques to provide citizen participa-tion opportunities for the public, either interactive or static. This evolution denotes that offering more convenient, open, effective approaches for citizen participation is one of the responsibilities of the government. In the next section, we will introduce several best practices in the United States in terms of digitized citizen participation.

BEST PRACTICES OF CITIZEN PARTICIPATION VIA DIGITAL GOVERNMENT IN THE UNITED STATES

According to a recent report of the Pew Internet and American Life Project, an estimated 68 million Americans have used government websites. Further, 25 percent of state and Federal government websites offer online transactions, such as tax filing and vehicle legislation renewal functions (*New York Times*, April 4, 2002). Meanwhile, some governments are striving to provide a more effective digitized system for encouraging a citizen's involvement in governmental affairs.

Below, we describe some best practices of citizen participation via digital government in the United States, including Minnesota's Department Results and Online Citizen Participation Opportunities, Santa Monica's Budget Suggestions, California's California Scorecard, Virginia Beach's EMS Customer Satisfaction Survey, and others.

Minnesota State Government's "Department Results"

In the Minnesota state government website, one of the linkages shows state government agencies' performance results as against their predetermined targets. This web page provides a list of major state agencies, as well as enabling visitors to click on links to see the key performance results of specific departments. The function of Department Results is to demonstrate what performance measures have been chosen by the specific department, how well the department achieves these targets, and how well the department satisfies "what citizens need and want." As stated on the state's Website (http://www.departmentresults.state.mn.us/):

> The executive branch of Minnesota state government is led by the Governor, 25 cabinet level commissioners and more than 1,300 managers — all charged with making sure that government provides what citizens need and want.

Each department has identified a few performance measurements to show whether they are getting results. The measures do not always tell the whole story about progress, but they can serve as indicators of success.

In terms of the content of performance results, in the Department of Children, Families and Learning, for example, measures indicate the results, but also communicate to citizens "Why is this indicator important?" "What is the agency doing?" and "Is the agency meeting the target?" Through the display of "department results," citizens can more clearly understand what the agency is doing, how well it is performing, and how their tax payments are being spent.

This performance review creates a feedback function to empower citizens to express their perceptions toward the agency's goals, performance indicators and targets.[1] After citizens visit and review the performance results of a specific department, they may provide comments regarding posted results. The feedback function asks citizens to comment on, first, whether reported results are based on appropriate indicators; second, what measures are most important to citizens; third, citizen's perceptions as to predetermined targets; and fourth, citizen's comments for improving the department's performance measurement in terms of indicators, measures, targets, etc.

In this respect, the feedback function not only provides a public sphere for comment by those interested in government's performance and productivity improvement, but also clarifies that state government recognizes that its performance improvement should be connected to citizen's concerns, needs, and desires; government's performance enhancement must be citizen-centered and citizen-driven. Within this mechanism, citizens are empowered to affect government's priorities in terms of performance measurement; it also means that government's performance measurement should reflect a citizen's preferences.

Minnesota's "Online Citizen Participation Opportunities"

The State of Minnesota was one of the first to practice direct democracy via information technologies. In its official website, a category called "tools of democracy" contains various linkages for citizen involvement in public affairs in the legislative, executive, and judicial branches. In particular, it creates an item for Online Citizen Participation Opportunities linked to an external directory called Interactive Minnesota, a website operated by a non-governmental organization, Minnesota E-Democracy, that hosts a variety of citizen participation forums, including state and local government issues.[2]

Even though Minnesota E-Democracy is a website hosted by a non-government, non-profit organization, within the official Minnesota state government's website citizens may also find linkages for e-democratic forums to express their ideas and opinions toward the state government. The state recognizes that this collaborative partnership between government and a non-profit organization is a different type of channel for providing residents with the opportunities to participate in state affairs.

City of Santa Monica's Budget Suggestions

Santa Monica's municipal web page is linked to an "Opinion Center" which enables citizens to give comments to the city government on specific topics or policies, in addition to the general comments form or feedback function.[3] Currently, projects asking for citizens' comments include the airport park, the civic center plan, and the living wage ordinance.

The conspicuous link in the opinion center is Budget Priority Suggestions.[4] The budget suggestions form not only offers a convenient electronic format for citizens to communicate their opinions, but also seeks citizens' suggestions and comments on the most important issues in residents' minds, and perceptions as to financial resource allocations, i.e., what programs or services should be funded to address issues suggested by citizens. Moreover, in formulating and reviewing the city's budget, residents' satisfaction is a measure employed to judge the budget.

Via this budget suggestion form, the city government promises that suggestions by citizens will be considered as the city staff and city council determine budget priorities for new fiscal year budgets, and as they review the spending for past years. This promise implies that the city government recognizes that citizens or residents, as well as city officials and the city council, are stakeholders in determining governmental budgets. Furthermore, residents' concerns and suggestions should be absorbed into municipal policy priorities and agenda setting. The city government website, therefore, is a tool to empower its citizens to play an active and decisive role in policy determination and resource allocation, and it enhances democratic value via electronic technologies.

California's "Innovation in Government"

The California Governor's office for "Innovation in Government" is a project that requires state agencies to provide more efficient and more effective services to citizens through information-based technological initiatives. It requires state agencies to respond to citizens' expectations that they be more accountable through digital government initiatives. Diverse initiatives in this project include e-California, e-Business Center, California Scorecard and Tracking Customer Satisfaction. Even though most of the initiatives are still in the testing and review stage, they are potentially important indicators of the future of digital government.[5]

With regard to citizen participation via digital government, California Scorecard is one of the important designs for improving citizen engagement. The California Scorecard, similar to Minnesota's Department Results, has as its goal to demonstrate agencies' performance and to enable citizens to understand state government's progress.[6] As described by the project: "It will provide an opportunity for Californians to better understand their changing state and for policy-makers and opinion-shapers to have quick and easy access to the most important measures being followed by state government."

As proposed by the project, this initiative "will provide an opportunity to engage the public in a dialog about government's role in improving the quality of life in California and the key measures of progress being made toward that goal."[7] Further, the California Scorecard will also provide a feedback form by which members of the public can express their opinions as to whether existing measures are appropriate for grasping government's achievements, as well as whether some measures should be added or dropped. In this respect, the California Scorecard has a function similar to Minnesota's Department Results in terms of systematically showing state agencies' performance and the measures they employ for evaluating results, as well as empowering state residents by listening to their voices on performance improvement and requiring that their concerns be reflected in governmental activities and priorities.

City of Virginia Beach's EMS Customer Satisfaction Survey

The Emergency Medical Services in the City of Virginia Beach provides an online customer satisfaction survey.[8] Visitors fill out the digitally formatted questionnaire, and express their opinions toward EMS services. The questionnaire is concerned with EMS employees' attitudes, responsiveness, service and information accuracy, and time saving, and includes visitors' comments for improving services.

Through this online satisfaction survey, the agency not only gathers current, instant and reliable customer information in terms of service satisfaction, but also enables citizens to present or voice feelings about the public services without regard to the limits of time and place. The electronic satisfaction survey creates a win-win situation for both the agency employing this technique and the citizen using this participation channel. If the survey results are indeed reflected in service enhancement, then this technique can be an effective strategy for pushing government progress and involving citizens in service monitoring.

Other Examples

In addition to the practices indicated above, other public agencies are striving to encourage citizen engagement via digital government initiatives. For example, there are several Citizen Involvement initiatives at Georgia state government's website, such as information as to polling places and elected officials, voter information guide, voter registration, and taxes.[9] Further, the Delaware E-Government Initiative offers some citizen participation services, including a polling place locator and ballot preview for elections, an online utility customer complaint form and a freedom of information request form.[10] In the city of San Jose, CA, an online feedback form asks a visitor to identify what he/she is submitting as a comment, suggestion, question or problem.[11] This function helps city government staff more easily classify feedback from visitors. In addition, the Prince William county government not only puts its County Accountability Reports on the official website, but also provides Citizen Participation channels with descriptions, applications and contact information via its information networks, such as police academy, fire academy and county volunteer program.[12] Residents in Prince William County are encouraged to dedicate themselves to involvement in public affairs, through the information published on the website, and the residents thus have more opportunities to participate. Finally, in Douglas County, NV, the county government places the electronic comments form on its website homepage.[13] Residents can easily find a channel to express their voice.

COMMON FEATURES AND PRINCIPLES

We can extract some common features from the best practices above, such as citizen as customer, recognizing a citizen's capacity, and direct participation.

Citizen as Customer

The experiences of the City of Virginia Beach's EMS Customer Satisfaction Survey, the unreleased California Tracking Customer Satisfaction, and some static text format citizen satisfaction survey results by such cities as Winston-Salem, NC, and counties such as Prince William County, VA, all demonstrate that government has begun to realize that the citizen should be recognized as the customer for government's services. Regarding citizens-as-customers was part of Osborne and Gaebler's Reinventing Government (1992), and the customer satisfaction survey via the Internet is an advanced practice. Further, the design of an online satisfaction survey not only means the transformation of public officials and employees' perceptions toward citizens, but also that the ultimate judgment as to service quality is via citizen or customer evaluations. In addition, the level of customer satisfaction has begun to be strongly connected with governmental resources allocation and reallocation.

Recognize Citizens' Capacity

A second feature common to the best practices above is government's recognition of the citizens' capacity in terms of participating in public affairs and policy making. Minnesota's Department Results asks citizens to provide their comments on performance measures, indicators and targets. The City of Santa Monica's Budget Suggestions opens to the public the determination of budget priorities that was previously controlled by the city council. The California Scorecard is designed to enable citizens to supervise the performance progress of state agencies. All of these practices denote that government realizes citizens have sufficient capacity, knowledge and competence to capably participate in setting the policy agenda and influencing policy decisions. Such governments are creating appropriate opportunities and channels for citizens to engage in public affairs.

Traditionally, public management scholars and practitioners have considered that policy making and agenda setting are professional matters that should rely on experts' professional knowledge to address problems. However, growing numbers of scholars and practitioners have begun to realize that in order to establish a counterbalance between the efficiency and effectiveness of public management, it is necessary to pay attention to citizens' concerns, needs and demands. Further, as Fischer (2000) points out, ordinary people are capable of participating in public policies due to their cultural rationality and local knowledge. In this respect, public policy making involving the citizen's knowledge will be more practical and feasible.

Direct Participation

The third common feature of electronic citizen participation mechanisms from the best practices would be "direct participation." The ultimate purpose of digital democracy is to address the underlying weakness and problems of representative democracy. Whether current digital citizen participation mechanisms can achieve this purpose or not, current digital mechanisms at least provide a convenient platform for the public to access public information and to contribute to public issues. Meanwhile, these mechanisms can help transcend the limits of time, place and even money, enabling a citizen to express his/ her opinion in public deliberations anytime, anywhere, and at virtually no cost. More-over, citizen opinions expressed through the Internet can be transmitted to government staffs directly.

Based upon common features of best practices in terms of citizen participation via digital government, we can develop guidelines for designing citizen participation mechanism through information networks. These recommended principles are to: operationalize direct policy involvement, enable the citizen to influence policy priorities, enhance government accountability, encourage participatory deliberation and shape digital citizenship.

Operationalizing Direct Policy Involvement

As described earlier, one of the purposes of digital government is to provide the opportunity for realizing direct democracy and for enhancing the public's democratic value in government. Accompanying the evolution of information technology, there are more and more approaches for citizens to participate in governance through information networks. The most important responsibility for digital government, however, is to construct a channel for operationalizing citizens' policy involvement.

Government must provide constructive public policies and productive public services to the public. Any policy that lacks endorsement by citizens may not be implemented smoothly and successfully. In this respect, an effective government needs active citizen participation in policymaking, and needs citizens' commitment to policy through participation.

What is the most direct way for the public to participate in public policymaking? The portion of people who participate in non-profit organizations concerned with public issues is relatively minor; most citizens are unorganized and silent toward governmental activities.

The City of Santa Monica provides a concrete channel for citizens to be involved in specific policies, rather than just submitting broad comments toward government's activities. The Internet mechanism provided for the city's citizens is convenient and easy. This implies that the government not only must provide approaches for citizens to be involved in specific and concrete policies, but also that the approach must be direct. Digital government is able to meet this commitment.

Enabling Citizens to Influence Policy Priorities

Digital government also has the capacity to enable citizens to influence policy priorities.

Santa Monica's online Budget Suggestions denotes that government could and should open its decision processes and information access to enable members of the public to express their concerns and contribute their wisdom in influencing policy priorities, and the digital government system could help achieve this goal.

In Minnesota's Department Results and California's California Scorecard, we find the same goal embedded in those digital government designs — enabling citizens to influence government's priorities. The common character of these two digital participation designs is that both ask the public to present their perceptions and concerns toward the measures of performance appraisal. Of course, performance measurement is only one part of government's activities. Although these governments only open performance measures to citizens' suggestions, the effect of performance measures is to guide and direct government's activities; further, performance measures indicate the relative weights of government's actions as well. In this respect, if the citizen is empowered with consulting rights to government's performance measures, then the individual has the capability to influence the direction of government activities.

Digital government is not only an effective instrument for increasing direct citizen participation in government, but is also expected to become an approach for empowering citizens in setting policy priorities.

Enhancing Government Accountability

Another principle of digital government is to enhance the accountability of governance. Significant examples are Minnesota's Department Results, California's California Scorecard, Virginia Beach's EMS Customer Satisfaction Survey, Winston-Salem's Citizen Satisfaction Survey Results and Prince William's County Accountability Reports. All of these digital governments either demonstrate their agencies' performance through the Internet or display their citizen satisfaction results on websites. These cases tell us that not only can the government highlight its productivity and achievements by applying information technology, but that the citizen can understand his/her government's performance and how well his/her taxes are spent by visiting the government's website and by expressing his/her satisfaction.

Scrutiny and enhancement of government accountability is an important dimension of digital government. Through online periodic demonstration of updated performance results, citizens can maintain sustained scrutiny and observation of government. If necessary, citizens can also instantly express opinions via an attached electronic feedback form or comment form. The electronic feedback form is a promising approach for accountability to the public.

The evolution of digital government can be seen as an instance of accountability to the citizen. It also helps educate citizens as to the importance of government performance and gives the public a tool to ask for improved government accountability.

Encouraging Participatory Deliberation

Because of the Internet's characteristics of convenience, instant communication and lack of geographic boundaries, various types of online forum and chatting techniques have been developed. These kinds of techniques have been applied in public or non-governmental organizations, e.g., Interactive Minnesota, to encourage citizens' participation through discussions in online forums. The advantage of an online forum is that through the construction of a policy or community forum and messages posted either by participants or by public officials, all participants can see and understand the process of discussion.

Most digital governments post e-mail lists of their elected and appointed officials and other members of the government on their website. This posting enables citizens to directly contact and express their opinion to an official or representative whom they consider responsible for their concerns. Through e-mail, public officials and citizens can contact and reply to each other directly. The traditional gap between public officials and citizens is reduced, putting public officials or representatives face to face with pressures from the public, thereby encouraging direct interaction and dialogue.

In appearance, both of the interaction approaches, online forum and e-mail, can be seen as helpful in shaping public dialogue. However, are these approaches helpful in constructing a new paradigm of public deliberation? The critical components of a healthy public deliberation should be, first, a context of participatory discourse; second, multiple policy stakeholders should be involved; and third, achieving a constructive consensus is its ultimate goal. Therefore, if we employ these three criteria to review the capacity of both the online forum and e-mail approach, none might satisfy the requirements.

In most situations, participants in online forums are critical of government's actions, but lack constructive suggestions. Further, the weakness of this kind of online forum mechanism is in approaching a consensus because participants face segments of a discussion. Even though the e-mail approach creates an opportunity for dialogue between public official and citizen, the discussion is still private; the conversation belongs only to the official and the citizen. This kind of conversation is difficult to define as public deliberation.

Nonetheless, encouraging participatory deliberation through an information network is still the purpose of digital government. Based upon the rapid evolution of information technology, it may be possible to construct an improved context of public deliberation through visual digital systems.

Shaping Digital Citizenship

Regardless of the function and type of citizen participation approach, the ultimate goal of digital government should be to shape a new digital citizenship to empower the citizenry. In the information age, citizens are facing a totally new and different world, as well as new types of interaction between themselves and governments or other organizations. Citizens are interfacing less frequently with "live" officials. Within this digital context, new human behavior patterns are being developed. Interactions between individuals, and between people and organizations, are being changed. Government must rethink this new digital citizenship.

Through the information network, citizen participation in government could become a direct mechanism and attempt to displace the position of elected political representatives. Because of the convenience of digital participation, citizens might ask for more flexible participation regulations, more empowerment, and higher degrees of political involvement, e.g., influencing policy priorities or being involved in decision-making on a virtual basis. Actively involving more citizens to increase the legitimacy of public policy is the duty of democratic governments. It is becoming necessary for contemporary governments to think about how to shape such digital citizenship. Getting instant deliberative consensus on policy issues from multiple policy stakeholders, through an information network, would be one such direction.

Because of the convenience of the Internet, it is now not difficult for governments to gather and collect the flow of public opinion. Governmental activities can, therefore, be more citizen-centered, citizen-oriented, and citizen-driven. If the citizen's endorsement is the premise of effective policy implementation, constructing a citizen-driven digital government, including digital citizenship, will be the responsibility of all governments.

In sum, we should attend to differences between traditional citizen participation in person, and participation via digital government systems. In terms of time spent in participation, participating in person is relatively time consuming and the participants need to adhere to a specific time schedule. In contrast, participating via digital government is a timesaving approach for participants, and they can submit their opinions anytime via the Internet. Further, participating in person requires some concrete meeting place for discussion, e.g., a conference room, while participating via digital government can be practiced anywhere via the Internet, without the limitation of place. Participating in person is bounded by territory, e.g., community and state. In contrast, digital participation has the ability to cross territorial boundaries, and enable participants to engage in local, state and even national issues without the limitations of space. With regard to participation, digital government strives to provide direct approaches for citizens who are interested in public issues. Participating in person generally offers only indirect participation in government. Even though citizens or residents can engage in public affairs through various organizational types, the ultimate participation in decision-making still needs some representatives, such as opinion leaders or elected officials, to convey the voices of their members or constituency. The vast majority of people only participate in government indirectly.

Furthermore, the digital participation mechanism owns the advantage of providing current, instant, and fast information exchanges; in contrast, due to the limited conditions described above, i.e., specific time schedule, place and territorial limitations, participating in person often suffers from a time lag following recognition of a problem. Digital participation also has the difficulty of information overload. Because every citizen can participate and express his/her comments or opinions via his/her computer and the Internet, those individual opinions may represent a huge information burden that the webmaster has to address. In terms of gaining consensus among participants, personal participation has an advantage in its consensus-oriented character. Most of the current digital participation mechanisms focus on individual expression of opinion only, rather than providing a collective consensus. The comparison between participating in person and participating via digital government systems is displayed in Table 1.

Table 1: Comparisons of participating in person and participating via digital government

	Participating in Person	Participating via Digital Government
Time spent	Time-consuming/ Specific time schedule	Time-saving/Anytime
Place requirement	Need concrete place	Virtual/Anywhere
Territorial requirement	Territorial boundary	No limit
Participatory type	Indirect participation	Direct participation
Information flow I	Time-lag	Current, instant, and fast
Information flow II	Information screening	Information overload
Consensus construction	Consensus-oriented	Opinion-expression only

CONCLUSION

In terms of why people do not trust government, Nye Jr. (1997) holds that " A major puzzle in the relationship between public dissatisfaction and government performance is the distance people say they feel from government." People are likely to trust the government close to, rather than far from, them. Digital government is not only an appropriate access point for letting citizens enter the government and understand what public agencies are doing, but it is also an effective instrument for reducing the distance between it's citizens and the government itself.

Through citizen participation, mutual understanding between the public and the government can be enhanced. Through the assistance of a digital information network, information exchanges could transcend limitations of time and space. The evolution of digital government is helpful for increasing democratic values of the contemporary citizenry.

It is necessary to identify some potential problems underlying citizen participation via digital government. The first is the impact of a webmaster's subjective screening and selection toward the opinions submitted by citizens. As noted above, almost every digital government has an electronic feedback or comment form provided for citizens to submit their comments. After the government agency receives comments from citizens, the webmaster must cope with these messages and information. The responsibility of the webmaster is to screen, select, eliminate, and arrange these individual messages as useful information, and then transmit it to his/her supervisor as policy references. Yet, a critical question remains: Is there any gap or difference between the webmaster's and citizens' perspectives toward these comments? Does the webmaster have the same perspective as citizens toward these messages? The webmaster screens and selects comments based upon his/her perceptions and professionalism. However, that is a subjective selection process. One possible result is that some constructive or useful suggestions are eliminated by a webmaster's limited knowledge, thereby reducing the momentum for a reform moment.

Second, one of the potential problems of digital government's citizen participation mechanism is that it creates a predicament of information overload. How are digital governments to apply the techniques of "data mining" to dig, explore, extract, and convert those discursive, unorganized opinions, suggestions and comments into usable policy information?

The third potential problem is related to the ethical issue in digital democracy. For instance, before the problem of the digital divide can be resolved (i.e. the existing gap of information accessibility and opportunity for policy participation between the information rich and the information poor), we must pay attention to the possibility of shaping a new societal class — "digital elitism" in policy making. Furthermore, public officials and elected representatives may focus too much on the latest public opinion flaws, overemphasizing "digital populism."

How to balance equality and justice with efficiency and effectiveness is a long-standing issue confronting public administration. Digital citizen participation might well help address this trade-off. We believe that citizen participation through digitized government systems could result in savings in time and money, both for governments and for citizens. We also have confidence that digital government's citizen participation mechanisms could enhance the legitimacy and feasibility of government's policies.

ENDNOTES

[1]   This function could be found at: http://www.departmentresults.state.mn.us/survey.html

[2]   Minnesota E-Democracy is a non-partisan citizen-based organization devoted to providing citizen participation channels through the use of information networks and improve democracy in Minnesota since 1994. Its official website is at http://www.e-democracy.org/; also, its brief history and primary goals can be found at http://www.e-democracy.org/about.html

[3]   The "Opinion Center" of Santa Monica city is at: http://pen.ci.santa-monica.ca.us/communication/opinion.htm

[4]   Residents in the city of Santa Monica can approach the budget suggestions form found at: http://pen.ci.santa-monica.ca.us/communication/cityforms/budget_suggestions_02.htm

[5]   According to the state government of California, some of the initiatives will be unveiled to the public by early 2003.

[6]   The description of "California Scorecard" can be found at: http://www.iig.ca.gov/projects/scorecard.shtml

[7]   See the description at: http://www.iig.ca.gov/projects/scorecard.shtml

[8]   The online customer satisfaction questionnaire is at: http://www.vbgov.com/dept/ems/adminisurvey.asp

[9]   The linkages of Citizen Involvement are placed at: http://www.georgia.gov/gta/cda/nav/front/0,1036,6-40,00.html

[10]   The citizen participation services are collected at: http://www.delaware.gov/agencies/egovernment/steering

[11]   The online feedback form is located at: http://www.ci.san-jose.ca.us/feedback.html

¹²   Residents can get the linkages by visiting the "Citizen Participation" web page at:
       http://www.co.prince-william.va.us/oem/cxo/Citizen_Participation.htm
¹³   Their homepage and comments form are located at: http://cltr.co.douglas.nv.us/

REFERENCES

Cullen, R. & Houghton, C. (2000). Democracy online: An assessment of New Zealand government websites. *Government Information Quarterly, 17*(3), 243-267.

Dunleavy, P. & Margetts, H. (2000). *The Advent of Digital Government.* London: University of College London.

Fischer, F. (2000). *Citizens, Experts, and the Environment: The Politics of Local Knowledge.* Durham: Duke University Press.

Fountain, J.E. (2001). *Building the Virtual State: Information Technology and Institutional Change.* Washington, D.C.: Brookings Institution Press.

Garson, G.D. (2000). *Information Systems, Politics and Government: Leading Theoretical Perspectives.* In Garson, G.D. (Ed.), *Handbook of Public Information Systems.* New York: Marcel Dekker, Inc. (pp. 591-609).

Korac-Kakabadse, A. & Korac-Kakabadse, N. (2002). Information technology's impact on the quality of democracy: Reinventing the 'democratic vessel.' In Heeks, R. (Ed.), *Reinventing Government in the Information Age: International Practice in IT-Enabled Public Sector Reform.* London: Routledge (pp. 211-228).

Leigh, A. & Atkinson, R.D. (2001). *Breaking Down Bureaucratic Barriers.* Washington, D.C.: Progressive Policy Institute.

New York Times. (2002). From parking to taxes: A push to get answers online. (April 4).

Nye Jr., J.S. (1997). In government we don't trust. *Foreign Policy, 108,* 99-112.

Osborne, D. & Gaebler, T. (1992). *Reinventing Government.* Reading, MA: Addison-Wesley.

Relyea, H.C. (2002). E-gov: Introduction and overview. *Government Information Quarterly, 19*(1), 9-35.

Shi, Y. & Scavo, C. (2000). Citizen Participation and Direct Democracy Through Computer Networking. In Garson, G.D. (Ed.), *Handbook of Public Information Systems.* New York: Marcel Dekker, Inc. (pp. 247-264).

West, J.P. & Berman, E.M. (2001). The Impacts of Revitalized Management Practices on the Adoption of Information Technology. *Public Performance and Management Review, 24*(3), 233-253.

Wyman, S.K., Beachboard, J.C. & McClure, C.R. (1997). *User and System-based Quality Criteria for Evaluating Information Resources and Services.* Available from Federal websites: Final Report. New York: Syracuse University.

Chapter XXI

Digital Government and Citizen Participation in International Context

Karin Geiselhart
University of Canberra, Australia

ABSTRACT

This book provides abundant evidence that the shift towards digital government is part of a sweeping set of changes. These are best viewed holistically, as they relate to pervasive shifts in the locus and purpose of many forms of control. These changes are visible in the gradual shift of terminology from 'government' to 'governance'. This chapter outlines the implications of this shift at the international level, and the role of digital technologies in global citizenship. Participation in these new regimes of global governance includes individuals as well as corporations, international institutions and non-government agencies.

The changes taking place are closely related to other aspects of globalisation, and the emerging patterns of communication and control all have correlates in the information systems that serve them. It is argued here that these patterns both influence and repeat at all scales. In the language of complex systems, these are fractal patterns. This and other concepts from complexity theory will be used to illustrate the growing interdependence of decision making at all levels, and the potential for these processes of governance to transform existing approaches to democracy. Digital participation is an essential element in these changes, and indicates vividly that all levels of governance are now interacting. This chapter conceptualises spheres of authority (Rosenau, 1997) as political attractors that can be simulated, where the rules of interaction are driven by the values of the actors (Theys, 1998). This perspective can help to understand new forms of individual and institutional participation in a systemic context.

These new forms of governance, like the Internet itself, may require a set of generic protocols that operate across borders and scale from the local to the global. Overt democratic indicators may help address the global democratic deficit. Examples such as the Global Reporting Initiative may be seen as the early stages of such protocols. It is likely that in the future, mathematical modelling of governance patterns will become as widespread (and contested) as climate modelling is now. The implications of such an approach are discussed in the context of global digital participation. The governance of the Internet itself, through the mechanisms of the Internet Corporation for Assigned Names and Numbers (ICANN), provides a case study of current processes and their degree of democratic accountability. These patterns are compared with the corresponding agency in Australia, the Australian Domain Administration (AuDA). Both highlight the need for structured protocols for citizen engagement if the information infrastructure is to serve democratic ends.

INTRODUCTION

'Democracy doesn't scale.' Vint Cerf, one of the founders of the Internet, in an answer to a question posed by Scott Aikens from the Minnesota E-democracy project, at the Internet Society Conference in 1996.

Issues of global governance have grown in importance over recent decades (Meyer and Stefanova, 2001). The traditional basis for international relations, the Westphalian system, acknowledged the rule of law through cooperation between sovereign states. This system is no longer adequate for managing situations where borders and issues are more permeable and less defined, both conceptually and physically.

Globalisation is both a cause and a result of issues overflowing borders. Trade, human rights and refugees, environment and climate change, financial markets, terrorism, crime and disease control are among the issues requiring international consensus and management. There is an increasingly urgent need for clearly defined governance processes that are not just adequately resourced and enforceable, but that also integrate solutions in ways that support sustainable and equitable development. Existing multi-lateral agencies, such as the World Trade Organisation, International Monetary Fund, and many others, are being encouraged to adopt more inclusive, democratic and sustainable policies and processes. Likewise, calls for better corporate governance focus on greater transparency and social accountability. The strongest evidence for a democratic deficit is growing inequalities and political instability, since this is not a policy direction likely to be sanctioned by the majority. This dynamic seems to repeat at throughout many levels and current regimes of government, one of the traits of a fractal pattern.

Deepening inequality has been recognised as a threat to global security (Thomas, 2001; Theys, 1998), even before the terrorist attacks on the United States of September 2001. Privatised, self-regulatory patterns of governance, most often associated with the neo-liberal reforms that have become widespread in liberal democracies at least since the

1980s, are now associated with a range of risks and complex emergencies (Turner, 2001; Dillon, 2000; Murphy, 2000). These are linked to the institutional arrangements and regimes that form an apex of power beyond the nation state. For example, the structural adjustment programs favoured by the World Bank have led to reduced public expenditure on health in lower-income countries, and health sector reform has resulted in adverse impacts on public health systems in many countries (Lee and Dodgson, 2000).

Thus, the shift towards growing private authority occurs with the compliance of the state, often with scarcely disguised disregard for democratic accountabilities[1]. In other situations, corporate authority has flowed into the spaces vacated by national governments or uncontrollable through current international agreements. This has been typified by global oligopolies and cartels in industries such as reinsurance, accounting, high-level consulting, mining and electrical products (Murphy, 2000). To these, the convergent industries of media, computing and telecommunications can surely be added (McChesney, 1999). One outcome of these arrangements is that 'globalization creates both a supply of and a demand for new forms of authority to provide those social goods that states are either incapable of or unwilling to provide' (Earnest, 2001).

On many issues, the impact of decision making outpaces the ability of current institutional arrangements to ensure equitable or even stable outcomes. This is one reason democracy has become a 'problem' for global governance (Murphy, 2000). One significant dimension of this problem is the withdrawal of participation from traditional opportunities for political and perhaps social engagement. This, too, is a pervasive problem that appears at scales from the organisational to the international, although with important exceptions. If we accept that creativity and change often occur at the boundaries of standard behaviour (Uncapher, 2001) in situations that are far from equilibrium (Stacey, 1996; Capra, 1996) then today's digital fringes may be seen as the primordial seas of democratic innovation and evolution.

This chapter explores the forms of participation that extend beyond the nation state, as part of a universal reach for renewal of democratic practice. The argument for an approach that sees democracy as a set of scalable communication protocols, subject to modelling as a complex system, is developed in the following sections. First is a perspective on global governance, followed by examples of the range of participation now available to individual cum global actors. This leads to a discussion of features that might allow global governance to be more adaptive and responsive to current crises. The author suggests that these general design features apply at all levels of governance, and are therefore useful for agency heads as well as heads of governments and transnational institutions. This leads to a discussion of democratic governance as a complex system and the suggestion that fractal patterns and attractors can be productively applied both metaphorically and mathematically. Then the management of the global electronic commons through ICANN and the smaller scale Australian AuDA is offered in illustration. The chapter concludes with implications for digital networks in efforts to achieve the holy grail of scaling democratic process in a globalised sphere.

REGIMES AND SPHERES OF AUTHORITY

It may be a homily that 'global governance is a site of struggle over wealth, power and knowledge' (Murphy, 2000). However, civil society and the growing role of non-government organisations (NGOs) form patterns of influence that repudiate the linear and hegemonic structures that currently dominate world issues. That is why 'sovereignty as the traditional principle of political formation is being supplemented by a network-based account of social organization whose principle of formation is emergence and whose science is increasingly that of complex adaptive systems' (Dillon, 2000). The next section elaborates on the new forms of participation available to citizens. This section prepares the ground for that analysis by outlining the changing landscape of international relations and the issues confronting global governance.

One popular view of the changing model of governance is Rosenau's proposal that 'spheres of authority' are arising as alternatives or complements to sovereign states. Rosenau (1997) describes a sphere of authority (SOA) as 'emergent authority relationships.'

Earnest (2001) discusses spheres of authority in some detail. He notes that, 'Spheres of authority may be temporal or enduring, local or global. What makes them unique is their ability to provide social goods and protections that states are either incapable of or unwilling to provide. SOAs encompass "traditional" units of analysis like intergovernmental and nongovernmental organizations, but include less structured forms of social behaviour such as transnational coalitions, issue networks, and global civil society. The critical common factor is that 'these SOAs create challenges to the authority of the contemporary nation-state in a wide range of issue areas, from the land mine ban to monitoring human rights conditions and governmental corruption.'

In this more fluid world of authority, change is the norm and allegiances change quickly. Citizen loyalties 'emerge and coalesce' dynamically as they use 'the technoscape and infoscape — to assert their claims to authority and legitimacy' (Earnest, 2001).

Because global issues by definition do not fall neatly under the jurisdiction of one authority, 'regime' is a more appropriate term for the structures that manage them. According to Krasner, (quoted in Meyer and Stefanova, 2001), 'a regime consists of principles, norms, rules and decision-making procedures around which actor expectations converge in a given issue-area.' These can arise around issues or areas. The most highly developed regimes include an institutional framework, a set of specific rules and norms and a more general set of shared expectations regarding acceptable behaviour.

However, much action takes place outside formal regimes. Indeed, some SOAs may be more influential because they are seen to be both leaderless and informal (Earnest, 2001). This is the phenomenon of the 'electronic herd' described in relation to international money markets (Friedman, 2000). Leaderless networks that both create and respond to each other and environmental factors co-exist with formal regimes. They interact with each other, providing a landscape of multiple influences that is now less tied to bonds of legitimacy and authority. They may more resemble medieval allegiances.

This dynamic situation is captured by the term 'emergence', which is also linked to the concept of path dependency, or sensitivity to initial conditions. These interactions are part of the creation of new norms, such as the pressures on the World Trade Organisation to give precedence to environmental treaties when they conflict with trade agreements (Bronkers, 2001). Much of the pressure from NGOs invokes a 'David and Goliath' friction, at least implicitly. Through a 'chorus of voices' many smaller players challenge the assumption that the biggest nations and corporate allies should determine the rules of the game. These form dynamics of scale within evolving power relationships.

Standard international relations analyses look at three levels of influence: the international, the regional and the national (Meyer and Stefanova, 2001). Thus, scale has always been an embedded organising assumption. More players and more levels are now relevant, through still within a Westphalian process that acknowledges the nation state as central. Thus the highest level of players concerned with corporate responsibility, particularly in relation to human rights and labour standards, now include the International Labor Organization (ILO), the World Bank (WB), the Organization of Economic Co-operation and Development (OECD) and the International Monetary Fund (IMF). These are supplemented by a second tier of business and civil society organisations that are gradually gaining a seat at the table, if not the right to help set the agenda. These would include Human Rights Watch, Amnesty, Public Citizen, Anti-Slavery International, Sweatshop Watch, the Clean Clothes Campaign and many others. The third tier (or sphere) includes more localised organisations which seek to influence the second tier, and when possible, the top level. The international labour movement has shown an agile solidarity in a number of high profile disputes.[2]

Viewed collectively, these organisations at all levels help maintain and change global norms and practices. This is happening to a much greater degree than previously, facilitated by globalisation and new communication technologies. Formal, regime based outcomes include the Global Compact proposed by the United Nations (Meyer and Stefanova, 2001) and the Global Reporting Initiative which a number of large corporations have agreed to. At a less institutionalised level, the self-organisation associated with anti-globalisation, genetically modified foods and cheaper anti-viral drugs to fight AIDS in developing countries are well-known examples. All these examples indicate the strong pressures to bring greater democratic pressures into global agreements.

Global governance has been defined as 'political management at the global level of a given area of human existence in the absence of global government' (Meyer and Stefanova, 2001). Their approach is consistent with the analysis above, as they note that in this 'interactive and multilayered process' nonstate actors, such as non-government organisations (NGOs), transborder interest groups, and transnational epistemic communities have growing influence, and the old levels of analysis on are no longer so useful.

The distinction between corporate governance and formal political structures is now also less clear. The spectacular collapse of Enron, the giant energy company, has led to disclosures about involvement of U.S. public officials at the highest levels. There have been claims that 21 agencies representing the U.S. government, multilateral development banks, and other national governments helped leverage Enron's global reach with $7.2 billion in public financing approved for 38 projects in 29 countries.'[3]

Thus, while the borders of control may be both blurring and in some cases, converging, in an ever-changing process of 'fragmentegration' (Rosenau, 2002), there is no clarity that these processes are leading towards greater democratic determination. The 'democratic deficit' continues to be cause of concern, both within and across cities, states and regions. As new norms are forged the creative edge is at the fringes, in situations far from equilibrium (Uncapher, 2001; Capra, 1996).

These emerging forms of global governance, both formal and defacto, all have digital correlates and manifestations. These can be used to analyse the direction and purpose of the various patterns. Over time, standards and norms may coalesce into patterns that are more democratic in their implications and enforcements. For the time being, the borders and jurisdictions become more 'fuzzy.' While a sovereign state may agree to (and even comply with) the principle of non-interference in another country's affairs, no such strictures apply to the trans-national companies that are, in effect, private global regimes. State sovereignty and international law are being re-interpreted in accordance with the current world system. While states remain key agents of international law, additional non-sovereign and even non-cohesive identities are winning a place at the table. The most dramatic rise has been in the number of non-government players, both corporate and civil. Corporate political power is certainly now a major factor in international laws and standard setting. These players command enormous resources to protect and expand their influence. Civil society can muster fewer dollars, but has the potential backing of large numbers of committed individuals. It is in the interest of both civil and corporate players to have secure, reliable and enforceable international agreements. The devil is in the detail as these players meet, enter into dialogue, debate or battle, and seek to entrench their own values and norms. This is how global governance is emerging, with variant regimes for different issues, both overlapping and intersecting. No wonder then that global governance is 'a process that must be understood by all students of international law in the 21st century' (Meyer and Stefanova, 2001).

The above discussion establishes the shifting sands of governance, where power is diffusing to and through new players. These operate at all levels simultaneously, but ultimately rely on the actions of individuals who may or may not represent a group at a particular time. The next section considers the relationship between the individual and digital participation beyond the nation state.

CITIZENS SANS FRONTIERS

A relatively recent suite of double-sided risks and opportunities has opened new realms of action and obligation to the masses. These can be embraced under the term globalisation, if it is defined to include all its manifestations of communication, consumption, mobility and the corresponding nuisances and dangers of homogenised media, disease vectors, terrorism, environmental as well as political refugees, etc. More than the political borders have become more permeable. The boundaries around the possible issues and approaches and techniques for influence and gaining an advantage have also collapsed. The continuum for engagement extends from a decision to donate to a distant cause through to terrorism on foreign soil. Between these extremes of charity and sociopathy lie traditional lobbying, consumer boycotts, and hactivism. Just as the WTO is free to determine fine detail of trade and production requirements in distant lands, so are some empowered individuals at liberty to take aim at and influence policies almost anywhere.

The previous section described how authority and governance is becoming more diffuse, moving to a wider set of actors, and operating across both larger and smaller scales. As legitimacy and obligation shift, so do the possible spheres for participation. There is no easy way of halting the petitions that now float around the Internet, often global in their supplications. There is also no way to slow consumer activism, which now has noticeable impact on corporate behaviour (Hertz, 2001).

Rosenau has argued that there is an increase in the skills, both analytic and emotional, that corresponds to the globalisation of participation. Lawrence Lessig has articulated the zeitgeist succinctly: 'We stand on the brink of being able to say, "I speak as a citizen of the world," without the ordinary person thinking, "What a nut"' (Lessig, 1999, quoted by Etzioni, 2001). A crucial aspect of global citizenship is that it applies at all levels simultaneously. Having U.S. citizenship does not release an individual from democratic obligations (and rights) at the local level. Likewise, engagement and action on trans-border issues becomes an extra layer of information need and another set of interactions and interdependencies for governments to facilitate. How to manage such change and complexity democratically is a key question for both citizens and governments. This paper suggests that modelling governance at all scales could be a valuable tool in this task.

Earnest (2001) has described the changing nature of the social contract in the face of globalising pressures and changing spheres of authority. Citizens become trapped by 'the twin pincers of privatization and bureaucratization' that create 'authority relationships without the commensurate institutions of consent.' However, voluntary engagement with civil organisations can provide a form of consent without obligation. Membership in organisations such as Greenpeace creates minimal demands, and consent can be withdrawn at any time.

A number of problems accompany new forms of digital participation. Such personal sovereignty is only available to those who are motivated and informed about their options. The flip side of participation, the ability to opt out of taxation systems, previously the privilege of corporate citizens (Martin and Schumann, 1997) has now been democratised to the level of 'digital expatriates,' who can access money laundering schemes accessible with a PC (O'Connor, 1995). Discussions about the 'digital divide' and the gap between the info-rich and info-poor (Lyon, 1988) can obscure a wider debate about the renovation of democracy. By identifying select groups of individuals as targets for a new form of welfare, efforts to ameliorate the digital divide can overlook the new kinds of literacy and learning that are needed to participate in a digital and globalised world (Warschauer, 2002).

Another concern, related to the new forms of literacy, is the lack of plural voices in the media, and the closing of the 'electronic commons' of ideas. While it is not possible to elaborate on these arguments here (for example McChesney, 1999), elements which drive this concern are the concentration of media ownership, the diminishing coverage of international news in the U.S. and in the aftermath of September 11, 2001, greater restrictions on government information flows. Rather than achieving a Lippmanesque ideal, as discussed in Aikens (1997), such trends are more likely to systemically undermine the legitimacy of their sources and promote alternative voices.[4]

In keeping with more diffuse, less formalised modes of governance, not all forms of participation fall neatly under the category of citizenship. That does not mean that they have no impact on structures that are more formal. The unintended consequences can be both widespread and powerful.

Sometimes the effects are indirect, as with Iranian women expressing themselves freely and often anonymously via web logs, or online journals. While few of these cyber diaries are about politics, many discuss social issues that cannot be normally talked about openly in the conservative Islamic country, such as choosing a boyfriend or attitudes towards sex. The Internet in Iran has grown rapidly to about 400,000 online in 2001 with 15m expected within four years. One man set up a site on blogging, and within seven months, there were over 1,200 of them. Many women have seized this opportunity to express themselves. As a result, some men are e-mailing a particular female blogger to say her writing has changed their attitude toward women (Hermida, 2002).

The borderless nature of the Internet is both cause and example of these trends. New communication technologies are best understood as an array of technologies, rather than a unified entity called 'the Internet' (Bimber, 2000). They offer a range of tools for expression and influence, from the very local to the global. The mutual interdependence of today's environment, both political and literal, means that influence can occur at several levels of governance simultaneously.

An Australian example is the recent defeat of a proposal to establish a charcoal factory on the south coast of New South Wales. The Premier overrode local opposition, decreeing it was 'not a local issue.' Community protest was strong, supplemented by help from other jurisdictions, such as the nearby Australian Capital Territory (ACT). This action was very much a face-to-face engagement, as Internet connectivity in the area is not high. The loosely assembled Charcoalition[5] used the web site to help distribute information both locally and farther afield, including an e-mail announcement about fund-raising dances, etc. This promoted citizen participation and understanding not available on the state government web site (Geiselhart, 2002). The issue had repercussions in Australia's most populous state, eventually gaining the support of the main opposition leader to seal its fate. The formally elected government, amid accusations of being less than fully disclosing on a number of issues related to the approval, lost both face and legitimacy. The international purchasers of the silicon (which was the ultimate product of the project) started receiving queries from the local activists. Had the company not withdrawn its plans, potential financiers may have become targets for communication and protest, with the aim of making financing unappealing. Similar approaches have worked to dampen investor enthusiasm for an aluminium smelter in Tibet. The Zapistas have also been taking their struggle in Mexico to the world via the Internet with some success (Cleaver, 1996). It is not always easy to identify clear or long-term impacts. However, there can be little doubt that both political and civil actors in coastal areas of Australia at the very least would have paid close attention to both the success of the community action and its techniques. Some international web sites on environmental activism linked to the Charcoalition web site, and offered support. At the time the project was cancelled, the author had placed an Internet classified ad, presumably seen primarily in North America, offering a free home stay 'down under' in exchange for substantial donations to the community group. This combined an element of international activism, commerce in the sense of exchange, and tourism.[6]

Other participatory efforts begin with no overt political agenda. The example of bird watchers, itself a globally diffuse yet participatory activity shows how cohesive action can emerge from individuals whose values may initially be united only by a desire to pursue their pastime. Garreau (2001) describes how the introduction of digital technology has led to changes in awareness, knowledge, and action. Annual bird counts, a simple yet cumbersome paper-based volunteer activity, became easier when the National Audubon Society moved it to the Web. As well as facilitating participation, individuals and clusters are modifying specific bird environments as a result, to enhance the birds' survival prospects. The collective consciousness that has consequently become more visible and robust has spread this modifying action to the largest private landowner in the U.S. (International Paper Co, according to Garreau) and the Department of Defense. Almost lyrically, Garreau describes this 'flocking together' as a leaderless but creative and spontaneous stewardship of a global ecological resource.

This too must be considered a form of governance, in the sense that it is an implicit rule-bound system that operates to manage and distribute resources in a consensual framework. Until the last few decades, the term governance was considered archaic. It has become popular once again, because it denotes forms of management without the connotations of democratic representation.

The dark networks of terrorism, child pornography and international money laundering can also be self-organising, sustainable, creative and scalable. These have been described in the literature on net war (Arquilla and Ronfeldt, 2001) and Internet activism (Meikle, 2002; Wray, 1998). Drug gangs deciding to cooperate and form partnerships to broaden their markets and profits[7] will also create international digital communication networks with more or less overt governance practices. These variations may all be seen as patterns driven by the values of the actors, as will be elaborated in the next section.

This analysis is not new. Indeed the international information infrastructure has often been described as a 'global nervous system.'[8] What may be new is the proposal that political formations can be mapped and simulated like weather patterns, using the scalable power of complex systems analysis.

While new communication technologies can facilitate participation (or criminal activity) in novel ways, they do not ensure a more able citizenry. It can be argued, as Rosenau does, that humans are now capable of both wider and deeper understanding of factual and contextual information across the globe, through higher skills. However, the complexity of the information has also increased, probably exponentially, from even 100 years ago. The digitally empowered are powerful but few in numbers, and the proportion of disengaged even among this group is great. Even for the committed or passionate, 'data smog' builds new barriers to meaningful understanding or action (Shenk, 1997).

On more formal levels of governance, the transparency and availability of information and its pricing, offers different hurdles for citizenship. For many institutional as well as individual actors, the stock market may be the most reliable measure of performance. However, this metric is not flexibly responsive to wider values, such as environmental costs and social externalities. Measurement and then dialogue about social indicators is hardly straightforward, but initiatives such as the Global Reporting Initiative and the Triple Bottom Line[9] indicate that these norms are shifting.

Online public spaces can provide flexible and interactive outlets for dialogue and document the dynamic as values shift and demands for transparency increase. The California Voters' Foundation[10] collects and disseminates information useful for informed decision-making, using the principle of 'digital sunshine'.

These examples describe the ever changing, multiply entwined and scalable 'spheres of authority' which become, consciously or otherwise, patterns of governance. The globalisation of risk in the form of terrorism, climate change and economic interdependence is driving the study of such phenomena as complex systems. The practical implications of this dynamic landscape of engagement/disengagement for governments on issues beyond their jurisdictional borders are discussed in the next section. These include approaches for engaging with quasi-citizens and brokering trans-boundary relationships as well as broader design principles. These features can provide systems of governance that are both digitally enabled and democratically sound. The author contends that only those versions of the networked model meeting democratic design criteria can help create adaptive global governance.

DIGITAL TECHNOLOGY AS A TOOL OF GOVERNANCE

The above sections described how sovereignty, legitimacy and participation are moving into new and more diffuse patterns. This section discusses how these new forms of participation, and their digital correlates, operate at the coalface of legitimacy: the government agency. While governments at all levels have tended to see new media as a means of service provision (Gualtieri, 1998; Musso et al., 2000; Geiselhart, 1999; Curtin et al., 2002) there has also been intense activity to incorporate these innovations into processes of consultation, policy development and evaluation (Coleman and Goetz, 2000). Thus, new forms of trans-national participation must be considered interactively with the structures that support or inhibit them. This section briefly describes the principles of the networked form of government, and then extends this approach to discuss how government agencies can facilitate feedback and participation on issues with trans-national ramifications. A supportive and receptive framework for digital citizenship may be viewed as a flywheel that helps prevent engagement from turning to hacktivism, cyber-terrorism or worse. Although it may seem counter-intuitive for government agencies or large bureaucratic organisations and corporations to move in the direction of less control, lessons from the networked model indicate the benefits. Richards (2000) outlines the elements of this new form of governance. While her observations are from a national level in Canada, the principles also apply at the transnational level using a complex systems approach, outlined in the section that follows.

Richards describes first how new media melds traditional government tools into a unified 'library, a news wire, a deliberation room and a voting booth.' In the new networked model, the key functions for government become those of partnership, coordination, engagement, and broker. Rather than seeing new media as an obligation to achieve massive participation, these approaches recognise that narrowcasting can be effective, as long as there is trust in the process. Her discussion of a 'distributed form of mass-participation, based on a platform of many associations talking to each other,' closely resembles Rosenau's spheres of authority.

For issues extending beyond national boundaries, the urgency and difficulty increase exponentially. As will be demonstrated in the examples of ICANN and AuDA, locating potential stakeholders and then engaging them meaningfully is not easy. A significant number of technophobes and techno-anarchists will always remain. More to the point, any process for reaching consensus will be attacked as either not inclusive enough or of having been hijacked by special interest groups. More deliberate and iterative forms of transparency can help create a resilient 'chorus of voices.'

The attempts driven by the Organisation for Economic Cooperation and Development (OECD) to achieve a legally binding Multilateral Agreement on Investment (MAI) were an example of national governments abrogating their duty to ensure wide public debate and approval. Some analyses have attributed the demise of the MAI in its originally proposed form to the actions of civil society using the Internet and accessing alternative media.[11] In Australia, there was much action from civil society against the MAI, but very little public coverage. Anecdotally, the author observed that even the politically active, academics and those involved with trade and competition issues were often unaware of the issue. While there was some presentation of these issues on relatively obscure government web sites, there was little effort to create public dialogue, even though the MAI would have had significant impacts at local levels.

Global issues require not just global solutions, but global checks and balances on decision-making. Separation of powers through trans-national spheres of authority is often inadequate, as it seldom includes formal procedures for public reporting and communicating to those who were not actively involved. This sense of accountability as reporting is an important element in achieving stability and trust in governance processes. Agencies which succeed in themselves becoming responsive to their internal stakeholders, who in turn have been authorised to meet with and listen to external voices, have the greatest potential of effectiveness and will be the least likely to implode. That is, organisations that interact with their own boundary dwellers will be able to innovate and adapt rapidly. This is very different from placing a few radical stakeholders on a nominal advisory panel, only to further marginalise their claims. It implies internal procedures for assuring a voice and external forms of transparency that effectively turn the organisation 'inside-out.' Digital media are made to order for this task, but shifting the internal norms to these forms of openness can be painfully difficult. Many agencies are reluctant to make public electronic submissions available online. Such measures empower through the ability to copy, store, search, document, analyse and measure responses. This can benefit not just local constituents, but a wider group of active 'sovereign individuals' who can collate this information across wider jurisdictions and feed it back through wider networks.

All aspects of the networked model have digital correlates. As well as coordinating information, brokering solutions and facilitating discussion, this includes archiving the history of an issue in easily searchable and accessible formats, and ensuring that all relevant background documents, research, reports, etc., are identified and made public. Particularly important for international participation are the links to the civil society groups, local and non-local, where critical dialogue can take place. This can avoid 'reinventing the wheel,' encourage local solutions and help build informed consensus. Inviting annotations for complex scientific or legal issues from opposing groups or 'outside' experts, and allowing public comment on these, can be a valuable step towards achieving informed discussion. Formal protocols for consultation and representation and policy incorporation of these can be developed, through iterative discussion with stakeholders. The entire process then has to be made fully transparent, using means and measures consistent with stakeholder needs. For more complex, multi-faceted issues such as the interfaces between human rights, environment and trade, the need for balancing digital techniques with public meetings, citizen juries and robust media coverage grows. Identification and cultivation of individuals with particular forms of expertise that transcend local applications can rapidly and efficiently expand the public knowledge base. Government managers that embrace this potential, rather than suppressing it, demonstrate synchronicity with a 'learning cities' approach. These techniques are widely used within governments or with visiting consultants, but the sharing of their expertise does not commonly spread to the electronic forms of public information and dialogue. It is generally limited to discussions with government officials with an occasional media article.

The full range of design and policy issues for digital government is considered elsewhere in this volume. The following protocols for democratic process are offered as preliminary and generic, as they apply to all scales of governance. The case study evidence is from a large government agency that was handling a number of significant change events rather badly. Shortly after this study, it was publicly revealed that they had been subject to one of the largest frauds ever in an Australian Commonwealth agency.

Thus, active planning for democratic inputs through the information systems can be one element of checks and balances. Greater openness to outside inputs is another. The NGOs attending the World Summit on the Information Society in Geneva[12] have complained that their participation has been restricted, while individual private firms have been given representation. They have called for clearer and more democratic procedures for broad participation and agenda setting. Communication audits can be useful in these contexts, but they should include all levels of possible participation, down to the local.

An example of openness on an issue with trans-national implications is the UK's Human Genetics Commission (HGC).[13] Apparently, the HGC chair, Baroness Kennedy, has kept her promise to make all the workings of the HGC plainly visible to the public, including the Register of Members Interests such as shareholdings and benefits, etc.

Table 1: Protocols for democratic information infrastructure/case study evidence (Geiselhart, 1999)

Protocol	Evidence from Major Case Study
Universal access	Universal access (via a PC)
Appropriate training	Training inadequate for developmental participation
Transparency of information, including feedback and agenda setting, strong freedom of information provisions. All major decisions fully textualised	Little availability of corporate minutes, decision processes, no internal FOI provisions
Deliberate creation and maintenance of a public space for communication, protected from commercial pressures	Limited public space available but not fully supported, no further development
Strong interactivity (open ended input)	Moves towards narrow inputs
Broadest and earliest possible participation in agenda setting and internal policy development	Participation in agenda setting and internal policy decreased
Minimisation of commercial in confidence protection	High levels of commercial in confidence protection
Freedom from direct or indirect censorship	Signs that surveillance and censorship were increasing
Maximisation of privacy protection	Possibility of anonymous communication removed
Equity in rights of transmission	Theoretically available, in practice upwards communication restricted to practical tasks
Provision for lateral and anonymous communication and ballots	Lateral communication widespread, ballots only for the industrial relations agreement
Availability of alternative forms and sources of information	Some availability of alternative views, information increasingly managed from above
Provision for localised information and dialogue	Local discussion possible, dialogue on non-work specific tasks dampened.
Mechanisms for reflective deliberation about the information system	Little such provision

By actively facilitating the knowledge and interactions that encourage the articulation of social values and networks, the networked manager encourages the emergence of political and community structures that are robust, influential and scalable. Another insight arising from this analysis is that the actors, both individual and institutional, become the distributed brain of the global nervous system. The networked approach can be seen as a way of sharing both expertise and control, thereby distributing risk, accountabilities and benefits.

These forms of openness have similarities to the open source software movement, databased policy, and the Cochran Collaboration of evidence-based medicine. All are facilitated through digital communications. More recently, this approach in the media has been termed 'open source journalism.' Ideally, the provisions for the separation of powers in a particular sphere of authority become driven by the transparency of the process. Simple rules create complex but adaptive and self-managing structures, as the following section sets forth.

GLOBAL GOVERNANCE AS A COMPLEX SYSTEM

With accelerating pace over the past 20 years, awareness has grown in first the physical, and lately the social sciences of a new and powerful way of modelling many kinds of systemic behaviour. [14] Some have taken this metaphorically (Zolo, 1992) while others have made serious efforts at mathematical modelling (Stocker et al., 2001; Biggs, 2001). There is interest in viewing global governance from this perspective. Complexity theory is showing that understanding and some form of control is possible without total determinism and predictability. These revelations suit modern, information driven governments, which are often caught up in changes that outpace their ability to adapt. Many institutions, including the administrative arms of representative government were developed for a simpler, self-reliant age. Physical systems, such as climate, are also undergoing rapid transformation. There is heightened recognition of the need to find new ways of harnessing citizen knowledge and consent to achieve rapid learning and flexible response.

This brief section argues that in addition to aiding in understanding and possibly prediction, modelling global governance could suggest methods for integration across scales. In particular, the author links the emerging forms of personal sovereignty to the challenges of democratic global governance. This offers a more positive response to the rather pessimistic quote that opens this paper. This argument for a complex systems approach is followed by one example of the proposed fractal model: the Internet Corporation for Assigned Names and Numbers (ICANN), and its Australian correlate, the Australian Domain Administration (AuDA).

Traditional Newtonian concepts influenced linear, hierarchical views of social structure and management, and are now yielding to the paradigm shift associated with complexity (Becker and Slayton, 2000). Recent work on simulating social models and the spread of ideas shows that while ideas spread from one-on-one exchanges, it is the collective and cumulative interactions that lead to major shifts in perception or values (Stocker, Green, and Newth, 2001). An essential observation of these systems is that a simple set of rules can generate very complex behaviours at many scales.

An 'attractor' is a pattern generated by complex systems. It forms behavioural loops that while dynamic are nonetheless recognisable. Social structures as well as biological events can form fractal patterns, which repeat at different levels. Thus, the incidence of industrial strikes has been found to follow a power law similar to the way fires spread in a forest (Biggs, 2001). These can be the ever different but similar patterns of bureaucratic procedures or the endless reshuffling of international accreditation. Work on government (Kiel, 1996) and on organisations (Theys, 1998) suggests that in human systems the rules of interaction are driven by the values of the actors. This implies democratic values produce different patterns of governance. These interconnections are now made more obvious through digital communications. The endless data of global networks could be as useful for monitoring democratic process as for catching terrorists.

Complex systems display sensitivity to initial conditions, which for humans may be read as the history of relevant events. There is a possible communication path from an individual in Iowa to the head of the World Bank, but the mapping of the rules onto the actors determines the degree of democratic governance. Ralph Nader has stated this simply as: Who gets to say? Who gets to know? Who gets to decide? There can be bifurcations, such as many believe occurred with the terrorists attacks on the United States of September 2001. Patterns can occur over time, and the much smaller World Trade Center attack in the early 1990s, as well as the bombing of a nightclub in Bali of 2002 may all be part of the 'pattern.' Identification of the values driving the patterns can assist in redirecting them for more sustainable outcomes, and avoiding counter-productive responses that incite further escalations.

Not all the patterns reflect democratic values. Some exclude citizen participation, while others have the potential to override national sovereignty. As this paper is being finalised, the capture of the Washington sniper reveals a possible 'cascade' from the September 11 attacks. Individuals form clusters, formal and informal. Organisational and institutional clusters, from a local Parent and Teachers Association to the World Trade Organisation and the United Nations, create spheres of authority and defacto systems of governance that increasingly have digital representation or at least a fingerprint. These may or may not include provision for information and decision-making, transparency, citizen participation, and accountable evaluation of the decision-making outcomes.

The observations of Dahl (1989) offer valuable hindsight. As well as suggesting widely accepted and generic criteria for democratic process, Dahl raised issues that are particularly relevant to questions about global governance and the forms of citizenship that could support it. These are his recognition that scale or size is a challenge for democracy; the dangers of control by intellectual elites; the role of democracy at the organisational level; the increasing power of trans-national corporate activities; and the potential of information technology to assist a modern transformation of democracy.

More recently, Picciotto (2000) suggested four general principles for a 'direct-democratic, deliberative public sphere' as transparency, accountability, responsibility, and empowerment. These, too, are generic and applicable at many levels of governance.

The following section is a case study of global governance and participation. It illustrates the influence of an initial set of values, and the shift of pattern that can occur when these change.

ICANN: TWO STEPS FORWARD?[15]

The governance of the Internet has been widely followed and discussed as an example of global governance and transnational civil society. The Internet may be considered an international public good, developed at public expense. Management of this global electronic commons suggests a sphere of authority with implications for many areas of life on a very immediate, practical and personal level. Accessibility, stability, security, interactivity and affordability of the global network all have household as well as governmental and corporate correlates and implications. Thus, decisions about the management of the Internet are relevant to a broad public spectrum. As a template for decision-making in the public interest, the Internet is one of many areas where global governance has the potential to set a democratic benchmark.

Most analyses of Internet governance have focussed on ICANN, the Internet Corporation for Assigned Names and Numbers. These names and numbers form the addressing system of the web addresses that are now a ubiquitous element in the information revolution. The history of ICANN has been told elsewhere (Mueller, 1999; Lindsay, 2001), and is part of a global story about the gradual convergence of both the technology and the regulation of telecommunications, computing and media (McChesney, 1999; Lessig, 1999) in the context of a global information society (Kleinwachter, 2001).

Neither a government nor a for-profit corporation, ICANN is a hybrid that interacts with both, and with individuals as well. ICANN may be the most prominent transnational institution with mechanisms for direct public representation, through its 'at large' elections. The early history of the Internet is relevant for understanding the idealistic underpinnings of ICANN.[16] A number of writers have considered ICANN as a template for global governance. These have mostly criticised the neo-liberal values that have come to dominate (Mueller, 1999; McDowell and Steinberg, 2001; Lindsay, 2001; Weinberg, 2001), but also hope for the approach (Kleinwachter, 2001).[17] Management of the domain name system is a global international issue, and ICANN's difficulties concern key aspects of democratic process, namely representation, legitimacy, access to information, participation, and decision-making. It is therefore an interesting case study of the challenges of scaling democracy, and of the opportunities, digital and otherwise, for citizen participation on a transborder issue.

The structures, networks, processes and accountabilities of ICANN illustrate both the potential and weaknesses of the emerging civil sphere, and highlight that digital participation is entwined with older forms. Conceptually ICANN fits the model of both a sphere of authority and a complex system in which the values of the actors determine the rules of interaction. The ambiguities of legitimacy and lapses of transparency and accountability that have characterised ICANN are typical of other attempts at global governance, with calls for similar remedies. The work of the Australian Domain Administration (AuDA) is offered as a fractal echo of ICANN values and processes.

From a global citizenship perspective, the membership of ICANN and participation in the at-large elections achieved far greater numbers than expected.[18] At the least, the at-large process has helped to raise awareness of the need to nurture civil society mechanisms throughout Asia (Kang, 2001). The Uniform Dispute Resolution procedures have undoubtedly also helped to curb potential excesses of cybersquatting on domain names.

The early days of the Internet coincided with an optimistic spirit and hopes that a new age was dawning. There was overt effort to create a universal network for communication, with the intention of fostering better scientific, social and political understanding. Developed as a cooperative project with corporate, government and university support, commercial concerns did not rank highly in the early development or management of the Internet's protocols or addressing system. The early 1960s were a time of relative largess in the United States government, before the Vietnam War detracted from projects that are more peaceful.

The early Internet actors came from different sectors, but their intentions were consistent with developing a global 'commons.' They were elites, but they shared a consensus about their task, and the values they articulated were generous and bold.[19] Initially one individual, Jon Postel, more or less established and maintained the limited number of domains that grew out of an initial 'root' addressing system for transferring packets of information over the network. Eventually administration of the root server was outsourced from a research institute to a private company (Lindsay, 2001).

The invention of the browser created a bifurcation in Internet evolution. Suddenly, hypertext became the norm, because it created a channel for much easier access to visual, audio as well as text materials and rapid cross-indexing to theoretically limitless oceans of information. The Internet became a mainstream resource and content grew exponentially. After that, in the early 1990s, the demand for domain names exploded and their commercial potential quickly grasped. While most content remained free, entrepreneurs started exploring the possibilities for returns on Internet investment through either familiar or novel business techniques such as brand recognition, demand aggregation through popular sites, and syndication. While there are no inherent legal rights in domain names, the possibilities for profit and therefore of dispute and legal challenges over this new but nebulous form of commercial real estate were soon obvious. By the time structured management of the addressing system became necessary, the main issues were 'definition and scope of property rights...in domain names, IP addresses, trademarks and zone file data' (Mueller, 1999). A subtle value shift had occurred that affected the rules for interaction.

ICANN has had a legitimacy problem from the beginning, and has been widely criticised as secretive and a captive of commercial interests that seek to maximise the rights of trademark and other intellectual property owners who help support it. Early open fora to establish a global basis for ICANN were quickly countered by a more narrow set of well-heeled stakeholders. Nor did ICANN put adequate effort into building a bottom-up network of distributed organisational support. Rather than consolidating broad based support, it leapt into policy making on the most divisive issues (Mueller, 1999).

Much rhetoric implied that ICANN was a technical, rather than policy body, and that its processes would build on the consensual bottom-up approaches that characterised Internet technical standards. The reality has been rather different, and has been linked to the neo-liberal values of ICANN's industry and government proponents. Highly politicised and under attack from many fronts, in mid-2002 ICANN was sued by one of its at large board members and had developed proposals for its own reform. While its President Stuart Lynn maintains that ICANN is not an 'exercise in global democracy,'[20] others maintain that if it fails to achieve broader participation it should be shut down. There is also an undeniable element of 'techno-refusniks' probably over-represented in the Internet community, of those who understand but will not accept any attempt to achieve consensus.

A communication map of the electronic and other mechanisms for public information and participation in ICANN would be extensive, as it has had a much higher profile than the purely technical activities of the Internet Engineering Task Force. The ICANN web site gives the appearance of an open organisation, with numerous discussion groups on meaty topics. However, there are no links to other sites and mailing lists that discuss its activities (such as icannwatch.org, or www.icannatlarge.com). Critics say there is just an 'illusion of legitimacy.' The board member, who is suing for access to financial documents, including contracts and other legal information, has claimed that he regularly hears about ICANN actions from outside bodies.[21]

On the face of it, however, ICANN supports democratic values and broad-based policy development. Meetings are held around the world, and are open to anyone. Participation is facilitated by intelligent, appropriate use of technology, including web cast and a number of mailing lists.[22] ICANN may be viewed as a sphere of authority.

But ICANN watchers report that these measures are inadequate, and that ICANN does not comply with many of the protocols listed earlier that contribute to open process. ICANN's inward focus shows in other ways. An insider who attended the Melbourne public ICANN meeting in 2001 said the Americans came in and proceeded to argue among themselves, and didn't really listen to statements from other countries.

International access to information about ICANN is through traditional media, but also online resources such as Computerworld.com, Salon.com, and Zdnet.com. Other stakeholder groups include the International Telecommunications Union (ITU), the International Trademark Association (INTA) and the World Intellectual Property Organization (WIPO).[23] Some claim the intellectual property 'maximisers' are gaining ground (Lessig, 1999; Mueller, 1999).

AuDA, the non-profit body that manages the Australian name system, has strong resemblances to ICANN, and important differences.[24] It was also set up under the auspices of the federal government, and has aimed for broad representation and consensus-based policy, with industry and consumer participation. There have similarly been denials that AuDA's staff and Board develop or alter policy.[25]

Just as ICANN could be taken over by the US Department of Commerce, so is AuDA subject to government 'last resort' powers.[26] There have likewise been complaints of AuDA being less than open, although much of the policy is on their web site and there is a discussion mailing list. The engagement process at AuDA has been open and accountable in patches, limited most likely by resource constraints. However, there have also been gaps in the policy process, which has not been fully evaluated or revised. Nearly a year passed between the first policy proposals that came out of advisory panels and their announcement as complete. During that time there was not another iteration with auDA's members, former panel members and other stakeholders, and vague or inadequate parts of the policy were instead ironed out by AuDA staff, lawyers or the Board.

There have been calls for clearer separation of AuDA's role as regulator of policy from its position as developer of policy, which its constitution says will be through advisory panels. Some have called for better procedures to provide full transparency of process, and ensure that unwarranted and unintended policy interpretations do not seep in after the policy panels have recommended them. Those associated with AuDA believe the domain name eligibility and allocation regime in Australia works fairly well for consumers and for consumers and industry alike. However, there are concerns that

AuDA staff and board have become less responsive to their stakeholders, that ad-hoc public meetings can easily result in over-representation by vested interests, and that the inter-dependencies between AuDA as industry regulator and those who supply its income, namely registrars and resellers of domain names, could become too cosy.

Even less than ICANN, AuDa is clearly not resourced to provide a public information role. The AuDA site offers little information about what the domain name space is, or links to other organisations that might explain, although there is a link to ICANN. It does not even use the word Internet on its home page, or discuss the importance of the name system. The documents on the web site are operational, rather than educational. The information is not layered, but is presented clearly enough for a specialist audience, such as registrars. AuDA did not budget or provide funding for placement of notices in newspapers informing the public that Panel discussion papers and policy papers were available for public comment. It has been left to other groups, including those with a stake such as registrars and the range of online and other media to present, interpret, summarise and disseminate this information. This means that opportunities for broader community involvement in the policy issues have been at a level of technical and legal detail that precludes most social groups beyond the industry and several very active NGOs and semi-academic networks.[27] The conversation, and sphere of its authority, is largely limited to a relatively elite group that is professionally engaged with the issues.

While the AuDA site says they will manage in the public interest, the public ramifications of domain name policy are not spelled out. The policy perspective AuDA offers is consistent with the neoliberal values that have increasingly dominated Australian (and American) politics for at least two decades: a for-profit model that is based in contractual arrangements, the promotion of competition, and industry self-regulation. The management model is hierarchical and instrumental, revealing a bureaucratic influence, rather than reflexive and networked.

There are also important differences between ICANN and AuDA.[28] While AuDA has a clear constitution, ICANN just has articles of incorporation. The entire AuDA Board is elected by members, whereas while some of ICANN's are appointed by their three supporting organisations. And there is perhaps a strong countervailing influence in the Australian Competition and Consumer Commission (the ACCC), which seems to willing to challenge the assertion that trade mark holders have superior IP rights in domain name system.

Australians interested in domain name issues have access to all the international online resources. In addition, information and discussion about AuDA is available through several mailing lists: AuDA's own publicly open list, the IAMEMS managed by ISOC-AU, and the LINK list, managed by Tony Barry.

Analysis

The above stories of ICANN and AuDA illustrate that problems of governance can repeat at every relevant scale. Given a certain harmony in the values in each group's administrative arm, it is possible to see them as fractal attractors that could be modelled mathematically. As an attempt at global governance, ICANN is flawed, but instructive. Espousing bottom up consensus comes with obligations to build the civic underpinnings that enable it. Failure to do this hampers the potential of participation to shift the outcomes towards the broader public good. Kang (2001) observed that the inadequacy of the public sphere limited Asian participation in the ICANN at large process. Without adequate resources, AuDA may also be unable to play a broader facilitating and educative role.

A uniform set of consultation and feedback mechanisms might benefit all levels, but also require reflective engagement. Once in place, they require procedures for monitoring to continue the feedback loops. Thus, with AuDA, the ability to comment on the process is available, but without formal obligations to discuss and review, this becomes a task for bolder individuals. AuDA's legitimacy may be weakened over time if there is no provision or capacity for wider public engagement.

The ICANN situation is not unique, as similar processes and patterns have been documented in many networks and spheres of authority, including the World Summit on the Information Society mentioned earlier. ICANN has been an experiment on the largest scale, but has tried to impose a bottom up process rather than become facilitator of it. There was great sensitivity to the initial conditions and actors. One can imagine that if ICANN had not had the influence of so many lawyers (including the mysterious Jo Sims), that a different model for its management might have emerged. AuDA is even less symbolic of these supposed bottom-up processes, with a role limited to administration. The struggle over ICANN continues, and its legitimacy and values has become a subject of parody (Kendall, n.d.). Attacks on Internet infrastructure mean it is now caught up in global terrorism.[29] As a sphere of authority, ICANN will find neutrality difficult to achieve.

Even generic democratic protocols require iterative implementation. Effective procedures such as the Request for Comment that helped develop the Internet's technical infrastructure and standards may not readily translate into more politically charged arenas. Further, the RFC process was based on a neo-liberal tradition of public and private sector decision-making and consultation processes (McDowell and Steinberg, 2001). Likewise, AuDA is partly shaped by the assumptions of hierarchical public sector processes that prevail in Canberra.

The Canadian Internet Registration Authority is said to be quite democratic in its workings, and it would be a mistake to assume that all patterns of governance for a particular sphere of authority are the same. Rather, their collective interaction creates the large attractor that envelops domain name management and becomes Internet governance. On this level, the design of the information infrastructure is relevant to a very wide global constituency, including those who are unaware that decisions are being made that could impact more widely. Disengagement, deliberate or incidental, suggests that there is much merit in the suggestion that a balance of elected representative and elite experts might provide a solid basis for democratic governance of the Internet (Weinberg, 2001). With appropriate separation of powers, check and balances and adequate education and democratically determined communication procedures, management of the global electronic commons might yet improve on rough consensus and running code.[30]

CONCLUSIONS — DEMOCRACY AS A SET OF PROTOCOLS

Computer networks have become integral tools for archiving, sharing, modelling and analysing information and decision flows at all levels of governance. It is now possible to digitally audit and map communication flows and networks. The control and management of these flows determines the answers to the core questions of democratic governance at all scales.

A complex systems approach suggests that digital participation is an emerging property of a global system. This paper has attempted to provide a response to the claim that 'almost no theories to assist in studying relationships between, for example, national associations and global nongovernmental organizations' (Ronit, 2001). One researcher of complexity in human systems has concluded that 'to manage the path of continuous readjustments is as important as to choose the goal' (Theys, 1998). The examples provided throughout this paper have sought to demonstrate that at every level of action there is potential to exercise personal sovereignty and direction setting. This is as important for the public administrator as for the citizen/consumer/activist. Governments, however, command collective resources. Ultimately, good government is expensive, bad government is unaffordable.

ENDNOTES

[1]   For United Kingdom case studies, see Monbiot (2000).

[2]   Including the dockworkers' dispute in Australia in 1999-2000.

[3]   Daphne Wysham, co-author of *Enron's Pawns: How Public Institutions Bankrolled Enron's Globalization Game*, quoted by the Institute for Public Accuracy http://www.accuracy.org, July 30, 2002.

[4]   See, for example, the Institute for Public Accuracy http://www.accuracy.org and Fairness & Accuracy In Reporting http://www.fair.org.

[5]   www.charcoalition.forests.org.au.

[6]   A coda to this example: While the charcoal factory was probably not a high profile issue, a by-election in the seat of Wollongong on the New South Wales south coast saw the first Green candidate enter the Australian House of Representatives (there is also a Green Senator). The seat had been held by Labor for 50 years. The state government that had approved the factory is Labor.

[7]   Intelligence Briefing, August 7, 2002, http://www.stratfor.com.

[8]   Beniger, 1986, 25, Margetts, 1996. There is a discussion of this in Geiselhart, 1999.

[9]   Global Reporting Initiative, http://www.globalreporting.org/; a definition of the Triple Bottom Line can be found at http://www.sustainability.com/philosophy/triple-bottom/tbl-intro.asp.

[10]   California Voters' Foundation www.calvoter.org.

[11]   How the Net killed the MAI, forwarded message posted to Link 6/5/98, from an article in The Globe and Mail, also a posting to Community and Civic Network discussion list, March 12, 1998.

[12]   See Civil Society Platform, http://www.geneva2003.org/.

[13]   http://www.hgc.gov.uk/.

[14]   Complexity-Related Application Papers http://www.calresco.org/related.htm.

[15]   This section is an abbreviated version of a longer paper in progress comparing ICANN and AuDa and their mechanisms for public participation.

[16]   History of the Internet http://www.nic.at/english/geschichte.html. Aikens (1997) also provided a brief history of the Internet.

[17]   For an overview of Internet governance, see Clark (2002).

[18]   It was expected that no more than 20,000 would sign up for the at large membership, but more than 160,00 joined (Kleinwachter, 2001).

[19]   Vint Cerf's lofty ode to the community of information sharing is in Hauben and Hauben (1997).

[20]   McGuire, D. (July 23, 2002). ICANN Forefather Wants More Democratic Internet Governance. http://www.washingtonpost.com/wp-dyn/articles/A51142-2002Jul23.html.

[21]   Auerbach, quoted in Weinberg (2001).

[22]   http://www.icann.org/shanghai/.

[23]   See Weinberg (2001).

[24]   This analysis is based on personal communications and local research with some of the parties involved in AUDA.

[25]   Chris Disspain, AuDA's CEO (November 2001). www.AuDA.org.au/list/dns/archive/112001/0069.html.

[26]   There are reserve powers of the Australian Communications Authority under telecommunications legislation.

[27]   These include the Internet Society of Australia, the Small Enterprise Telecommunication Enterprise Limited, the Australian Consumers' Association, the Consumers' Telecommunication Network, Australian Telecommunications Users Group (ATUG) and the Communications Law Centre.

[28]   The agreement governing the relationship between ICANN, AuDA and the Australian Government is at www.icann.org/cctlds/au/sponsorship-agmt-25oct01.htm.

[29]   Internet Attack Probed, Seen Hard to Trace, by Elinor Mills Abreu Reuters.com, October 23, 2002.

[30]   David Clark's quote about the IETF standard setting process, quoted in Lindsay (2001), 'We reject kings, presidents and voting. We believe in rough consensus and running code.'

REFERENCES

Aikens, G. S. (1997). *American Democracy and Computer-Mediated Communication: A Case Study in Minnesota*. PhD thesis, Cambridge University. Available at: http://aikens.org/phd.

Becker, T. & Slayton, C. D. (2000). *The Future of Teledemocracy*. Westport: Praeger.

Beniger, J.R. (1986). *The Control Revolution - Technological and Economic Origins of the Information Society*. Cambridge, MA: Harvard University Press.

Biggs, M. (2001). Fractal Waves: Strikes as Forest Fires. Sociology Working Papers, (November 2001). Available at: http://www.sociology.ox.ac.uk/swps/2001-04.html.

Bimber, B. (2000). The Study of Information Technology and Civic Engagement. *Political Communication, 17*, 329-333.

Bossomaier, T. & Green, D. (1998). *Patterns in the Sand: Computers, Complexity and Life*. Sydney, Australia: Allen Unwin.

Bronckers, M. C. E. J. (2001). More power to the WTO? *Journal of International Economic Law, 4*(1), 41-65.

Capra, F. (1996). *The Web of Life: A New Synthesis of Mind and Matter*. New York: Harper Collins.

Clarke, R. (2002). An Overview of Internet Governance. Available at: http://www.anu.edu.au/people/Roger.Clarke/II/Governance.html.

Cleaver, H. (1996). The Zapatistas and the Electronic Fabric of Struggle. *Internet Society Conference: Transforming Society Now*. Montreal, Canada. (June).

Coleman, S. & Gotze, J. (2000). *Bowling Together: Online Public Engagement in Policy Deliberation*. Available at: http://bowlingtogether.net/about.html.

Curtin, G., McConnachie, R., Sommer, M. & Vis-Sommer, V. (2002). American E-Government at the Crossroads: A National Study of Major City Uses. *Journal of Political Marketing, 1*(1).

Dahl, R.A. (1989). *Democracy and its Critics*. New Haven and London: Yale University Press.

Dahlberg, L. (2002). Democratic Visions, Commercial Realities? The Corporate Domination of Cyberspace and the Prospects for Online Deliberation. In *Antepodium*, (April). Available at: http://www.vuw.ac.nz/atp/articles/Dahlberg_0204.html.

Dillon, M., & Reid, J. (2000). Global Governance, Liberal Peace, and Complex Emergency. *Alternatives — Social Transformation and Humane Governance, 25*(1), 117-143.

Earnest, D. (2001). *Will No One Rid Me of This Meddlesome State? Social Inequality and the New Social Contract*. Paper prepared for delivery at the 42nd Annual Convention of the International Studies Association, Chicago, IL (February 20-24). (Author's draft).

Etzioni, A. (2001). Beyond Transnational Governance. *International Journal, 56*(4), 595-610.

Friedman, T. (2000). *The Lexus and the Olive Tree*. New York: Anchor Books.

Garreau, J. (2001). Flocking Together Through the Web: Bird Watchers may be a Harbinger of a True Global Consciousness. *The Washington Post*, (May 9).

Geiselhart, K. (1999). *Does Democracy Scale? A Fractal Model for the Role of Interactive Technologies in Democratic Policy Processes*. PhD thesis, University of Canberra, Australia. Available at: http://www.bf.rmit.edu.au/kgeiselhart.

Geiselhart, K. (2002). Charcoal Factory a Black Mark on Information Policy. *Canberra Times*, (February 24).

Gualtieri, R. (1998). *Impact of the Emerging Information Society on the Policy Development Process and Democratic Quality*. OECD Public Management Service. Available at: http://www.oecd.org/puma/gvrnance/it/itreform.htm.

Hauben, M. & Hauben, R. (1997). *Netizens — On the History and Impact of Usenet and the Internet*. Los Alamitos, CA: IEEE Computer Society Press.

Hermida, A. (2002). Web Gives a Voice to Iranian Women. Available at: http://news.bbc.co.uk/hi/english/sci/tech/newsid_2044000/2044802.stm.

Hertz, N. (2001). *The Silent Takeover: Global Capitalism and the Death of Democracy*. London: Heinemann.

Kang, M. (2001). Beyond Underdevelopment of the Public Sphere: Democratizing Internet Governance in Asia. *Info — The Journal of Policy, Regulation and Strategy for Telecommunications, 3*(4), 348-358.

Kendall, D. (n.d.). *ICANN Animation*. Available at: www.paradigm.nu/icann.

Kiel, D. (1994). *Managing Chaos and Complexity in Government*. San Francisco, CA: Jossey-Bass.

Kleinwachter, W. (2001). The Silent Subversive: ICANN and the New Global Governance. *Info — The Journal of Policy, Regulation and Strategy for Telecommunications, 3*(4), 259-287.

Lee, K., & Dodgson, R. (2000). Globalization and Cholera: Implications for Global Governance. *Global Governance, 6*(2), 213-236.

Lessig, L. (1999). *Code and other Laws of Cyberspace.* New York: Basic Books.

Lindsay, D. (2001). *Should we Believe in Rough Consensus? ICANN and the Problem of Legitimacy in Managing the Domain Name System (DNS).* Paper presented at the Communications Research Forum, Canberra, Australia (26-27 September).

Lyon, D. (1988). *The Information Society — Issues and Illusions.* Cambridge: Polity Press.

Margetts, H. (1996). The Implications for Democracy of Computerisation in Government. In P. Hirst and S. Khilnani (Eds.), *Reinventing Democracy,* (pp. 70-84). Blackwell Publishers. Oxford and Cambridge, MA: The Political Quarterly Publishing Co.

Martin, H.P. & Schumann, H. (1997). *The Global Trap - Globalisation and the Assault on Democracy and Prosperity.* Patrick Camiller: Translator. Sydney, Australia: Pluto Press.

McChesney, R. (1999) *Rich Media Poor Democracy.* Urbana: University of Illinois Press.

McDowell, S. D., & Steinberg, P. E. (2001). Non-State Governance and the Internet: Civil Society and the ICANN. *Info — The Journal of Policy, Regulation and Strategy for Telecommunications, 3*(4), 279-298.

McGuire, D. (2002). ICANN Forefather wants more Democratic Internet Governance. *Washington Post* (July 23).

Meikle, G. (2002). *Future Active: Media Activism and the Internet.* Sydney, Australia: Pluto Press.

Meyer, W. H. & Stefanova, B. (2001). Human Rights, the UN Global Compact, and Global Governance. *International Law Journal, 34*(3), 501 (21p).

Monbiot, G. (2000). *Captive State: The Corporate Takeover of Britain.* London: Pan Books.

Mueller, M. (1999). ICANN and Internet Governance: Sorting through the Debris of 'Self-Regulation.' *Info — The Journal of Policy, Regulation and Strategy for Telecommunications, 1*(6), 497-520.

Murphy, C. N. (2000). Global Governance: Poorly Done and Poorly Understood. *International Affairs, 76*(4), 789(15).

Musso, J., Weare, C. & Hale, M. (2000). Designing Web Technologies for Local Governance Reform: Good Management or Good Democracy? *Political Communication,* 17, 1-19.

O'Connor, F. (1995). *Doing Small Business on the Information Super Highway or How to go Offshore for Less than $10,000.* Unpublished, Australian Taxation Office, Moonee Ponds CATA Team.

Picciotto, S. (2000). Liberalization and Democratization: The Forum and the Hearth in the Era of Cosmopolitan Post-Industrial Capitalism. *Law and Contemporary Problems*, (Autumn)*63* I(4)157.

Richard, E. (2000). Lessons from the Network Model of Online Engagement of Citizens. Paper presented to LENTIC colloquium, Brussels. Canadian Policy Research Networks. Available at:www.cprn.org.

Ronfeldt, D. & Arquilla, J. (2001). Networks, Netwars and the Fight for the Future. *First Monday, 6*(10). Available at: http://www.firstmonday.org/issues/issue6_10/ronfeldt/index.html.

Ronit, K. (2001). Institutions of Private Authority in Global Governance: Linking Territorial Forms of Self Regulation. *Administration & Society, 33*(5), 555-578.

Rosenau, J. (n.d.) Order and Disorder. Paper sent to author.

Rosenau, J. (1990). *Turbulence in World Politics: A Theory of Change and Continuity.*
Princeton, MA: Princeton University Press.

Rosenau, J. (1997). *Along the Domestic-Foreign Frontier: Exploring Governance in a
Turbulent World.* Cambridge, UK: Cambridge University Press.

Rosenau, J. (2002). The Complexities and Contradictions of Globalization. Article sent
to author.

Shenk, D. (1997). *Data Smog: Surviving the Information Glut.* London: Abacus.

Stacey, R. (1996). *Strategic Management and Organisational Dynamics.* (2nd ed.).
London: Pitman.

Stocker, R., Green, D. & Newth, D. (2001). Consensus and Cohesion in Simulated Social
Networks. *Journal of Artificial Societies and Social Simulation,* 4(4). Available
at: http://jasss.soc.surrey.ac.uk/4/4/5.html.

Theys, M. (1998). The New Challenges of Management in a Wired World. *European
Journal of Operational Research, 109*(2), 248-263.

Thomas, C. (2001). Global Governance, Development and Human Security: Exploring the
Links. *Third World Quarterly, 22*(2), 159-175.

Turner, B. S. (2001). Risks, Rights and Regulation: An Overview. *Health, Risk & Society,
3*(1), 9-18.

Uncapher, W. (2001). Boundary Politics: Scale, Networks and Cyberspace Research,
Association of Internet Researchers . Minneapolis, MN.

Warschauer, M. (2002). Reconceptualizing the Digital Divide. *First Monday,* 7(7).
Available at: http://www.firstmonday.org/issues/issue7_7/warschauer/index.html.

Weinberg, J. (2001). Geeks and Greeks. *Info — The Journal of Policy, Regulation and
Strategy for Telecommunications, 3*(4), 313-332.

Wray, S. (1998). *Electronic Civil Disobedience and the World Wide Web of Hacktivism:
A Mapping of Extraparliamentarian Direct Action Net Politics.* Paper presented
at The World Wide Web and Contemporary Cultural Theory Conference, (November), Drake University.

Zolo, D. (1992). *Democracy and Complexity* (David McKie, Trans.). University Park, PA:
Pennsylvania State University Press.

Chapter XXII

The Future of
Digital Government

Christopher Corbett
University of Victoria, Canada

ABSTRACT

This chapter explores the challenges that we will collectively face as we make choices about the use and implementation of enabling technology for e-government. "The construction of informed government policy that protects citizens' freedoms while accomplishing the critical work of a professional civil service within a democratic government," will be the central theme of public administration in the next decade. This chapter focuses on the target date 2012.

"Advanced applications of information technology in government are well-integrated combinations of policy goals, organizational processes, information content, and technology tools that work together to achieve public goals." (Dawes, Bloniarz, Kelly and Fletcher, 1999)

DIGITAL GOVERNMENT —
WHERE ARE WE?

In February 2002, the White House released the President's E-Government Strategy (U.S. Government, 2002). The document noted that in 2002, the United States' government spending on information technology was 48 billion dollars. This spending would increase by more than eight percent to 52 billion dollars in 2003. There can be no dispute that the United States Government is taking digital government seriously. If this spending trend by government were to continue, the expenditures in 2012 would be approximately 106 billion dollars!

However, in terms of prioritizing digital government, the United States Government is not unique. Around the world, significant resources are being devoted to digital government, aiming toward similar goals. These goals have been articulated in the "White House E-Government Strategy" document. Primary goals are to:

- Make it easy for citizens to obtain service and interact with the federal government;
- Improve government efficiency and effectiveness; and
- Improve government's response to citizens.

To implement these goals, managers must take into account six critical factors that form the backbone of e-government strategic planning.

Factor One: Moore's Law

Moore (1965) speculated that the speed of microprocessors would continue to double every two years, while the price remained the same. Nearly four decades later the trend continues, perhaps because Moore's law is in part self-fulfilling in that it tends to set expectation within the microprocessor industry and among consumers.

Significance: The lowering cost of computational power and memory is a significant factor shaping the future because it leads to the pervasiveness of computing devices. Further, the increasing capacity of desktop computing will increase the processing capability of professional groups and organizations toward whom e-government is directed. However, the combination of these two factors will not have an impact on the digital divide if government e-service providers do not ensure that their citizen-focused information and service sites are consistently accessible to citizens using very basic (often older) equipment with minimal bandwidth.

Factor Two: Metcalf's Law and Kelly's Extension

Metcalf's Law states that the usefulness of a network increases exponentially with the number of users. At the time Metcalf made his observation he was considering proprietary organizational and inter-organizational networks. Kelly's (1999) extension extends Metcalf's Law by holding that the value of the Internet increases to the power of the number of users.

Significance: Metcalf and Kelly emphasized the impact of changes that come with an increase in the number of participants on a network, particularly the impact on work functions. Metcalf's law is related to the e-government concept of universal service, lessening and eventually eliminating the need for agencies to maintain expensive paper processes in parallel to e-processes. As computer networks have shifted from a proprietary network standard to an open standard like TCP/IP, it has been increasingly possible to envision the sort of e-government portals which cross agency lines and even unite similar functions across levels of government or even internationally.

Reflecting Moore's and Metcalf's laws, the growth of participation on the Internet has made impressive gains just from 1997 to 2002. From a review of a number of the Nielsen-Net Ratings on the NUA website (http://www.nua.ie/surveys/about/index.html), it is reasonable to expect the movement of participation on the Internet from 50 to 60 percent of households[1] in 2002 to relative ubiquity by 2012. This represents a growth of approximately 4 percent per year.

Significance: The numbers indicate that Canada and the United States are continuing to aggressively market the value of the Internet to the citizens of their respective countries. Given the social network dimension of the Internet, the change is likely to be more dramatic than was the impact of technology such as the television and VCR. While the recruitment of individuals to the Internet will take time, it is essential to understand that as the volume of users grows, the value to new users grows and hence, the draw will increase. The probable outcome of this is that the needs and uses of the Internet will continue to be developed in new and innovative ways involving social interaction. This in turn will set the context for citizen expectations of e-government — expectations that will not be satisfied with passive civics information servers.

Factor Three: Worldwide Use of the Internet

It is estimated that there were 162,128,493 active domains on the Internet in July 2002 (Internet Software Consortium, 2002). The number of Internet users worldwide has been climbing steadily from 1995 (16 million users) to 2002 (580 million users).

Significance: Utilization to 2002 was weighted heavily to the G7 nations, Scandinavia and the English-speaking countries. It is expected that this weighting will continue for the coming decade. Use of the Internet will reach near-ubiquity on or before 2012 in these countries. Eastern Europe and Russia will be slower to develop but even there, there are significant points of participation. The rate of uptake in the Spanish-speaking world within Central and South America is extremely slow as is participation within Africa. These discrepancies in participation draw lines for an enduring global digital divide.

Factor Four: The Growth of the Use of the Internet by Government

As the number of Internet users grows, the volume of web content also grows. A government organization is no different in the production of digital files. Staff and consultants produce organization-centric materials digitally and now, frequently these pages are posted to the web. This for the first time will reveal to the public the general level of coordination and cooperation that exists between government organizations. It is clear that there are large numbers of disparate government web pages and data resources. In the United States, it was estimated in 2002 that there were over 35 million web pages online at over 22,000 websites (U.S. Government, 2002). This means that the average US government website is comprised almost 1,600 web pages. In this context, the current volume might be considered as 87,500 400-page desk references. Integrating this with other information would suggest that 20,460 (93 percent) provide access to documents and 11,880 (54 percent) have databases.

Overall, 60 percent of government website users say government sites enhanced their relations with at least one level of government. Half of government website users (49 percent) say the Internet has improved the way they interact with the Federal government; 44 percent say it has improved the way they interact with their state government; and 30 percent say the Internet has improved the way they interact with local government (West, 2001).

Significance: The United States has established a commitment to the provision of e-services via the Internet and World Wide Web. The steps taken so far have harvested the easier functions associated with placing pages online. Still relatively, few complete transactions can be executed by clients entirely online. Thus far, government websites do not tend to attract the interest of the majority of web users in the United States. Of those 41 percent of total Internet users that do use a government web page, only 60 percent feel the experience was of benefit when dealing with a Federal, State, or local government topic. No level of government can state that the impact of the government's direct involvement in the Internet has had a positive impact upon more than 15 percent of the U.S. population. These limitations of interest and participation threaten to set constraints on achievement of the goals of e-government.

Factor Five: Privacy, Confidentiality and Security

Concern about privacy and the use of private information is consistent across a majority of the U.S. population (Alan, 2000; Harris Interactive, 1999, 2001; Koontz, 2000). While there is a generalized concern with privacy, it is difficult to identify a pattern in the online behaviors of individuals that clearly demonstrate this concern in specific settings. For example, website visitors wish to have opt-out privacy policies instead of opt-in. However, it is not clear that a sufficient volume of individuals avoid websites with opt-out requirements to change the behavior of organizations on the web.

Nowhere is this lack of concern for privacy requirements more disturbing than on government websites. Koontz (2000) acknowledged that Federal government websites do not meet the basic privacy requirements set down by the FTC Fair information Principle.

> *As of July 2000, all of the 65 websites in our survey collected personal identifying information 3 from their visitors; 85 percent of the sites also posted a privacy notice. A majority of these Federal sites (69 percent) met FTC's criteria for Notice. However, we found that a much smaller number of sites implemented the three remaining principles- Choice (45 percent), Access (17 percent) and Security (23 percent). Few of the Federal sites — 3 percent — implemented elements of all four of FTC's fair information principles. Finally, a small number of sites (22 percent) disclosed that they may allow third- party cookies; 14 percent actually allowed their placement (Koontz, 2000).*

Several key elements associated with privacy must be considered. The first is the extent that individuals should be permitted an "envelope" about themselves, which shields their life event stream from personal comparison against society's norms. Secondly, some would argue that privacy is also required to prevent inappropriate conclusions being drawn based upon a surface level of data analysis..

Finally, the provision of public information may be used to intentionally or unintentionally control the behavior of citizens. Different portions of society regarding the web-based publishing of what is acknowledged to be public information have raised concerns. Several examples of the use of public data that caused citizens to react negatively were in New Hampshire (James, 2000).

Significance: The population has been clear about its concern for privacy; however, government and business have been slow to respond with actions that bring hard or unpleasant consequences for inappropriate use of personal information. While some efforts are being made to develop voluntary privacy agreements and government is working to establish good practices, it is not clear that these measures can keep pace with an increasingly imaginative population of individuals exploiting the Internet. Nor can the measures keep up with a much larger group of service providers who do not have a sufficient understanding of the issues to avoid intentional and unintentional acts which violate privacy. While privacy concerns are not unique to e-government, they tend to be magnified in an e-government context because of the ease of privacy invasion on a routinized, massive basis.

Factor Six: Inexpensive Networked Devices, Mobile Networks and the Plethora of Data

The pervasiveness of computing devices, including mobile devices that can record geographic location, will create "digital track" of the individual as he or she proceeds through their day. Questions of intrusion will take a significant portion of the dialogue as vendors argue, for instance, that advertisements splashed to cell phones offer significant market opportunities that should be protected as part of commercial free speech. Likewise, access to financial information is possible from many electronic devices, from smart cards to ATM machines; these financial transactions now leave an auditable trail. As devices are more networked and databased, the possibilities for both benefit and abuse escalate. Where national databases on individuals were once the subject of controversy if not abhorrence, now they are routinely accepted, particularly in the post-9/11 United States. These trends both increase the potential of what e-government may accomplish through networked databases and also alert civil libertarians to the dangers of a possible surveillance state disguised under the banner of e-government services.

PERSONAL CRYSTAL GAZING

Digital government is the use of computers and the Internet to establish communications and services between government and: individual citizens (for example, voting); special groups (for example, drivers licensing); other government bodies (for example, the FBI); and business (for example, purchasing). These communication relationships are known as: citizen to government, government to citizen, government to government, and government to business, respectively. After considering the trends embodied within the six key factors, the following sections relate the special challenges and findings expected for each service area in the year 2012.

Expectations of Citizen to Government Internet Usage

By 2012, the first wave of Internet provided government to citizen (G to C) "applications/services suites" will have been rolled out to all Federal, State and local governments in the United States and Canada. This timeframe represents the end of the first cycle of uptake of the Internet by the late adopter government organizations. The second and in some cases, third generation of digital government application/service packages will be in the implementation process among early and middle adopting government offices.

G to C initially might be seen to represent the low hanging fruit available for the basic provision via the Internet of services/applications to the public. It will include electronic versions of documents and applications, access to web enabled databases and application, completion and issuance of permit and licenses of all kinds. These will include but not be limited to driving licenses, hunting permits, mining exploration permits, building permits, census taking and applications to vote. These will be available every day of the year and every hour of the day. Given the implementation of an Internet-based system the bricks and mortar costs of operating and maintaining government offices will increasingly come into question. How should government determine the value of providing services to citizens who do not choose to use the Internet? This question will have come to the surface over the years but now with ubiquity reached or nearly reached the question of bricks and mortar will be square on the shoulders of government. The challenge will be to determine the extent that citizens want services, the expectations they have for these services and the probability these services can be provided at the quality level expected and at a price that meets budget requirements while increasing value to government.

Incentives

In general, the business of government is not expected to change because of the digital revolution. However, how the business is done, when it may be transacted, who may participate, and where the transactions occur will all change in the next ten years. The full impact of change will not be known, but our future hand will have been tipped so we may read the cards. The next ten years will reshape citizen, civil service, political and business expectations of government and enable a rigorous testing of our collective vision of democratic freedom and worldwide collaboration. Digital government will test the limits of our concepts of government because the revolution is taking place in a domain where the former constraints of physical objects and geographic space are not the primary design restrictions.

The business of government is confirmed by noting the United Nations list of distinct roles that national governments can play in an information society (2002). These are:

- To deliver government programs and services to the citizens;
- Interact with citizens in support of the democratic process;
- Formulate and sustain policies and regulatory systems; and
- To use information infrastructure to enhance the machinery of government.

What is most appealing about the goals of digital government is the clear desire on the part of the majority of politicians and civil servants is to improve the relationship between the government and its citizens (U.S. Government, 2002). In digital government, this is to be accomplished by providing a consistent and reliable face on government using the Internet and evolving Internet based capabilities. From the public's perspective the use of the Internet is intended to provide a government that is always ready and available to serve the public. From the civil service perspective, digital government offers an opportunity to reinvent government through the reengineering of current business processes.

Complexity

What is not clear is the extent that those leading the reinvention of government towards digital government fully understand the complexity of the interrelationships within and between departments and levels of government. As a system, the government is a family of interlocking relationships, agreements and interpretations held together by higher order democratic concepts, laws and societal norms. While it may seem difficult to believe, this complex system is in a state of equilibrium, changing a system from a current equilibrium state to a new preferred state of equilibrium is extremely challenging. This is not to imply that change is not desirable, or cannot be made. It is intended to identify the significant probability of arriving at an alternative location to the identified preferred state of equilibrium. It is necessary to emphasize the real probability of arriving at a state that is less desirable than the stable position of equilibrium you chose to leave. Once released, the genie cannot be put back in the bottle and consequently, great care is required to understand the issues and carefully chart the course. Government is not a business and failure does not simply redistribute capital and expertise from one group of shareholders so another group of shareholders can try again. When government fails, the same citizen shareholders must shoulder the burdens created by the failure, enduring the service gap while implementing the repairs and financing the "bail-out."

This note of caution is founded upon the belief that government policies and programs direct and redistribute a significant portion of a country's wealth. Thus a small percentage of the population representing the civil service working at the "business of government" have a significant impact upon how 30 to 50 percent of the income of the nation is redistributed (Drucker, 2001). This makes the policy and procedure development and maintenance process of government a singularly important lever in the business and individual lives of the citizens of any country. The digital government initiative offers many opportunities for intentional and/or unintentional alterations in the incentive structure of a nation.

The digital government initiative will present opportunities to influence the policies and procedures through which benefits are distributed. Consequently, the business process reengineering incorporated into the digital government process and intended to provide opportunities to realign the incentives within government for the improvement of government services to the citizens will also receive significant attention from companies, political organizations and lobby groups. It will be the intention of all parties to benefit from the business process reengineering of digital government and this can only be accomplished through a clear understanding of the outcomes from different changes.

Global

To add challenge, the digital government initiative among democratic nations holds its own complications because administrative policies, industrial standards and legal procedures must be examined, developed or enforced before we fully understand the implications of our actions. This brings into conflict variations in public policy, business practice and national law between countries with different traditions supported by alternative, sometimes contradictory, national perspectives. In the case of the planet, the United States is a dominant force and consequently, changes in its incentive structures tend to have consequences outside the United States. Former Canadian Prime Minister Pierre Trudeau characterized the relationship between the United States and Canada as friendly but having the problem of the mouse [Canada] sleeping with the elephant [the United States]. The mouse must react to the slightest twitch of the elephant for fear of being rolled over.

Who Will Critique

There are too few applied researchers working within the intersecting domain of social science, public administration and information science to effectively foreshadow and study the consequences of digital government (Dawes, Bloniarz, Kelly and Fletcher, 1999). The vast majority of information systems have been specified and designed by individuals with a business and technology background. Consequently, they tend to have little understanding of the critical difference between business and government functions. In addition, many in government have little appreciation of technical challenges associated with automating office processes and tend to believe that these things have all been successfully implemented in the private sector. Because something is easy to say does not make it easy to do.

One need only look at the project management literature to see that failure in technology projects averages between 50 to 70 percent (McConnell, 1998; Standish Group, 1994). Industrial pages informing technology buyers (as opposed to site promoting technology vendors) also document the challenges associated with successful implementation of complex information systems. For example, according to Jim Erricson (2001) and Tom Kaneshige (2002) a number of independent technology assessment companies are identifying Client Relationship Management Systems (CRM) failure rate of 55 to 70 percent. They believe that it is a combination of vendors along with the press hyping the potential of technology that miss directs the attention of so many buyers from the true challenges of implementation. Further, it is suggested that the hype is not countered in the media because there is little if any incentive for the vendors, press or failed implementation companies to report the failure accurately.

The consequence of these challenges is to fail to realize that the most significant challenge is the difficulty of articulating and defining the current management or administrative process, not the technology. While the senior management may feel confident that their organizations are working with accurate and coherent data and following procedures and policies as prescribed, they will be shocked to discover the magnitude of the approximations and judgment used in the execution of the average job by the civil service (Corbett, Sherman and Tate, in press).

Government vs. Business Incentives

Finally, in terms of incentives, it is extremely difficult to articulate an objective function that adequately characterizes government in the same way that the profit motive characterizes business. Profit is an easily determined measure. While this may seem to be a fantastic statement in 2002 with government and citizens demanding a renewal of ethical behavior from the corporate sector driven by the outright misrepresentation of financial status by Enron and their accounting firm, Arthur Andersen, it is nonetheless true. What has become clear through the debacle is that public accounting of status must be carried out by organizations that are independent of both the organization being evaluated and their suppliers who share collective and complimentary incentives. Given this level of complication associated with the determination and representation of the "simple" notion of profit as the primary objective function of business, what complications will arise by 2012 when the growing need for policy interoperabilitybetween business and government must incorporate value for money measures of government which include such concepts as freedom, or equality? Then extend this notion to incorporate the global requirements for policy interoperability.

GOVERNMENT TO CITIZEN (G TO C) AND CITIZEN TO GOVERNMENT (C TO G)

Citizen to Government: A Problem with Trust

In 2012, the Internet is ubiquitous in the industrial world. Citizens, directly through their home connection to the Internet or indirectly through an employer, a friend or a public facility, have access to Government information and services online. The population of citizens without easy access still tends to be those who are at the lower end of the socio-economic curve. Meaning that it is much more likely that someone without easy access to the Internet is someone who needs the social services provided by government. The digital divide continues to exist in that there are still individuals who do not have the skills necessary to use a browser and a World Wide Web search engine to find a specific, basic topic of interest or more importantly of benefit to themselves. More important the analogue divide (Corbett and Longo, 2001) (illiteracy and innumeracy) continues to rise in the population. The hope that the Internet and free Internet based educational services would solve these problems has yet to find significant support based upon evidence.

Significant expenditures have been made by governments to provide Internet based services and much progress has been made in providing basic services. Yet, challenges remain in the development and provision of strategies that aid citizens in quickly finding specific government information. While use of the Internet by citizens is common, the use of government services on the Internet is not as common. This gap, which was clear in all early data, in terms of the number of people online versus the number that had visited a government website was never considered to be an indication that government online would not reach a significant portion of the population. While the digital divide was identified and discussed most never considered the analogue divide (Corbett and Longo, 2001) or the notion that citizens would, for reasons of their own, not want to use government services online. I have decided to call this the "Internet Leap of Faith."

The Internet Leap of Faith is the willingness of a user of the Internet to provide information to an entity[2] represented on the Internet. Many individuals who use the Internet are still unwilling to provide personal financial information (their bank card) to make Internet purchases.

The willingness of that person to provide information is based upon their assessment of the risk and possible damages within the context of alternatives and the risks and possible damages resulting from those alternatives. There are different risks and rewards associated with reading a page online, purchasing something online, and providing personal information online. While many would prefer to assume that a citizen would be more likely to provide information to a government site than a private business or individual, this is unclear. It is entirely reasonable that citizens will believe that businesses managing personal data will be responsive to issues of customer trust, while governments managing personal data will not. The public understands the incentive system for business and is likely to trust the incentive system for business. While there are failures of trust in business, it is also clear from the record that Arthur Andersen, as a company, died for failure to meet the obligations associated with public trust. The requirements and incentives for public trust have been well communicated.

However, the incentive system within government is not well understood, or is expected by many to be based upon secret agreements with special interest groups and lobbyists with disbursements of; cash, future considerations, private safety nets or votes made in back rooms (Barnes and Gill, 2000). Arguments have been made that the Internet will only increase the power of the current elites who are sophisticated enough to use the power of the Internet to reinforce their current position and network (Norris, 1999). This refutes the mobilization theory, "more people will become politically active online," and supports the reinforcement theory, "more people will continue to choose what has traditionally interested them." Following the logic of reinforcement theory, we should ask what people will go to the government website. Is it possible that "Government online" is a service that is only valuable to other civil servants? Will the numbers show that the reinvention of government was a rationalization of the government to justify a massive investment in technology and systems but framed within the context of reaching out to citizens when in fact it is clear that citizens did not ask to be reached and in fact would rather be left alone. Are the "hits" registered on government websites? Are those hits intended to imply interest from the citizens and justify further government investment? Alternatively, are they simply indications that government staff is using the Internet instead of an intranet or a book to review government documents?

The work of Putnam (1993) initiates an important discussion of social capital and the need for fundamental levels of trust in order to maintain social cohesion in communities. The level of social cohesion is essential to keep down the costs of transactions among individuals and businesses. As evidenced on its website, (http://www.worldbank.org/poverty/scapital/index.htm) the World Bank has been using the idea of social capital in work intended to harness the power of social relationships within communities.

Government to Citizen: "Enabling the Digital Citizen"

In 2012, the transition from "bricks to clicks" is taking longer than expected. In some cases, this is because the complexity of government is taking much longer to understand than expected. In other cases, it is because government purchased technology without fully understanding the risk of failure. The consequence has been a great deal of failure and sky rocketing costs which jeopardize the business cases which were made to cost justify each digital government project during the effort to raise funding between 2000 and 2005. For example, this clipping from Reuters:

> *SACRAMENTO, Calif. (Reuters) - California Gov. Gray Davis accepted the resignation of one official on Thursday and suspended another in a growing scandal surrounding a $95 million software deal with Oracle Corp. for*

software few state agencies wanted or needed.
The moves came as state troopers were called to secure the shredders and
trash at California's Department of Information Technology.
Oracle renewed an offer to rescind the controversial deal, although, in a
statement, the world's No. 2 software vendor stood by its projection that its
contract would eventually save the state money.
Davis suspended Department of Information Technology Director Elias
Cortez and accepted the resignation of Director of eGovernment Arun
Baheti for their roles in approving the contract that could cost taxpayers
$41 million in wasted spending. (O'Mara, 2002)

These highly publicized projects have lead to a high level of exposure for senior civil servants and politicians who are being asked to explain why their estimates and planning were so poor. In cases where technology projects were public private partnerships (P3s) the corporations involved will also be questioned and the public will suspect that greed, sloth and graft are central to the true story that is hidden from their view.

Consequently, problems of trust are still the primary problem of government and overshadow much of the work carried out. The citizen's trust in government began to decline in the 1960s and continued to drop into single digits in the United States in 1985 (Bok, 1997). Trust remained in the single or near single digits throughout the 1990s and through the first decade of the 21st century. A clear finding by Bok (1997) and supported by a New Zealand Government study (Barnes, 2000) confirmed that the trust of the public in government was not related to the performance of government. This indicates that to change the level of trust of the public in the government is more complicated than reducing a deficit or delivering a project on time and on budget. Further, it is not clear that the Trust proposition is symmetrical, i.e., that government failure to deliver on the deficit or a project may increase the level of distrust in government. To add to the possibility of miscommunication between government and the public, is the fact that significant proportions of the civil service trust the government.

The Front Office

In transforming the provision of service from human civil servant to the Internet, a by-product will be the loss of human contact associated with the transaction from the staff of government. The underlying notion is that citizens will accept the removal of the human contact in exchange for efficiency or effectiveness. This implies that the working model for government in 2012 will be "the automat." A vision of the future of eating[3] in the first half of the 20th century, automats were restaurants where patrons served themselves by selecting items from an array of coin-operated vending machines. The vending machines were the face of the organization that was intended to provide "good food cheap." The cooks, who created the food, worked diligently in kitchens behind the scenes and were nearly invisible to the patrons. In many cases, a server was present within the automat to assist the patrons, maintain the condiments, clean up as required and provide status reports to the kitchens on the inventory within the vending machines.

This author thinks this "clicks and mortar" model of government service delivery, he has called the "GovernMat," will be acceptable in 2012 because there will be significant levels of household and business access to the Internet, which will ensure the vast majority of citizens will connect to government directly through their personal connection to the Internet. Consequently, the GovernMat will be provided to meet the egalitarian requirement to provide Government Internet based services to citizens who are not connected or who for some reason require assistance. Assistance might include: confirmation of identity papers; collection of physical documents produced by government; aid to members on the wrong side of the digital divide; voter registration; and direct user education. GovernMats will be provided to the citizens through Government-to-Government partnerships and through public private partnerships. A single GovernMat office may represent one or more levels of Government. Indeed, given there were approximately 87,504 local government units (U.S. Census Bureau, 1997)[4] in the United States in 2002, it is highly likely that a logical strategy would be to partner with local government offices to provide the services of State and Federal organizations. To benefit by a comparison of availability, worldwide in 2002, there were approximately 30,000 McDonald's Restaurants, where customers could receive fast food.

GovernMats will be much heralded for the savings they provide to Government through the closing down and sale of properties and buildings no longer required to support the direct provision of service to the public. The consolidation of multiple government offices into a single GovernMat office will be identified as a demonstration of the improved efficiency of government. GovernMat offices will become the icon for "fast-government."

Finally, the movement to online services has increased the expectations of the public for prompt service without regard for the problems of government. People using the Internet have high expectations for quality of service and ease of use and will quickly reject a site that does not measure up (Gaudin, 2002).

The Back Office — Magnitude of the Challenge

In 2002, there were 22,000 government offices in the United States with websites displaying 35 million pages (U.S. Government, 2002). For argument's sake, let us say they represented 25 percent of the government offices and 10 percent of the content of government.[5] In 2012, there are 88,000[6] government offices (Federal, State and local) providing 350 million pages of information to the Internet. Remaining consistent with 2002 percentages, 50 percent of these sites will provide access to online databases.

In 1999, there were 20,160,000 government employees in the United States (Bureau of Economic Analysis, 1999). Thus, government composed approximately 15 percent of the U.S. workforce. These civil servants directed Federal outlays of approximately $1,703,000,000,000 and State outlays of $814,000,000,000 resulting in total outlays of $2,517,000,000,000 (Bureau of Economic Analysis, 1999). To place this dollar amount in context, imagine it as approximately the same amount as the revenue of the world's largest 20 company's: Wal-Mart Stores, Exxon Mobil, General Motors, BP, Ford Motor, Enron, DaimlerChrysler, Royal Dutch/Shell Group, General Electric, Toyota Motor, Citigroup, Mitsubishi, Mitsui, ChevronTexaco, Total Fina Elf, Nippon Telegraph & Telephone, Itochu, Allianz, Intl. Business Machines, and ING Group.

If the ratio of 75 civil servants to 1,000 population[7] is stable, then 2012 will see approximately 23 million civil servants[8] working for approximately 304,764,000 United

States citizens.[9] This provides the basis for the communication of approximately 22,857,300 civil servants working in Federal, State and local governments to communicate with the 304,764,000 citizens in the United States. To place this in perspective, the *Fortune* magazine online database[10] lists Wal-Mart, the world's largest company, with 1,269,585 employees, while the total number of employees in the *Fortune* list of the World's 100 Largest Companies total 3,415,895 (*Fortune*, 2001).

The number of pages does not assume that the U.S. will adopt the multilingual policies of most governments in the rest of the world. If this were to happen then, at a minimum, we would expect to see a doubling of the number of pages to provide Spanish language content, since the percentage of the population with Hispanic heritage would equal approximately 15 percent of the total population (U.S. Census Bureau, 2000).

While the authoring of Spanish language content would produce little in the way of additional creative effort, it would be the case that indexing and organizing the information would add a significant level of complexity to the interface of the Internet services provided and the obligations within the GovernMat offices to provide bilingual or multilingual support. In 2012, the proportion of the U.S., population that is Hispanic (15 percent) has eclipsed the proportion of the population that is Black. It is reasonable to believe that this portion of the population will have generated an equally strong voice in the affairs of the country.

Key Requirements for Government to Citizen in 2012

In 2012, there are significant challenges that must be addressed to meet the collective needs of the Internet-connected citizen and the GovernMat offices. These are:

1. *Indexing the "variety of government"*
   - Government structure must be organized and represented in a fashion that will serve the needs of the average citizen. This requires relative stability of the mental model of government and government services so the average citizen can "interface."
   - The author's Digital Government Paradox notes that the information technology of digital government facilitates the adaptation of the organization of government and programs making it more flexible while the broadening of the interface to the public increases the pressure to remain constant. As the burden of understanding the government's programs shifts from a professional civil service to the Internet based documentation provided to the public on the Internet the need for stability in the presentation of information to the public will increase. This is needed to avoid confusion within and between users of the information.

2. *Usability*
   - A broad range of "average" citizens must manipulate the interface to the digital government Internet system using the broadest imaginable range of hardware and software systems.
   - The frustration and errors associated with poor interface design will reduce the usability of digital government thereby significantly increasing the cost of operations increasing dissatisfaction, reducing the willingness of users to use the digital government interface and increasing the need for more service personnel.

3. *Flexibility*

    • The ongoing changes which result from government business process reengineering (BPR), supply chain management (SCM), enterprise resource planning (ERP) and developing a knowledge management system (KMS) for various levels of government is going to induce dramatic levels of change which increase the problems of maintaining a stable citizen interface. An example from government would be this from Information and Regulatory Affairs, "In the last six months, OMB has cleared 41 significant federal regulations aimed at responding to the terrorist attacks of September 11th. These rules address urgent matters such as homeland security, immigration control, airline safety, and assistance to businesses harmed by the resulting economic disaster experienced in several regions of the country (Graham, 2002)."

4. *Security and privacy*

    • Intentional release of information and unintentional release of information will require new significant levels of investment in order to contain the challenges presented by personnel. Security and privacy will be a much greater burden than expected.

    • It will be "obvious" to government employees to save money by combining databases into increasingly broad profiles of citizens.

    • The fact that civil servants trust themselves is a significant barrier to creating high quality security and privacy systems.

    • The fact that there is little consequence associated with Government errors when compared to Private sector errors increases the risk of greater damage coming from breaches in government controlled information systems.

5. *Support*

    • There must be someplace for the average e-citizen who cannot perform using the government's systems to go to get help and support on an alternative basis.

    • There must be trained individuals capable of supporting government in the use of the systems being built.

    • The complexity of the new systems and the speed in which they operate will increase the difficulty in bringing a new person in and training them.

6. *Experience*

    • Given the broad demand for the development of digital government systems, there is sure to be a poverty of experienced professionals to work through the problems and to design and manage the projects.

    • Key challenges will be associated with a failure to understand and consequently, manage the risks and uncertainties of project management.

    • There is a failure to recognize the significant complexity involved and the lack of "business of government" knowledge of most technical people. This results in the use of business models as equivalents for government models.

7. *Training*

    • There will be significant, ongoing training associated with the civil service staff required to be able to assist the citizens with private and business questions associated with government online.

8. *Storage of old websites*
   • For legal reasons, the government kept copies of documents stored in an archive. To what extent must the government maintain copies of earlier versions of its websites?
   • What strategies have been developed to synchronize these earlier versions with other key linked sites?
9. *Sustainability*
   • It is entirely possible that the ongoing maintenance costs of the new digital government system will equal or exceed the costs of operating the former system.
   • Organizations that assume future savings will pay for the investment in digital government have not been reading the broad technical literature.
10. *Increased stress within the civil service*
    • While stress was a major concern in 2002 (Daniels, 2002), in 2012, the stress in the backroom of government has increased due to the constant public surveillance permitted by the transparency of government processes explained and documented online. E-mail attacks have become commonplace.
    • The position in hierarchy for most government managers and the increase in the number of individuals watching their work may increase the stress on workers in the ranks of the civil service. The transparency of the Internet may create increased pressure due to (what the author calls) "the surveillance effect." High pressure comes from having instructions, policies and procedures under permanent scrutiny by citizens, interest groups, politicians and companies interested in "optimal interpretations" of government rules and regulations (Marmot, Shipley & Rose, 1984; Clarke, Breeze, Sherlicker et al., 1998; Clarke, Shipley, Lewington et al., 1999).[11]
11. *Government is not business*
    • There is a needed trend on the radar screen at this time that would direct our attention to the fundamental differences between government and business. The assumption that business models can and should be used for the development of digital government is misdirecting our attention from those variables and consequences which are not measured by business models yet provide the substantive benefits of government. The notion that performance cannot improve except where there is measurement would suggest that an unintended consequence of the use of business models by government is the erosion of the basic rights and benefits provided to the citizens who are most needy and deserve a disproportionate share of government assistance.
    • While it is fair to say that many aspects of government could be well served by taking a more business like approach, many projects for government have failed to succeed simply because traditional business objective functions like profit could not be used to focus the efforts of government service providers. Cost savings could be used to provide some guidance, but increasingly it became difficult to balance the justification to cut each most costly client from the service until the cost met the budget available.
    • The founding fathers were concerned with the notion of inclusiveness, participation and the obligation of government to provide access for all citizens. Consequently, the precision available to business is to accept that some people

would like the service, but for whatever reason choose not to purchase. This clean opportunity to force choice is not available to government, so additional costs must often be incurred to ensure inclusiveness and the basic obligation of service to every citizen.

GOVERNMENT TO BUSINESS RELATIONS (G TO B): DOING BUSINESS WITH GOVERNMENT

The subject of Government to Business (G to B) seems to offer a greater opportunity for savings and government improvements (Cairncross, 2001). Business transactions between different parties on the Internet have shown a growing trend during the late 1990s and early 2000s. A significant volume of the Internet transactions will continue to be Business to Business (B to B) transactions. These have been successful because all parties in the B to B family of transactions have a clear purpose of making improvements to productivity that can be demonstrated on the bottom line. It is reasonable to assume that a logical offshoot of the B to B technical infrastructure will be the B to G purchasing infrastructure. These relationships may be coordinated in a variety of ways but for our purposes be considered to fall within three basic categories. The first is the automating of transactions between current buying and selling parties already doing business. The second is through an intermediary working to provide a "seller's" portal. The third is through an intermediary working to establish a "buyer's" portal (Wyld, 2001).

In 2012, different levels of Federal, State and local governments will have combined their purchasing power. In addition, they will have used the Internet to enhance their monopsonistic power to bring down the cost of purchasing goods and services consumed by government. Producers of goods and services will be working to collectively negotiate vendor industry monopolies/oligopolies because vendors will discover they need to produce vending monopolies to protect their profitability. This will lead to American versions of Japanese Keiretsu.

Within the context of a government's purchase of services and products it will become increasingly easy for Freedom of Information legislation to provide citizens and citizen groups access to the business practices of government. This will include the extent that civil servants and other government officials follow the policies and procedures required. The increase in the openness (transparency) of government will both increase the professionalism of civil servants but will also move some government programs to higher levels of government decision making to ensure civil servants continue to have control. Alternatively, confidential work will be downloaded to contractors of government enterprises specifically designed to carryout activities within a context of secrecy and without the need to comply with government rules. Signals of this strategy are being evidenced in early 2000 with the creation of non-governmental organizations which carry-out the work of government but are not required to meet the same obligations and transparency of government.

GOVERNMENT TO GOVERNMENT RELATIONS (G TO G): THE DIGITAL WORLD

Federal, State and Local Government

The use of G to G will most certainly be of interest between Federal, State and local governments. In most circumstances, the benefits available are similar to the B to B transactions, relating the reduction in the costs of transactions between the parties and an increase in the clarification of responsibilities in order to reduce redundancy. However, there are additional benefits to government in that cooperative use of data and information collection systems may reduce the number of disparate data systems within Federal State and Local information systems.

The increasingly collaborative nature of relationships between agencies will increase the need to restructure government to better take advantage of the opportunity. In Britain, this is known as "joined-up thinking," the use of the opportunity to restructure to flatten organizations and reduce redundancy of activities within government (Cairncross, 2001). However, joined up thinking has also surfaced turf wars within Government which are similar to those which take place in the private sector.

The movement of data for government purposes must be questioned from the perspective of fair use and the obligation of government organizations to state clearly at the initiation of a transaction, how the data will be used and shared. In these situations, the challenge for each level of government is to determine, in concert with the population, what happens when a citizen refuses to agree to information sharing beyond the explicit purpose of the primary government transaction. To what extent should the government be allowed to use its monopoly power to force or coerce its clients to agree to the release of data? To what extent can the desire to reduce the costs of providing services be accepted as sufficient justification for the breach of individual confidentiality?

In 2012, the debates will have become heated between the levels of government, special interest groups and citizens in the allocation of blame associated with failures to achieve productivity improvements (cost savings) for government. A key focus of these arguments will be that savings are not possible because some level of government will not comply with a cost saving sharing of information. In the hard politics that will be associated with the negotiation between levels of government, some concern should exist for the lower level of government in each negotiation. This is because the higher level of government, in many cases, holds additional bargaining power that may leave the outcome associated with negotiation a foregone conclusion. The logical flow of costs will move from Federal to State to local and finally to the citizen.

International

In 2002, the growing use of the Internet suggests that most of the industrial world has made preliminary investments in digital government by providing basic information services to citizens via the Internet. It is clear there is an interest in providing an ongoing investment in using the Internet for improving relations with the citizens within a country and in producing productivity gains or savings for government through business process reengineering.

However, in 2012, on a worldwide basis, the pressures of digital government more likely fall within the context of a nation's global competitive advantage, which includes issues of bargaining power and comparative efficiency (Bakos and Treacy, 1986). For example, the arguments will be variations of those we see developing between Europe and the United States in terms of privacy in 1998 to 2002 (Davies, 1998). In these cases, European countries have demanded a higher level of privacy assurance by companies working in Europe than are demanded by the U.S. of it own companies. In these cases, Europe may use these privacy regulations to limit the business of U.S.-based firms wishing to transfer data to and from European operations to the United States for business purposes. The situation demonstrates that the regulation of digital government may be used to shape trade policy and agreements.

IMPROVED PRODUCTIVITY AND SAVINGS TO GOVERNMENT FROM DIGITAL GOVERNMENT INITIATIVES

In 2002, a critical assumption that government has made is that digital government will provide savings through improvements in the organization of government and delivery of government services. This is a digital government yields productivity argument. This requires an accounting system that tracks costs associated with specific government activities and that is capable of making detailed cost comparisons. These audit systems and rules that are necessary to maintain them will be in place by 2012. This will be a consequence of the increasing openness of government through the Internet.

Many organizations characterize savings as costs that have been moved off their bottom line. In other words, an improvement in efficiency within the organization would be seen in the same light as finding a newer lower cost supplier. Both events may cut production costs and consequently, both are equally good from the organization's perspective. Digital government is expected to generate savings for the Government. These must be examined carefully to ensure that the savings identified by government are not simply the movement of government costs to other government departments, other levels of government or the citizenry. For example, an online form that is printed by the citizen at home, completed as a hard copy, then mailed to the appropriate government office is a transfer of paper and printing costs from government to the citizen. This author does not suggest that the citizen is unwilling to take on this cost in exchange for personal efficiency. It is simply important to note that savings, which accrue to government because of digital government, must be watched carefully to ensure that savings are not the result of shifts of cost within the value chain. This would be the case if savings in digital government were demonstrated by looking at narrow cost centers and not the actual full activity cost of a specific service. Activity cost would include all the costs in the provision of a service to a citizen.

The cost of maintaining a working knowledge is often not included in the cost of providing web-based services. It is the effort expended by the client in executing search strategies/behaviors in order to find a target document or form. This represents the shift in the need for knowledge from the civil servant who used to provide the service efficiently by having specialized training about the government and its policies and procedures to the citizen. The management of this cost will be extremely difficult and require the creation of a useful government Internet indexing strategy that can be used by citizens who have a variety of mental models about how the information of government might be organized.

In 2012, there will be a new, professional group of consultants and not-for-profit organizations that help citizens find what they want or need to do with government. The new consultants are a result of: not addressing the digital divide; transferring the costs of understanding government to the citizen via the Internet, and increasing instead of decreasing the complexity of government. For those on the right side of the digital divide, the world will be a better place.

SUMMATION ABOUT THE FUTURE

In this summary for the chapter, it seems best to highlight the most interesting research questions that lay before us. These research topics will best be framed as a series of paradoxes. This author hopes these cause good questions to be asked and answered.

Paradox One: Democratization Paradox — Transparency May Not Be Democratizing But Lead to Elitism

The increasing volume of government data, procedure and policy made available to the public increases the significance of the effort to understand them. Competency will require individuals to understand the implications of changes made to procedures and policies and will require ongoing investment in the knowledge of the domain and interrelationships. For example, tax regulations began as a family of policies and procedures requiring individuals and organizations to pay taxes to the government. As time passed, the dialogue between the government and taxpayers required the development of an ever-increasing body of detail refining the language, clarifying special cases and interpreting intent. What was initially intended to be a communication between government and the population has become an arcane body of knowledge that is only understood by a small group of specialists. These specialists have become an elite group of optimizers for citizens and business but due to their costs have excluded the vast majority of citizens from the discussion of policies and procedures. This trend is continuing with privacy, security and management information systems in general.

- *Synopsis* — The democratization of government information may require the creation of new elites to maintain intellectual mastery of the data, procedures and policies. Therefore, the increasing volume of detail about dealing with the government will require significant intellectual (personal time) or financial (consultants' time) investment on the part of the citizen. In either case, an elite will be born.

Paradox Two: Integrity Paradox — Openness May Lead to the Loss of Judgment

The availability of data, policies and procedures will increase the number of observers who may measure the performance of the civil servant's work by comparison with the written specification of the policy or procedure. This will increase the pressure on civil servants to follow "to the letter" the policies and procedures, whether or not the outcome of following "to the letter" will result in an outcome that is consistent with their understanding of the original intent of the policy or procedure. The focus of this paradox is that the openness of the process will reduce the willingness of the individual civil servant to use their judgment to adjust "the system" to allow exceptions they believe are consistent with the original intent of the policy, procedure, or regulation. A logical consequence of this will be an upward ratcheting of the stress on the civil servant, correlating with the increase in complaints from the public. Increased levels of scrutiny will be associated with: increased fear of deviation; surface conformity and procedural compliance in disregard of intent; and increased levels of measurement dysfunction.

- *Synopsis* —To the average citizen, the increasing openness of government should be correlated with an increasing willingness on the part of government civil servants to discuss the policies and procedures and to be "reasonable" in their interpretation. However, the increase transparency is more likely to reduce the desire of civil servants to risk reprimand by applying judgment.

Paradox Three: Internet Paradox — Social Technology Reduces Social Involvement

There is an ongoing concern that the Internet may reduce social involvement and psychological well being (Kraut, Lundmark, Patterson, Kiesler, Mukopadhyay and Scherlis, 1998). This suggests that individual users of the Internet are more likely to be depressed and withdrawn from social contact within their household and community because of the time they invest on the Internet. Initial indications were that users tended to find themselves socially isolated as a consequence of Internet usage (Kraut et al., 1998) however more recent studies have found that there appears to have been some adaptation in behaviors which more reasonably suggest that people are just like themselves on the Internet (Murray, 2002).

- *Synopsis* — The use of the Internet may cause individuals to exchange their involvement from local physical communities to virtual communities. It is not clear where this results in a net gain or loss of social capital. The possibility of individuals using the Internet to withdraw from the physical community to participate in socially less accepted practices (based upon the community's standards) are increasing.

Paradox Four: The Productivity Paradox

Despite significant efforts to find measures of improved productivity related to information technology there has yet to be any indication of a broad gain. Individual case studies are available to show that there are cases where improved productivity has been created with information technology. However, on the broader basis of an industry wide productivity gain there is no evidence that productivity will be the result of investment. There are several ways this might be explained.

- *Synopsis* — The promised increase in productivity associated with information technology is often promised but not delivered. This suggests that something is wrong with how we choose, implement or measure the impact of information technology.

CONCLUSION

The pathway we will follow in the development of digital government is of course unknown. While key characteristics of the future are clear, the weight of influence from each is uncertain. While we understand that society will evolve, fundamental human characteristics will be slow if not impossible to shift. Many of the issues are associated with the availability of data in electronic form. Issues will include: the storage of increasing volumes of data, the management of the data, the utilization of the data to answer questions that we have today, as well as the architecture of the data in order to answer questions we generate in the future. Attitudes about the worth of data in the office place will be difficult to shift. New rules are being implemented for employees that are handling the same data in a new way. To what extent shall these changes to digitize systems require the reinvention of government business processes.

Humans are curious and individuals will work diligently to exploit digital government in new and novel ways. Identity theft and invention are simple examples. These fringe activities will be the source of significant cost to the systems being implemented. Foreshadowing the problems associated with poor regulation and enforcement we can see that rules makers in government tend to believe that written rules can adequately control human behavior. That is to say, many managers and administrators fail to see the difference between natural laws that are self-enforcing, for example, gravity, and human regulations that do require enforcement, for example, speeding. A casual observer need only look to the Enron Corporation and Arthur Andersen accounting debacle of 2002, or the Florida "dangling chad" debates in the 2000 Presidential Election to identify the limitless capacity of human beings to "make distinctions" depending upon their personal motivation. In addition, there are unforeseen events that exert great influence. September 11, 2001 stands out as a milestone. How the world will change as it comes to grip with the practical reality of terrorism is uncertain but we know it has changed many perspectives and practices.

It is our good fortune to be uncertain. For these issues provide our opportunity to shape the future and to continue the difficult process of bringing together public policy, social science and information technology.

ENDNOTES

[1]   The current percentage estimates are from the Nielsen-Net Ratings. Internet universe is defined as all members (two years of age or older) of U.S. households, which currently have access to the Internet.

[2]   Entity is used here in the accounting context and would include a person or an organization including for profit, not for profit or government.

[3]   Automats were in operation from the early 1900s to the late 1960s. (See http://www.theautomat.com/inside/history/history.html.)

[4]   1997 Census of Governments, Volume 1, *Government Organization*. U.S. Department of Commerce Economics and Statistics Administration, U.S. Census Bureau, 1997.

[5]   This is a simple guess and is not intended to accurately reflect the specific numbers of offices of pages but is instead intended to represent the degree of complexity

associated with the problems of information management and services delivery by government.

[6]   This is an underestimate, as the U.S. Census of Government identifies approximately 87,504 government units in 1997. The figure of 87,504 counts the Federal Government and each State-Government as a single unit in the count. Given the count does not include State or Federal agencies of their sub organizational structures it is fair to say this estimate is conservative.

[7]   In 2000, Japan produced an international review of the ratio of civil servants to population comparing multiple countries using 1998 data. It was estimated that the civil service rate in the United States was 67 per thousand for administrative staff and rose to 75 per thousand citizens when defense forces were added. Civil servants are expected to communicate with the 280,000,000 citizens in the United States. This estimate is rounded from the U.S. Census estimate for 2001.

[8]   This is the equivalent to the entire population of Canada in 1999.

[9]   This represents the Middle Series estimate for 2012. Annual Projections of the Total Resident Population as of July 1: Middle, Lowest, Highest, and Zero International Migration Series, 1999 to 2100. Population Estimates Program, Population Division, U.S. Census Bureau, Washington, D.C. 20233. Internet Release Date: January 13, 2000. Revised Date: February 14, 2000. http://www.census.gov/population/projections/nation/summary/np-t1.txt.

[10]   The number of employees includes part-time employees; data as of December 1, 2001. *Fortune*'s usual summer-to-summer calculations for employee growth and turnover were extended to 17 months to capture layoffs after September 11. http://www.fortune.com/lists/bestcompanies/index.html.

[11]   Findings in the original Whitehall Study were repeated again in Whitehall II. Findings generally indicated the inverse relationship between an individual's sense of control in the work place and their health.

REFERENCES

Alan, F. (2000). *ChoicePoint Public Opinion Survey: Public Records and the Responsible Use of Information.* Westin/ORC International.

Bakos, Y.J. & Treacy, M.W. (1986). Information technology and computer strategy: A research perspective. *MIS Quarterly*, (June).

Barnes, C. & Gill, D. (2000). Working Paper # 9, *Declining Government Performance? Why Citizens Don't Trust Government* (Working Paper # 9, May). New Zealand: State Services Commission.

Bok, D. (1997). Measuring the performance of government. In S. Nye, P.D. Zelikow & D.C. King (Eds.), *Why People Don't Trust Government*. Cambridge, MA: Harvard University Press.

Bureau of Economic Analysis, Bureau of Labor Statistics, National Agricultural Statistics Service, National Center for Health Statistics, U.S. Census Bureau, Bureau of Justice Statistics, Energy Information Administration, and Social Security Administration. (1999) Retrieved on August 15, 2002 from http://www.fedstats.gov/qf/states/00000.html.

Cairncross, F. (2001). The rise of Cisco government. *Network World* [online]. Retrieved on July 5 from http://www.itworld.com/Tech/3494/NWW010507cairncross/.

Clarke, R., Breeze, E., Sherliker, P., Shipley, M., Youngman, L., Fletcher, A., Fuhrer, R., Leon, D., Parish, S., Collins, R., & Marmot, M. (1998). Design, objectives and lessons from a pilot: 25 year follow up re-survey of survivors in the Whitehall study of London Civil Servants. *J Epidemiology & Community Health, 52,* 364-369.

Clarke, R., Shipley, M., Lewington, S., Youngman, L., Collins, R., Marmot, M. & Peto, R. (1999). Underestimation of risk associations due to regression dilution in long-term follow-up of prospective studies. *Am J Epidemiolg, 150,* 341-353.

Corbett, J.C. & Longo, J. (2001). *Analogue Divide, Knowledge Worker Divide: Identifying a Citizen's Readiness for the Knowledge Economy.* Unpublished. E-Government Forum, Centre for Public Sector Studies, University of Victoria at Victoria, B.C.

Corbett, J.C., Sherman, G. & Tate, R. (in press). *Managing Complexity: Using the Internet to Support and Improve Inter-Jurisdictional Health Information Standards.* Amsterdam: MEDNET.

Daniels, C. (2002). The Last Taboo It's not sex. It's not drinking. It's stress — and it's soaring. *FORTUNE,* (October 28).

Davies, S. (1998). Europe to U.S.: No privacy, no trade. *Wired Magazine,* (May).

Dawes, S.S., Bloniarz, P.A., Kelly K.L. & Fletcher, P.D. (1999). *Some Assembly Required: Building a Digital Government for the 21st Century (SUNY National Science Foundation Grant 99-181).* New York: University of Albany, Center for Technology in Government.

Drucker, P. (2001). *Management Challenges for the 21st Century.* New York: Harper Collins Publishers.

Ericson, J. (2001, August 2). The 'Failure' of CRM: Looking for Someone to Blame. *Line56 The E-Business Executive Daily,* [Online] Available at: http://www.line56.com/.

Fortune. (2001, December 1). Retrieved on September 30, 2002 from: http://www.fortune.com/lists/bestcompanies/index.html.

Gaudin, S. (2002). Failing grades for many fortune 100 web sites. *Datamation.* Retrieved on October 24 from: http://itmanagemement.earthweb.com/ecom/article/0,,11952_1487841,00.html.

Graham, J.D. (2002). OIRA's 2002 Report to Congress — Statement as Administrator, Office of Information and Regulatory Affairs before the Subcommittee on Energy Policy, Natural Resources and Regulatory Affairs, United States House of Representatives. Retrieved on March 12 from: http://www.white house.gov/omb/inforeg/graham-house-testimony-3-12-02.html.

Harris Interactive. (2001). *Consumer Privacy Attitudes and Behaviors Survey: Wave II.* Privacy Leadership Initiative. Retrieved July 2001: http://www.bbbonline.org/.

IBM/Harris Interactive. (1999, October). *Multi-National Consumer Privacy Survey.* Author.

Internet Software Consortium. (2002). Retrieved on July 9, 2002 from: http://www.isc.org/ds/host-count-history.html.

James, G. (2000). *Privacy Hits the Fan in New Hampshire.* Retrieved on December 28 from: http://www.upside.com/Opinion/3a4a67261.html.

Kaneshige, T. (2002). Second round of CRM failures looms — Best practices advises companies on CRM for the long run; earlier missteps snowball into giant messes. *Line56 The E-Business Executive Daily,* Retrieved on October 17 from: http://

www.line56.com/.

Kelly, K. (1999). *New Rules for the New Economy.* New York: Penguin.

Kennedy, J. F. (1962). *Address at Rice University on the Nation's Space Effort.* Houston, TX: Author.

Koontz, L. D. (2000). *Internet Privacy: Comparison of Federal Agency Practices with FTC's Fair Information Principles.* Testimony as Director, Information Management Issues, before the Subcommittee on Telecommunications, Trade and Consumer Protection, Committee on Commerce, House of Representatives, and United States General Accounting, October 11.

Kraut, R., Lundmark, V., Patterson, M., Kiesler, S., Mukopadhyay, T. & Scherlis, W. (1998). Internet Paradox: A Social Technology That Reduces Social Involvement and Psychological Well-Being? *American Psychologist, 53*(9), 1017-1031.

Marmot, M.G., Shipley, M.J., & Rose, G. (1984). Inequalities in death-specific explanations of a general pattern. *Lancet,* I, 1003-6.

McConnell, S. (1998). *Software Project Survival Guide.* Redmond, WA: Microsoft Press.

Moore, G.E. (1965). Cramming more components onto integrated circuits. *Electronics, 38*(8).

Murray, B. (2002). Time has taught us to build better Web bonds. *Monitor on Psychology, 33*(4).

Norris, P. (1999). Who surfs? Democracy.com. In E.C. Kamarck & J.S. Nye (Eds.), *Governance in a Networked World.* NH: Hollis Publishing Company.

O'Mara, J. (2002, May 3). *California governor suspends official in Oracle deal.* Reuters Limited.

Putnam, R. D., Leonardi, R. & Nanetti, R.Y. (1993). *Making Democracy Work: Civic Traditions in Modern Italy.* NJ: Princeton University Press.

Standish Group. (1994). *The CHAOS Report.* http://www.pm2go.com/sample_research/chaos_1994_1.php.

United Nations. (2002, May). *DPEPA - Benchmarking E-government: A Global Perspective Assessing the Progress of the U.N. Member States.* New York: Author.

U.S. Census Bureau. (1997). *Census of Governments Volume 1, Government Organization.* U.S. Department of Commerce Economics and Statistics Administration. Washington, DC: Author.

U.S. Census Bureau. (2000). *Projections of the Resident Population by Race, Hispanic Origin and Nativity: Middle Series, 2011 to 2015* ((NP-T5-D). Washington, DC: Population Projections Program, Population Division. Available at: http://www.census.gov/population/projections/nation/summary/np-t5-d.txt

U.S. Government. (2002). *Implementing the President's Management Agenda for E-Government: E-Government Strategy - Simplified Delivery of Services to Citizens.* WA: Author.

West, D. (2001). *Global E-Government Survey.* Providence, Rhode Island: Brown University. World markets Research Centre. Available at: http://www.worldmarketanalysis.com/.

Wyld, D.C. (2001). The auction model: How the public sector can leverage the power of e-commerce through dynamic pricing. In M.A. Abramson & G.E. Means (Eds.), *The Business of Government: E-Government 2001.* Lanham, MD: Rowman & Littlefield Publishers, Inc.

About the Authors

Alexei Pavlichev is a doctoral student in the Public Administration program of North Carolina State University, USA. His academic interests include information technology and geographic information systems. He holds a Master of Public Administration degree from the American University. He may be contacted at aypavlic@unity.ncsu.edu.

G. David Garson is a full professor of Public Administration at North Carolina State University, USA, where he teaches courses on geographic information systems, information technology, e-government, research methodology, and American government. He has been an author, coauthor, editor, or coeditor of two dozen books and author or coauthor of more than 50 articles, primarily on topics related to computing and information management. Professor Garson received his undergraduate degree in political science from Princeton University (1965) and his doctoral degree in government from Harvard University (1969). He may be contacted at David_Garson@ncsu.edu.

*   *   *   *   *

Barbara Allen, **Luc Juillet**, **Mike Miles**, **Gilles Paquet**, **Jeffrey Roy**, and **Kevin Wilkins** are research fellows at the Centre on Governance at the University of Ottawa, Canada, and they may be contacted at the Centre at www.governance.uottawa.ca.

Ronald E. Anderson is professor at the University of Minnesota in the Department of Sociology (USA). He also serves as co-editor of *Social Science Computer Review* and was chair of ACM's SIGCAS (Special Interest Group on Computers and Society) from 1989 to 1993. He has held numerous offices within ACM and was chair of the Task Force for the Revision of the ACM Code of Ethics.

Paul M. A. Baker, PhD, is the associate director of Research Policy at the Georgia Centers for Advanced Telecommunications Technology (GCATT), and an adjunct professor at the School of Public Policy, Georgia Institute of Technology, USA. He may be contacted at paul.baker@gcatt.gatech.edu or at his website, www.gcatt.gatech.edu.

Christopher Corbett holds an interdisciplinary PhD in public administration and health information science. These competencies are directed in the development and implementation of knowledge management/decision systems to solve complex problems experienced by public and private health organizations. Solutions often incoporate the development of collaborative systems for decision-making where health professionals and managers work with each other and Web shared information resources to address specific challenges. In addition to his consulting, Dr. Corbett is the director of the E-Government Forum within the Centre for Public Sector Studies at the University of Victoria (Victoria, B.C.), and an adjunct professor in the Graduate School of Public Administration. As a decision scientist his research includes the development of governance and accountability systems that support resource allocation decision-making within and between government organizations. A specific interest includes the development of evaluation methods to determine the success of e-government strategies and their implementation.

David H. Coursey is an associate professor at the Askew School of Public Administration and Policy, Florida State University, USA. He founded and directs the School's government information technology concentration in the MPA program. He has consulted in the development of more than 100 e-government applications and is a regular speaker for *Government Technology* magazine's conferences. His research appears in *Public Administration Review, Journal of Public Administration Research and Theory* and other major journals.

Patricia Diamond Fletcher is an associate professor in the Policy Sciences Graduate Program at UMBC, USA. She has published extensively in the area of government information policy and electronic government. She recently participated in an NSF funded project studying new models of multi-partner collaboration for electronic government projects. She spent the past year on sabbatical leave from UMBC to conduct research at the U.S. General Accounting Office. While at the GAO, she worked with the IT Policy Team and was involved in two studies initiated by the Senate Committee on governmental affairs on information policy, privacy law, security act compliance, and strategic planning at U.S. Federal agencies. Fletcher received her MLS and PhD from the School of Information Studies at Syracuse University.

Laura Forlano is a doctoral candidate in Communications at Columbia University, USA. Forlano is the project manager for the Information Technology and International Cooperation program at the Social Science Research Council and the Technology Columnist for *GothamGazette.com*, a New York City news and policy website. Forlano has consulted for international organizations including the World Bank, United Nations and International Telecommunication Union. She received a BA in Asian studies from Skidmore College, a Diploma in International Relations from The Johns Hopkins University School of Advanced International Studies Bologna Center and a Master of International Affairs from the Columbia University School of International and Public Affairs. She can be contacted at lef45@columbia.edu.

Joshua M. Franzel is holds a Master's in Public Administration from Florida State University with a specialization in technology policy. He also holds a bachelor's degree in political science with a minor in history from the University of Delaware. Within his field, he has been an assistant to U.S. Representative Michael Castle (DE), a legislative fellow for the Delaware State Legislature, a graduate policy analyst for the Florida Office of Program Policy Analysis and Government Accountability, and a Web developer for Renegade Webheads and Imager Software Consultants. Mr. Franzel is currently working on a PhD in public administration, with specializations in policy analysis and international communications at American University.

Jon Gant is an assistant professor, Maxwell School of Citizenship and Public Affairs, School of Information Studies, Syracuse University, New York, USA. He may be contacted at gant@maxwell.syr.edu.

Karin Geiselhart has been a teacher, federal bureaucrat and researcher. She completed a PhD on electronic communication patterns within a key government agency and she has managed a government website. Until recently she was a post-doctoral research fellow in electronic commerce at RMIT University, where she continued her work on electronic democracy and looked at how non-profits are using new technologies. This chapter she includes in this book is part of a book in preparation on electronic empowerment and complexity theory. She is now working for the Australian National Office for the Information Economy. She is a dual national, born and educated in the United States, but a long-term Australian resident. She may be contacted at karin@case.org.au.

Richard Groper is an instructor in the Department of Political Science at California State University, Fullerton, USA. His research interests include the influence of the Internet upon the political process. He has written and published numerous articles in this area. His teaching areas include state and local politics, campaigns and elections and political behavior. Professor Groper may be reached at rgroper@fullerton.edu.

Franklin Maxwell Harper is the National Civic League's Web manager (USA), responsible for the creation and maintenance of the organization's online presence. Since 1998 Max has held a variety of software engineering positions with firms ranging from start-ups to corporate behemoths. Most recently, he worked as a Java engineer with a Denver Internet security firm, creating enterprise-scale Web-based applications. Max earned a BA in international relations and environmental studies from Carleton College (Northfield, MN). While there, he studied international environmental politics and law, and worked as a research intern for the Minnesota Center for Environmental Advocacy. He lives in Denver with his wife Cindy, who is working towards a master's degree in Landscape Architecture at the University of Colorado, Denver. He may be contacted at mharper@ncl.org.

Henry B. Hogue joined the staff of the Congressional Research Service of the Library of Congress (USA) in 2001 after receiving his doctorate in public administration from American University. His areas of research include government organization, government management, and the presidential appointments process. He previously earned his MSW at San Francisco State University and practiced social work in Northern California and Maryland.

J. William Holland is a 28-year veteran of the Georgia Bureau of Investigation (USA) and its Georgia Crime Information Center. Dr. Holland currently serves as GBI assistant deputy director for Plans and Program Development. Dr. Holland has extensive experience in operational, developmental, and policy issues related to information technology and its role in meeting the mission critical needs of the criminal justice community. He has served on numerous national committees in the area of standards and information sharing, including both the FBI's Electronic Fingerprint Transmission Specifications committee and the National Institute of Standards and Technology group for the electronic transmission of fingerprint images. Dr. Holland serves as his state's director of the National Criminal History Improvement Program (NCHIP) and since 1996 has served as chairperson of the Georgia Criminal Justice Records Improvement Subcommittee. In 2001, that subcommittee was expanded to serve as the state's Task Force on Criminal Justice Integration. Dr. Holland received his PhD in 1996 from Georgia State University. He is married and has two sons, ages 21 and 17.

Keven Holland is the Help Desk administrator for the eMaryland Marketplace, USA. His primary responsibility is to answer questions and assist users of the eMaryland Marketplace, whether suppliers or agencies, via e-mail or telephone.

Marc Holzer is chair and professor of Public Administration at Rutgers University— Campus at Newark, USA. Dr. Holzer also serves as director of the PhD program in public administration and as executive director of the National Center for Public Productivity. He is the author or editor of 14 books and is widely published in professional journals, compendia, and symposia. He may be contacted at mholzer@pipeline.com.

Lung-Teng Hu is a PhD student of the graduate department of Public Administration at Rutgers University—Campus at Newark, USA. His current research interests include performance measurement of digital government services and knowledge management in the public sector. He may be contacted at hulung_teng@hotmail.com.

Donald S. Ijams is senior management analyst, Tucson Police Department (USA), and chairman, Tucson GIS Cooperative. He may be contacted at dijams1@ci.tucson.az.us.

Mark E. Krysiak is the deputy director of procurement for the Maryland Department of General Services, USA. He is also the director of the eMaryland Marketplace, Maryland's eProcurement initiative. He has been involved in the project from its inception. Mark is responsible for general oversight of the eMaryland Marketplace and continues to guide the project forward. He was instrumental in writing and presenting legislation that moved eProcurement forward as a state initiative. He may be contacted at mark.krysiak@dgs.state.md.us.

Patrick R. Mullen is senior analyst, U.S. General Accounting Office. The views expressed in this chapter represent the opinions of the author and not necessarily those of the U.S. General Accounting Office. He may be contacted at mullenp@gao.gov.

Costas Panagopoulos is a doctoral candidate in the Department of Politics at New York University, USA, where he also serves as executive director of the Department's

372 About the Authors

Master's Program in Political Campaign Management. He is a graduate of Harvard College, where he earned his degree in government *magna cum laude*. He may be contacted at costas@post.harvard.edu.

Harold C. Relyea has been a senior staff member of the Congressional Research Service of the Library of Congress since 1971. His principal areas of research responsibility include the office and powers of the President, executive branch organization and management, congressional oversight, and various aspects of government information policy and practice. An undergraduate of Drew University, he received his doctoral degree in government from The American University. In addition to his CRS duties, Dr. Relyea has authored numerous articles for scholarly and professional publications in the United States and abroad. Currently preparing a book on national emergency powers, his recently published titles include *The Executive Office of the President* (1997) and *United States Government Information: Policies and Sources* (2002). He has served on the editorial board of *Government Information Quarterly* since it was founded in 1984, and has held similar positions with several other journals in the past.

Carole Richardson is assistant professor in the Department of Public Administration, School of Public Affairs, American University, USA. Her areas of interests include eGovernment, the digitial divide, cyberdemocracy, and eLearning. She may be contacted at caroler@american.edu.

Shannon Howle Schelin is a doctoral student in the Public Administration Program at North Carolina State University, USA. The University of North Carolina School of Government also employs her as the program manager for the Center for Public Technology. She may be contacted at schelin@iogmail.iog.unc.edu.

Seok-Hwi Song is a PhD student of the Graduate Department of Public Administration at Rutgers University—Campus at Newark, USA. His fields of interest are organizational communication using e-government strategies, internal communication patterns and productivity, and accountability in the public sector. He may contacted at whossong@yahoo.com.

David Spitzer is the business development manager for eMaryland Marketplace, USA. He conducts presentations of the eMaryland Marketplace system to interested groups throughout Maryland, contacts suppliers and invites them to take part in the system, and acts as a liaison between the supplier community and the DGS Department of Procurement and Contracting.

Genie N.L. Stowers is professor and director of the Public Administration program at San Francisco State University, USA. Her primary research interests are in the areas of e-government and online education. She has researched Internet applications for government and teaching online since 1995, publishing in both academic and professional association outlets. She has also completed two reports for the PricewaterhouseCoopers Foundation for the Business of Government and is currently working on a third. Her current focus is on measuring the performance of early e-government efforts, assessing the effects of increased security concerns on e-government efforts and structuring/ designing websites for maximum usability.

Carla Tucker is the deputy director of the eMaryland Marketplace, USA. She was brought onto the project early on and has been instrumental in the evolution of the initiative. She also oversees all aspects of the system, including end-user training. She also has the responsibility of setting up using agencies and their staff in eMaryland Marketplace so that they may post bid solicitations and/or purchase through online catalogs of statewide contracts.

Index

O

objective information 67
Oceans Act 81
Office of Information and Regulatory
    Affairs (OIRA) 7
Office of Management and Budget
    (OMB) 24
Office of Technology Assessment (OTA)
    23
one-stop-shopping 277
online auctions 161
open for business 54
outsourcing 69

P

page hits 70
paper bid 152
paper-based transaction 150
Paperwork Reduction Act (PRA) 24
parcel and land use information 251
participation-driven e-government 112
performance measurement 69
platform for privacy preferences project
    (P3P) 140
political participation 293
politically viable 100
President's e-government strategy 344
President's management agenda (PMA)
    54
privacy act 136
privacy Issues 239
privatization 202
public access to data warehouses 239
public electronic network (PEN) 170
public key infrastructure (PKI) 143
public managers 279
Public Policy Institute of California
    (PPIC) 293
public services broker 120
public-private partnership (P3) 13, 202
push technology 106

R

raison d'être 92
reconnaissance attempts 177

record-keeping policies 137
reidentification risks 141
request for proposal (RFP) 154
restricted areas on government
    websites 100
return on investment (ROI) 242, 273
reverse auction 160
reversed digital divide 283
root compromise attempts 177

S

seamless stage 122
SEARCH group 186
security 136
security breaches 219
security issues 174, 239
security program management 143
sensitive information 57
SHWASHLOCK project 170
smart card 120
Snow Fighter 249
social capital 292
sphere of authority (SOA) 323
stovepipe approach 3
system failures 220

T

technical developments 18
technology hype 243
three-digit code 151
tools of democracy 310
transaction 172
transactional presence 39
transactional stage 122
transmission control protocol (TCP) 19

U

U.S. Department of Justice 187
United Nations (UN) 35, 116
usability 105
user compromise 177

V

vendor participation 162
vertical integration 172